# The Beginning Forecaster

# The Beginning Forecaster:

## The Forecasting Process Through Data Analysis

Hans Levenbach
James P. Cleary

LIFETIME LEARNING PUBLICATIONS
Belmont, California

A division of Wadsworth, Inc.

Designer: Richard Kharibian
Developmental Editor: Kirk Sargent



Printed in the United States of America

2 3 4 5 6 7 8 9 10——85 84 83 82

**Library of Congress Cataloging in Publication Data**

Levenbach, Hans.
The beginning forecaster.

Bibliography: p.
Includes index.
1. Forecasting. 2. Forecasting—Statistical methods. I. Cleary, James P. II. Title.
CB158.L48 303.4 81-4282
ISBN 0-534-97975-0 AACR2

# Contents

*"The earth is degenerating these days. Bribery and corruption abound. Children no longer mind parents. Every man wants to write a book, and it is evident that the end of the world is approaching fast."*
Assyrian Tablet, 2800 B.C.

# Preface

In recent years the need for improved statistical forecasting techniques in business and government has become increasingly clear. This need is in part due to the uncertainty and frequency of change in the economic and financial climate. The clear need for improved techniques has accompanied development of improved computer systems and the desire to apply this technology to the planning and management of change. Fortunately for the professional forecaster, computer-based techniques have greatly simplified access to data bases and quantitative techniques so that a wide variety of methods can be applied in a relatively short time at a reasonable cost. Still, the forecaster can easily be overwhelmed by a multitude of forecasting techniques that are not readily classifiable into easy-to-understand methodologies. Moreover, the manager or user of the forecasting process has been offered little guidance in how to make effective and appropriate applications of these powerful (often newly-discovered) techniques.

*The Beginning Forecaster* describes a number of basic forecasting methods applicable to a wide variety of forecasting problems; the beginner will also find that the methods explained in this book provide initial models for measuring the improvements resulting from building increasingly complex models. Likewise, managers and other forecast users will find in this book a comprehensive treatment of how to evaluate basic forecasting methods, together with a guide to using, interpreting, and communicating practical forecasting results.

*The Beginning Forecaster* is the first volume of a two-volume work. Volume 2, *The Professional Forecaster*, extends topics of the first volume that will be of interest to the experienced forecaster. It describes up-to-date statistical forecasting tools. A forecaster experienced in modern data analysis, including robust/resistant methods and the basics of regression analysis, may proceed directly to Volume 2. However, we think experienced forecasters can also benefit from beginning with Volume 1 since its development forms the basis for Volume 2.

In both volumes, we have emphasized the following:

- Establishment of a *process* for effective forecasting. Specific methods and techniques are presented within the context of the overall process.
- Selection of the forecasting and analytical techniques most *appropriate* for any given problem. The methods discussed, many representing the current

state of the art, are the ones that have proved to be most useful and reliable to us as practicing forecasters.

- Refocusing the attention of practitioners away from the *mechanistic execution of computer programs* and towards a greater understanding of data and the processes generating data.
- Preliminary *analysis of data* before attempting to build models. Computer-generated graphic displays enable you to see in one picture what you might otherwise have to glean from a stack of computer printouts.
- Use of *robust/resistant methods* in addition to traditional methods to provide insurance that a few bad data values do not seriously distort the conclusions that are reached. Experience with a wide variety of practical applications has convinced us that data are rarely well-behaved enough for the direct application of conventional modeling assumptions. The robust/resistant methods produce results that are less subject to the distortions caused by a few outlying data values. By comparing traditional and robust results, the practitioner is in a better position to decide which are most appropriate for the problem at hand.
- Performance of *residual analyses* to determine what the "unexplained" variation might tell about the adequacy of the model. As in data analysis, the importance and usefulness of displaying data in residual analyses are emphasized throughout as essential in all phases of any effective model-building effort.

In addition, both volumes show how the results from the traditionally diverse fields of time series and econometric modeling can be combined into a decisive forecast and presented as an authoritative, credible package.

A number of forecasting methods useful to analysts are not covered explicitly in either volume. The omitted methods are typically useful when data are scarce or nonexistent. As an example, the whole area known as technological forecasting, which requires a grounding in probabilistic (in contrast to statistical) concepts, is not treated. Likewise, new-product forecasting for which data would be unavailable also falls in this category. Since our volumes deal with exploratory data analysis along with confirmatory modeling, we have concentrated instead on techniques for which a reasonable amount of data are available or can be collected.

Some practitioners may feel that we have given greater emphasis to data-analytic concepts than is necessary. However, many practicing forecasters and writers on forecasting methods tend to concentrate on making models more complex rather than keeping them simple: sources of forecast errors are difficult to analyze with increasingly complex models. Our experience suggests that, in practice, the undoing of many forecasting efforts begins with flaws in the quality and handling of data, rather than in the lack of modeling sophistication. Thus an objective of *The Forecasting Process* is to place greater emphasis on data-analytic methods (much of it intuitive and graphical) as a key to improved forecasting.

The *Beginning Forecaster* is divided into three parts. The first part includes seven chapters which deal with approaching a forecasting problem. Chapters 1 through 4 discuss the forecasting process in general and describe the modeling process used throughout the book. These chapters consider the integration of practical forecasting experience, method selection, costs of applying the method, the matching of a forecast to a user's needs and limitations, and forecast accuracy. Chapters 5 through 7 describe the premodeling, data-analytic process every forecaster should perform in any forecasting application.

The second part contains thirteen chapters, five of which are concerned with the development of regression analysis basic to all quantitative forecasting, with specific forecasting techniques, and with their uses and interrelationships. Chapter 8 treats forecasting with classical exponential smoothing models, which have a long history of successful application to short-term forecasting. Chapter 9 takes a first look at trend and seasonality through a two-way table analysis and provides a descriptive tool for identifying the percent that each component is of the total variation. Chapter 10 deals with data-adjustment tools for examining forecasting data in the context of the model assumptions. Chapter 11 provides a subjective method for projecting a cyclical component. Chapters 12 through 15 contain the basics of regression analysis, the interpretation of output from a model, confidence limits, and the key role of residual analysis. Chapters 16 and 17 introduce robust methods useful to forecasters. Chapters 18 and 19 deal with analyzing trending, seasonal and cyclical data, and describe several seasonal adjustment procedures. Chapter 20 provides two case studies on forecasting with regression models.

The third part contains five general chapters dealing, respectively, with the presentation and tracking of forecasts (Chapters 21–22) and the management of the forecasting function (Chapters 23–25). The latter chapters should help the technical forecast manager or user understand a particular forecasting technique as an aspect of management.

The examples are predominantly drawn from the experience of the authors in the telecommunications business. While this may be distracting to some readers, it should be noted that the characteristics of the data are what is important for the example, not the fact that the data are telephone-related. Other data sets from nontelecommunications sources have also been used throughout to make certain points or illustrate a particular technique.

Hans Levenbach
James P. Cleary

# Acknowledgments

The authors are indebted to a number of people in forecasting organizations throughout the Bell System whose involvement and contribution can only be indirectly recognized. Over the last decade several members of the technical staff at Bell Laboratories have made significant contributions to the methodological and computer software development of statistical forecasting in the Bell System. In particular, the efforts of Bill Brelsford and Dave Preston stand out in this regard. Their software contributions are reflected in the forecasting courses taught at the Bell System Center for Technical Education (BSCTE) and in the modeling work of many practicing forecasters in the Bell System.

The BSCTE courses provided a great deal of impetus to the introduction of improved quantitative forecasting techniques in the Bell System. This widespread acceptance of statistical forecasting by upper level management at AT&T and the Associated Telephone Companies has necessitated the introduction of management techniques in forecasting, to maximize forecast usefulness at minimum cost to the System. Some of the techniques discussed in this book are representative of this practice.

There are a number of individuals who have assisted the authors in their review of the manuscript. Ms. Shubha Tuljapurkar, formerly of Pacific Northwest Bell, made a thorough review of an early version and provided many practical insights. The following members of AT&T's Analytical Support Center commented on at least one chapter apiece: Cathy Cridge, Steve Safran, and Monty Shultes. Margaret Rowe and Sherry McArdle Karas were instrumental in organizing the data files, running examples on the computer, and generating many of the visuals via computer graphics. Joe McCabe and Pamela Siegel of New York Telephone, and Bill Cleveland and Lorraine Denby of Bell Laboratories were also very helpful in reviewing specific chapters. The authors are particularly appreciative of the efforts of Drs. Bob Brousseau and Min-te Chao, who thoroughly reviewed and made significant comments on the entire manuscript!

The authors would like to express their appreciation and indebtness to the late Sir Ronald A. Fisher, F.R.S., Cambridge, and to Hafner Publishing Co. for permission to reprint Table IV from their book, *Statistical Methods For Research Workers;* to Professor E. S. Pearson and the *Biometrika* trustees for permission to reproduce the materials in Appendix A, Tables 1, 3, and 4; and to Professors J. Durbin and G. S. Watson for the values in Appendix A, Table 5.

The authors would also like to express their appreciation to the editorial and production staff of Lifetime Learning Publications for their courteous cooperation in the production of this book; to Lenore Pahler, Joan Mendez and various members of the AT&T Word Processing Staff, who typed the manuscript; and above all to Kirk Sargent for his numerous and valuable editorial suggestions for improving the text.

Lastly, the authors owe thanks to the management of the respective organizations in which they worked as forecasters and forecast managers. The Residence and Business forecasting organizations, the Analytical Support Center, and the Demand Analysis group at AT&T have over the years provided initiative in the development of courses and the implementation of quantitative techniques like those described in both volumes. However, any errors, obscurities or omissions remain the sole responsibility of the authors. Any procedures described in this book should not necessarily be interpreted as representative of official forecasting practices of AT&T or its Associated Telephone Companies.

H. L.
J. P. C.

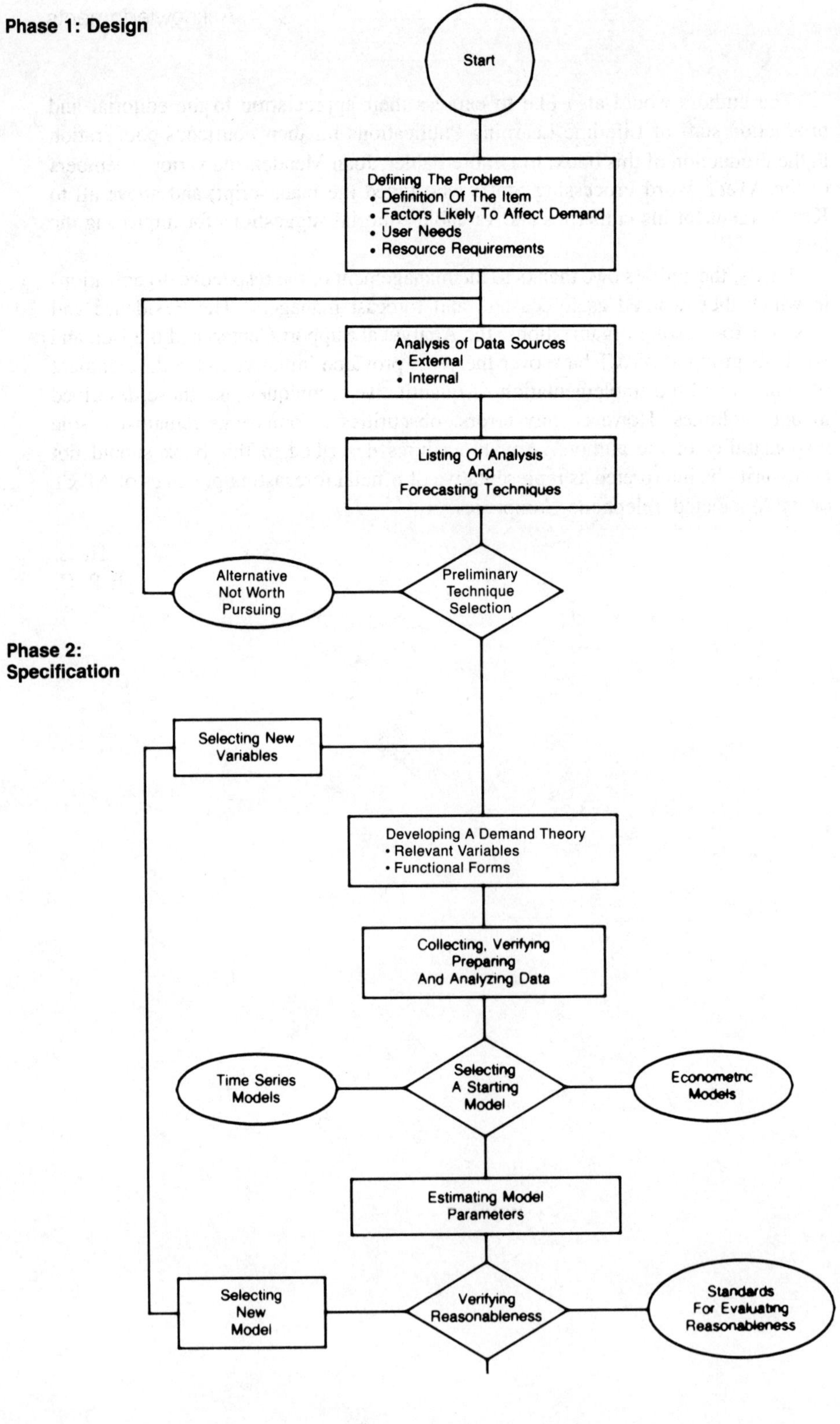
Phase 1: Design
Start
Defining The Problem
• Definition Of The Item
• Factors Likely To Affect Demand
• User Needs
• Resource Requirements
Analysis of Data Sources
• External
• Internal
Listing Of Analysis And Forecasting Techniques
Alternative Not Worth Pursuing
Preliminary Technique Selection
Phase 2: Specification
Selecting New Variables
Developing A Demand Theory
• Relevant Variables
• Functional Forms
Collecting, Verifying Preparing And Analyzing Data
Time Series Models
Selecting A Starting Model
Econometric Models
Estimating Model Parameters
Selecting New Model
Verifying Reasonableness
Standards For Evaluating Reasonableness

**Phase 3: Evaluation**

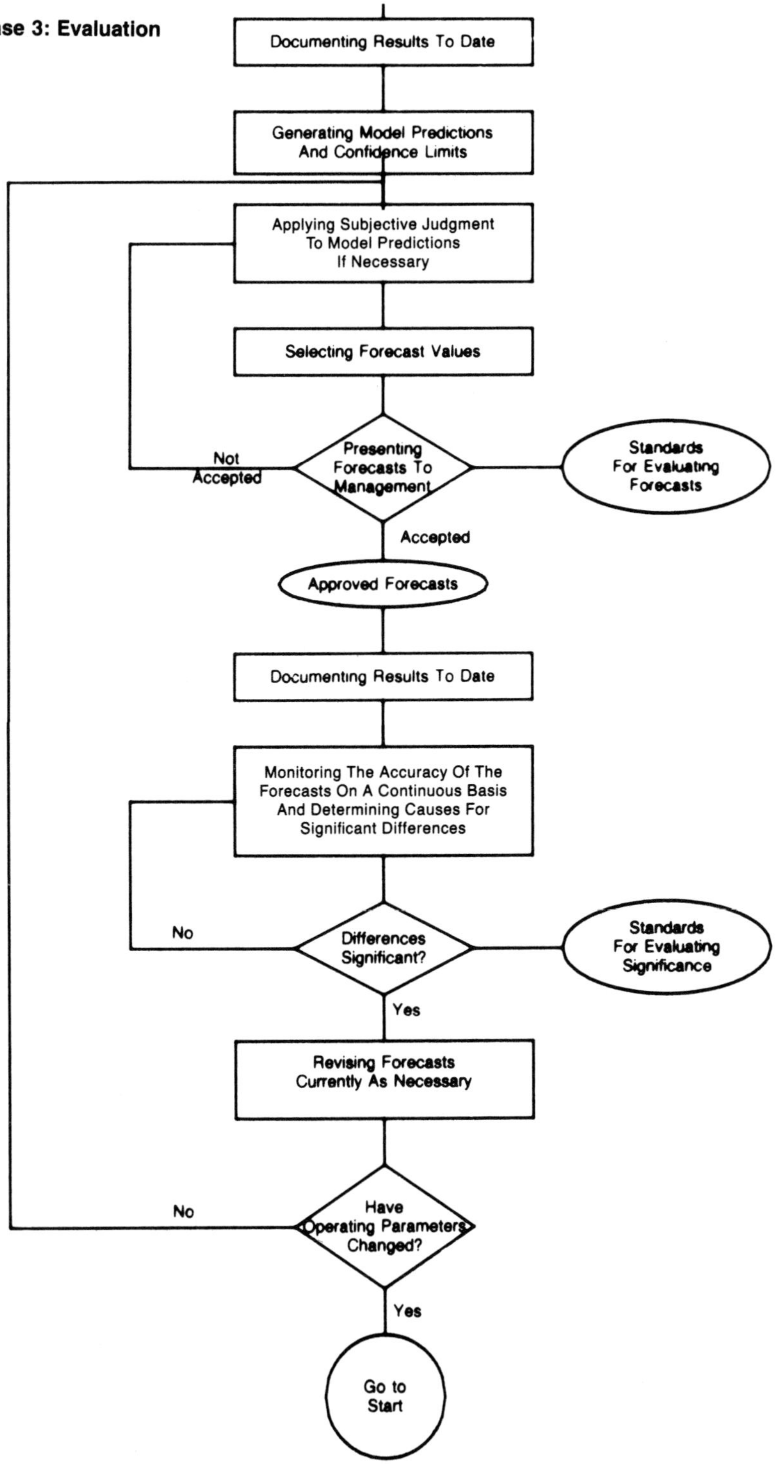

# The Beginning Forecaster

# Part 1

## Approaching a Forecasting Problem

CHAPTER **1**

# Why Is Forecasting a Process?

As you begin to read this book, you may find it helpful to keep the following in mind:

- A grasp of mathematical and statistical knowledge, while necessary for the forecaster, will not in itself ensure successful forecasting.
- For the best results, apply such knowledge within a sound framework—a forecasting process.
- Following a sound process, which describes the sequence of activities to be followed, can reduce chances of inadvertently overlooking a key step.
- Omission of a key step, whether deliberate or inadvertent, can jeopardize a forecaster's credibility, and credibility is a forecaster's livelihood.

This chapter describes

- What a forecasting process is.
- Why it is a necessary approach in the forecasting profession.
- How, when, and by whom forecasting is done.

## FORECASTING DEFINED

Probably the simplest definition of forecasting is that it is a process which has as its objective the prediction of future events or conditions. More precisely, forecasting attempts to predict change. If future events represented only a readily quantifiable change from historical events, future events or conditions could be predicted through quantitative projections of historical trends into the future. Methodologies that are used to describe historical events with mathematical equations (or a model) for the purpose of predicting future events are classified as quantitative projection techniques. However, there is much more to forecasting than projecting past trends.

Experience and intuitive reasoning quickly reveal that future events or conditions are not solely a function of historical trends. Even familiar abstractions such as trend, cycle, and seasonality, while extremely useful to business forecasters, cannot be completely relied upon when it comes to predicting future events. In the commercial world, goods and services are bought by individuals for innumerable reasons. Therefore, business forecasting must include other ingredients to complement quantitative projection techniques.

A forecast is not an end product but rather an input to the decision-making process. A forecast is a prediction of what will happen under an assumed set of circumstances. Often, a forecast is a prediction of future values of one or more variables under "business as usual" conditions. In planning activities, this is often referred to as the status quo, or, the "base case." Forecasts are also required for a variety of "what if" situations and for the formulation of business plans to alter base case projections that have proved unsatisfactory.

## Learning from Actual Examples of Forecasting

As a unifying thread throughout this book, we shall frequently examine practical forecasting problems drawn from our experience in forecasting for the telephone industry. Where appropriate, we shall also use time series (data about changes through time) from other sources, to illustrate forecasting methods and to compare or contrast results.

The forecasting problems we shall borrow from telephone-industry experience arise from the requirement for accurate one- and two-year-ahead forecasts of revenues, products, and services. Specifically, throughout the book we shall develop forecasts of revenues to be derived from toll calls made by business customers.

The telecommunications industry involves a number of considerations common to many forecasting applications (Figure 1.1). For example, the overall state of the economy, as measured by nonfarm employment, is known to influence the demand

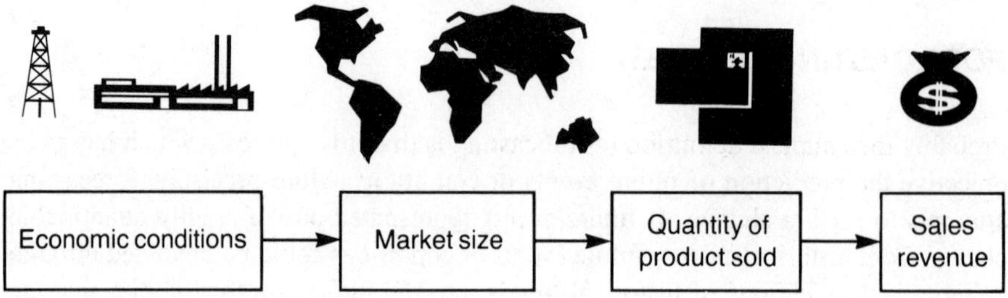


**Figure 1.1** A generic forecasting problem.

for business telephone service. For other industries, different measures of economic activity, such as interest rates, industrial production, the unemployment rate, Gross National Product, volume of imports versus exports, inflation rates, or other variables, may have special significance in determining the size of some market at a designated time.

The market that generates telephone toll revenues may be viewed, in part, as the number of business telephones from which calls can be made (Figure 1.2). Toll messages (calls) may be viewed as the quantity of service rendered (or product sold). There is not a one-to-one correspondence between revenues and messages because additional factors, such as the distance between the parties, time of day, duration of calls, and whether or not an operator is needed, allow for variation in the revenue per message.

The revenue-quantity relationship in the most general sense is similar to what would be encountered in forecasting revenues from passenger-miles of transportation, mortgage commitments from housing starts, and revenues from barrels of crude oil after refining. In each instance, the revenue depends on the mix of the products sold. However, for financial planning purposes, very accurate total revenue forecasts can be derived without the necessity of forecasting every product or product combination and multiplying that by the sales price.

In this book we shall analyze and forecast variables by using basic forecasting techniques. We shall begin the analysis with classical approaches and follow them with robust/resistant solutions (those which safeguard against unusual values and departures from assumptions) to the same problems. In *The Professional Forecaster,* more advanced techniques, including the ARIMA method (Autoregressive-Integrated-Moving Average, or Box-Jenkins) and econometric modeling with multiple variables and equations, will be applied as well.

## Forecasting as a Process

The process of forecasting is not an exact science but is more like an art form. As with any worthwhile art form, the forecasting process is definitive and systematic,

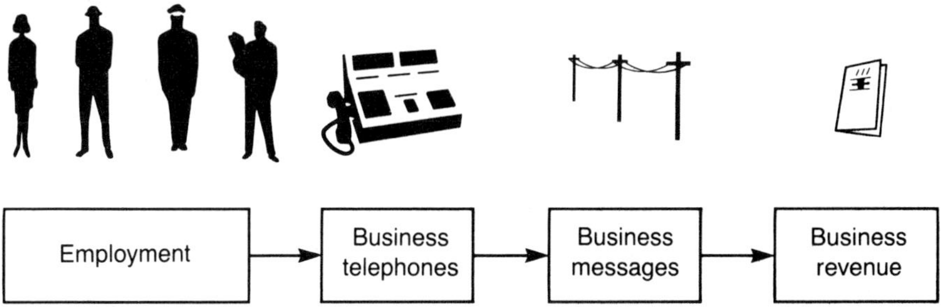


**Figure 1.2** A telecommunications forecasting problem.

and is supported by a set of special tools and techniques that are dependent upon human judgment and intuition.

For example, business forecasting generally attempts to predict future customer demand for a company's goods and services. Once forecasting needs are identified, a data-gathering network capable of continuously providing pertinent information about market conditions must be established. The data that have been gathered are then placed into some form of data base for easy analysis. Data gathering and analysis precede and also follow the production of the forecast.

The starting point for the forecasting process is to identify all the things that will be needed to put a forecast together. These are inputs: typical inputs might be

- Finding sources of data about the item to be forecast.
- Obtaining information about external conditions—that is, about those factors in the environment influencing a forecast.
- Determining the needs of the user of the forecast.
- Gathering the human and financial resources required to produce a forecast.
- Listing projection techniques.

These are not only inputs to the forecasting process but also inputs to the judgment that is applied throughout the process.

The forecasting process also requires knowledge about the outputs of the process:

- Formatting the output of the final product.
- Presenting the forecast to the forecast users.
- Evaluating the forecast on an ongoing basis.

The forecast user will generally specify the format of the forecast output and consult with the forecaster about the kinds of analyses and/or variables that should be considered.

The end product of the forecasting process is clearly the forecast itself. A forecast should not be considered as being permanent or never changing. The dynamic nature of any market (customer demands for goods and services) dictates that the forecasting process be reviewable and repeatable at some future time. Since the value of any forecast is based on the degree to which it can provide information to a decision-making process, the view of a market and its demands on a company within that marketplace (as expressed in terms of a forecast) must be current to be useful.

The process by which forecasting is done is emphasized for several reasons. First, of primary importance to anyone who makes a forecast is that better forecasts will result if the proper process has been meticulously followed.

Second, a structured method for forecasting leads to a better understanding of the factors that influence demand for a product or service. The forecaster who has a good handle on demographic, economic, political, land-use, competition, and pricing considerations will develop expertise in making or evaluating forecasts for these considerations and relating them to the demand for a company's services.

A third reason for emphasizing the process of forecasting is that it focuses attention on selecting the right methodology for a given forecast. For example, one goal is to be certain not to use short-range methods for long-range forecasts. Instead of focusing first on the numbers they hope will result from a forecast, forecast managers and users should decide which method is likely to produce the most accurate forecast.

## WHAT ARE FORECASTING MODELS?

A forecasting model is a job aid for forecasters: it attempts to create a simplified representation of reality. The forecaster tries to include those factors which are critical and exclude those which are not. This process of stripping away the non-essential and concentrating on the essential is the essence of modeling in the forecasting profession.

Although simplified, models permit the forecaster to estimate the effects of important future events or trends. In the telecommunications industry, for example, there are thousands of reasons why subscribers want their telephones connected or disconnected, or place calls over the switching network. It is beyond the scope of the forecaster to deal with all these reasons. Therefore, a forecaster attempts to distill these many influences into a limited number of the most pertinent factors.

As an example, consider a forecasting model for telephone demand in Detroit, Michigan; the model might look like Figure 1.3. This model assumes that the automobile industry creates jobs for people who then buy homes or rent apartments and want telecommunications services. The telephone forecaster's job, for instance, is to determine the relationships between employment levels, household growth, land use, and telephone demand.

Models are usually designed by using mathematical equations to represent the real situation being analyzed. Such an equation might take the form

$$\begin{aligned}\text{Telephone demand} = b_0 &+ b_1 \text{ (Number of employees)} \\ &+ b_2 \text{ (Number of housing starts),}\end{aligned}$$

where $b_0$, $b_1$, and $b_2$ are coefficients determined from data. Models such as these simplify the analysis of some problems, but, of course, sacrifice the ability to account for all the factors that cause people to behave as they do. Notice that the model summarized in the equation does not include information on the prices of other goods and services. There is a trade-off between simplicity and completeness in every model-building effort.

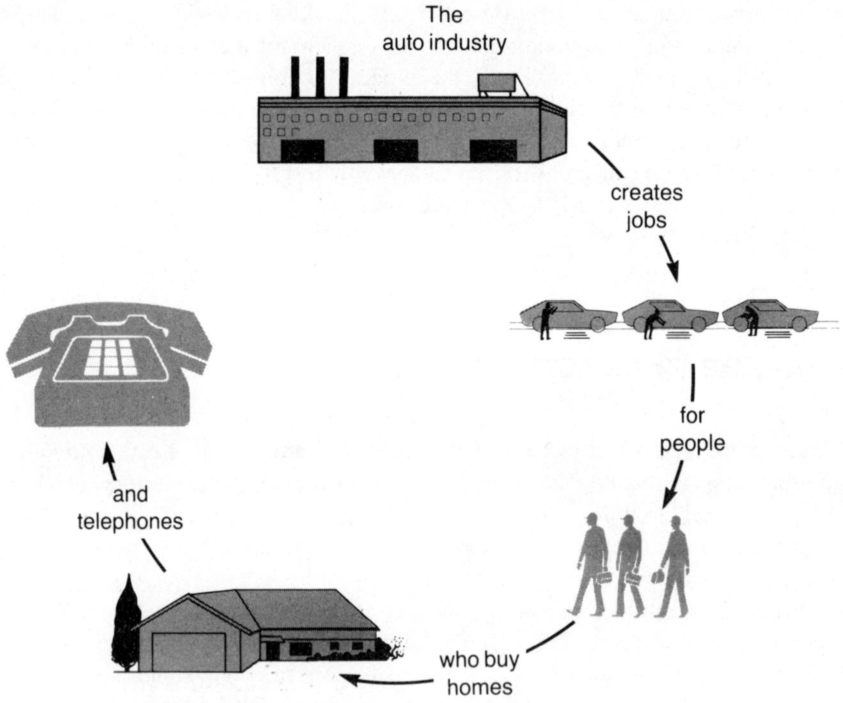


**Figure 1.3** A forecasting model: the demand for telephones in Detroit.

Just as the forecasting process is tangible and structured, so are modeling or projection techniques. They perform the same task regardless of the data they use: while some of the inputs to the forecasting process are dependent upon the nature of the given situation, projection techniques are not. For this reason, the forecaster must exercise sound judgment in selecting and using the projection techniques for any given forecast. Through a systematic process of elimination, the forecaster can identify those projection techniques which will provide the greatest assistance in the development of the forecast output.

## HOW TO DEVELOP A FORECAST

The process for developing a specific forecast consists of seven basic steps:

1. Set down basic facts about past trends and forecasts.
2. Determine causes of changes in past demand trends.
3. Determine causes of differences between previous forecasts and actual behavior.

4. Determine factors likely to affect future demand.
5. Make the forecast for some future period and provide the user with a measure of its accuracy and reliability.
6. Follow up on the accuracy of the forecast continually and determine the reasons for significant differences from the forecast.
7. Revise forecasts when necessary.

For anything which is to be forecast, there is a "start" point for the first forecast made of that product, but there is no "end" point until either the product no longer exists in its original form or there is no longer a need to forecast it. The first forecast utilizes all of the steps of the forecasting process. All following forecasts are revisions or extensions in time of the original forecast.

## WHO MAKES THE FORECAST?

In this book, we assume that the forecaster and the person in need of a forecast are different people. This distinction is, of course, not a necessity, but rather a recognition that businesses tend to specialize their functions. Professional forecasting requires the development of unique knowledge and skills to support the planning function. This has resulted in the significant growth of lucrative forecasting and consulting firms in the past decade.

### Role of the Forecaster

The forecaster is an advisor. The completed forecast must meet the requirements of the user in terms of timeliness, format, perhaps methodology, and presentation. In the forecaster–problem-solver partnership, the problem-solver is knowledgeable about the environment surrounding the problem and variables that should probably be considered. The forecaster is knowledgeable about the forecasting process and specific forecasting methods most appropriate for the problem. In large businesses, the volume and complexity of required forecasts is usually sufficient to support full-time forecasting staffs.

### How Planners Use Forecasts

The diversity of business activities today has created work for a variety of planners—each with a special set of problems. The problems may be viewed in terms of a business's function and a time period for that function.

*Executive managers* are concerned with current performance but even more concerned with future direction—what is called strategic planning. In which markets should the business operate over the next five to ten years? An executive manager must identify and analyze key trends and forces that may affect the formulation and execution of strategies, including economic trends, technological developments, political climates, market environments, and assessment of potential competitors. In addition to strategic planning, executive managers are concerned with financial planning, for which they need short-term (one to three months), medium-term (up to two years), and long-term (greater than two years) forecasts.

*Marketing managers* are concerned with short- and long-term forecasts of demand for products and services. Forecasting methods suited to products and services have existed for some time. In forecasting a new product, these methods are applicable if analogous products exist or if careful market trials can be conducted. The demand for the product can then be related to the economic or demographic characteristics of the people in the market areas. These relationships can then be used to predict the product's acceptance in other areas having their own economic and demographic characteristics.

For *planners of competitive strategies,* forecasting techniques can be used to forecast the total market—for example, total gasoline consumption, passenger-miles of traffic between cities, automobile purchases by size (sedan, compact, subcompacts), computer storage requirements, or other such variables. Given the total market, each firm within it will then estimate its market share on the basis of product differences, price, advertising, quality of service, market coverage (including the size of a sales force), geography, and other factors specific to the market for the product or service. In many cases, market share is also estimated by using quantitative models.

*Production and inventory control managers* are generally concerned with short-term forecasts. In inventory control, exponential smoothing models find extensive application. (This technique is like a weighted moving average, in which the most current data are given the greatest weight.) For extremely complex inventory systems, these models provide forecasts which are closely monitored for deviations between estimated and actual inventories. Sometimes minor deviations can be modeled and used to alter future predictions. Large deviations are "flagged" as exceptions, for scrutiny and reevaluation of the model generating the forecasts.

## SUMMARY

- Forecasting is a structured process which produces a specific output, namely advice about the future. The steps of the forecasting process are independent of the item to be forecast and the input parameters.
- The purpose of the forecasting process is to identify and evaluate systematically all factors which are most likely to affect the course of future events and to

produce a realistic view of the future. Since the future is not "completely predictable," the systematic structure of the forecasting process establishes the foundation on which the most important ingredient (human judgment and intuition) is based.

- This chapter has emphasized the need to think of forecasting as a process. A properly trained forecaster is one who does the right things in the correct sequence.

The next chapter will present detailed steps in the forecasting process. This will be followed by discussions that can help you improve your data analysis capabilities, build and evaluate quantitative models, and improve your management of these analytical functions and the forecasts they will lead to.

## USEFUL READING

The books and articles listed at the end of each of the following chapters are those cited within the text; they are described in the Bibliography at the back of the book.

CHAPTER **2**

# How to Start Making a Forecast

This chapter deals with the first two stages of the forecasting process:

- Defining the parameters that will govern the forecast.
- Making first choices of alternative projection techniques.

The considerations help the forecaster answer the question:

- Can cost-effective forecasts be provided to assist planners or managers in making their decisions?

The specific operations that must be performed in these and other stages of the forecasting process are diagrammed in a flowchart in the front of this book. Each chapter will highlight those flowchart operations relevant to that chapter, thus emphasizing the iterative nature of the forecasting process.

## DEFINING PARAMETERS

Suppose that you are in charge of making the forecast that was used as an example in Chapter 1—a toll revenue forecast for telephone company use during the next two years. How do you begin to plan your work?

### Defining User Needs, Forecastable Items, and the Forecaster's Resources

First, a forecaster will want to identify forecast users and their information needs. For example, the toll revenue forecast is needed to determine the expected net income and return on investment for a "base case" (described in Chapter 1). You would want to be certain too that you had an understanding of what products or services should be measured in your forecast.

Next, a forecaster's own practical needs must be recognized; if they are overlooked, the quality of the forecast will be diminished. So you would want to consider

- The forecaster's time.
- Clerical time.
- Expense dollars for computer operations.
- Transportation for field visits.

## Identifying Factors Likely to Affect Changes in Demand

A forecaster also needs information about the economic environment in which a business operates: what factors have caused the demand for a product or service in the past and are likely to affect the demand in the future? For example, in the marketing environment, demand for a product may need to be forecast along with a measure of the effect a change in price of a product or service will have on the demand for it. Or the forecaster may need to consider demographic, economic, and land-use factors. In particular, factors such as income, market potential, and habit are usually an integral part of a formal demand theory.

- *Income* measures a consumer's ability to pay for a company's goods or services. The price of its goods or services and the prices of its competitors' are certainly important.
- The *market potential* represents the total market for products or services of the type being forecast. This might be the number of households or business telephones.
- Finally, *habit* is crucial because innovation and change create new products and services, thus causing people's tastes and habits to change; these changes must be monitored. For example, the introduction of air transportation caused people to change travel habits; the impact on the railroad industry was tremendous.

The beginning forecaster can develop a simple demand theory without building complex models. For example, the forecaster may be required to project the sales of a product or service per household. A total sales forecast can be obtained by multiplying the forecast of this ratio by an independent forecast of the number of households. In this way, an important relationship can be modeled that uses relatively simple forecasting methods. This gives a first approximation which may provide valuable and timely information to decision makers.

In addition to these demand factors, supply considerations may also need to be taken into account. In forecasting basic telephone services, it is important to recognize that a corporate charter requires a telephone company to serve customer demand. Its management does not have the option of meeting only a part of the demand. In other industries, where this isn't so, the interaction of demand and supply must be evaluated by the forecaster and the forecast user before arriving at the final forecast.

### A Car-buying Analogy

At first glance, the first two stages of the forecasting process as depicted in the Flowchart may appear somewhat complex, so an analogy of buying a new car may help simplify its analysis.

The first stage in defining a car buyer's problem (definition of the item) is seemingly straightforward—a new car. It may later turn out that other alternatives (used car, public transportation) provide more appropriate solutions to the real problem; the potential car buyer doesn't overlook this possibility but wants to do some preliminary checking to see if the assumption that a car is needed will hold up.

Therefore the potential buyer defines the car's users and their requirements. In this example the users are family members, and their needs will be determined as part of the forecasting process. The needs primarily relate to the use to which the car will be put: the car might be needed for commuting, for family chores, for vacation trips, or for teenager transportation. The intended use will strongly influence the selection of the type of car to be purchased.

Potential constraints also need to be considered: these include family size and the family's financial limitations (including money for a down payment, the availability of financing, the cost of insurance, and maintenance and operating costs). To help in a basic understanding of these things, the potential buyer might read publications relating to new car quality, consult books, talk to friends for advice about their experiences, and go to several dealers to discuss prices and terms of sale. This leads to a listing of alternative solutions.

The problem-definition stage concludes with a determination of the costs versus the benefits of alternative solutions. What this modest forecast will have taught the potential car buyer is to look for solutions in which benefits exceed costs. But has the car buyer been sufficiently accurate in measuring costs and benefits? There are, after all, numerous alternative ways of generating any forecast.

## ANALYSIS OF DATA SOURCES

Since all forecasting methods require data, the forecaster proceeds to analyze the availability of data from sources both external (outside a business or industry) and internal (within the company or its industry). For example, one potential source of internal data is corporate books, which normally contain a rich history of revenues, expenses, capital expenditures, product sales, prices, and marketing expenses.

The availability of external data is improving rapidly. Most of the required demographic data (age, race, sex, households, and so forth), forecasts of economic indicators, and related variables can be obtained from the data banks of computer firms, and from industry and government publications. A partial listing of data sources for marketing and social sciences is given in Armstrong (1978, pp. 448–51). Intriligator (1978, pp. 72–73), and Sullivan and Claycombe (1977, pp. 12–14) summarize some useful external data sources. Another overall reference for data sources at the national and international levels is the *Statistical Yearbook,* published annually by the United Nations.

## CHOOSING ALTERNATIVE PROJECTION TECHNIQUES

The commonly used projection techniques can be classified as being either qualitative or quantitative.

### Qualitative Techniques

The qualitative techniques provide the framework within which quantitative techniques (including forms of quantitative analyses, such as decision trees and linear programming) are brought to bear on a particular problem. The objective of qualitative techniques is to bring together in a logical, unbiased, and systematic way all information and judgments which relate to the factors of interest. These techniques use human judgment and rating schemes to turn qualitative information into quantitative estimates. Qualitative techniques are most commonly used in forecasting something about which the amount, type, and quality of historical data are limited.

Common qualitative techniques include the Delphi method, market research, panel of consensus (focus groups), visionary forecast, and historical analogies (Armstrong, 1978). These techniques are generally not treated in this book, but treatments of these subjects may be found in Makridakis and Wheelwright (1978), Sullivan and Claycombe (1977), and Wheelwright and Makridakis (1980).

### Quantitative Techniques

If appropriate and sufficient data are available, then quantitative projection techniques can be employed. Such quantitative techniques can be further classified into two more categories, statistical and deterministic.

- *Statistical (stochastic) techniques* focus entirely on patterns, pattern changes, and disturbances caused by random influences. This book treats some of these, including summary statistics (Chapter 7), moving averages and exponential smoothing (Chapter 8), time series decomposition (Chapters 9, 18, and 19), and regression models and trend projections (Chapter 12). The ARIMA models and other sophisticated time series techniques are taken up in *The Professional Forecaster.*

- *Deterministic (causal) techniques* incorporate the identification and explicit determination of relationships between the factor to be forecast and other influencing factors. These include anticipation surveys, input-output models, econometric models, and leading indicators (Chambers et al., 1974; Wheelwright and Makridakis, 1980). Leading indicators are discussed in this book in Chapter 11, in connection with cycle forecasting. Econometric techniques are taken up in *The Professional Forecaster.*

Within the listings of statistical projection techniques, there are essentially two approaches. The approach treated in this volume is best illustrated by the *time series decomposition* technique. The primary assumption on which this methodology is based is that the data can be decomposed into several unobservable components such as trend, seasonality, cycle, and irregularity, and that the components can then be analyzed and projected into the future on an individual basis. The forecast is then merely the combination of the projections for the components.

A second approach is associated with the *Box-Jenkins* and *econometric time series modeling* methodologies. Their theoretical foundations are grounded primarily in statistical concepts and do not assume that the data are represented by the superposition of separate components. Rather, the data have an overall representation in which the components are not separately identifiable or specified.

There is often a further distinction made between time series and econometric methods: although they have strong similarities in their mathematical representation, they differ vastly in their estimation methodologies.

### Time Series and Econometrics

A *time series* is a set of chronologically ordered points of raw data, such as the revenue received, by month, for several years. An assumption often made in the time series approach is that the factors that caused demand in the past will persist into the future.

Time series analysis can help to identify and explain any regularly recurring or systematic variation in the data owing to *seasonality.*

- Sales forecasters typically deal with monthly seasonality. This is usually related to weather and human customs.
- Economic forecasters more often deal with quarterly time series.

Time series analysis also helps to identify *trends* in the data and the growth rates of these trends.

- By trend is meant the basic tendency of a measured variable to grow or decline over a long time period. For many consumer products, the prime determinant of trend is growth in numbers of households.

Finally, time series analysis can help to identify and explain *cyclical patterns* that repeat in the data roughly every two, three, or more years.

- A cycle is usually irregular in depth and duration and tends to correspond to changes in economic expansions and contractions. It is commonly referred to as the "business cycle."

The concepts of trend, seasonality, and cycle are abstractions of reality. In Chapter 11 it will be seen how these concepts can be effectively used to make a "turning-point analysis and forecast."

The econometric approach may be viewed as a "cause-effect" approach. Its purpose is to identify the factors responsible for demand. The econometric models of the U.S. economy, for example, are very sophisticated and represent one extreme of econometric modeling. These models are built to depict the essential quantitative relationships that determine output, income, employment, and prices.

It is general practice in econometric modeling to remove only the seasonal influence in the data prior to modeling. The trend and cyclical movements in the data should be explicable by using economic and demographic theory. The Detroit model, discussed in Chapter 1, is an example of how an econometric system is used in the telecommunications industry. The growth in revenues might be analyzed, projected, and related to business telephones in service, a measure that is related to the level of employment. It is not necessarily assumed that the factors that caused demand in the past will persist in the future. Rather, the factors believed to cause demand are identified and forecast separately.

## PRELIMINARY SELECTION CRITERIA

After generating a list of alternative projection techniques, it is often possible to reject some of these techniques immediately. Some of the considerations that go into such a preliminary selection include

- The time horizon of the forecasts.
- The accuracy requirements.
- The level of detail in the forecasts.
- The quantity of forecasts required.

Other considerations include the willingness of users to accept given techniques and approaches and the ease with which the methods or forecasts match their planning processes. The specific strategy for completing the preliminary selection is the subject of Chapter 3.

### Time Horizon

A *time horizon* refers to the period of time into the future for which forecasts are required. The periods are generally short-term (one to three months), medium-term (three months to two years), and long-term (more than two years). Wheelwright and Makridakis (1980) also refer to the immediate term (less than one month). The business revenue forecasting example requires both short- and medium-term forecasts.

### Accuracy Requirements

The *accuracy requirements* that a forecaster must deal with are normally related to the cost of forecast error. In an inventory control problem in which the inventory consists of numerous relatively inexpensive parts that are readily available (let us say boxes and mailing labels), the accuracy requirement will be less than for an inventory of very expensive parts with long lead times between order placement and delivery (for example, airplane engines and airplane fuselages). In the latter case, the production line could be affected adversely and sales could be lost to competitors if the inventory is not adequate. Alternatively, too great an inventory will cause a manufacturer to have unnecessarily high carrying charges, which might result in the need to raise prices to maintain profitability.

Each situation determines its own accuracy requirements. It is not uncommon for the forecast user to expect accuracy levels that realistically cannot be achieved. It is up to the forecaster, as advisor, to state what can be done. The user may well have to establish contingency plans to deal with the potential imprecision in the forecast. An objective accuracy level for the telephone revenue forecast example used in this book is less than 1.5 percent for monthly forecasts, less than 1.0 percent for annual forecasts, and less than 2.0 percent for two-year-ahead forecasts.

### Levels of Detail and Quantities of Forecasts

Methods or forecasts that are appropriate for large-scale demand may not provide satisfactory results if applied to an individual product. For example, the projected total of automobile sales for all manufacturers may be related to certain large-scale economic variables such as real income or Gross National Product. This relationship may not be adequate to help an individual manufacturer (a custom car maker, for example) to determine its share of the market; much less does it enable the manufacturer to determine future sales for a given model.

Related to the level of detail is the quantity of forecasts that may be required of the forecaster. As the forecast process moves from executive management to production-line management, the quantity of required forecasts usually grows in a nonlinear manner. These could number in the thousands. A forecaster generally lacks resources to devote the full range of modeling techniques to that many forecasts. Instead, simple, more mechanical procedures must be applied. Checks for reasonableness must then be established to make sure that the total of the parts is in reasonable agreement with more sophisticated forecasts based on large-scale demand levels.

## SUMMARY

Problem definition begins with

- A statement of the problem in specific terms.
- A demand theory stating what causes demand.
- A listing and preliminary evaluation of alternative solutions.

Problem definition is a critical phase of any project. It is necessary in this stage to define what is to be done and to establish the criteria for successful completion of the project or forecast.

- It is essential to agree on the required outputs, time, and money to be devoted to solving a problem, the resources that will be made available, the time when an answer is required and, in view of the above, the level of accuracy that may be achievable.
- Data analysis, forecasting, and model-building steps should only begin after these kinds of agreements are reached.

If the prospects for reasonably accurate forecasts are good, the forecaster proceeds to the next phase of the process.

## USEFUL READING

ARMSTRONG, J. S. (1978). *Long-Range Forecasting: From Crystal Ball to Computer*. New York, NY: John Wiley and Sons.

CHAMBERS, J. C., S. K. MULLICK, and D. D. SMITH (1974). *An Executive's Guide to Forecasting*. New York, NY: John Wiley and Sons.

INTRILIGATOR, M. D. (1978). *Econometric Models, Techniques, and Applications*. Englewood Cliffs, NJ: Prentice-Hall.

MAKRIDAKIS, S., and S. C. WHEELWRIGHT (1978). *Forecasting Methods and Applications*. New York, NY: John Wiley and Sons.

SULLIVAN, W. G., and W. W. CLAYCOMBE (1977). *Fundamentals of Forecasting*. Reston, VA: Reston Publishing Co.

WHEELWRIGHT, S. C., and S. MAKRIDAKIS (1980). *Forecasting Methods for Management*, 3rd ed. New York, NY: John Wiley and Sons.

CHAPTER **3**

# Is There a Best Technique to Use?

This chapter describes the factors that must be considered before deciding on the most appropriate projection technique to solve a forecasting problem (see the flowchart). These factors can be classified in terms of

- Characteristics of the data.
- Minimum data requirements.
- Time period to be forecast.
- Accuracy desired.
- Applicability.
- Computer and related costs.

## SELECTING ALTERNATIVE PROJECTION TECHNIQUES

Suppose that you have made some basic determinations about the direction your forecast should take. Now you need to take a closer look at projection techniques. To select projection techniques properly, the forecaster must have

- An understanding of the nature of the forecasting problem.
- An understanding of the nature of the data under investigation.
- A listing of all potentially useful projection techniques, including information regarding their capabilities and limitations.
- Some predetermined criteria on which the selection decision can be made.

We explained how to make first approximations of some of these things in Chapter 2. The forecaster now must take the process a step further through data gathering, data preparation, and preliminary data analysis. The forecaster reviews literature and discusses similar problems with other forecasters to assess successes and failures of alternative approaches. Staff or company colleagues may be available for consultation; otherwise, industry associations, minutes of professional association meetings, and discussions with organizations such as the Conference Board (a nonprofit business research organization—see Conference Board, 1978) and government agencies may be helpful. If the scope of the project is large and requires extensive and ongoing consultations, consulting firms might be contacted for assistance. After conducting this initial research, the forecaster and the user are in a good position to select the most appropriate approach to solving the forecasting problems. Through the following discussions, imagine that you must select projection techniques for a telecommunications forecast of the kind introduced in Chapter 1; this will be considered as an illustrative example. First, however, notice what is compared in Table 3.1.

The first decision criteria shown at the left in Table 3.1 relate to the characteristics and amount of data. Beneath these are four selection criteria that relate to the inherent characteristics of various techniques in terms of

- The capability of handling the time horizon.
- Accuracy.
- Applicability.
- Computer costs.

These four parameters differ from the first two since they are influenced more by the requirements, resources, and objectives of the project than by the nature of the data. Let's examine each criterion in the table.

### Data Characteristics

The pattern of data that can be recognized and handled is assessed in this part of the table. In the telecommunications example, the revenue series can be characterized in two ways: Figure 3.1 shows it to be markedly trending (having a tendency to grow or decline over time), while Figure 3.2 shows that the annual changes in revenue are highly cyclical. These two versions of the revenue series show how the nature of the data is critical in the selection of appropriate projection techniques.

A major factor influencing the selection of projection techniques relates specifically to the variable for which the forecast is being developed: namely, identification and understanding of historical patterns of data. If trend, cyclical, seasonal, or irregular patterns can be recognized, then techniques which are capable of handling those patterns can be readily selected. Questions to be asked include:

- Were there any data collection or input errors which could distort the analysis? (These might be evident as data gaps, discontinuities, or "oddball" data values.)

**Table 3.1** Comparison of analysis and forecasting techniques.

| | | Qualitative | | | | | Quantitative | | | | | | | | | | |
|---|---|---|---|---|---|---|---|---|---|---|---|---|---|---|---|---|---|
| | | | | | | | Statistical | | | | | | | Deterministic | | | |
| | | Delphi method | Market research | Panel consensus | Visionary forecast | Historical analogue | Summary statistics | Moving average | Exponential smoothing | ARIMA (Box-Jenkins) | TCSI decomposition (Shiskin X-11) | Trend projections | Regression model | Econometric model | Intention-to-buy, Anticipation survey | Input-output model | Leading indicator |
| Pattern of data that can be recognized and handled | Horizontal | Not applicable | | | | | X | X | X | X | X | X | X | X | X | X | X |
| | Trend | | | | | | X | X | X | X | X | X | X | X | X | X | X |
| | Seasonal | | | | | | X | X | X | X | X | | X | X | | | |
| | Cyclical | | | | | | X | | | X | X | | X | X | | | |
| Minimum data requirements | | Not applicable | | | | | 5 Points | 5 - - 10 Points | 3 Points | 3 yrs. by mo. | 5 yrs. by mo. | 5 Points | 4 yrs. by mo. | 4 yrs. by mo. | 2 yrs. by mo. | > 1000 | 5 yrs. by mo. |
| Time horizon for which method is most appropriate | Short term (0 - - 3 mos.) | | X | X | | | X | X | X | X | X | X | X | X | X | | X |
| | Medium term (3 mos. - - 2 yrs.) | X | X | X | X | X | X | X | X | X | X | X | X | X | X | X | X |
| | Long term (2 yrs. or more) | X | X | X | X | X | X | | | | | X | X | X | | X | |
| Accuracy (scale of 0 to 10: 0 smallest 10 highest) | Predicting patterns | 5 | 5 | 5 | 5 | 5 | 2 | 2 | 3 | 2 | 7 | 4 | 8 | 2 | 2 | 2 | 2 |
| | Predicting turning points | 4 | 6 | 3 | 2 | 3 | NA | 2 | 2 | 6 | 8 | 1 | 5 | 7 | 8 | 0 | 5 |
| Applicability (scale of 0 to 10: 0 smallest 10 highest) | Time required to obtain forecast | 4 | 8 | 4 | 3 | 5 | 1 | 1 | 1 | 7 | 5 | 4 | 6 | 9 | 5 | 10 | 3 |
| | Ease of understanding and interpreting the results | 8 | 9 | 8 | 8 | 9 | 10 | 9 | 7 | 5 | 7 | 8 | 8 | 4 | 10 | 3 | 10 |
| Computer costs (scale of 0 to 10: 0 smallest 10 highest) | Development | Not applicable | | | | | 0 | 1 | 1 | 8 | 6 | 3 | 5 | 8 | NA | 10 | 4 |
| | Storage requirements | | | | | | 4 | 1 | 1 | 7 | 8 | 6 | 7 | 9 | NA | 10 | 2 |
| | Running | | | | | | 1 | 1 | 1 | 9 | 7 | 3 | 6 | 8 | NA | 10 | NA |

*Note:* This table is a subjective adaptation of material presented in Chambers, Mullick, and Smith (1974, pp. 63–70) and Wheelwright and Makridakis (1980, pp. 292–93).

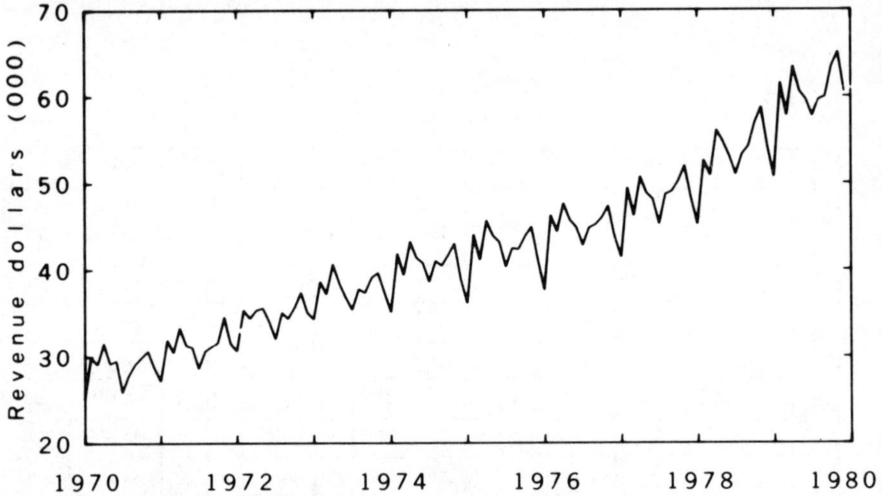


**Figure 3.1** Time series plot of telephone toll revenue for the telecommunications forecasting problem.

- Are the data smooth or irregular?

The purpose of the foregoing analysis is to determine the true starting point for the forecast itself—i.e., the specific method or model to use. Not all projection techniques are appropriate for all forecasting situations. For instance, if the data are relatively stable, a simple exponential smoothing approach may be quite adequate. Other exponential smoothing models are appropriate for trending and seasonal data: the same model is not applicable in all cases. Notice, for example, that the simple exponential smoothing model can handle nontrending, nonseasonal data. Brown's linear exponential smoothing model is appropriate for data with linear trend. The Holt-Winters seasonal exponential smoothing model is appropriate for series that exhibit seasonal patterns.

As the forecast horizon increases, the cyclical pattern of the data may become a significant feature of the overall trend. In these cases, the need to relate the variable to be forecast to economic, market, and competition factors increases, since simple trend projections may no longer be appropriate.

## Minimum Data Requirements

In the telecommunications example, ten years of monthly data are available and the full time period is considered appropriate for forecasting future revenues. The full range of statistical methods may be considered, based on the amount of available data.

The selection of a given technique assumes that the patterns of the time series

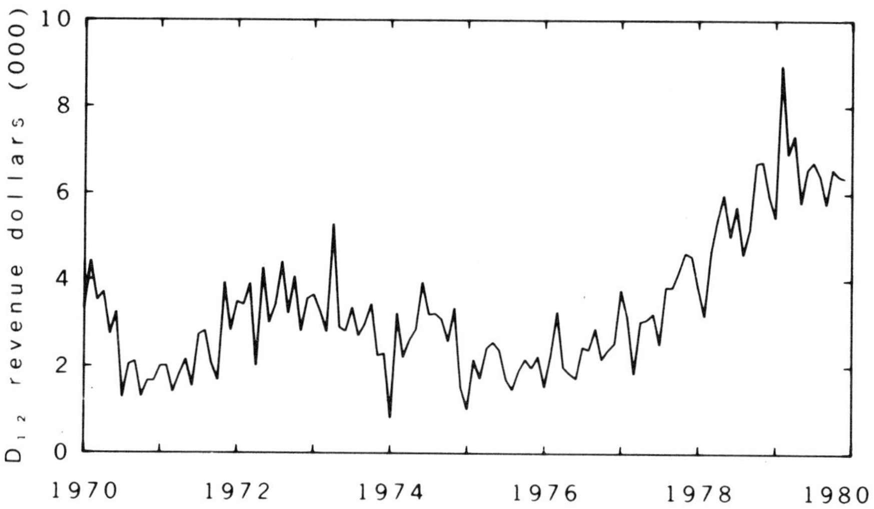


**Figure 3.2** Time series plot of annual changes of telephone toll revenue for the telecommunications forecasting problem.

are such that the forecaster can make certain judgments as to what portion, if any, of the historical data are representative of patterns that will most likely occur throughout the forecast period. Thus the amount of relevant historical data and the patterns of that relevant data serve to reduce the number of projection techniques that can be considered useful. An extensive list of potentially useful projection techniques and their uses will be presented shortly.

## Time Horizon

The time horizon for a forecast has a direct bearing on the selection of forecasting methods. In general, the longer the time horizon, the greater the reliance on qualitative methods.

For the short and medium terms, a variety of quantitative methods can be applied. As the horizon increases, however, a number of these techniques become less applicable. For instance, moving averages and exponential smoothing, and univariate ARIMA time series models are poor predictors of turning points; beyond two years into the future their use is not recommended. However, econometric and transfer function models may be more useful here. Regression models are appropriate for the short, medium, *and* long terms. Summary statistics, moving averages, trend–cycle–seasonal–irregular (TCSI) decomposition, and trend projections are quantitative techniques that are appropriate for the short and medium time horizons. The more complex Box-Jenkins (ARIMA) and econometric techniques are also appropriate. Input-output (I-O) models are not appropriate for short-term forecasting since they are usually based on cross-sectional data that are not very current.

Table 3.1 compares the various projection techniques on a scale of zero to ten for the next three selection criteria: accuracy, applicability, and costs. The scaling represents a subjective evaluation in which a score of zero represents the low end of the range and a score of ten represents the high end of the range. The material is adapted from similar tables in Chambers et al. (1974, pp. 63–70) and Wheelwright and Makridakis (1980, pp. 292–93).

## Accuracy

The objective in the telephone revenue-forecasting example is to provide very accurate short-term and medium-term forecasts (up to two years). However, even two-year-ahead forecasts require great accuracy. Since a business cycle is approximately three to four years in duration, we shall assume that a turning point is expected in the second year but not the first.

Accuracy is relative: you will have whatever precision can be attained through the application of the various projection techniques. If it becomes apparent that the projection technique you plan to use will not meet your original precision objectives, the "go–no go" decision must be reevaluated. Assuming these objectives are attainable, then further assessment of relative precision will require you to examine your selection of data and their compatibility with the specific projection techniques you have chosen for the forecast.

For instance, experience has shown that the technically sophisticated ARIMA (Box-Jenkins) class of time series models can provide very accurate short-term forecasts. For a long-range forecast (say for a six-year plan), the forecaster will also want to make use of regression or econometric models. In the short term, the inertia or momentum of existing consumer behavior often resists sudden, dramatic change. Over a six-year period, however, customers can find new suppliers, and their needs may change as their suppliers change. Therefore, in the long term it is essential to relate the item being forecast to its "drivers" (as explanatory factors are called).

The accuracy of regression (or econometric) models during volatile forecast periods depends to some extent on the accuracy with which explanatory factors can be predicted. While these models can also be used in the short term, they are costlier and more complex than simpler ARIMA models, and they are seldom more accurate. This is particularly true when economic or market conditions are stable.

For forecasts between the medium and long terms, simple trend, regression, and econometric models are used increasingly. Certain trend projection techniques are relatively inexpensive to apply, but the forecasts they produce are often not as accurate as those resulting from econometric methods.

When sufficient data exist and the need for accuracy is great, as when predicting company revenues, the use of both ARIMA and regression (or econometric) models is recommended. Then the generally superior short-term forecasting abilities of ARIMA models balance with the econometric models, which are superior in relating the item to be forecast to economic conditions, price changes, competitive activities, and other explanatory variables.

When both ARIMA and econometric models yield similar forecasts, the analyst can be reasonably certain that the forecast is consistent with assumptions made about the future and has a good chance of being accurate. When the forecasts produced by two or more methods are significantly different, take this as a warning to exercise greater care: careful judgment will be more critical if you must decide to accept one or the other of these, or perhaps some combination of different methods producing different forecasts. It is also important to advise the people who have asked you to make the forecast that the risks associated with such forecasts are greater than when different methods produce consistent forecasts.

The methods that have the highest expected prediction accuracy for one-year-ahead forecasts (assuming no turning point) are the ARIMA and econometric models. Other methods suitable for one-year-ahead forecasts are regression models, time series decomposition, trend projection, and exponential smoothing, all described in this book.

For predicting turning points and—therefore—forecasts two years ahead, time series decomposition, econometric models, ARIMA models, and multiple regression models are suitable methods.

## Applicability

Applicability of projection techniques is generally something a forecaster bases on experience with time series, techniques, the forecasting process, and cost. Forecasts are frequently needed in a relatively short time; exponential smoothing, trend projection, regression models, and time series decomposition methods have an advantage in this regard.

Ultimately a forecast will be presented to management executives for approval; ease of understanding and interpreting the results is therefore an important consideration. Regression models, trend projections, time series decomposition, and exponential smoothing models all rate highly on this criterion.

## Computer and Related Costs

Computer costs are rapidly becoming an insignificant part of technique selection, and in recent years the proliferation of computer packages has lessened the need for forecasters to develop software. Moreover, machine charges for different system configurations (large mainframe, minicomputer, or microprocessor) and different computer services (in-house versus vendor) are hard to compare. Since within the next few years desk-top computers (microprocessors) will almost certainly become commonplace for many forecasting organizations, other criteria will likely overshadow computer cost considerations in the future.

While computer costs are decreasing, certain labor-intensive costs associated with forecast development and implementation cannot be ignored. Start-up costs for developing forecasts for new products and services, analysis, and modeling work tend to escalate, especially when the experience level of the forecasting staff is low. The maintenance of a complex forecasting system, on the other hand, is relatively less costly provided adequate programming documentation and standards are kept current.

For computing costs some of the major considerations include:

- Processing costs.
- Connect-time and data storage costs.
- Supplementary charges for use of software packages and data base retrievals.
- Maintenance and support charges.
- Special hardware needs, such as terminals, cathode-ray tube devices, and plotters.
- Minimum charges (a consideration that can increase costs of small jobs).

## ROLE OF JUDGMENT

As part of the final selection, each technique must be rated by the forecaster in terms of its general reliability and applicability to the problem at hand, its relative value in terms of effectiveness as compared to other appropriate techniques, and its relative performance (accuracy) level.

Now that selection criteria have been established, the forecaster can proceed to reduce the list of potentially useful projection techniques even further. An understanding of data and of operating conditions are the forecaster's primary inputs now. This knowledge must, however, be supplemented by a thorough knowledge of the techniques themselves. To see why this is so, let's look again at the telecommunications application.

Figures 3.1 and 3.2 depict a telecommunications revenue series as well as the changes in revenue over the same period in the prior year. Figure 3.1 is dominated by trend and Figure 3.2 is dominated by cycle. What projection techniques should be used in planning a forecast of these data?

Bear in mind first that a greater number of techniques are appropriate for the time horizon one year ahead than are appropriate for two-year-ahead forecasts. As one approaches forecasts two or more years ahead, the moving average, exponential smoothing, Box-Jenkins, and time series decomposition methods become less applicable.

Also apparent is that a greater number of techniques handle trending data than handle cyclical data. If we assume a turning point will occur in the second year, the moving average, exponential smoothing, and trend projection techniques are no longer applicable.

In terms of expected forecast accuracy for the one-year-ahead forecasts, the

ARIMA, econometric, regression, and time series decomposition approaches look most promising. With a turning point in the second year, the time series decomposition, econometric, and regression models look most promising.

If we consider time constraint and the desire to present an easily understood method, regression and time series decomposition approaches appear promising, followed by trend projection and exponential smoothing for the one-year-ahead forecasts.

The time series decomposition and linear regression methods appear most promising for the two-year-ahead forecasts.

Different conclusions might result, however, under the following circumstances:

- Shorter time horizons are involved.
- Computer costs are important.
- Accuracy requirements are less stringent.
- Time is not a constraint.
- Ease of understanding and explaining forecast methods is not important.

## A LIFE-CYCLE PERSPECTIVE

Figure 3.3 provides broad recommendations of forecasting methods related to a *product's life cycle* (Chambers et al., 1974). The life cycle begins with the decisions and actions taken before the product is introduced. The techniques used to forecast a product's future at this stage include the Delphi method, market research related

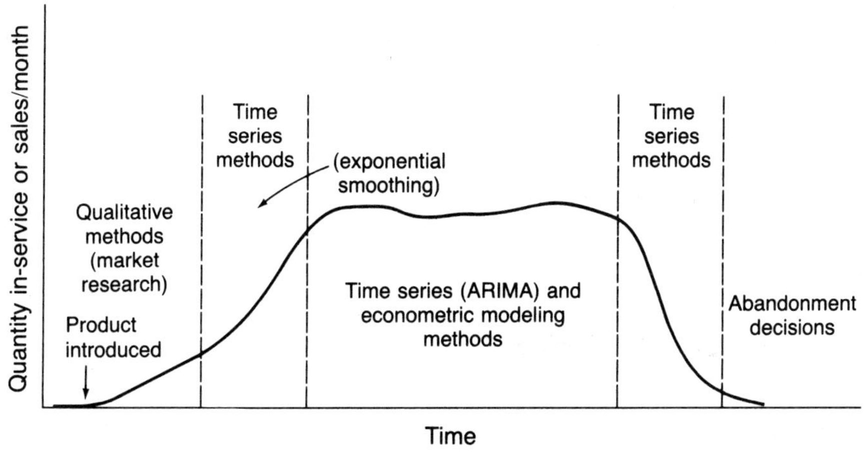


**Figure 3.3** The life cycle of a product.

to the characteristics of the market and consumers' willingness to pay, panel consensus, visionary forecasts, historical analogues, decision trees, and other methods that can be applied with little or no historical data about the product. These techniques are presented in Wheelwright and Makridakis (1980).

*Product introduction* begins the next phase of the product life cycle. Quite often supply limitations, pipeline backups, and lack of customer awareness result in only a gradual buildup of the quantity of products sold. At this time, qualitative and market-research estimates may be refined.

The next stage in the life of a successful product is *rapid growth*. The product fills a need not otherwise met in the marketplace, or its price-performance characteristics are superior to its competitors, and it is adopted rapidly—faster, in fact, than would be accounted for by average growth in market or economic conditions.

At this stage, to project the product's future, time series methods become applicable. For less than thirty months of data, exponential smoothing techniques may be tried. For thirty or more months of data, ARIMA models can be built. When forty or more months of data are available, research shows that ARIMA models are superior to exponential smoothing models in terms of forecasting performance (see, for example, Geurts and Ibrahim, 1975; Granger and Newbold, 1977; Groff, 1973; Makridakis and Hibon, 1979; Newbold and Granger, 1974; and Reid, 1971).

As the product enters a *mature stage,* with three and preferably four or more years of data available on sales, prices, economic factors, market size, and so forth, econometric modeling techniques can be applied. These techniques offer an explanatory capability the time series methods lack. Whether or not this is an important consideration depends on the circumstances that have created the need for the forecast; in the mature phase a product is frequently modified, or its price may be adjusted, to maintain its competitiveness.

As new technology or other competitive products with superior price-performance characteristics also enter the market, demand for the "mature" product drops. The *fall-off* is greater than can be attributed to economic or market size considerations. Once again, time series methods may be more responsive in projecting the rapid decline of the product's sales.

In the final stage of the life cycle, the product is about to be abandoned. It is no longer profitable and its past history may not help in determining when it will be withdrawn. Financial considerations, or plans to introduce customers to a new product, will determine the product's fate.

## A MULTI-METHOD APPROACH

Projection techniques are used during the forecasting process to describe the historical behavior of a time series in a simplistic, mathematical way and then, using that same mathematical model, to predict the future characteristics of the data. To describe the complexities of reality in terms of simplified models, clearly no single model can be considered universally adaptable to any given forecasting situation. The assumptions and theories on which the projection techniques are based limit their appropriateness and reliability.

The forecaster should be careful to avoid using techniques where the data characteristics do not match the assumptions of the method. Thus a basic principle is to utilize more than one projection technique. By observing this principle during the actual development of a forecast, the forecaster can be reasonably sure of avoiding biases which are inherent in any one projection technique or its use.

The purpose of using more than one technique is to ensure that the forecasting approach will be as flexible as possible and that the forecaster's judgment (which is so critical to the forecasting process) is not overly dependent upon one particular projection technique. It is not uncommon to see forecasters develop a preference for one forecasting technique over another, and then to use that technique almost exclusively even in a new situation. Such a preference can be easily established because of the highly specialized nature of some of the techniques.

Some forecasters always use the most statistically sophisticated techniques that can be found. In many cases, this tendency can greatly reduce the effectiveness of the forecasting process because some of the more sophisticated techniques are unresponsive to drastic pattern changes in the time series. The degree of forecast precision for the projection techniques is not necessarily a direct function of the degree of sophistication.

We recommend that two or more projection techniques be used to describe the historical behavior of the data and to predict this for the future. In essence, one is able to evaluate alternative views of the future. It is also necessary to provide a risk level associated with each alternative. A comparison can be made of the alternative views of the future and hence increase the chances that the selected forecast level is reasonable.

## SUMMARY

To summarize the techniques selection process, the forecaster must

- Perform a general analysis on the time series.
- Perform a screening procedure that reduces the list of all available projection techniques to a list of those projection techniques that are capable of handling the data in question.
- Perform a detailed examination of the techniques that are still considered appropriate.
- Make the final selection of two or more techniques that are considered to be the most appropriate for the given situation.

Table 3.1 provides guidance on the relative abilities of a number of forecasting methods to handle the patterns in the data, the minimum amount of data required, the time horizon, accuracy, applicability, and costs.

- Careful analysis of the data in terms of the qualities shown in the table will indicate if the characteristics of the data match the requirements (assumptions) of the forecasting methods.
- A multi-method approach is recommended since the use of a single technique is neither the desirable nor practically attainable objective of the technique selection process.

## USEFUL READING

CHAMBERS, J. C., S. K. MULLICK, and D. D. SMITH (1974). *An Executive's Guide to Forecasting*. New York, NY: John Wiley and Sons.

CONFERENCE BOARD (1978). *Sales Forecasting*. New York, NY: The Conference Board.

GEURTS, M. D., and I. B. IBRAHIM (1975). Comparing the Box-Jenkins Approach with the Exponentially Smoothed Forecasting Model Application to Hawaii Tourists. *Journal of Marketing Research* 12, 182–88.

GRANGER, C. W. J., and P. NEWBOLD (1977). *Forecasting Economic Time Series*. New York, NY: Academic Press.

GROFF, G. K. (1973). Empirical Comparison of Models for Short-Range Forecasting. *Management Science* 20, 22–31.

MAKRIDAKIS, S., and M. HIBON (1979). Accuracy of Forecasting: An Empirical Investigation. *Journal of the Royal Statistical Society* A 142, 97–145.

NEWBOLD, P., and C. W. J. GRANGER (1974). Experience with Forecasting Univariate Time Series and the Combination of Forecasts. *Journal of the Royal Statistical Society* A 137, 131–46.

REID, D. J. (1971). Forecasting in Action: A Comparison of Forecasting Techniques in Economic Time Series. *Proceedings, Joint Conference of the Operations Research Society,* Long-Range Planning and Forecasting.

WHEELWRIGHT, S. C., and S. MAKRIDAKIS (1980). *Forecasting Methods for Management,* 3rd ed. New York, NY: John Wiley and Sons.

CHAPTER **4**

# Do the Forecasting Assumptions Hold Up to Scrutiny?

This chapter deals with the final phase of the forecasting process:

- Evaluating the alternatives.
- Determining the reliability of the forecasts.
- Recommending the forecast values. This involves:
- Selecting the final forecast values.
- Packaging and presenting the forecast for approval.

Once one or more forecasting techniques have been selected, the forecaster uses the computer to estimate the model parameters and to assess the reasonableness of the model (see the Flowchart). It should be evident that the model-building process has similarities to general problem solving in other disciplines.

## PARAMETER ESTIMATION

After narrowing down the possible alternatives, the forecaster must determine the parameters of a forecasting model. These parameters may be ratios such as housing units per acre or market penetration rates. Similarly, the potential car buyer doublechecks the parameters that make a certain car seem right, including the specific model, color, engine size, and extras such as power steering, power brakes, and a stereo radio.

Model parameters may also be coefficients estimated statistically from data by computer. Computer time sharing provides immediate access to, flexibility, and breadth of potentially useful forecasting techniques.

## VERIFYING REASONABLENESS

Next, the car buyer attempts to validate the manufacturer's claims concerning ease of parking, comfort, noise level, braking, and acceleration. This is done by taking a road test. Forecasters also validate models through diagnostic checking. There are a number of analytical tools available (e.g., residual analysis and forecast tests) to determine if it is possible to improve on an initial model. These tools will, of course, be presented throughout the book.

As a result of the road test, the car buyer may decide to try a different make, model, or engine. The forecaster might decide to add new data, try a different method, or replace one time series such as the reciprocal of an unemployment rate with another series such as total employment in a revenue model.

The diagnostic checking stage usually means a number of iterations around a program loop. New variables can be considered, transformations of variables can be made to improve the models, and some techniques should be rejected at this stage because of their

- Inability to provide statistically significant results.
- Inability to achieve the desired objectives of accuracy.

In evaluating alternatives, the forecaster will find patterns or characteristics of the models that will influence the final selection of the models for use. For example, which techniques are more accurate in predicting turning points? In predicting stable periods? Which techniques have the best overall accuracy in the forecast test mode? Do some techniques tend to overpredict or underpredict in given situations? Are the short-term predictions of one model better than another? Do you actually need long-term predictions? Do the coefficients of one model seem more reasonable than those of another either in sign or magnitude?

## DOCUMENTING RESULTS TO DATE

A vital part of forecasting is the documentation of the work at various stages of the process. The chore of documentation can be minimized by advance planning and continuous record keeping. The forecaster's documentation is as essential as the proof that a car has been serviced in compliance with a warranty would be for someone wanting to buy or sell a used car. The forecaster must write down the specific steps taken and the assumptions made. Only then can the forecaster and the manager have a meaningful analysis of results when the actual data are compared.

If work has been documented, it will be possible to specify a reason or set of reasons for the forecast's differing from actual accomplishments. The reasons would go a long way toward helping the manager evaluate the forecaster's performance.

Moreover, without documentation it will not be possible to learn from past experiences. Without documented methods and assumptions, it is not possible to determine where some problem lies.

From a manager's viewpoint, documentation also simplifies staff turnover problems. If the original forecaster is unavailable, a new forecaster will not have to reconstruct a forecast from scratch. A model or case study will exist and a body of information will be available for use.

The users of the forecast will also appreciate the additional documentation. Instead of simply having a set of numbers, they will have the kind of information they need to assist them in making decisions about their area of responsibility.

## GENERATING MODEL PREDICTIONS AND CONFIDENCE LIMITS

The forecaster now reaches the stage where actual forecasts are produced, tested, and approved. This effort begins with a generation of predictions from the models that have survived the selection process.

In addition, the forecaster provides estimates of the reliability of the forecast in terms of limits at specified levels of confidence. Alternatively, reliability can be expressed as the likely percent (amount of) deviation between a forecast and actual performance. For example, suppose that new car purchases for the year are forecast to be 10 million plus or minus 700,000 at about a 90 percent confidence level. Another way of stating this might be that in a particular forecasting model, average annual deviation (absolute value) between what is forecast and actual new car sales is 7 percent.

One way forecasters can test the validity of their models is to work backward through a time series, generating predictions from the models over prior time periods for which the actual results are known. In this way it is possible to monitor the performance of the models and determine the likely forecast accuracy.

Table 4.1 illustrates how a forecaster could summarize forecast errors in a model with actual data from 1964 through 1979. A prediction from the model for 1975 is generated. Actual data through 1974 show that the prediction is 8.7 percent greater than the 1975 actual value. An additional year of actuals is then added to the model and 1976 is predicted. This time the prediction is only 1.2 percent greater than the actual.

This process can be continued and some average performance can be calculated. In this hypothetical example, the average absolute one-year-ahead forecast error for five periods is 4.3 percent. It might be useful to consider the median absolute percent error (here 3.8 percent) as well, to ensure that a very large miss one year doesn't unduly distort the average value. With this model, the forecaster might expect the one-year-ahead prediction to be within 4 percent of the actual value, on the average.

**Table 4.1** Summary of one-year-ahead forecast errors from a hypothetical model with data from 1964 through 1979.

| Historical fit | Percent error |
|---|---|
| 1964–1974 | −8.7 |
| 1965–1975 | −1.2 |
| 1966–1976 | +5.7 |
| 1967–1977 | +3.8 |
| 1968–1978 | −2.3 |
| Average absolute percent error = | 4.3 |
| Median absolute percent error = | 3.8 |

*Note:* Percent error = (Actual − Forecast) / Actual.

At this point, monitoring procedures can be established to determine the accuracy of the forecast. Likewise, the owner monitors a car's performance after purchase. Since the "forecast" the car buyer was attempting to make was whether a car would fulfill all projected contingencies, monitoring that forecast would entail measuring how family members use the car, its mileage, its maintenance costs, and so on: the buyer would also monitor factors such as changed public transit availability or cost, since those entered into the original definition of a car-buying forecast.

The forecaster does the same thing. Assumptions and results are continuously monitored.

## RECOMMENDING THE FORECAST NUMBERS

The final steps of the process entail relating predictions from various models to the final forecast. The forecaster has several decisions to make. The forecaster recognizes that the various models are abstractions from the real world. The future will never be exactly like the past. The predictions from the models must be viewed as job aids in making a subjective judgment about the future.

### Role of Judgment

Judgment plays an important role in the final determination of the forecast values and, later on, in the determination of when a forecast should be revised. Analogously, once the car buyer has purchased the car, subjective judgment comes into play if the car buyer realizes that the purchase was not a good decision. For example, during "verification" and "confidence" checks, suppose that the car buyer discovers a flaw so great that the dealer agrees either to repair the car or to exchange it for a slightly different model: the buyer needs to exercise judgment not called for in the original forecast in order to reconcile expectations and reality.

In an actual forecasting situation, it may become apparent that the actuals have exceeded the estimates for the last three months. Experience may suggest that a model's predictions be modified upwards by a given amount to account for the current deviation and the forecaster's expectation of whether or not that pattern will continue.

Subjective judgment in forecasting should be based on all available information, including changes in company policy, changes in economic conditions, contacts with customers, and government policy considerations. This judgment is a real measure of the skill and experience of the forecaster. For this reason data and processes are only as good as the person interpreting them. This judgment operates on many inputs to reach a final forecast.

Judgment is, by far, the most crucial element when trying to predict the future. Informed judgment is what ties the forecasting process and the projection techniques into a cohesive effort that is capable of producing realistic predictions of future events or conditions.

Informed judgment is an essential ingredient of

- The selection of the forecasting approach.
- The selection of data sources.
- The selection of the data collection methodology.
- The selection of analysis and projection techniques.
- The use of analysis and projection techniques during the forecasting process.
- The identification of influencing market and company factors which are likely to affect the future of the item to be forecast.
- The determination of how those factors will affect the item in terms of the direction, magnitude (amount or rate), timing, and duration of the expected impact.
- The selection of the forecast presentation methodology.

Informed judgment, therefore, plays a significant role in minimizing the uncertainty associated with forecasting. Automatic processes, models, or statistical formulas are sometimes used in computing future demand from a set of key factors. However, no such approach is likely to reduce the reliance upon sound judgment substantially. Judgment must be based on a comprehensive analysis of market activities and a thorough evaluation of basic assumptions and influencing factors.

Statistical approaches can provide a framework of information around which analytical skills and judgment can be applied in order to arrive at and support a sound forecast. To quote from Butler et al. (1974, p. 7):

> In actual application of the scientific approaches, judgment plays, and will undoubtedly always play, an important role. . . . The users of econometric models

> have come to realize that their models can only be relied upon to provide a first approximation—a set of consistent forecasts which then must be "massaged" with intuition and good judgment to take into account those influences on economic activity for which history is a poor guide.

The limitations of a purely statistical approach should be kept clearly in mind. Statistics, like all tools, may be valuable for one job but of little use for another. An analysis of patterns is basic to forecasting and a number of different statistical procedures may be employed to make this analysis more meaningful. However, the human element is required to understand the differences between what was expected in the past and what actually occurred, and to predict the likely course of future events.

### Selecting Forecast Values

Since future events and conditions cannot be predicted consistently with complete accuracy, the end product of the forecasting process can best be described as giving advice. In most cases, that advice is provided in the form of a single "best bet" figure which represents either the data value at some specific time or the cumulative value of a series of data points at the end of a specific period of time.

The "best bet" figure can be illustrated best with the median of a hypothetical frequency distribution. There is an even chance that the future outcome will fall above or below that median. Its primary weakness, however, is that the planning and decision-making processes assume that the forecast precisely describes the future, when in fact it cannot perform such a feat.

Decision making involves the assessment and acceptance of risk. Therefore, forecasters can assist decision makers by providing forecast levels and associated probability statements that indicate the chance of each of those levels being exceeded. This does not mean that the forecaster takes a "shotgun approach" to predicting the future by incorporating the extreme alternatives at either end of the range. It simply means that the forecaster should provide the "best bet" figure, and state the associated risk levels on each side of the "best bet." If a view of the future is presented in this format, the decision maker has much more information on which to assess the risk associated with decisions.

The probabilities associated with the alternative views of the future are, of course, highly subjective. In the physical sciences, probabilities are developed through some form of scientific sampling process over a long period of time. Such is not the case when it comes to quantifying the probabilities of future events or conditions in the business world. A multitude of influencing factors can enter into the picture after the forecast is made and thereby completely change the course of future events.

The principle of using more than one projection technique can again provide substance to the forecasting process by giving a certain degree of objectivity in the development of risk levels. It is clear, therefore, that the projection techniques play an important role in the decisions on the forecast level which is ultimately produced.

## Forecast Presentation and Approval

Normally, it is necessary to obtain user acceptance and higher management approval of a forecast. When a car buyer presents his or her selected car to friends and family, the buyer tries to convince them that the car is a beauty and that its cost doesn't exceed what had been planned for. Besides, won't the neighbors be jealous? The buyer hopes to receive approval, especially since the relatives agreed to help in financing the purchase.

The forecaster must also present a forecast for approval. With pride of authorship, the forecaster thinks it is a beauty and is worth what it cost to produce. The managers will approve, hopefully, but never with much enthusiasm. After all, if things go wrong, it is your forecast!

## The Forecast Package

After the forecast has been developed, it must then be documented and communicated to people who need the information. The purpose of the forecast package is to communicate the forecast to others and, at the same time, provide credibility to the forecast in the form of supporting documentation. Such a package should include

- The forecast.
- A display of the forecast which analytically relates it to the past data (through graphical and/or tabular display of the historical data and the forecast on the same page).
- Appropriate documentation of the rationale and assumptions regarding external and company factors which are likely to influence the item under study during the forecast period.
- Appropriate documentation on the approach that was used to make the forecast and on the projection techniques used during the forecasting process.
- A delineation of specific potential decision points related to risk levels and the significance of particular assumptions.

The value of a forecast is a function of its usefulness to decision makers in the face of future uncertainty. Therefore, the forecaster's job is not completed by merely developing the forecast. The product must also be sold to the decision maker. The supporting documentation should emphasize the quality of

- The process.

- The inputs used during the process.
- The judgment that was applied throughout the process.

An example of a forecast presentation is given in Chapter 21.

## SUMMARY

The forecaster has now reached the end of the forecasting process.

- After selecting the forecasting methods for study, the forecaster evaluates each method. This process is called diagnostic checking and often results in modifications of the initial models until acceptable models are obtained.
- A variety of test statistics and graphical analyses are reviewed to decide when the model is acceptable.

After passing these tests, predictions are generated from the models.

- Informed judgment, important throughout the process, is used to select the forecast values from among the possible candidates.
- Estimates are made of the precision of the forecast and a presentation is made to gain acceptance of the forecast.
- The forecasts are monitored to ensure their continuing relevance and forecast changes are proposed when necessary.

## USEFUL READING

BUTLER, W. F., R. A. KAVESH, and R. B. PLATT, eds. (1974). *Methods and Techniques of Business Forecasting*. Englewood Cliffs, NJ: Prentice-Hall.

CHAPTER **5**

# Why Stress Data Analysis?

Analysis of data is basic to the forecasting process. Analysis is essential for

- Summarizing and exposing detail in time series data so that the forecaster can effectively select a good starting model.
- Comparing a number of traditional and innovative analytical tools to increase one's understanding of "good" data. "Good" data are data that are typical or representative of the problem being studied. Such data are accurate in terms of reporting accuracy and also have been adjusted, where necessary, to eliminate unrepresentative or extreme values.

## COMPONENTS OF A TIME SERIES

It is commonly assumed in practice that the total variation in a time series is composed of several basic *unobservable* components: a long-term trend plus a cyclical part, a seasonal factor, and an irregular or random term (Figure 5.1). In any given time series, one or more of these components may predominate.

In Chapter 2 we defined a trend as a prevailing tendency or inclination with time. When the term "trend" is applied to a straight line, it is often referred to as "slope." A trend may fall or rise and can have a more complicated pattern than a straight line: the Federal Reserve Board index of industrial production, depicted in Figure 5.2, is a good example of a time series that is predominantly trending upward. Trending data are often modeled with exponential smoothing models (Chapter 8) and regression methods (Chapter 12).

Figure 5.3 depicts a time series strongly dominated by seasonal effects—namely, monthly changes in telephone connections and disconnections. The seasonality results from the installation of telephones coincident with school openings and removal of telephones coincident with school closings each year. Thus, the seasonal peaks

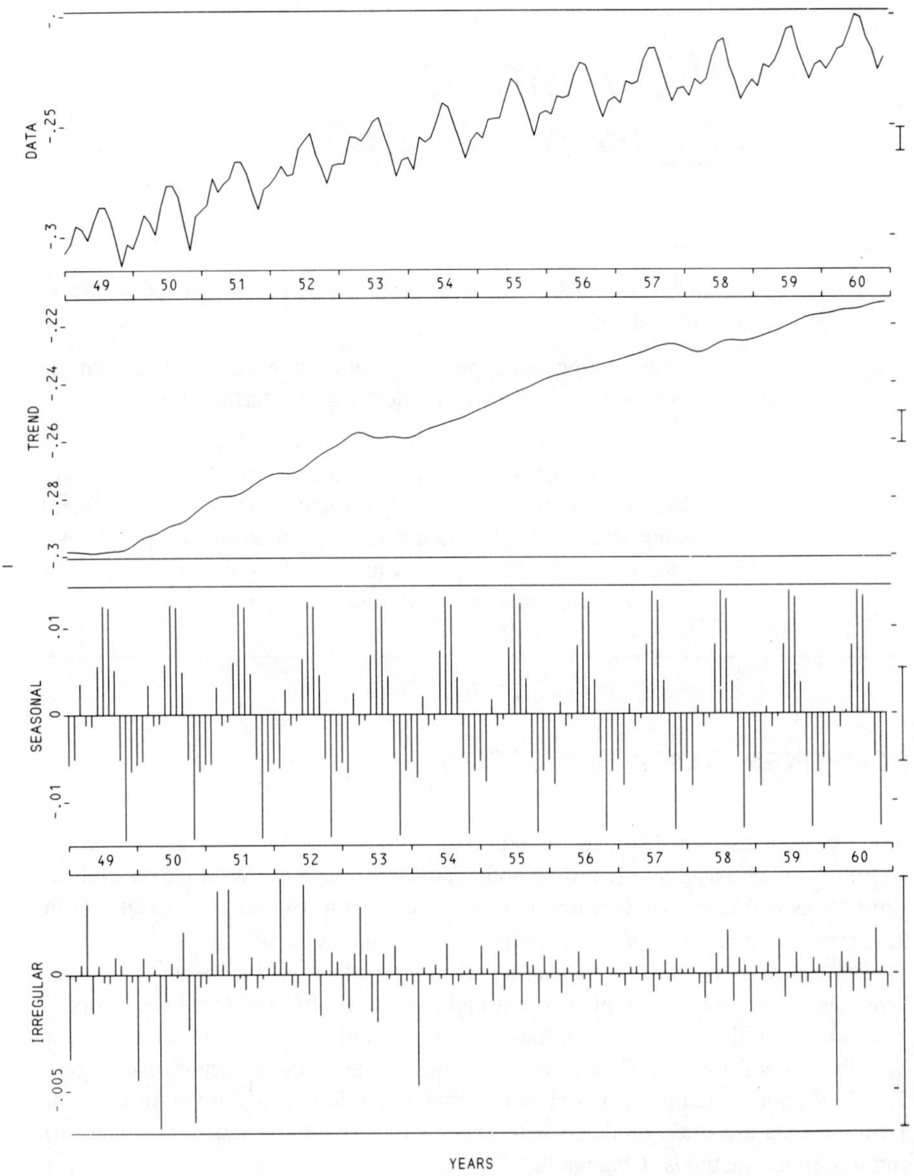


**Figure 5.1** A time series decomposition into trend-and-cycle, seasonal, and irregular variation parts.

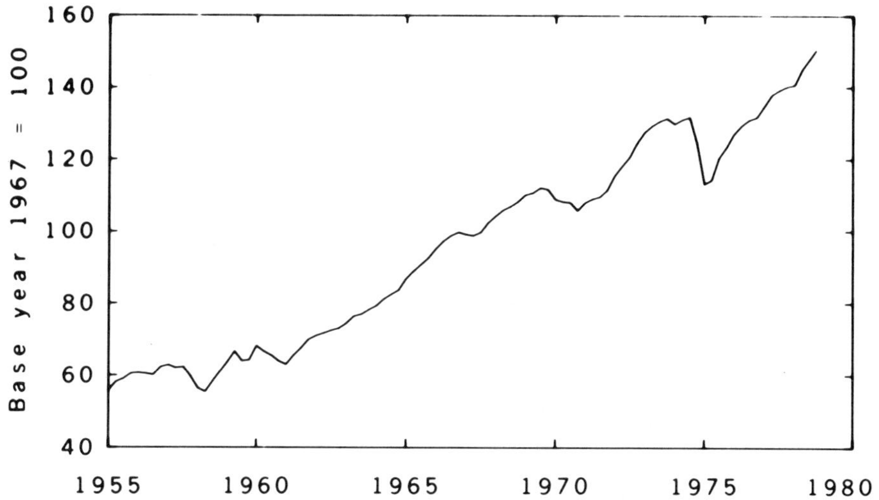


*Source:* Board of Governors of the Federal Reserve System.

**Figure 5.2** Time plot of the FRB index of industrial production.

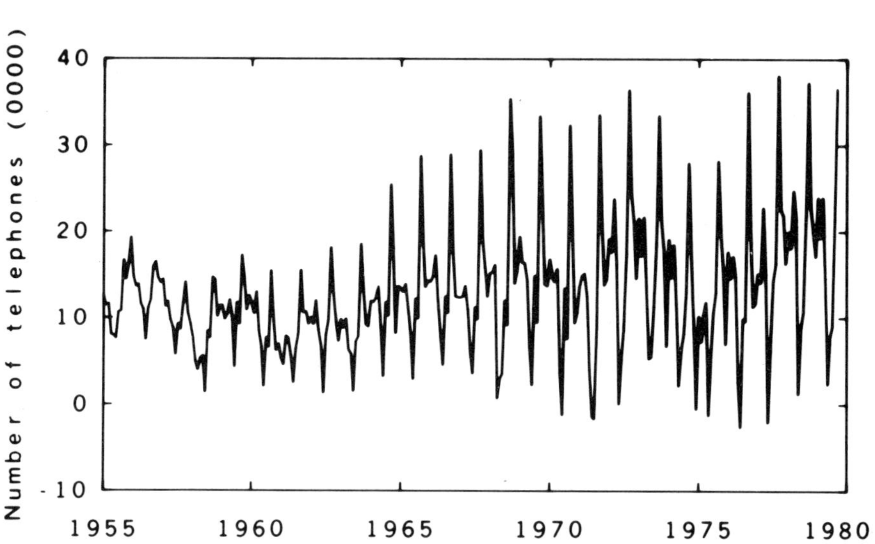


**Figure 5.3** Time plot of monthly gain in a main telephone series.

and troughs appear with regularity each year. The trend in the net gain in telephones is related to the growth in households and the increasing use of telephones by former nonusers. Thus both trend and seasonal effects are superimposed on each other, as well as some residual effects which are not readily discernible from the raw data. Seasonal decomposition is the subject of Chapters 18 and 19.

The definition of cycle in forecasting is somewhat specialized in that the duration and amplitude of the cycle are not constant. This characteristic is what makes cycle forecasting so difficult. Although a business cycle is evident in so many economic series, its quantification is one of the most elusive in time series analysis (Chapter 11). In practice, trend and cycle are sometimes considered as a single pattern, known as the trend-cycle.

Other time series data are not strongly dominated by seasonal and trend effects, such as the University of Michigan Survey Research Center's index of consumer sentiment shown in Figure 5.4. In this case, the dominant pattern is a cycle corresponding to contractions and expansions in the economy. (Compare Figure 5.4 with the index of industrial production and housing starts in Figures 5.2 and 5.8, respectively.) Of course, a large irregular pattern is present in this series because there are many unknown factors that significantly affect the behavior of consumers and their outlook for the future.

The *irregular* is the catch-all category for all patterns that cannot be associated with trend, cycle, or seasonal effects. Except for some cyclical variation, the plot of the consumer sentiment index does not suggest any systematic variation that can be readily classified.

Irregulars are nontypical observations which may be caused by unusual or rare events, errors of transcription, administrative decisions, and random variation. The irregulars most often create the greatest difficulty for the forecaster since they are generally unexplainable. A thorough understanding of the source and accuracy of the data is required to recognize the true importance of irregularity.

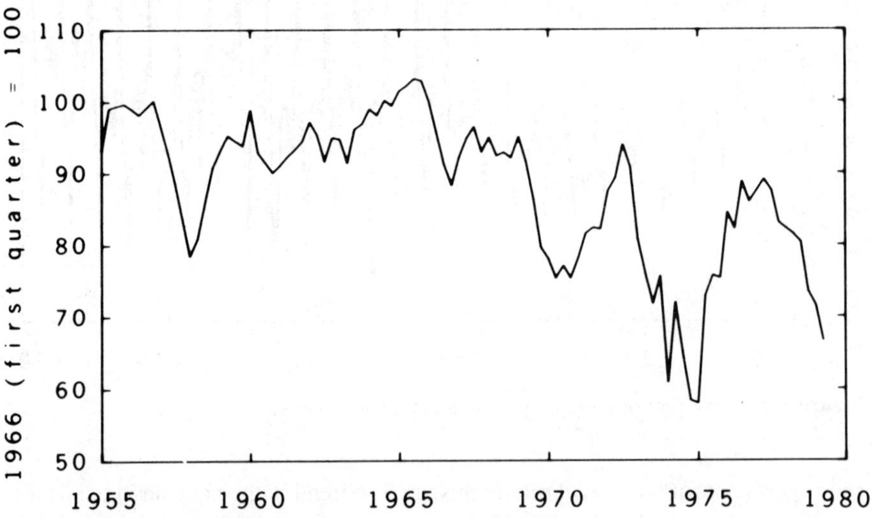


*Source:* University of Michigan, Survey Research Center.

**Figure 5.4** Time plot of the University of Michigan Survey Research Center's index of consumer sentiment (quarterly).

An example of an irregular—an unusual or rare event arising in a time series—is depicted in Figure 5.5, which shows a monthly record of telephone installations for the Montreal area from 1958 through 1968. Although dominated by trend and seasonality, the September 1967 figure is greatly reduced because of the influence of Montreal's World's Fair (Expo '67). Residential telephone installations normally accompany a turnover of apartment leases during September in Montreal, Canada. However, a large number of apartments were held for visitors to Expo that year. The dotted line depicts what might have happened under normal conditions in the absence of this "unusual" event.

Another example—this one is of a transcription error—is shown in Figure 5.6, which shows a series of monthly telephone message volumes. The general upward trend is quite evident and the unusual value in 1973 is due to a keypunch error.

Figure 5.7 shows an example in which an administrative decision influenced a time series. The series represents the number of "main" telephones (telephones for which separate numbers are issued) in service in a specific telephone exchange. The saturation (or "filling-up") of a neighboring exchange for a period in 1976 necessitated a transfer of new service requests from that exchange to the one depicted in the figure. This distorted the natural growth pattern. Any modeling effort based on these data must be preceded by an adjustment to account for this unusual event.

The components of a time series need not occur simultaneously and with equal strength. For example, many time series do not exhibit seasonality, while others, such as the weather, are not affected by the business cycle.

The purpose of analyzing time series data is to *expose* and *identify* these components. If appropriate, it is also desirable to correct, adjust, and transform data

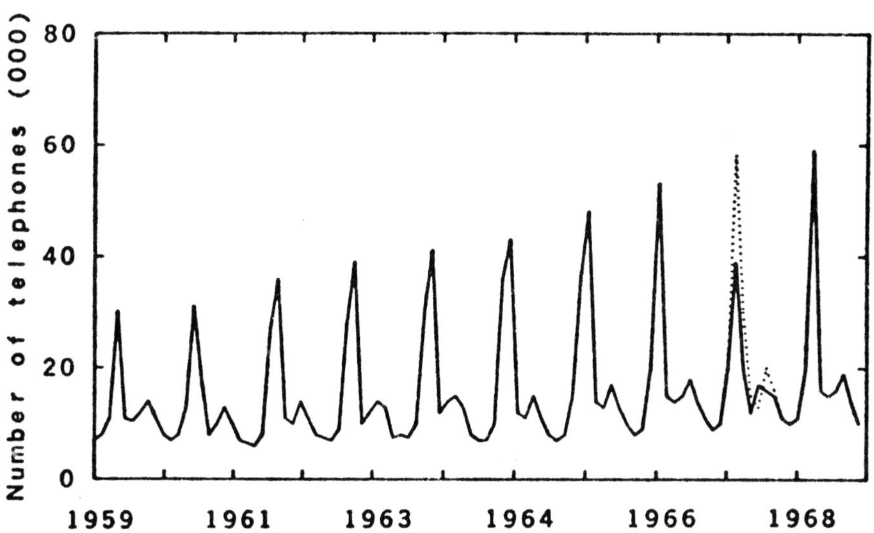


**Figure 5.5** Impact of Expo '67 on monthly connections of main telephones in Montreal, Canada.

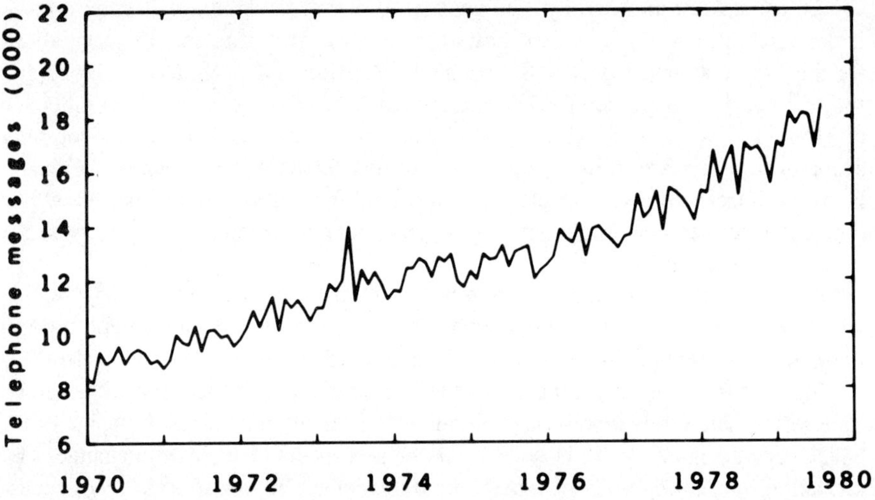


**Figure 5.6** Time plot of a monthly telephone toll message series with a transcription error in 1973.

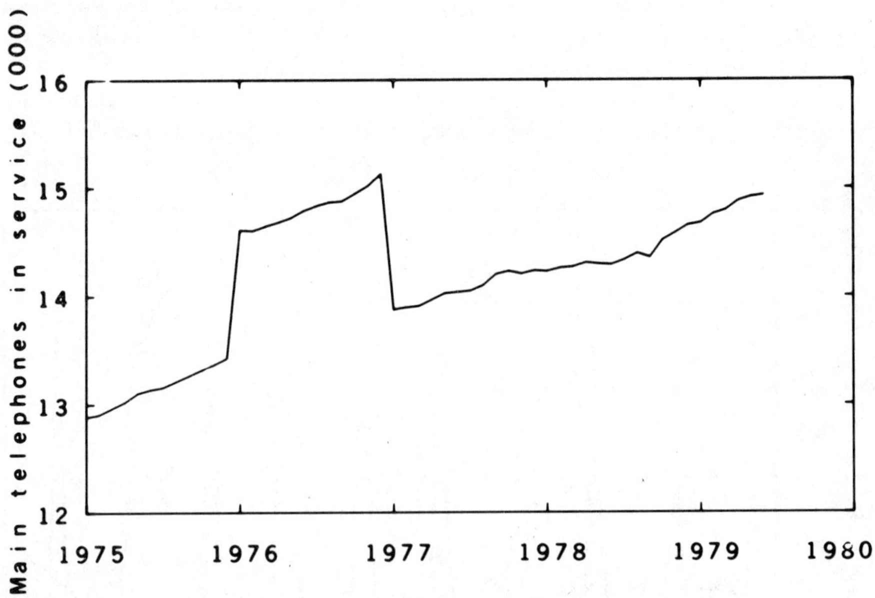


**Figure 5.7** Time plot of main telephones in service in a telephone exchange.

prior to the modeling process. Exposing key components increases understanding of the data-generating process, in practice, and thus improves the likelihood of successfully predicting these patterns in the forecast period.

## JUDGING THE QUALITY OF DATA

The analysis of data for forecasting purposes requires a careful consideration of the quality of data sources. A model or technique based on historical data will be no better than the quality of its source. There are several criteria that can be applied to data to determine appropriateness for modeling. The first of these is

- Accuracy: Proper care must be taken that the required data are collected from a reliable source with proper attention given to accuracy.

*Survey data* exemplify the need to ensure accurate data: survey data are collected by government and private agencies from questionnaires and interviews to determine future plans of consumers and businesses. The quarterly index of consumer sentiment, shown in Figure 5.4, is the result of an analysis made by the Survey Research Center at the University of Michigan. These data have certain limitations because they reflect only the respondent's anticipation (what they expect others to do) or expectations (what they themselves plan to do), not firm commitments. Nevertheless, such information may be regarded as a valuable aid to economic forecasting either directly or as an indication of the state of consumer confidence concerning the economic outlook.

Another criterion of appropriateness of data is

- Conformity: The data must adequately represent the phenomenon for which it is being used. If the data purport to represent economic activity, the data should show upswings and downswings in accordance with past historical business cycle fluctuations. Data that are too smooth or too erratic may not adequately reflect the patterns desired for modeling.

The Federal Reserve Board (FRB) index of industrial production for the United States, depicted in Figure 5.2, is an example of a cyclical *indicator of the economy*. It is evident that the time series variation is consistent with historical economic expansions and recessions. The FRB index measures changes in the physical volume or quantity of output of manufacturers, minerals suppliers, and electric and gas utilities. The index does not cover production on farms, in the construction industry, in transportation, or in various trade and service industries. Since the index of industrial production was first produced by the FRB in 1920, it has been revised from time to time to take account of the growing complexity of the economy, the availability of more data, improvement in statistical processing techniques, and refinements in methods of analysis.

Still another criterion is

- Timeliness: It takes time to collect data. Data collected, summarized, and published on a timely basis will be of greatest value to the forecaster. Often preliminary data are available first, so that the time delay before the data are declared "official" may become a significant factor.

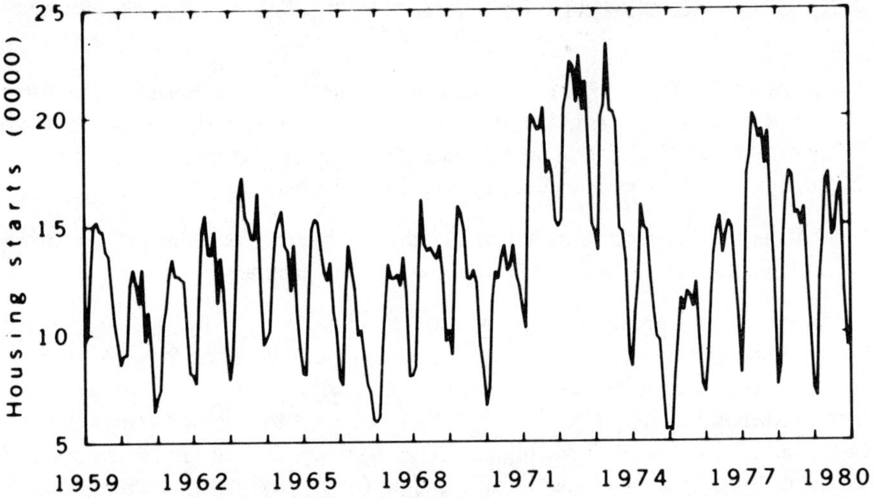


*Source:* U.S. Department of Commerce, Bureau of Census.

**Figure 5.8** Time plot of monthly housing starts in the United States.

Demographic data may fall in this category for many users. The monthly housing starts shown in Figure 5.8 are demographic data reported by contractors and builders for use by government and private industry. Such *external data* are, of course, subject to adjustment because of data collection delays and reporting inaccuracies.

A final criterion is

- Consistency: Data must be consistent throughout the period of their use. When definitions change, adjustments need to be made in order to retain logical consistency in historical patterns.

The monthly increase in telephone gain, depicted in Figure 5.3, is an example of data that would be made available to telephone company forecasters. Such data, called *internal data,* are obtained from corporate books or from other company records made available to a forecaster's organization. Their definitions may vary because of changes in the structure of the company organization, accounting procedures, or product and service definitions. As part of the forecasting process, throughout this book various kinds of internal data will be related to economic indicators, survey data, and external data in a number of forecasting examples and case studies.

## UNDERSTANDING DATA

With "good" data in hand, a forecaster can start the important task of exploratory data analysis. *Exploratory data analysis* means looking at data, absorbing what the data are suggesting, and using various summarizations and display methods to gain insight into the process generating the data. It is only a first step and not the whole story.

Exploratory data analysis is like detective work (Erickson and Nosanchuk, 1977; Hartwig and Dearing, 1979; McNeil, 1977; and Tukey, 1977). It requires tools and understanding. Without an important tool such as fingerprint powder, a detective cannot find fingerprints. Without an understanding of where criminals will place their fingers, no fingerprints can be found. Exploratory data analysis uncovers indicators that are generally quantitative in nature; some are accidental, some are misleading. A planned forecasting and modeling effort that does not include provisions for exploratory data analysis often misses the most interesting and important results.

*Simple summarization* procedures provide a useful initial step in any modeling process. Many macroeconomic variables, such as the U.S. Gross National Product (GNP), employment, and industrial production are dominated by a strong trend. This pattern can be quantified in many cases by fitting a simple curve, such as a straight line, through the data. Certain sales data show strong peaks and troughs within the years, corresponding to a seasonal pattern. When seasonality is removed from these data, the secondary effects become apparent and may be important.

Inspection of time series data often indicates strong trend patterns. The fitting of trend lines is a simple and convenient way of exposing detail in data. A useful way of presenting the FRB index shown in Figure 5.2 is to compare it to some trend line, such as an exponential or straight trend line. This type of analysis brings out sharply the cyclical movements of the FRB index, and it also shows how the current level of output compares with the level that would have been achieved had the industrial sector followed its historical growth rate.

Although this may not be the best or final trend line for the data, the straight line is a simple summarization tool. In order to assess the value of this simple procedure, the deviations (data minus trend line) of the FRB data from the fitted straight line are depicted in Figure 5.9. It is evident that elimination of "trend" in the data now highlights the cyclical patterns corresponding to economic expansions and contractions.

## LOOKING AT RESIDUALS

By considering the deviations from a fit, known as *residuals,* it is possible to expose other characteristics of the data without being distracted by the dominant trend. In the previous example based on FRB data, the residuals show a cyclical pattern which can be related to economic contractions and expansions. The recession in 1974–1975 is very dramatically shown by its plunge below the trend level. Also, the steady recovery to more normal growth is apparent in the last three years.

Implicit in this simple analysis is a model, characterized by the linear trend. However, the analysis is preliminary in that its summaries are based on a simple model that exposes residuals for more detailed analysis and possibly further mod-

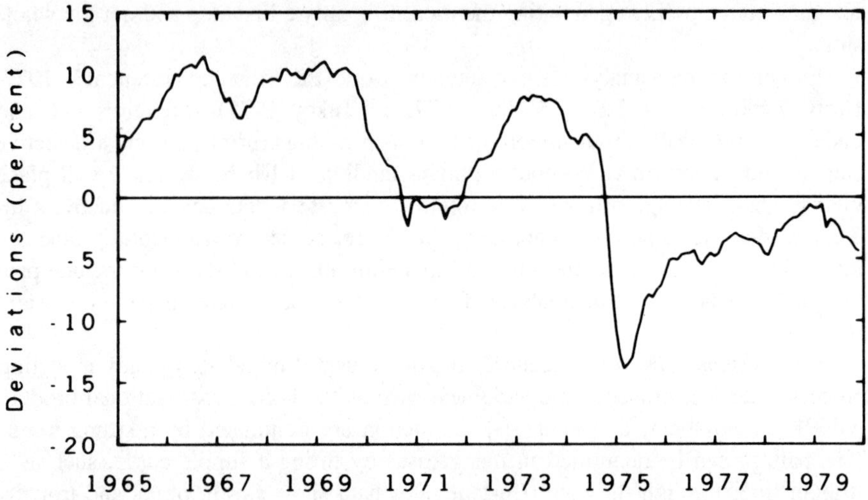


**Figure 5.9** Time plot of the deviations of the FRB index of industrial production from a straight line trend.

eling at a later stage. This process is typical of the *iterative* procedure one follows in summarizing and exposing data.

During residual analysis, it may become apparent that certain individual observations or small sequences of them are in some sense extreme. Such unusual values, called *outliers,* can severely impact on the results of an analysis. Outliers are not expected to recur or to influence the data in the same way again, so that their effect should be negated by replacing them with more "typical" values.

This is particularly true when the objective is to use statistical forecasting techniques to extrapolate past results into the future. For example, the extremely severe snowstorms of 1977 and 1978 prohibited many people from getting to work. As a result, residential telephones were used more often and revenues increased significantly as people called their offices to say they would not be in, called friends and relatives to determine if they were safe, and so forth. For forecasting purposes, it is necessary to adjust downwards the 1977 and 1978 revenues to more typical revenues so as not to overstate the expected revenues in 1979.

On the other hand, if one is attempting to build a model to explain past results, one should think long and hard before adjusting past data. These may be useful in understanding how extreme or unusual events affect the process of generating data. If one wanted to know the impact of severe weather on telephoning habits, the 1977–1978 data provide excellent indications and as such should not be adjusted.

A residual analysis can be an effective procedure for isolating outliers. Among the unusual events that create outliers in business data, the most commonly occurring are related to weather, strikes, or changes in the observance of holidays. These events have predictable effects, so appropriate adjustments can generally be made.

More often, the reasons for unusual values are unknown and must be investigated. Even with the assistance of statistical methods, extensive subjective judgment is often required in selecting replacement values.

Residual analysis in the context of regression modeling is treated in Chapter 15.

## SUMMARY

Data analysis is important in the preanalysis and diagnostic checking (residual analysis) stages of model building.

- It is also a lone-standing process that has significant value outside the realm of model building, too—that is, in the evaluation and interpretation of data.
- Data analysis should be performed to improve your understanding of what the data are trying to tell you.
- It can also be applied effectively in presenting the results of a study to management.

In terms of statistical methodology, much data analysis is informal. Like the modeling process

- Data analysis is open-ended and iterative in nature.
- The steps you may take will not always be clearly defined.
- The nature of the process will depend on what information is revealed to you at various stages.

At any given stage various possibilities may arise, some of which will need to be separately explored. To the beginner, such a process may seem inefficient and interminable; but in practice, a reasonable course will often become apparent, especially with experience.

## USEFUL READING

ERICKSON, B. H., and T. A. NOSANCHUK (1977). *Understanding Data*. Toronto, Canada: McGraw-Hill-Ryerson Ltd.

HARTWIG, F., and B. E. DEARING (1979). *Exploratory Data Analysis*. Sage University Paper on Quantitative Applications in the Social Sciences, 07-016. Beverly Hills, CA: Sage Publications.

McNEIL, D. R. (1977). *Interactive Data Analysis*. New York, NY: John Wiley and Sons.

TUKEY, J. W. (1977). *Exploratory Data Analysis*. Reading, MA: Addison-Wesley Publishing Co.

CHAPTER **6**

# The Importance of Graphical Displays of Data

---

Forecasters will understand their data better if they also understand that data can be displayed in a variety of ways.

- Not only does it help to display raw data, results of an analysis of the data can also be shown graphically.
- Analyses, such as seasonally adjusted data, differenced or smoothed data, transformed data (e.g., logarithms and square roots), fitted values, and residuals, can all be generated effectively as "cheap-and-dirty" plots on high-speed printers and terminals; higher quality output is produced by CRT (cathode-ray tube) devices; highest quality output is produced with microfilm or penplotters.

Most of the visuals shown in this book were generated by computer graphics on microfilm by using the GR-Z graphics software package (Becker and Chambers, 1977).

---

## GRAPHICAL DISPLAYS

Graphical forms of data displays are often easier to interpret than tabular forms of the same data. It is easier for the human eye and brain to extract a piece of information from a graph than a table. Graphical displays are flexible in their ability to reveal alternative structures present in data or to see relationships among variables. A wise choice in the scale of a graphical display can also make the difference between seeing something important in the data or missing it altogether. For example, rates of growth and changing rates of growth are easier to interpret from charts with a logarithmic scale than an arithmetic scale.

Some useful tools for displaying data include time plots, scatter diagrams, low-resolution displays, stem-and-leaf diagrams, histograms, and box plots. The latter two are discussed in Chapter 7.

The most commonly used graphical representations of time series data include the time plot and scatter diagram.

## Time Plots

A *time plot* is simply a graph in which the data values are arranged sequentially in time. Since the values in a time series are arranged sequentially in time, the corresponding values must be plotted at equally spaced time intervals. These time intervals may be days, weeks, months, quarters, or years. A number of time plots were displayed in Chapter 5.

Another use of time plots arises when a time series is reexpressed in another form. When analyzing trending data, the percent changes (annually or quarterly) of a time series can be considered as a new time series. For example, Figure 6.1 shows a plot of the seasonally adjusted GNP in billions of 1972 dollars for some recent years. Figure 6.2 shows the annualized percent changes from previous quarters. Clearly, trend is essentially removed in the latter graph and attention is focused on the GNP growth rate, a comprehensive measure of the vitality of the economy.

The GNP is the most important and widely used indicator of the nation's economic health. It measures the market value of all the goods and services produced

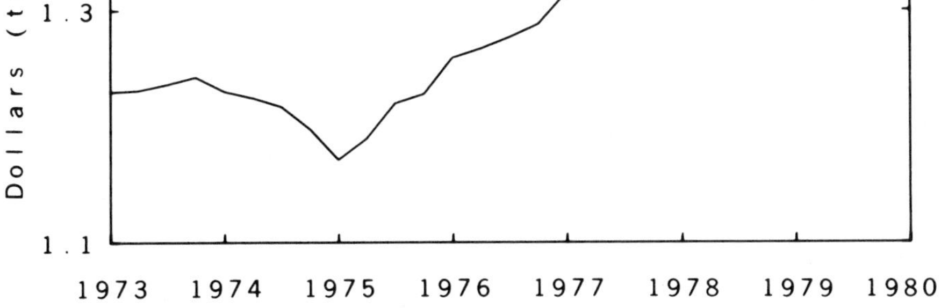


*Source:* U.S. Department of Commerce, Bureau of Economic Analysis.

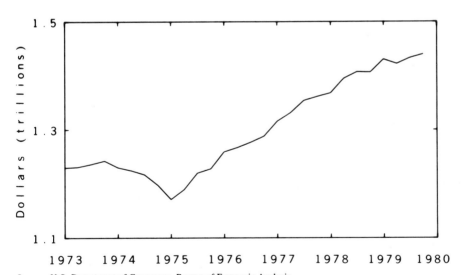

**Figure 6.1** Time plot of U.S. Gross National Product; seasonally adjusted (quarterly) in 1972 constant dollars.

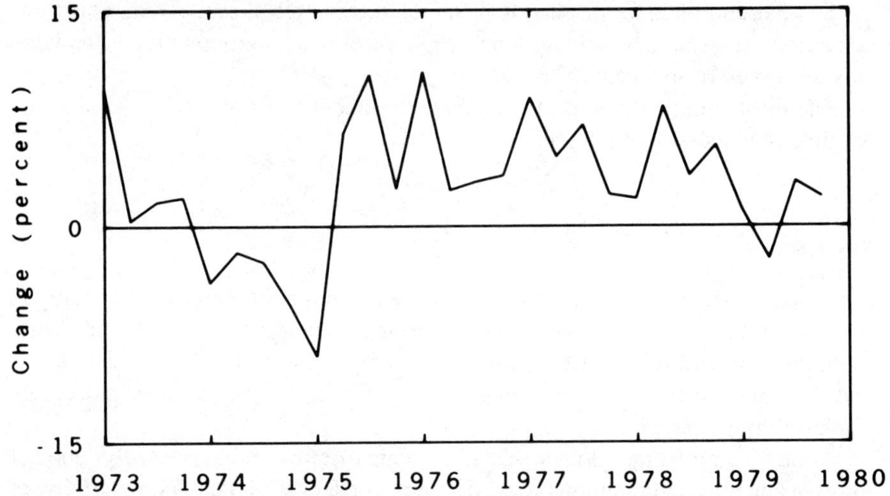


**Figure 6.2** Time plot of the percent change from the previous quarter in the annual rates for GNP.

in the economy. Estimates of GNP are released quarterly by the U.S. Department of Commerce and are expressed in terms of seasonally adjusted annual rates. Because inflation distorts the validity of current-dollar data as a measure of "real" economic activity, GNP is also published in constant-dollar (1972) terms. All these forms of the GNP can be viewed as time series and displayed as time plots.

## Scatter Diagrams

When the points of one variable are paired with corresponding values of a related variable, a linear or nonlinear relationship between the variables can be depicted in a *scatter diagram*. One variable is plotted on a horizontal ordered-number scale and the other variable is plotted on a vertical ordered-number scale. Such a plot is a valuable tool for studying the relationship among two or more sets of variables.

As a prelude to regression analysis (finding the line that best fits the points of the scatter diagram), an analyst may search for variables that are related to one another in a linear or functional manner: if an independent variable has been plotted against a variable that is dependent on it, the variables will have a functional (linear) relationship. As part of modeling, scatter diagrams can suggest if certain relationships among variables may be assumed linear on the basis of physical, economic, or even intuitive hypotheses. After regression, scatter diagrams play a role in the graphical analysis of residual series to help verify if assumptions are reasonable, and if, moreover, a proposed statistical model will give acceptable answers (i.e., will have a good fit to the data).

In our telecommunications example, consider the problem of forecasting telephone toll revenues from toll message volumes. In general, the amount of revenue would depend on the number of messages, the duration of the calls, and the rates charged for the calls. Toll message data were shown in Figure 5.6 of Chapter 5; toll revenues corresponding to these message volumes were shown as a time plot in Figure 3.1. Notice the similarity of the trend and seasonal patterns in the time plots. These two time series will be analyzed and modeled in detail throughout the book.

For example, for each toll revenue value you can associate a corresponding toll message value. In this case, it would simply mean associating the January 1976 toll revenue value with the January 1976 toll message value and so forth. These data are plotted in Figure 6.3 as a scatter diagram, in which the revenues are represented on the vertical axis and the message volumes are represented on the horizontal axis. The scatter diagram suggests that, *on the average,* toll revenues increase as toll message volumes increase. However, for a given number of toll messages, the toll revenue data have a good deal of *variability* depending on distance, operator assistance, time of day, duration of call, and possibly other factors.

A tight scatter is apparent, as may be expected. However, it is also apparent from the time plots that both series have similar seasonal patterns. If this were not the case, the diagram might appear much less smooth. Alternatively, a scatter diagram can also be plotted between toll revenues and toll message volumes that have been adjusted for seasonal variation. Such a scatter diagram would appear even smoother because small seasonal differences have been removed.

It is sometimes necessary to relate trend-cycle patterns in two series that have

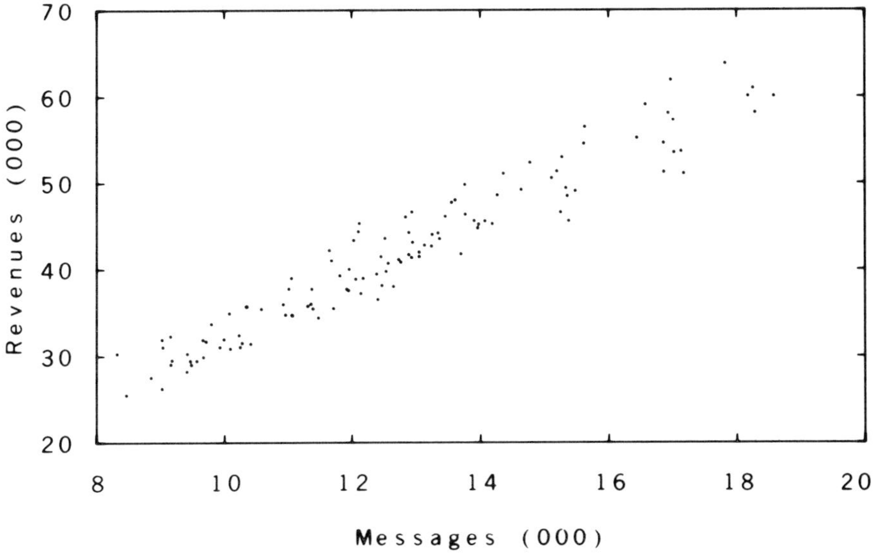


**Figure 6.3** Scatter diagram of telephone toll revenue and message volumes.

different seasonal patterns, such as data about the increase in the number of main telephones and housing starts. For example, Figure 6.4 shows a scatter diagram between monthly main-telephone gain and U.S. housing starts. The broad scatter suggests a weak relationship between the variables. In fact, such broadly dispersed scatter diagrams are not likely to give rise to good forecasting models.

Any relationship between the trend characteristics of the main-telephone gain and housing starts is obscured by the differences in their seasonal characteristics. Here, it would be useful to remove seasonal influences first in both series before plotting a scatter diagram, by taking "differences of order twelve" on both time series (see Chapter 10). This will reduce or even remove the seasonal influence in the relationship. The resulting scatter diagram (Figure 6.5) between the "differenced" series shows a much clearer linear pattern, which is likely to produce better modeling results and possibly more accurate forecasts. A comparison of the forecasts resulting from these two ways of relating quarterly main gain to quarterly housing starts will be summarized in a case study in Chapter 20.

## Low-Resolution Displays

The human eye can perform a smoothing of data without the computer. It can also selectively isolate certain data characteristics and make visual comparisons with other sets of data. Thus with some training, forecasters and managers can make very effective uses of graphical summaries in their work.

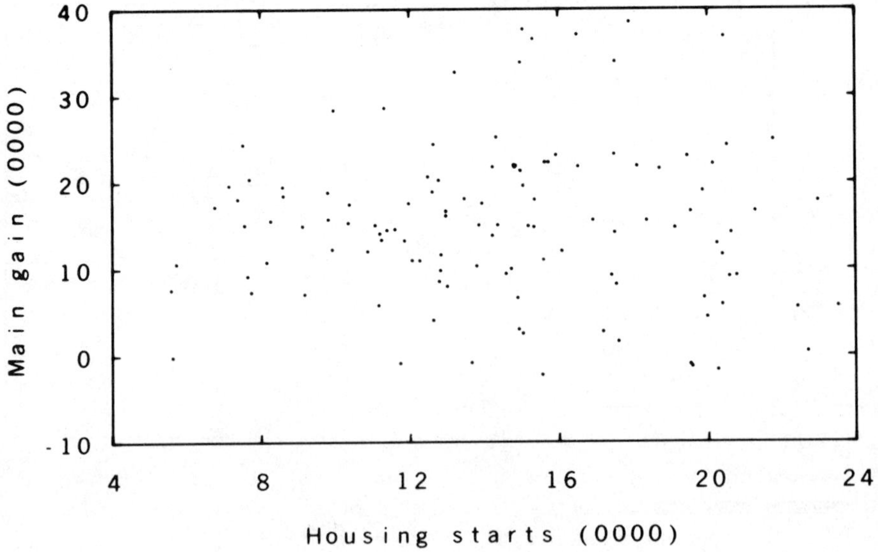


**Figure 6.4** Scatter diagram between monthly main-telephone gain and housing starts.

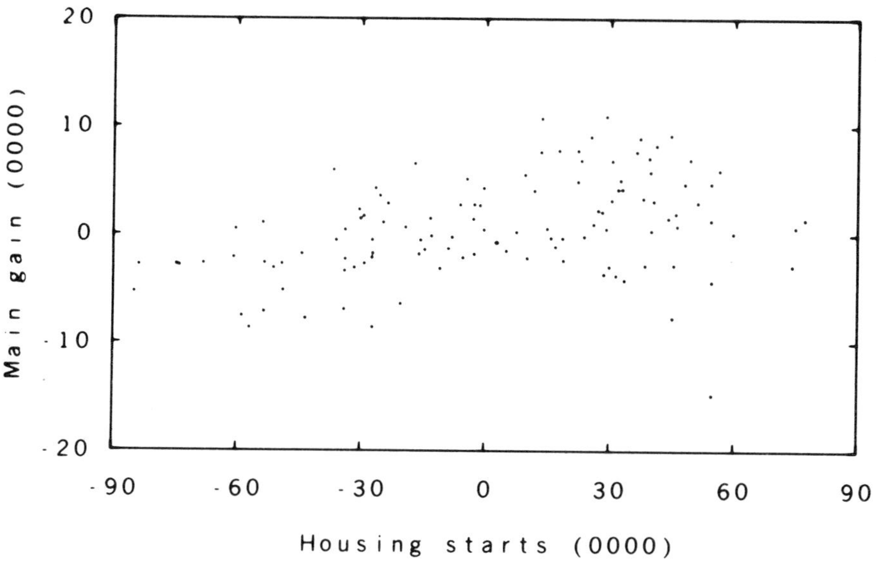


**Figure 6.5** Scatter diagram between monthly main-telephone gain and housing starts—differenced data.

Time plots and scatter diagrams allow one to analyze relationships with time and between variables, respectively. The object of making a *low-resolution display,* on the other hand, is to compare in a single display certain trend and/or seasonal patterns for one or more series without cluttering up the diagram.

For example, seasonal patterns can be displayed by first scaling the monthly data within each year into a number (say ten) of equal subintervals. These intervals are based on all the data, and are calculated as

(Largest value − Smallest value)/10.

Each monthly value is translated into a corresponding number of asterisks (0 to 10) depending upon the subinterval into which the data value falls. The strongest month in the year will have the greatest number of asterisks. Thus shifts in the strongest (or weakest) month over time can be readily detected by a shift in the peak (or trough) month on the display.

Likewise, evidence of a changing seasonal pattern in telephone data owing to changes in school openings and closings can be demonstrated with a display showing telephone gain (i.e., the difference between connections and disconnections of telephones) for individual months over time. As can be noted in Figure 6.6, the gain in telephones shifts the seasonal pattern to a high in September and a low in June from a high in October and a low in June. This normally can be ascribed to changing opening and closing dates of universities and schools.

```
VBL:          1 1955         2 1956         3 1957         4 1958         5 1959         6 1960         7 1961
MIN:                 7.59           7.44           5.72           1.39           4.32           2.06           2.49
MAX:                19.34          16.55          14.51          14.72          17.27          15.47          15.55

JANUARY    43 *****       80 *********   99 **********  46 *****       55 ******      72 ********    21 ***
FEBRUARY   33 ****        68 *******     63 *******     26 ***         42 *****       62 *******     15 **
MARCH      34 ****        71 ********    70 ********    19 **          47 *****       82 *********   41 *****
APRIL       3 *           45 *****       45 *****       29 ***         60 *******     47 *****       39 ****
MAY         3 *           39 ****        34 ****        31 ****        43 *****       33 ****        24 ***
JUNE        0 *            0 *            0 *            0 *            0 *            0 *            0 *
JULY       26 ***         41 *****       40 *****       53 ******      57 ******      42 *****       29 ***
AUGUST     27 ***         51 ******      32 ****        46 *****       38 ****        33 ****        43 *****
SEPTEMBR   77 ********    93 **********  66 *******     99 **********  99 **********  99 **********  99 **********
OCTOBER    58 ******      99 **********  96 **********  97 **********  80 *********   60 *******     61 *******
NOVEMBER   73 ********    79 ********    53 ******      65 *******     51 ******      31 ****        63 *******
DECEMBER   99 **********  72 ********    39 ****        75 ********    64 *******     36 ****        51 ******

VBL:          8 1962         9 1963        10 1964        11 1965        12 1966        13 1967        14 1968
MIN:                 1.31           1.51           3.22           2.92           4.55           3.58           0.70
MAX:                18.17          18.55          25.44          28.79          28.96          29.47          35.38

JANUARY    51 ******      48 *****       39 ****        40 *****       39 ****        34 ****        41 *****
FEBRUARY   46 *****       42 *****       38 ****        39 ****        42 *****       34 ****        42 *****
MARCH      63 *******     49 *****       40 *****       42 *****       52 ******      39 ****        44 *****
APRIL      43 *****       28 ***         47 *****       32 ****        31 ****        28 ***          0 *
MAY        31 ****        25 ***         25 ***         20 ***         13 **           9 *            6 *
JUNE        0 *            0 *            0 *            0 *            0 *            0 *            8 *
JULY       39 ****        33 ****        38 ****        36 ****        32 ****        29 ***         32 ****
AUGUST     49 *****       36 ****        31 ****        26 ***         24 ***         24 ***         24 ***
SEPTEMBR   99 **********  99 **********  99 **********  99 **********  99 **********  99 **********  99 **********
OCTOBER    68 *******     69 *******     67 *******     63 *******     53 ******      60 *******     81 *********
NOVEMBER   48 *****       45 *****       22 ***         41 *****       32 ****        47 *****       38 ****
DECEMBER   35 ****        43 *****       47 *****       44 *****       32 ****        34 ****        42 *****
```

**Figure 6.6** Low-resolution display for main-telephone gain by year across months.

Low-resolution displays also provide a comparison of trend patterns over time. In this case, the scaling is based on the values for the Januarys, Februarys, etc., taken separately. The data for the telecommunications example, displayed in Figure 6.7, provide a comparison in a single diagram of trend patterns among four series with widely different scales. It is evident that the toll revenue (REV) and toll message (MSG) series have similar trend patterns while the business telephone (BMT) and nonfarm employment (NFRM) data have quite different trend-cycle structures. It would be more useful to compare similar characteristics for different series. One such comparison can be most effective when the data are expressed as percent changes. Such a visual display for the telecommunications example gives a quick comparison of correlations and similarities that could be suggestive of model relationships (Figure 6.8). Notice that as percent changes, the first two and last two series appear quite similar. This observation will be used effectively in the case studies developed in Chapter 20.

As another example, a composite time series such as the FRB index of industrial production could be shown in relation to its components. The low-resolution displays ("star charts") would show, in a single display, how the components vary in this decomposition. Similar plots may be useful for displaying a price index, for example, in relation to its components.

Low-resolution displays are a direct tool for visually comparing several series simultaneously or graphically displaying a common characteristic. However, it is not possible to make accurate numerical comparisons because the resolution in scale has been replaced by the capability of making overall visual comparisons. They are generally used in the early stages of exploratory data analysis to identify unusual patterns or shifts in basic patterns and to uncover possible outliers.

## Stem-and-Leaf Displays

A *stem-and-leaf display* is a simple device for depicting frequencies as well as actual values in a single diagram. Table 6.1 shows the stem-and-leaf display for a simplified data set consisting of some travel time data (to be discussed in detail in the next chapter). The data themselves are not important for the moment.

The "stem" is a vertical column: its unit divisions are multiples of ten. The "leaves" are horizontal rows of numbers; each of the numbers in a "leaf" represents a unit within the corresponding "tens" category, i.e., the first number is 3. By entering each number in this manner and ordering the numbers, one gets a visual impression of the distribution of the data, and, as well, an ordering of the data.

Frequent values stand out (e.g., 10, 11) as well as atypical values and absences. For example, there are no values in the 33–39 range. Notice that the "leaves" have been ordered. The right-hand column provides a count that is useful as a check to see that all values are entered. A cumulative count will also turn out to be useful in the quick calculation of certain statistics, such as the interquantile difference (discussed later).

| VBL: | 1 REV | 2 MSG | 3 BMT | 4 NFRM |
|---|---|---|---|---|
| MIN: | 25.16 | 8.24 | 491.20 | 6645.00 |
| MAX: | 63.42 | 18.50 | 523.94 | 7282.00 |
| JAN 1970 | 0 * | 1 * | 0 * | 65 ******* |
| FEB 1970 | 12 ** | 0 * | 5 * | 70 ******** |
| MAR 1970 | 10 ** | 11 ** | 13 ** | 80 ********* |
| APR 1970 | 16 ** | 6 * | 20 *** | 87 ********* |
| MAY 1970 | 10 ** | 8 * | 25 *** | 90 ********** |
| JUN 1970 | 11 ** | 13 ** | 23 *** | 99 ********** |
| JUL 1970 | 1 * | 6 * | 25 *** | 85 ********* |
| AUG 1970 | 7 * | 10 ** | 27 *** | 85 ********* |
| SEP 1970 | 10 ** | 12 ** | 35 **** | 77 ******** |
| OCT 1970 | 12 ** | 10 ** | 34 **** | 72 ******** |
| NOV 1970 | 14 ** | 6 * | 34 **** | 71 ******** |
| DEC 1970 | 9 * | 8 * | 34 **** | 73 ******** |
| JAN 1971 | 5 * | 5 * | 34 **** | 44 ***** |
| FEB 1971 | 17 ** | 8 * | 36 **** | 44 ***** |
| MAR 1971 | 13 ** | 17 ** | 39 **** | 52 ****** |
| APR 1971 | 21 *** | 14 ** | 43 ***** | 56 ****** |
| MAY 1971 | 16 ** | 13 ** | 41 ***** | 64 ******* |
| JUN 1971 | 15 ** | 20 *** | 40 ***** | 73 ******** |
| JUL 1971 | 9 * | 11 ** | 37 **** | 63 ******* |
| AUG 1971 | 14 ** | 18 ** | 36 **** | 59 ****** |
| SEP 1971 | 15 ** | 19 ** | 44 ***** | 51 ****** |
| OCT 1971 | 16 ** | 16 ** | 41 ***** | 52 ****** |
| NOV 1971 | 24 *** | 17 ** | 38 **** | 55 ****** |
| DEC 1971 | 16 ** | 13 ** | 37 **** | 59 ****** |
| JAN 1972 | 14 ** | 15 ** | 39 **** | 34 **** |
| FEB 1972 | 26 *** | 19 ** | 38 **** | 35 **** |
| MAR 1972 | 24 *** | 25 *** | 44 ***** | 49 ***** |
| APR 1972 | 26 *** | 19 ** | 49 ***** | 55 ****** |
| MAY 1972 | 27 *** | 25 *** | 49 ***** | 65 ******* |
| JUN 1972 | 23 *** | 30 **** | 47 ***** | 74 ******** |
| JUL 1972 | 18 ** | 18 ** | 49 ***** | 58 ****** |
| AUG 1972 | 25 *** | 30 **** | 52 ****** | 68 ******* |
| SEP 1972 | 24 *** | 26 *** | 60 ******* | 62 ******* |
| OCT 1972 | 27 *** | 29 *** | 61 ******* | 74 ******** |
| NOV 1972 | 31 **** | 26 *** | 59 ****** | 79 ******** |
| DEC 1972 | 25 *** | 22 *** | 58 ****** | 81 ********* |
| JAN 1973 | 23 *** | 26 *** | 62 ******* | 52 ****** |
| FEB 1973 | 35 **** | 26 *** | 65 ******* | 54 ****** |
| MAR 1973 | 31 **** | 35 **** | 68 ******* | 64 ******* |
| APR 1973 | 40 ***** | 32 **** | 72 ******** | 71 ******** |
| MAY 1973 | 34 **** | 36 **** | 71 ******** | 79 ******** |
| JUN 1973 | 30 **** | 37 **** | 73 ******** | 90 ********** |
| JUL 1973 | 26 *** | 29 *** | 74 ******** | 79 ******** |
| AUG 1973 | 32 **** | 40 ***** | 79 ******** | 85 ********* |
| SEP 1973 | 31 **** | 35 **** | 85 ********* | 78 ******** |
| OCT 1973 | 36 **** | 39 **** | 85 ********* | 84 ********* |
| NOV 1973 | 37 **** | 35 **** | 83 ********* | 87 ********* |
| DEC 1973 | 31 **** | 29 *** | 82 ********* | 87 ********* |
| JAN 1974 | 26 *** | 33 **** | 83 ********* | 53 ****** |
| FEB 1974 | 43 ***** | 32 **** | 84 ********* | 51 ****** |
| MAR 1974 | 37 **** | 41 ***** | 85 ********* | 59 ****** |
| APR 1974 | 47 ***** | 40 ***** | 90 ********** | 65 ******* |
| MAY 1974 | 42 ***** | 44 ***** | 86 ********* | 76 ******** |
| JUN 1974 | 40 ***** | 42 ***** | 87 ********* | 86 ********* |
| JUL 1974 | 35 **** | 37 **** | 85 ********* | 76 ******** |
| AUG 1974 | 41 ***** | 44 ***** | 88 ********* | 79 ******** |

**Figure 6.7** Low-resolution display for the four series in the telecommunications example.

| | | | | | | | | |
|---|---|---|---|---|---|---|---|---|
| SEP 1974 | 39 | **** | 43 | ***** | 91 | ********** | 68 | ******* |
| OCT 1974 | 43 | ***** | 46 | ***** | 89 | ********* | 69 | ******* |
| NOV 1974 | 46 | ***** | 36 | **** | 86 | ********* | 68 | ******* |
| DEC 1974 | 35 | **** | 34 | **** | 81 | ********* | 59 | ****** |
| JAN 1975 | 28 | *** | 39 | **** | 79 | ******** | 23 | *** |
| FEB 1975 | 49 | ***** | 36 | **** | 77 | ******** | 18 | ** |
| MAR 1975 | 41 | ***** | 46 | ***** | 76 | ******** | 21 | *** |
| APR 1975 | 53 | ****** | 44 | ***** | 73 | ******** | 24 | *** |
| MAY 1975 | 49 | ***** | 44 | ***** | 66 | ******* | 34 | **** |
| JUN 1975 | 47 | ***** | 49 | ***** | 66 | ******* | 40 | ***** |
| JUL 1975 | 39 | **** | 41 | ***** | 64 | ******* | 34 | **** |
| AUG 1975 | 45 | ***** | 46 | ***** | 66 | ******* | 40 | ***** |
| SEP 1975 | 44 | ***** | 47 | ***** | 71 | ******** | 25 | *** |
| OCT 1975 | 48 | ***** | 48 | ***** | 70 | ******** | 27 | *** |
| NOV 1975 | 51 | ****** | 37 | **** | 69 | ******* | 28 | *** |
| DEC 1975 | 41 | ***** | 40 | ***** | 65 | ******* | 30 | **** |
| JAN 1976 | 32 | **** | 42 | ***** | 65 | ******* | 3 | * |
| FEB 1976 | 55 | ****** | 44 | ***** | 65 | ******* | 3 | * |
| MAR 1976 | 50 | ****** | 54 | ****** | 65 | ******* | 10 | ** |
| APR 1976 | 58 | ****** | 51 | ****** | 67 | ******* | 17 | ** |
| MAY 1976 | 53 | ****** | 50 | ****** | 59 | ****** | 21 | *** |
| JUN 1976 | 51 | ****** | 57 | ****** | 58 | ****** | 30 | **** |
| JUL 1976 | 45 | ***** | 45 | ***** | 59 | ****** | 37 | **** |
| AUG 1976 | 51 | ****** | 55 | ****** | 59 | ****** | 35 | **** |
| SEP 1976 | 52 | ****** | 56 | ****** | 66 | ******* | 25 | *** |
| OCT 1976 | 54 | ****** | 53 | ****** | 68 | ******* | 26 | *** |
| NOV 1976 | 57 | ****** | 51 | ****** | 66 | ******* | 29 | *** |
| DEC 1976 | 48 | ***** | 48 | ***** | 63 | ******* | 31 | **** |
| JAN 1977 | 42 | ***** | 52 | ****** | 64 | ******* | 0 | * |
| FEB 1977 | 63 | ******* | 53 | ****** | 64 | ******* | 2 | * |
| MAR 1977 | 55 | ****** | 67 | ******* | 65 | ******* | 11 | ** |
| APR 1977 | 66 | ******* | 58 | ****** | 67 | ******* | 21 | *** |
| MAY 1977 | 61 | ******* | 61 | ******* | 61 | ******* | 31 | **** |
| JUN 1977 | 59 | ****** | 68 | ******* | 62 | ******* | 43 | ***** |
| JUL 1977 | 52 | ****** | 54 | ****** | 62 | ******* | 42 | ***** |
| AUG 1977 | 61 | ******* | 69 | ******* | 66 | ******* | 47 | ***** |
| SEP 1977 | 62 | ******* | 68 | ******* | 72 | ******** | 43 | ***** |
| OCT 1977 | 65 | ******* | 66 | ******* | 74 | ******** | 48 | ***** |
| NOV 1977 | 70 | ******** | 62 | ******* | 73 | ******** | 52 | ****** |
| DEC 1977 | 60 | ******* | 57 | ****** | 72 | ******** | 55 | ****** |
| JAN 1978 | 52 | ****** | 68 | ******* | 73 | ******** | 24 | *** |
| FEB 1978 | 71 | ******** | 67 | ******* | 73 | ******** | 26 | *** |
| MAR 1978 | 67 | ******* | 83 | ********* | 78 | ******** | 40 | ***** |
| APR 1978 | 80 | ********* | 71 | ******** | 80 | ********* | 53 | ****** |
| MAY 1978 | 77 | ******** | 79 | ******** | 73 | ******** | 64 | ******* |
| JUN 1978 | 73 | ******** | 84 | ********* | 75 | ******** | 77 | ******** |
| JUL 1978 | 67 | ******* | 67 | ******* | 76 | ******** | 69 | ******* |
| AUG 1978 | 73 | ******** | 85 | ********* | 80 | ********* | 76 | ******** |
| SEP 1978 | 75 | ******** | 83 | ********* | 88 | ********* | 71 | ******** |
| OCT 1978 | 82 | ********* | 84 | ********* | 91 | ********** | 78 | ******** |
| NOV 1978 | 87 | ********* | 80 | ********* | 89 | ********* | 85 | ********* |
| DEC 1978 | 75 | ******** | 71 | ******** | 87 | ********* | 85 | ********* |
| JAN 1979 | 66 | ******* | 86 | ********* | 89 | ********* | 54 | ****** |
| FEB 1979 | 95 | ********** | 84 | ********* | 91 | ********** | 57 | ****** |
| MAR 1979 | 85 | ********* | 97 | ********** | 95 | ********** | 65 | ******* |
| APR 1979 | 99 | ********** | 92 | ********** | 98 | ********** | 74 | ******** |
| MAY 1979 | 92 | ********** | 96 | ********** | 93 | ********** | 86 | ********* |
| JUN 1979 | 90 | ********** | 96 | ********** | 95 | ********** | 97 | ********** |
| JUL 1979 | 85 | ********* | 83 | ********* | 95 | ********** | 90 | ********** |
| AUG 1979 | 90 | ********** | 99 | ********** | 99 | ********** | 92 | ********** |

**Figure 6.7** *(continued)*

| VBL: | 1 | PCTREV | 2 | PCTMSG | 3 | PCTBMT | 4 | PCTNFRM |
|---|---|---|---|---|---|---|---|---|
| MIN: | | 2.37 | | 0.02 | | 1.38 | | 4.07 |
| MAX: | | 17.34 | | 15.46 | | 2.27 | | 3.14 |
| JAN 1970 | 86 | ********* | 67 | ******* | 37 | **** | 76 | ******** |
| FEB 1970 | 99 | ********** | 52 | ****** | 37 | **** | 82 | ********* |
| MAR 1970 | 76 | ******** | 99 | ********** | 37 | **** | 72 | ******** |
| APR 1970 | 73 | ******** | 67 | ******* | 37 | **** | 68 | ******* |
| MAY 1970 | 53 | ****** | 70 | ******** | 37 | **** | 58 | ****** |
| JUN 1970 | 66 | ******* | 76 | ******** | 37 | **** | 54 | ****** |
| JUL 1970 | 18 | ** | 63 | ******* | 37 | **** | 46 | ***** |
| AUG 1970 | 37 | **** | 56 | ****** | 37 | **** | 38 | **** |
| SEP 1970 | 36 | **** | 61 | ******* | 37 | **** | 39 | **** |
| OCT 1970 | 14 | ** | 34 | **** | 37 | **** | 25 | *** |
| NOV 1970 | 22 | *** | 62 | ******* | 37 | **** | 26 | *** |
| DEC 1970 | 25 | *** | 48 | ***** | 37 | **** | 26 | *** |
| JAN 1971 | 37 | **** | 29 | *** | 99 | ********** | 29 | *** |
| FEB 1971 | 29 | *** | 65 | ******* | 93 | ********** | 24 | *** |
| MAR 1971 | 16 | ** | 43 | ***** | 85 | ********* | 22 | *** |
| APR 1971 | 22 | *** | 55 | ****** | 77 | ******** | 18 | ** |
| MAY 1971 | 33 | **** | 37 | **** | 65 | ******* | 25 | *** |
| JUN 1971 | 18 | ** | 50 | ****** | 67 | ******* | 24 | *** |
| JUL 1971 | 54 | ****** | 33 | **** | 59 | ****** | 29 | *** |
| AUG 1971 | 51 | ****** | 58 | ****** | 54 | ****** | 24 | *** |
| SEP 1971 | 31 | **** | 48 | ***** | 53 | ****** | 24 | *** |
| OCT 1971 | 21 | *** | 39 | **** | 50 | ****** | 32 | **** |
| NOV 1971 | 69 | ******* | 75 | ******** | 44 | ***** | 36 | **** |
| DEC 1971 | 49 | ***** | 35 | **** | 42 | ***** | 38 | **** |
| JAN 1972 | 70 | ******** | 79 | ******** | 47 | ***** | 44 | ***** |
| FEB 1972 | 55 | ****** | 84 | ********* | 41 | ***** | 44 | ***** |
| MAR 1972 | 69 | ******* | 56 | ****** | 46 | ***** | 52 | ****** |
| APR 1972 | 24 | *** | 37 | **** | 49 | ***** | 55 | ****** |
| MAY 1972 | 75 | ******** | 81 | ********* | 51 | ****** | 57 | ****** |
| JUN 1972 | 48 | ***** | 66 | ******* | 50 | ****** | 58 | ****** |
| JUL 1972 | 64 | ******* | 51 | ****** | 58 | ****** | 50 | ****** |
| AUG 1972 | 80 | ********* | 72 | ******** | 66 | ******* | 68 | ******* |
| SEP 1972 | 53 | ****** | 49 | ***** | 65 | ******* | 70 | ******** |
| OCT 1972 | 70 | ******** | 89 | ********* | 72 | ******** | 83 | ********* |
| NOV 1972 | 38 | **** | 60 | ******* | 75 | ******** | 86 | ********* |
| DEC 1972 | 59 | ****** | 62 | ******* | 76 | ******** | 84 | ********* |
| JAN 1973 | 63 | ******* | 75 | ******** | 79 | ******** | 78 | ******** |
| FEB 1973 | 45 | ***** | 45 | ***** | 85 | ********* | 81 | ********* |
| MAR 1973 | 38 | **** | 58 | ****** | 80 | ********* | 76 | ******** |
| APR 1973 | 83 | ********* | 83 | ********* | 77 | ******** | 76 | ******** |
| MAY 1973 | 38 | **** | 67 | ******* | 77 | ******** | 73 | ******** |
| JUN 1973 | 39 | **** | 37 | **** | 84 | ********* | 76 | ******** |
| JUL 1973 | 54 | ****** | 68 | ******* | 82 | ********* | 82 | ********* |
| AUG 1973 | 35 | **** | 61 | ******* | 85 | ********* | 77 | ******** |
| SEP 1973 | 41 | ***** | 50 | ****** | 82 | ********* | 76 | ******** |
| OCT 1973 | 48 | ***** | 58 | ****** | 80 | ********* | 68 | ******* |
| NOV 1973 | 24 | *** | 55 | ****** | 79 | ******** | 67 | ******* |
| DEC 1973 | 28 | *** | 48 | ***** | 79 | ******** | 63 | ******* |
| JAN 1974 | 0 | * | 37 | **** | 74 | ******** | 58 | ****** |
| FEB 1974 | 39 | **** | 34 | **** | 71 | ******** | 52 | ****** |
| MAR 1974 | 23 | *** | 31 | **** | 67 | ******* | 49 | ***** |
| APR 1974 | 27 | *** | 46 | ***** | 69 | ******* | 49 | ***** |
| MAY 1974 | 33 | **** | 44 | ***** | 64 | ******* | 52 | ****** |
| JUN 1974 | 55 | ****** | 31 | **** | 62 | ******* | 51 | ****** |
| JUL 1974 | 44 | ***** | 49 | ***** | 56 | ****** | 52 | ****** |
| AUG 1974 | 41 | ***** | 23 | *** | 52 | ****** | 48 | ***** |

**Figure 6.8** Low-resolution displays for the telecommunications example, showing percent changes of the four series.

| | | | | | | | | |
|---|---|---|---|---|---|---|---|---|
| SEP 1974 | 39 | **** | 45 | ***** | 48 | ***** | 43 | ***** |
| OCT 1974 | 28 | *** | 34 | **** | 45 | ***** | 38 | **** |
| NOV 1974 | 40 | ***** | 3 | * | 42 | ***** | 32 | **** |
| DEC 1974 | 11 | ** | 24 | *** | 35 | **** | 22 | *** |
| JAN 1975 | 3 | * | 38 | **** | 30 | **** | 18 | ** |
| FEB 1975 | 18 | ** | 25 | *** | 25 | *** | 14 | ** |
| MAR 1975 | 13 | ** | 26 | *** | 21 | *** | 8 | * |
| APR 1975 | 21 | *** | 16 | ** | 7 | * | 4 | * |
| MAY 1975 | 25 | *** | 0 | * | 3 | * | 4 | * |
| JUN 1975 | 23 | *** | 32 | **** | 0 | * | 0 | * |
| JUL 1975 | 13 | ** | 20 | *** | 0 | * | 4 | * |
| AUG 1975 | 7 | * | 9 | * | 0 | * | 8 | * |
| SEP 1975 | 15 | ** | 24 | *** | 3 | * | 2 | * |
| OCT 1975 | 18 | ** | 14 | ** | 4 | * | 3 | * |
| NOV 1975 | 14 | ** | 4 | * | 8 | * | 6 | * |
| DEC 1975 | 22 | *** | 35 | **** | 9 | * | 20 | *** |
| JAN 1976 | 12 | ** | 12 | ** | 13 | ** | 30 | **** |
| FEB 1976 | 18 | ** | 44 | ***** | 16 | ** | 36 | **** |
| MAR 1976 | 37 | **** | 45 | ***** | 19 | ** | 42 | ***** |
| APR 1976 | 13 | ** | 39 | **** | 26 | *** | 47 | ***** |
| MAY 1976 | 12 | ** | 28 | *** | 25 | *** | 39 | **** |
| JUN 1976 | 10 | ** | 40 | ***** | 23 | *** | 43 | ***** |
| JUL 1976 | 24 | *** | 19 | ** | 28 | *** | 59 | ****** |
| AUG 1976 | 21 | *** | 41 | ***** | 26 | *** | 50 | ****** |
| SEP 1976 | 29 | *** | 40 | ***** | 28 | *** | 56 | ****** |
| OCT 1976 | 17 | ** | 20 | *** | 34 | **** | 56 | ****** |
| NOV 1976 | 19 | ** | 76 | ******** | 32 | **** | 57 | ****** |
| DEC 1976 | 25 | *** | 41 | ***** | 34 | **** | 57 | ****** |
| JAN 1977 | 50 | ****** | 53 | ****** | 35 | **** | 52 | ****** |
| FEB 1977 | 29 | *** | 41 | ***** | 36 | **** | 55 | ****** |
| MAR 1977 | 11 | ** | 60 | ******* | 37 | **** | 57 | ****** |
| APR 1977 | 26 | *** | 35 | **** | 38 | **** | 61 | ******* |
| MAY 1977 | 29 | *** | 57 | ****** | 41 | ***** | 69 | ******* |
| JUN 1977 | 32 | **** | 53 | ****** | 45 | ***** | 73 | ******** |
| JUL 1977 | 23 | *** | 48 | ***** | 43 | ***** | 63 | ******* |
| AUG 1977 | 41 | ***** | 70 | ******** | 49 | ***** | 72 | ******** |
| SEP 1977 | 40 | ***** | 58 | ****** | 48 | ***** | 79 | ******** |
| OCT 1977 | 45 | ***** | 63 | ******* | 47 | ***** | 85 | ********* |
| NOV 1977 | 49 | ***** | 58 | ****** | 50 | ****** | 86 | ********* |
| DEC 1977 | 53 | ****** | 49 | ***** | 52 | ****** | 87 | ********* |
| JAN 1978 | 45 | ***** | 79 | ******** | 53 | ****** | 89 | ********* |
| FEB 1978 | 27 | *** | 71 | ******** | 54 | ****** | 88 | ********* |
| MAR 1978 | 51 | ****** | 68 | ******* | 59 | ****** | 94 | ********** |
| APR 1978 | 55 | ****** | 57 | ****** | 59 | ****** | 98 | ********** |
| MAY 1978 | 65 | ******* | 80 | ********* | 58 | ****** | 98 | ********** |
| JUN 1978 | 53 | ****** | 70 | ******** | 60 | ******* | 99 | ********** |
| JUL 1978 | 68 | ******* | 60 | ******* | 62 | ******* | 90 | ********** |
| AUG 1978 | 47 | ***** | 69 | ******* | 63 | ******* | 93 | ********** |
| SEP 1978 | 54 | ****** | 64 | ******* | 65 | ******* | 92 | ********** |
| OCT 1978 | 73 | ******** | 81 | ********* | 66 | ******* | 93 | ********** |
| NOV 1978 | 70 | ******** | 79 | ******** | 64 | ******* | 97 | ********** |
| DEC 1978 | 66 | ******* | 61 | ******* | 64 | ******* | 94 | ********** |
| JAN 1979 | 64 | ******* | 75 | ******** | 65 | ******* | 95 | ********** |
| FEB 1979 | 98 | ********** | 72 | ******** | 67 | ******* | 96 | ********** |
| MAR 1979 | 74 | ******** | 54 | ****** | 67 | ******* | 89 | ********* |
| APR 1979 | 71 | ******** | 91 | ********** | 69 | ******* | 83 | ********* |
| MAY 1979 | 54 | ****** | 71 | ******** | 72 | ******** | 84 | ********* |
| JUN 1979 | 66 | ******* | 44 | ***** | 73 | ******** | 82 | ********* |
| JUL 1979 | 72 | ******** | 74 | ******** | 69 | ******* | 82 | ********* |
| AUG 1979 | 64 | ******* | 54 | ****** | 70 | ******** | 76 | ******** |

**Figure 6.8** *(continued)*

**Table 6.1** A stem-and-leaf display of travel-time data.

| Tens digit | Unit digit | Number of orders |
|---|---|---|
| 0 | 33444566666777888999 | 20 |
| 1 | 000000111111223344678 | 21 |
| 2 | 012337 | 6 |
| 3 | 02 | 2 |
| 4 | 0 | 1 |
| 5 | | 0 |
| 6 | | 0 |
| 7 | | 0 |
| 8 | | 0 |
| 9 | | 0 |
| | | (Total: 50) |

When the data are concentrated, as these are, it is often desirable to split each tens unit of the stem into two ranges (0 to 4 and 5 to 9). This is illustrated in Table 6.2. The absence of data in the 35–39 range becomes more apparent. Additional information can be added by the use of symbols to identify various qualities of data that may be helpful in understanding differences in data. For example, a circle might be used to indicate whether a travel-time value represented the first trip of the day (which usually takes longer than others because it begins at the service company's garage).

Stem-and-leaf displays are useful in that they

- Show inherent groupings.
- Show unsymmetric trailing off, going farther in one direction than another.
- Highlight unexpected popular or unpopular values.
- Show "about where" the values are centered.
- Show "about how widely" the values are spread.

## Autocorrelations and Correlograms

Data sequences one or more time periods apart are often statistically related. This effect is known as *serial correlation* or *autocorrelation* and plays a significant role in the analysis of many types of time series and forecast modeling applications.

When stock prices, sales volumes, population counts, and other data are measured or observed sequentially in time, the data may contain information about important sequential relationships that you should extract or quantify. An objective of autocorrelation analysis is to develop tools for describing the association or mutual dependence between values of the same time series at different time periods. A

**Table 6.2** A stem-and-leaf display with split stem.

| Range | Unit digit | Number of orders |
|---|---|---|
| 0–4 | 33444 | 5 |
| 5–9 | 566666777888999 | 15 |
| 10–14 | 000000111111223344 | 18 |
| 15–19 | 678 | 3 |
| 20–24 | 01233 | 5 |
| 25–29 | 7 | 1 |
| 30–34 | 02 | 2 |
| 35–39 | | 0 |
| 40–44 | 0 | 1 |
| 45–49 | | 0 |
| | | (Total: 50) |

$$\text{Median} = \frac{\text{25th + 26th observations}}{2} = \frac{10+10}{2} = 10$$

useful graphical tool for displaying these autocorrelations is the *correlogram*. Patterns in a correlogram can be used to analyze corresponding patterns in the data, such as seasonality, and help in the specification of time series and econometric models. Correlograms can be interpreted in terms of autocorrelation coefficients.

Given $n$ discrete values of a time series $\{y_t;\ t = 1, \ldots, n\}$, a commonly used formula for the *first sample autocorrelation coefficient* ($r_1$) is

$$r_1 = \frac{\sum_{t=1}^{n-1} (y_t - \bar{y})(y_{t+1} - \bar{y})}{\sum_{t=1}^{n} (y_t - \bar{y})^2},$$

where $\bar{y}$ is the average (arithmetic mean) of the $n$ values of the time series. The subscript in observation $y_t$ denotes the "time" $t$; thus, $y_{t-1}$ is the observation one period earlier.

In a similar fashion the formula for the *sample autocorrelation coefficient* ($r_k$) between observations a distance *k periods apart* is given by

$$r_k = \frac{\sum_{t=1}^{n-k} (y_t - \bar{y})(y_{t+k} - \bar{y})}{\sum_{t=1}^{n} (y_t - \bar{y})^2}$$

There are a number of closely related ways in which the sample autocorrelation coefficient at lag $k$ is calculated. The differences are usually minor and have only theoretical value.

Table 6.3 shows a numerical example of the calculations involved in obtaining the first two sample autocorrelations of a simple trending series.

The interpretation of a correlogram is an art and requires substantial experience. Some common correlograms arise for time series with the following characteristics:

- Pure randomness.
- Low-order serial correlation.
- Trend.
- Alternating and rapidly changing fluctuations.
- Seasonality.

A *random time series* is one in which there is no time dependence between data values any number of time periods apart. Thus the autocorrelations would be zero at all lags, except at lag 0. At lag 0, the series is perfectly related to itself and has the maximum value 1. For a sampled random series, a correlogram will depict sample estimates of correlations of the data. Hence the correlogram shown in Figure 6.9 would be unity at lag 0 (shown by the column of pluses at the far left) and be

**Table 6.3** An illustrative example of the calculation of sample autocorrelations.

| Time period | Data $y_t$ | $y_t - \bar{y}$ | $(y_t - \bar{y})^2$ | $y_{t-1}$ | $(y_{t-1} - \bar{y})$ | $(y_t - \bar{y})(y_{t-1} - \bar{y})$ |
|---|---|---|---|---|---|---|
| 1 | 0 | −6 | 36 | NA* | NA | NA |
| 2 | 2 | −4 | 16 | 0 | −6 | 24 |
| 3 | 3 | −3 | 9 | 2 | −4 | 12 |
| 4 | 4 | −2 | 4 | 3 | −3 | 6 |
| 5 | 6 | 0 | 0 | 4 | −2 | 0 |
| 6 | 7 | 1 | 1 | 6 | 0 | 0 |
| 7 | 8 | 2 | 4 | 7 | 1 | 2 |
| 8 | 9 | 3 | 9 | 8 | 2 | 6 |
| 9 | 10 | 4 | 16 | 9 | 3 | 12 |
| 10 | 11 | 5 | 25 | 10 | 4 | 20 |
| Sum: | 60 | 0 | 120 | | | 82 |

$\bar{y} = 60/10 = 6$;

$r_0 = 1$ (always);

$r_1 = 82/120 = 0.68 =$ First autocorrelation coefficient;

$r_2 = 50/120 = 0.42 =$ Second autocorrelation coefficient.

*NA = No data available.

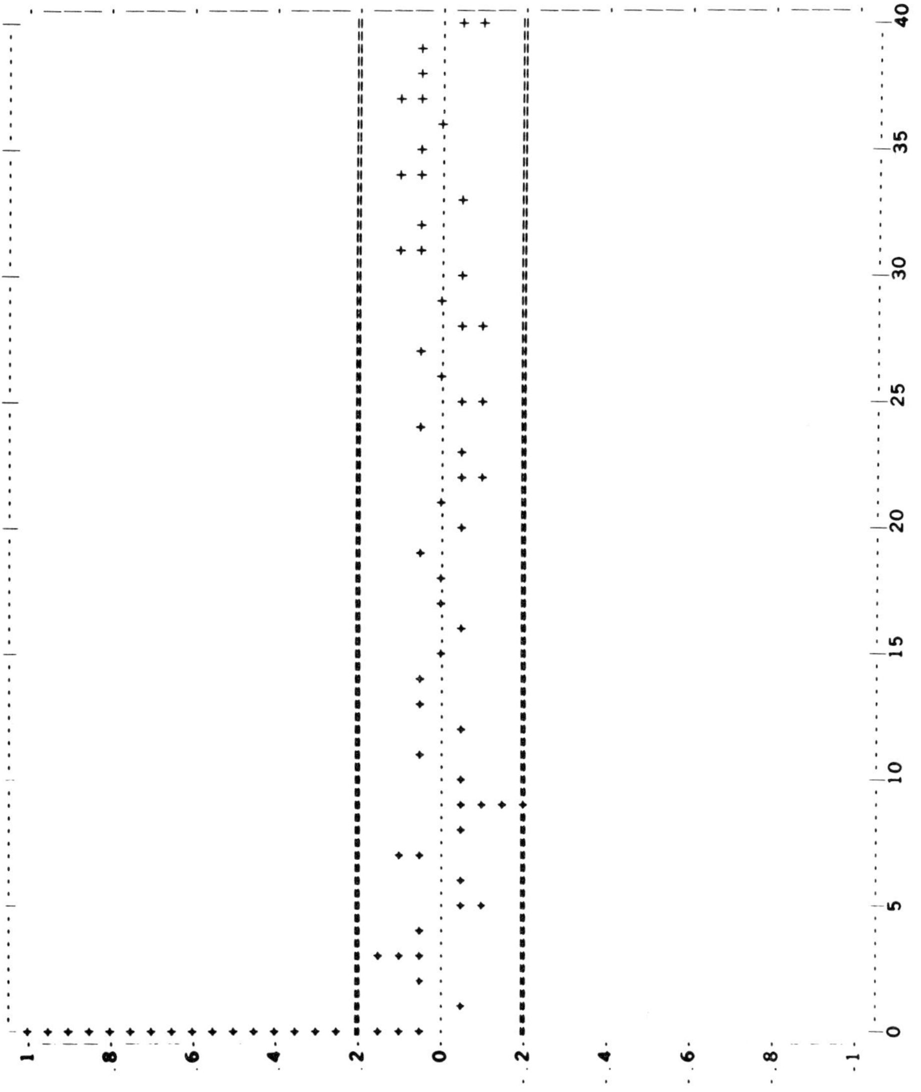


**Figure 6.9** A correlogram of a random series.

very close to zero for all nonzero values $k$ of the lag (there are forty of these plotted on the abscissa in the figure).

A random series appears to have no systematic pattern that can be exploited for forecasting. It should be noted that a "random" series is not necessarily "normally" distributed (see Chapter 7 for a discussion on how data are "distributed").

Many time series, even after a certain amount of "differencing," exhibit short-term correlations (or "memory") in their pattern. Thus autocorrelation at shorter lags is greater than autocorrelation at longer lags. For a time series having this low-order dependence, a correlogram would show a decaying pattern. Figure 6.10 shows a correlogram of telephone toll revenue data. In this case, the strong trend in the data induces a "memory" pattern, and the correlogram corroborates this. Thus a correlogram can help identify structure in data; the pattern is not unique to the individual time series, however.

Other time series have a tendency to show periodicities in a fairly regular way. This means that correlograms for these series will also show this periodicity. A seasonal series like the main-telephone gain is a very special kind of periodic series in which the highs and lows correspond to a seasonal pattern. It is interesting to notice that correlograms of seasonal data will have their very own seasonality pattern: notice the high autocorrelation at lag 12 and at multiples of 12 for the main-telephone-gain data displayed in Figure 6.11.

Correlograms and their interpretations play a major role in ARIMA time series modeling. They are also used in the analysis of residuals from regression models. As part of the diagnostic checking process, an analyst either confirms or rejects the hypothesis that the residuals are randomly distributed.

## SOFTWARE CONSIDERATIONS

All statistical computer packages and many desk-top computers nowadays contain some capability for displaying and summarizing data graphically. In your planning, you should make certain they can generate time plots and scatter diagrams on a printer plotter. Fewer software systems can provide output to selected high quality graphics devices, however, and this limitation should be considered carefully.

Among widely available statistical software packages, time plots and bivariate (scatter) plots are available through the P6D program in the University of California Biomedical Computer Programs (BMDP) (Dixon and Brown, 1979), the subprogram SCATTERGRAM in the Statistical Package for the Social Sciences (SPSS) (Nie et al., 1975) or the PLOT PROC subprogram in the Statistical Analysis System (SAS) (Barr et al., 1976). In SAS the PLOT option in PROC UNIVARIATE produces a stem-and-leaf plot (or a vertical bar chart) as part of the output and PROC AUTOREG provides a way to calculate autocorrelations.

McNeil (1977, Chapter 3, Section 7) discusses computer algorithms (using APL

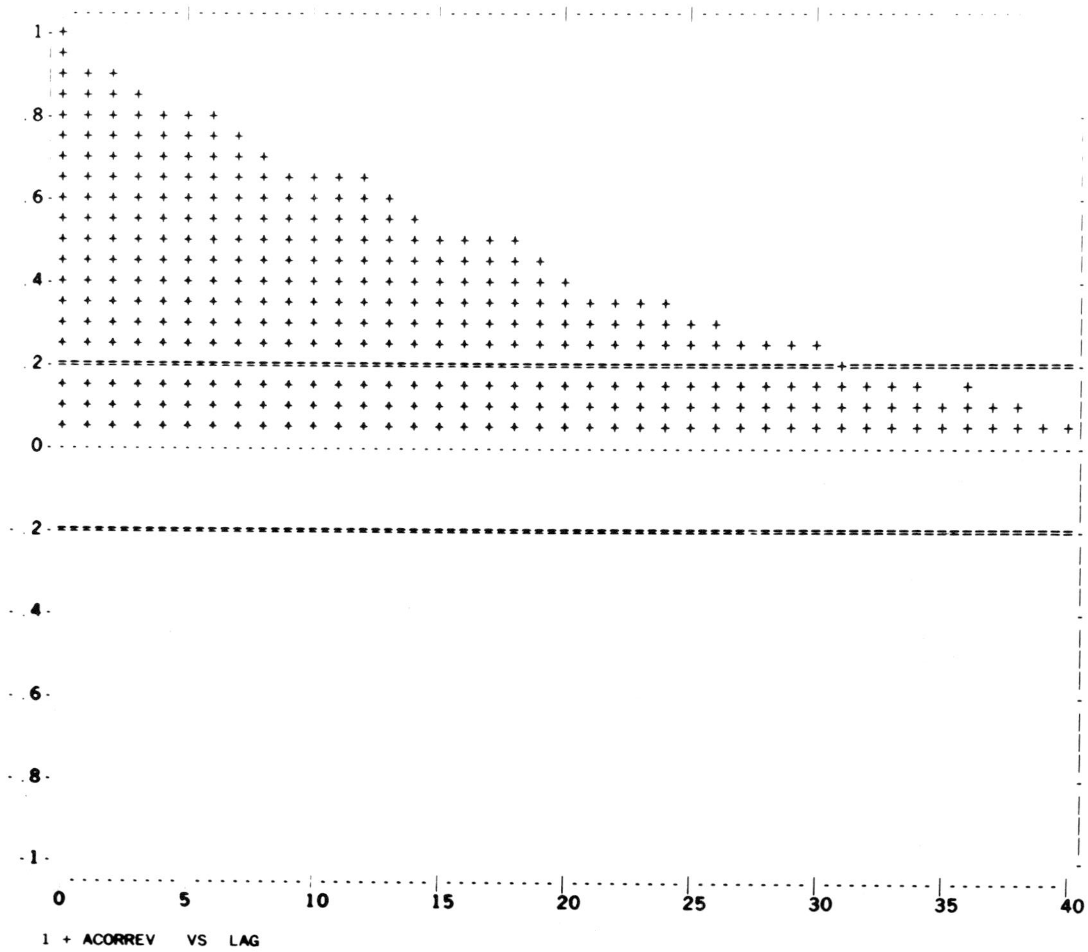


**Figure 6.10** A correlogram of monthly toll revenue data.

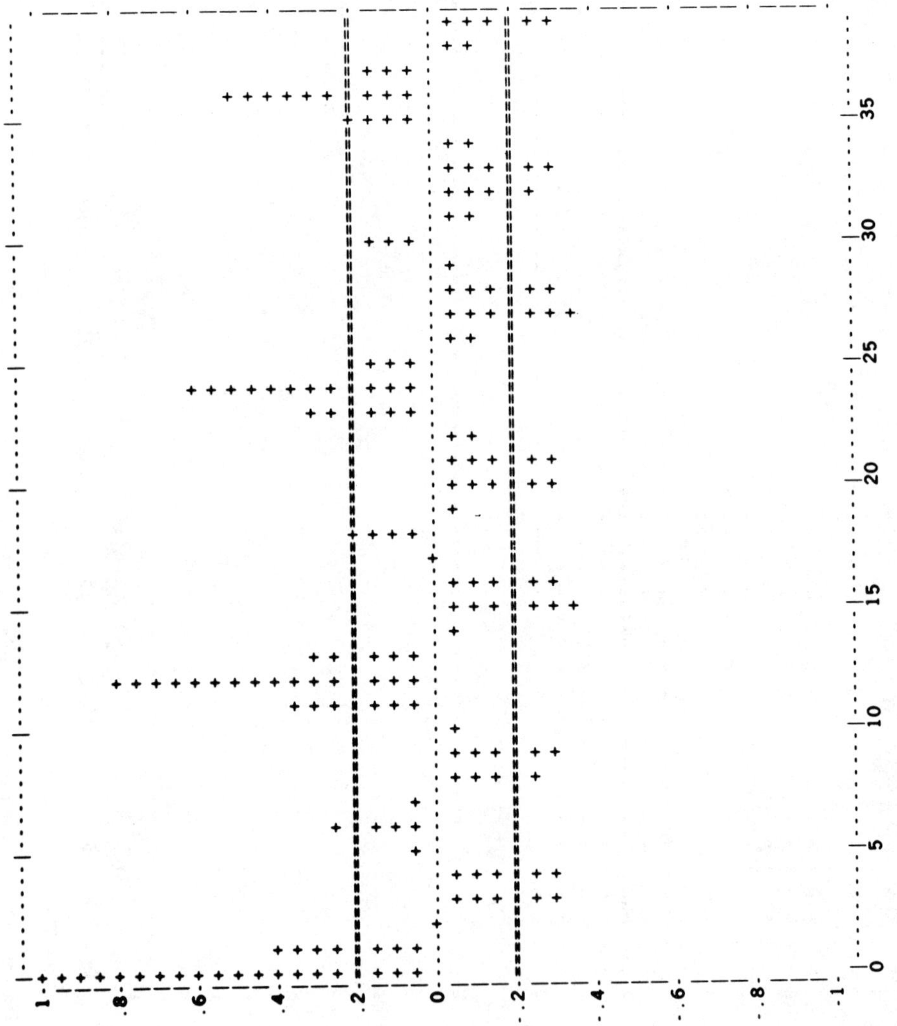


**Figure 6.11** A correlogram for the monthly main-telephone-gain data.

functions and FORTRAN subroutines) for "line and scat," which can be used for time plots and scatter plots, respectively. In Chapter 1, Section 7 he gives a program listing for the stem-and-leaf plot in APL and FORTRAN.

In addition, many time series analysis and forecasting tools are available in the statistical and econometric software systems of a large number of commercial time-sharing firms. Through these service bureaus forecasters can often obtain access to software packages other than BMDP, SAS, or SPSS, such as Interactive Data Analysis (IDA) (Ling and Roberts, 1980), Minitab (Ryan, Joiner, and Ryan, 1976), SCSS (Nie et al., 1980), and SIBYL/RUNNER (Makridakis and Wheelwright, 1978).

## SUMMARY

Effective graphical displays and summaries that help forecasters understand their data include

- Time plots that provide a visual indication of the predominant characteristics of a time series—trend-cycle, seasonal, and/or irregular.
- Scatter diagrams that are useful for studying relationships among variables and are widely applied in regression analysis.
- Low-resolution displays which allow you to concentrate on the overall trend and seasonal patterns of one or more series without worrying about accurate numerical comparisons.
- Stem-and-leaf displays that show groupings of data values, distribution or spread of the data, and unsymmetric trailing off at the low or high end. Central tendency, missing values, and unusual values can also be identified with this display.
- Autocorrelograms that show the strength of the relationship between data values separated by one or more periods. Seasonality can be identified with such plots, but they are more frequently used in the analysis of residuals from regression models. In this instance, the analyst looks for the absence of autocorrelation, i.e., a random pattern.

This chapter has stressed the importance of graphical tools for all aspects of the model building phases—exploratory as well as confirmatory. Additional uses for graphical displays will become evident in subsequent chapters.

## USEFUL READING

BARR, A. J., J. H. GOODNIGHT, J. P. SALL, and J. T. HELWIG (1976). *A User's Guide to SAS 76*. Raleigh, NC: SAS Institute, Inc.

BECKER, R. A., and J. M. CHAMBERS (1977). GR-Z: A System of Graphical Subroutines for Data Analysis. *Proceedings of Computer Science and Statistics, Tenth Annual Symposium on the Interface*. National Bureau of Standards Special Publication 503, 409–15.

DIXON, W. J., and M. B. BROWN (1979). *BMDP-79 Biomedical Computer Programs P-Series*. Los Angeles, CA: University of California Press.

LING, R. F., and H. V. ROBERTS (1980). *User's Manual for IDA*. Palo Alto, CA: The Scientific Press.

McNEIL, D. R. (1977). *Interactive Data Analysis*. New York, NY: John Wiley and Sons.

MAKRIDAKIS, S., and S. C. WHEELWRIGHT (1978). *Interactive Forecasting—Univariate and Multivariate Methods*. San Francisco, CA: Holden-Day.

NIE, N. H., C. H. HALL, M. N. FRANKLIN, J. G. JENKINS, K. J. SOURS, M. J. NORUSIS, and V. BEADLE (1980). *SCSS: A User's Guide to the SCSS Conversational System*. New York, NY: McGraw-Hill Book Co.

NIE, N. H., C. H. HALL, J. G. JENKINS, K. STEINBRENNER, and D. H. BENT (1975). *SPSS: Statistical Package for the Social Sciences*, 2nd ed. New York, NY: McGraw-Hill Book Co.

RYAN, T. A., B. L. JOINER, and B. F. RYAN (1976). *Minitab Student Handbook*. North Scituate, MA: Duxbury Press.

CHAPTER **7**

# Summarizing Batches of Data

The previous chapter discussed data displays, which reveal a great deal about patterns in data. This chapter deals with the analysis of the distribution of data, which is an important analytical step often overlooked in forecasting. It is important to recognize that:

- Summaries are required to quantify information about the shape or distribution of data.
- Summarizing data is part of the data analysis process. Assuming that an arithmetic mean is representative of a "typical" value may not be appropriate when the data have outliers (unusual data values).
- Assuming inappropriate distributions for data can result in misleading tests of significance. Hypothesis testing assumes that data are "normally" distributed, for example, and this may not be the case in reality.

## TABULATING FREQUENCIES

Suppose that an analyst has been asked to determine the meaning of a set of numbers dealing with the travel time between a central garage and customers' locations for fifty service orders (visits) (Table 7.1). The following questions are to be answered:

- Where are most of the data values concentrated?
- What fluctuations are present in the data?
- Are there any extreme or unusual data values—values that don't seem to fit?
- Can the overall behavior of the data be described?

It is clear that the data displayed in Table 7.1 are not very enlightening. The analyst decides to condense the raw data by placing it into *cells* or *classes*. These

**Table 7.1** Travel times (in minutes) from a garage to customers' locations for fifty service orders.

| | | | | | | | | | |
|---|---|---|---|---|---|---|---|---|---|
| 11, | 23, | 11, | 8, | 11, | 10, | 9, | 6, | 7, | 8 |
| 23, | 7, | 32, | 10, | 12, | 7, | 14, | 10, | 6, | 11 |
| 9, | 10, | 11, | 10, | 40, | 13, | 5, | 9, | 6, | 27 |
| 14, | 21, | 11, | 6, | 17, | 4, | 30, | 10, | 6, | 3 |
| 4, | 4, | 16, | 22, | 20, | 3, | 13, | 8, | 18, | 12 |

cells can be either numerical or attributive (e.g., designated as either a "business" or "residence" service order) in nature. The first count and display of the data are shown in Table 7.2. The relative percent that each class is of the total number of orders suggests that between 9 to 11 minutes is the typical or most frequent travel time. Most of the observations are clustered within 3–14 minutes. The one observation between 39–41 minutes looks very unusual, and all values beyond 26 minutes look suspect because they are so far from the apparent average. Perhaps there were extenuating circumstances that caused these travel times to be so great. But how does the analyst determine if some of the data are truly "unusual"?

## Relative Frequency Distributions

The procedure for counting the number of occurrences of a given characteristic in a grouping of data gives rise to frequencies. These frequencies, when considered as

**Table 7.2** A frequency distribution for the fifty service-order travel times shown in Table 7.1.

| Interval (in minutes) | Number of service orders | | Relative percent of orders |
|---|---|---|---|
| 3–5 | ~~IIII~~ I | 6 | 12 |
| 6–8 | ~~IIII~~ ~~IIII~~ I | 11 | 22 |
| 9–11 | ~~IIII~~ ~~IIII~~ ~~IIII~~ | 15 | 30 |
| 12–14 | ~~IIII~~ I | 6 | 12 |
| 15–17 | II | 2 | 4 |
| 18–20 | II | 2 | 4 |
| 21–23 | IIII | 4 | 8 |
| 24–26 | | | |
| 27–29 | I | 1 | 2 |
| 30–32 | II | 2 | 4 |
| 33–35 | | | |
| 36–38 | | | |
| 39–41 | I | 1 | 2 |
| | | (Total: 50) | |

fractions, can be displayed as a *relative frequency distribution.* Table 7.2 is an example of a relative frequency distribution.

A grouping interval needs to be selected before tallying the data. The grouping interval will depend on the range of variation, the number of data values, and the palatability of the display to the user.

In Table 7.2 the intervals have a width of two minutes. An interval of one minute rather than two would result in a long table without providing added information. These groupings should be uniquely defined so that there is no ambiguity into which cell a given tally goes.

The relative frequencies are then determined by counting the number of data values in a cell divided by total number of data values recorded.

In the first cell, for example, there are six orders out of fifty giving a relative frequency of 12 percent. This information is then appropriately summarized as a relative frequency distribution in the last column.

Table 7.3 is another relative frequency distribution, but it has an additional column—the cumulative percent of orders. Once the 21–23-minute interval is reached, 92 percent of the observations have been counted. This reinforces the suspect nature of the remaining observations.

Several points need to be considered in establishing class intervals. The units should be meaningful. It should be decided first whether the number or attribute class is most appropriate. Also, the amount of data as well as the range of values of interest should be considered. If the data are integer-valued, the class intervals should not be fractional.

Many analysts use what is called "the 10/15/20 rule" for guidance in selecting the size of class intervals. The total range of data (maximum value minus minimum value) is computed first, and the result is then divided by 10, 15, and 20. For a small

**Table 7.3** The cumulative frequency distribution of the service-order travel times.

| Interval (in minutes) | Number of orders | Cumulative number of orders | Cumulative percent of orders |
|---|---|---|---|
| 3–5 | 6 | 6 | 12 |
| 6–8 | 11 | 17 | 34 |
| 9–11 | 15 | 32 | 64 |
| 12–14 | 6 | 38 | 76 |
| 15–17 | 2 | 40 | 80 |
| 18–20 | 2 | 42 | 84 |
| 21–23 | 4 | 46 | 92 |
| 24–26 | | 46 | 92 |
| 27–29 | 1 | 47 | 94 |
| 30–32 | 2 | 49 | 98 |
| 33–35 | | 49 | 98 |
| 36–38 | | 49 | 98 |
| 39–41 | 1 | 50 | 100 |

group of data (50 or so), a class interval in the range resulting after division by 10–15 is preferred; for a large group of data, take a class interval resulting from division by 15–20. Select the minimum value as the initial lowest class boundary. Add other classes according to whichever interval formula you have used. An example of this procedure is shown in Table 7.4.

The resulting graph of the frequency distribution can take the form of a *histogram,* as is shown in Figure 7.1. In a histogram, data are plotted as bars rather than as a single graph-line. Figure 7.1 shows that there are a very few long travel times (above 25 minutes) and that the times around the median (10 minutes) are the most typical. The distribution is said to have a "tail" skewed to the right. However, the shape of the histogram can be sensitive to the choice of class intervals. Figure 7.2 demonstrates the fact that it is often desirable to select several class intervals to be certain that the results are reasonable. (For the service order example, fractional intervals make little sense since the data are composed entirely of whole numbers.)

A relative frequency distribution can be turned into a *cumulative frequency distribution* when one is interested in quantities such as the proportion of items below (or above) a given standard value. Another situation requiring a cumulative frequency distribution arises when investigating whether a distribution follows some particular mathematical form. This will be touched on again in the section on quantile-quantile plots.

## The Normal Distribution

The primary reason many analysts construct histograms is to compare them with a normal ("bellshaped") probability distribution. The normal distribution, which is deeply rooted in all statistical theory, looks symmetrical and is completely specified by two parameters ($\mu,\sigma$); it is tabulated in Appendix A, Table 1.

**Table 7.4** An illustration of the 10/15/20 rule.

- Compute range = Maximum value − Minimum value:
  Range = 40 − 3 = 37.
- Compute range divided by 10, 15, and 20:
  Range/10 = 3.7; Range/15 = 2.47; Range/20 = 1.85.
  Class length of 3 will yield between 10 and 15 classes.
- Select initial lower class bound not more than minimum value:
  Initial lower class bound = 3.
- Increment this bound by length of class interval to obtain subsequent lower class bounds:
  (3 − 5, 6 − 8, 9 − 11, . . .
- Upper class bound is highest possible value that is less than the subsequent lower class bound:
  . . . 33 − 35, 36 − 38, 39 − 41).

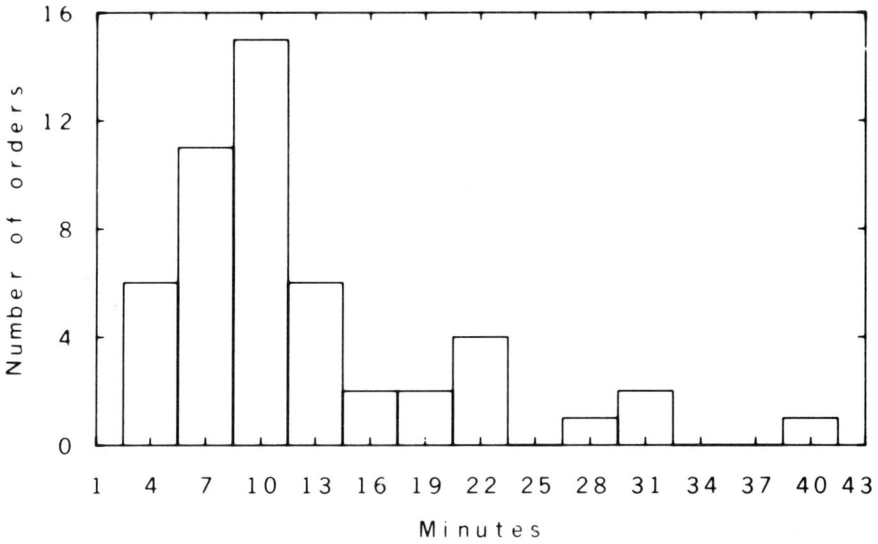


**Figure 7.1** A histogram plot of the frequency distribution for fifty service-order travel times.

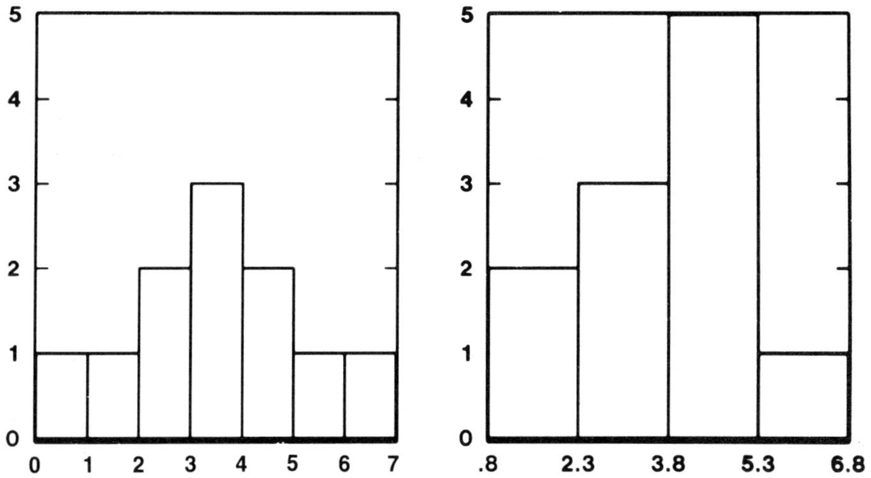


**Figure 7.2** Two histograms using the same data but different class intervals.

In general, probability distributions are used to make statements about the probability that a certain portion of the data or that a statistic falls within a specified range. For a normal distribution with mean $\mu$ and standard deviation $\sigma$, the interval $(\mu - 1.64\sigma, \mu + 1.64\sigma)$ contains 90 percent of the distribution. Similarly, there is about a 68 percent probability that a random observation from a normal distribution will be between plus and minus one standard deviation ($\sigma$) of the mean ($\mu$).

The use of confidence limits about the fitted values in regression theory is derived from the normal distribution. This subject is treated in Chapter 14.

## DISPLAYING SUMMARY MEASUREMENTS

While time plots, scatter diagrams, and low-resolution displays are useful for revealing overall patterns, it is often desirable to condense some features of the data into a few meaningful numbers. These summary measures are called *statistics*.

While statistics can be used for many purposes, they are commonly used for:

- Simply describing some aspect of the data that needs to be highlighted for a particular application, such as measures of central tendency or dispersion.
- Summarizing salient features of a frequency distribution, such as its percentiles.
- Comparing two or more frequency distributions.
- Confirmatory analysis, such as hypothesis testing.

There are a number of familiar ways, as described in elementary statistics texts, for summarizing data with statistics. The histogram has already been introduced. There are a number of other techniques that have sprung up in recent years as a result of the increased flexibility of computers in handling, analyzing, and displaying data. Much of this "new look" can be attributed to Tukey (1977). Other elementary books that emphasize exploratory data analysis include Erickson and Nosanchuk (1977), Hartwig and Dearing (1979), and McNeil (1977).

### Central Tendency

The *location,* or central tendency, of a group of data is the center of the data when arranged in order of size of the measure. One measure of location or central tendency is the median. Other commonly used measures of location are the mode, the arithmetic (sample) mean or average, and the midmean. The reason no single measure of location is always the best is that each provides its own perspective and insights, and in practical situations outliers or unusual data values can seriously distort the representativeness of certain statistics.

As an example, consider the following set of numbers:

$$\{1.1, 1.6, 4.7, 2.1, 3.1, 32.7, 5.8, 2.6, 4.8, 1.9, 3.7, 2.6\}.$$

The arithmetic mean is 5.56, and the median is 2.85. It is noteworthy that the mean, which is theoretically the "best" statistic for estimating central tendency for normally distributed data, has been severely distorted by the outlying value 32.7. The mean of the data, excluding the outlier, is 3.1, and appears much more representative.

One simple way to make the arithmetic mean less sensitive to extreme outliers is first to delete or "trim" a proportion of the data from each end and then calculate the arithmetic mean of the remaining numbers. Such a statistic is called a *trimmed mean*. The midmean, for example, is a 25-percent trimmed mean since 25 percent of the data values are trimmed from each end (i.e., the mean is taken of the values between the 25th and 75th percentiles). This will be discussed more in Chapter 16. A thorough treatment of measures of location and their properties under varying realistic assumptions of distribution may be found in Andrews et al. (1972).

## Dispersion

Besides measures of location for a freqnency distribution, certain measures of *scale* or dispersion are useful. Some commonly used measures are range, standard deviation, and modifications of these. The range is simply the difference between the largest and smallest value in the data set.

The (sample) standard deviation is the most commonly used measure of dispersion, though, like the mean, it can be misleading when there are outliers. The standard deviation is the square root of the (sample) variance that has the formula

$$\sum_{i=1}^{n}(y_i - \bar{y})^2/(n - 1),$$

where $y_1, y_2, \ldots, y_n$ are the $n$ data values and

$$\bar{y} = \sum_{i=1}^{n} y_i/n$$

is the sample mean. Historically, its popularity is due primarily to its theoretical advantages in formal statistical theory.

Other measures of dispersion include the *MAD statistic* (MAD stands for median of the absolute deviations from the median of the data), the sample variance of a truncated sample, and the *interquartile difference* (IQD), which is the difference between the 75th and 25th percentiles. The 25th percentile is $(n + 1)/4 = 13/4 = 3.25$; i.e., between the third and fourth smallest value. The 75th percentile is $3(n + 1)/4 = 9.75$; i.e., between the ninth and tenth value in the ranked data.

The calculation of a MAD is illustrated in Table 7.5. The "data" there are the same numbers used earlier to explain "median" and "arithmetic mean." The MAD is calculated by first ranking the data from smallest to largest (Column 2) and picking the median [it is $(2.6 + 3.1)/2 = 2.85$, since there is an even number of data values]. Deviations from the median are calculated next (Column 3), and the result is reranked (Column 4). The midvalue of the latter set of numbers is the MAD [it

**Table 7.5** Calculation of the median absolute deviation from the median (MAD).

| Data ($n$) | Data, ranked | | Deviations from the median | Absolute deviations from the median, ranked | |
|---|---|---|---|---|---|
| 1.1 | 1.1 | | −1.75 | 0.25 | |
| 1.6 | 1.6 | | −1.25 | 0.25 | |
| 4.7 | 1.9 | | −0.95 | 0.25 | |
| 2.1 | 2.1 | | −0.75 | 0.75 | |
| 3.1 | 2.6 | | −0.25 | 0.85 | |
| 32.7 | 2.6 | Median | −0.25 | 0.95 | MAD = 1.1 |
| 5.8 | 3.1 | | 0.25 | 1.25 | |
| 2.6 | 3.7 | | 0.85 | 1.75 | |
| 4.8 | 4.7 | | 1.85 | 1.85 | |
| 1.9 | 4.8 | | 1.95 | 1.95 | |
| 3.7 | 5.8 | | 2.95 | 2.95 | |
| 2.6 | 32.7 | | 29.85 | 29.85 | |

First quartile = 1/4 ($n$ + 1) = 13/4 = 3.25.
Median = (2.6 + 3.1)/2 = 2.85.
Midmean = (2.1 + 2.6 + 2.6 + 3.1 + 3.7 + 4.7)/6 = 3.13.
Third quartile = 3/4 ($n$ + 1) = 39/4 = 9.75.

is (0.95 + 1.25)/2 = 1.1]. For practical use the MAD and IQD are scaled by dividing by 0.6745 and 1.35, respectively. For normally distributed data this scaling makes these measures good approximations of the theoretical standard deviation ($\sigma$) if the number of observations is large.

The conventional sample mean and standard deviation do not offer much protection against outliers. Statistics based on the median or the mean of truncated data appear to be much more "resistant" to outliers. A statistic is said to be *resistant* if no change of a small fraction of the data can produce a large distortion of a total calculated value—i.e., it is resistant to "weird" or unusual values. The arithmetic mean is clearly not resistant since its value can be changed by arbitrarily increasing only one of its terms. The median, on the other hand, is quite resistant. Chapter 16 will deal more thoroughly with techniques for ensuring against unusual values.

In the data we used for these examples—the twelve numbers with the single outlier—the standard deviation is 8.6, the MAD is 1.1, and the interquartile range is 2.75. For normally distributed data, the standard deviation can be approximated by dividing the MAD by 0.6745 (= 1.63) or by dividing the IQD by 1.35 (= 2.04). The mean plus three standard deviations is 31.35 [5.55 + (3)(8.6) = 31.35], which almost encompasses the outlier of 32.7. This is because the calculation of the standard deviation gives equal weight to all observations. However, if one considers the median plus three times 1.63 (= 7.74), then 32.7 is clearly very far away from the bulk of the data.

## The Box Plot

A frequency distribution can be described by its percentiles. The *p*th percentile is the value which exceeds *p* percent of the data. In particular, the median is the 50th percentile; i.e., it is the value which exceeds 50 percent of the data. For example, the stem-and-leaf display described in Chapter 6 shows that the median of the travel-time data is 10 minutes. The distribution does not have a symmetrical shape, so it becomes essential to summarize the distribution with more than one percentile.

While percentiles can be used to summarize a frequency distribution, it is often desirable to describe a distribution with the smallest set of numbers possible. Rather than simply write down a sequence of such numbers, there is a graphical device, called the *box plot,* which is a five-number summary of a distribution (McGill et al., 1978, and Tukey, 1977). A box plot concisely depicts the median, the upper and lower quartiles, and the two extremes of any group of data. The upper and lower quartiles are respectively the 25th and 75th percentiles.

A box plot for the travel-time data previously discussed is shown in Figure 7.3. Fifty percent of the data values are tightly grouped (these are depicted with the box, which includes all data falling between the 25th and 75th percentiles; these quartiles are also called hinges). The upper tail appears longer than the lower tail. The median value is slightly lower than the midrange of the box. The upper extreme value appears to be an outlier since it is so far away from the bulk of the data. Since there may be

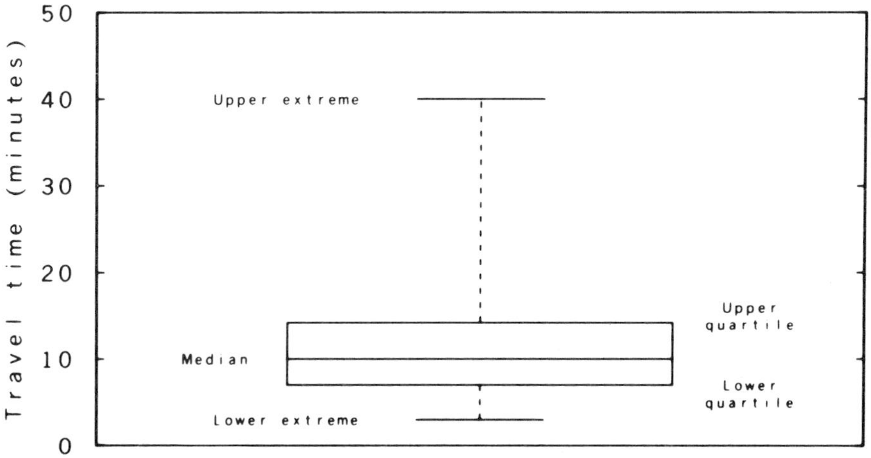


**Figure 7.3** The box plot of the service-order travel-time data.

data values along the "whisker," this conclusion needs to be confirmed with additional analyses. This plot gives a surprising amount of information for such a simple display.

The simple box plot summarizes the distribution in terms of five quantities. In addition, the distance between the quartiles is the interquartile range, a measure of dispersion. A missing link in this plot is the number of data values in the distribution, which impacts on the reliability of the estimate of the median. To indicate sample size, a *notched box plot* can be drawn in which the depth of the notch can be made proportional to the square root of the sample size (McGill et al., 1978).

Figure 7.4 shows a notched box plot for the annual variation in the twelve monthly values for the main-telephone-gain data across nine years. The changes in level as well as the variation of the data within years are summarized in a single display. Evidently, the difference between the high and low values within a year is increasing over time. Moreover, while the median values reflect the cyclical pattern of the economy (the 1970 and 1975 recessions), the range spanned by the interquartile range of the monthly values (the height of the box) varies considerably over time. These kinds of information can provide the forecaster with some insights about the nature of variation in data.

The single comprehensive box plot may not be enough by itself, however. One weakness is its inability to identify or discern data from two different populations. Figure 7.5 shows box plots for the travel times for three categories of service orders. It shows that there are really two distributions, one from the subset of nonkey telephone orders and the other from the orders for key telephone sets (a "key"

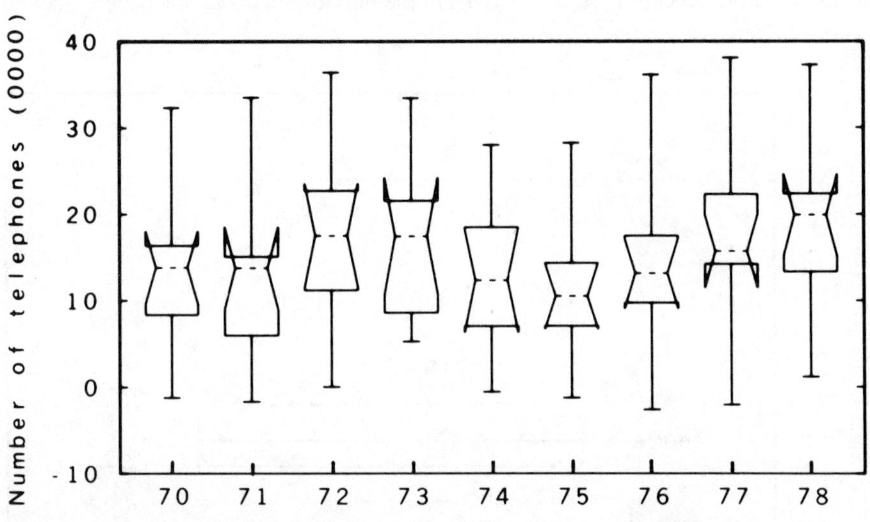


**Figure 7.4** A notched box plot showing the annual variation in the twelve monthly values for the main-telephone-gain data.

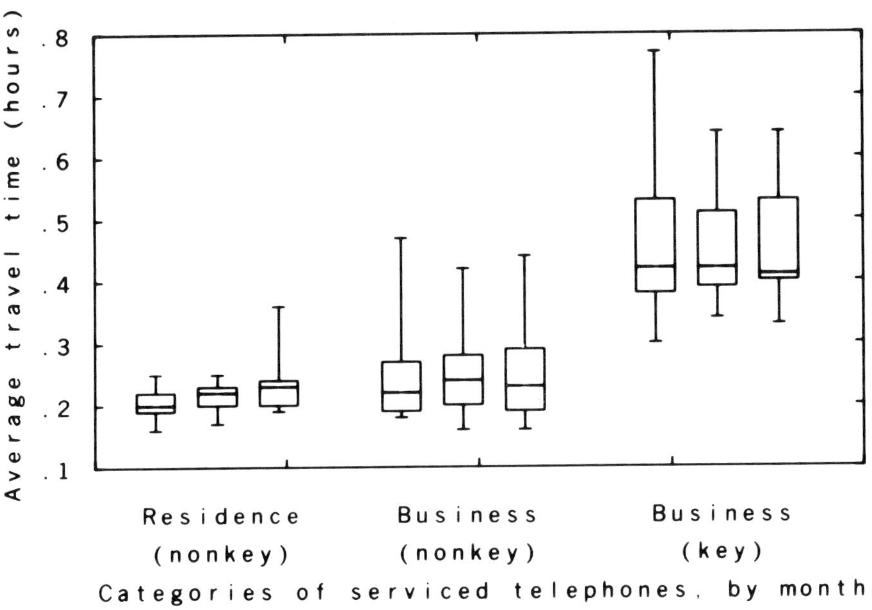


**Figure 7.5** Box plots for the travel times for three categories of service orders.

telephone set is one linked to a multiple set of telephone numbers). The difference in the type of work that is required to service "key" and "nonkey" orders results in two separate distributions. A single box plot would clearly mask these differences.

The box plot can also be used to identify potential outliers. In the terminology of Tukey (1977), a "step" is defined as 1.5 times the interquartile range (height of the box). Inner fences are values one step above the top and one step below the bottom of the box. Outer fences are values two steps above and below the box. A value outside an inner fence can be an outlier, but a value outside an outer fence is much more likely to be one.

## The Quantile-Quantile Plot

The Q-Q (quantile-quantile) plot is useful for determining if two data sets have the same probability distribution. The quantiles (percentiles) of one distribution are plotted against the quantiles of the second distribution. If two data sets have the same probability distribution, the Q-Q plot will be linear.

For example, the quantiles of an empirical data set can be compared to the quantiles of the standard normal distribution ($\mu = 0, \sigma = 1$) to test for normality. Each value corresponds to a quantile which can be compared to the same quantiles of the normal curve.

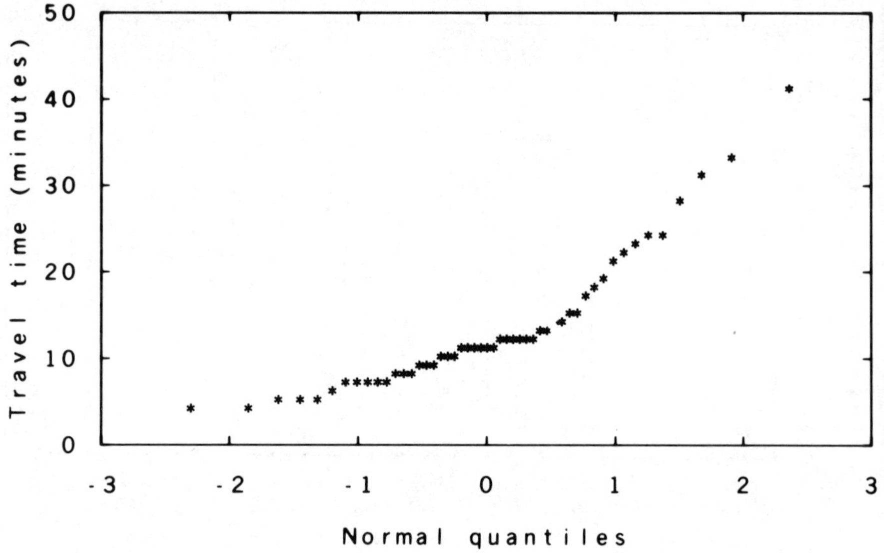


**Figure 7.6** A quantile-quantile (Q-Q) plot for the service-order travel-time data.

A Q-Q plot for the travel-time data we have been using in this chapter is shown in Figure 7.6. This plot shows an upper tail in the empirical distribution that is much longer than that of the normal distribution. The tails of many data sets are longer than those of the normal distribution, but generally by a lesser amount than in this example.

## SOFTWARE CONSIDERATIONS

Frequency tabulations are widely available in a number of software packages, such as Program P2D in BMDP (Dixon and Brown, 1979), PROC FREQ in SAS (Barr et al., 1976), and subprogram FREQUENCIES in SPSS (Nie et al., 1975). The P2D program in BMDP prints out a simple printer-plot version of the box plot. In SAS the PLOT option causes PROC UNIVARIATE to produce a box plot as part of the output. The BMDP program P5D prints a normal or half-normal probability plot of the data. The PROC RANK in SAS can be used to construct normal probability plots. A normal probability plot is also produced in SAS through the PLOT option in PROC UNIVARIATE. McNeil (1977, Chapter 1, Section 7) provides APL functions and FORTRAN subroutines for programming the box plot.

## SUMMARY

In this chapter, the key points about tabulating frequencies are that:

- Summaries are necessary to quantify information inherent in the "shape" or distribution of data.
- Frequency distributions can be calculated and plotted to show what percentage each interval is of the total number of data.
- Cumulative frequencies or percentiles can be used to determine if a given data set follows a normal probability distribution.

Several measures are useful for summarizing distributions. These include:

- Statistics used to describe central tendency such as the mean, median, and trimmed mean.
- Measures of dispersion, such as the standard deviation, median absolute deviation, and range.
- The box plot, which is a convenient way of visually displaying a five-number summary of a distribution.
- The quantile-quantile plot, which is frequently used to determine if a data set, especially residuals from a regression model, follows a normal distribution. If it does, hypothesis testing can be carried out or confidence limits can be constructed.

The summarizing measurements discussed in this chapter provide important insights into understanding the shape of data—one of the early steps in model building or analysis. This may necessitate adjustments of the data (using methods to be discussed in Chapter 10) so that a particular forecasting or analytical technique can be applied. When data suggest nonnormal distributions with possible outliers, robust/resistant methods should also be considered (Chapters 16 and 17).

## USEFUL READING

ANDREWS, D. F., P. J. BICKEL, F. R. HAMPEL, P. J. HUBER, W. H. ROGERS, and J. W. TUKEY (1972). *Robust Estimates of Location: Survey and Advances*. Princeton, NJ: Princeton University Press.

BARR, A. J., J. H. GOODNIGHT, J. P. SALL, and J. T. HELWIG (1976). *A User's Guide to SAS 76*. Raleigh, NC: SAS Institute, Inc.

DIXON, W. J., and M. B. BROWN (1979). *BMDP-79 Biomedical Computer Programs P-Series*. Los Angeles, CA: University of California Press.

ERICKSON, B. H., and T. A. NOSANCHUK (1977). *Understanding Data*. Toronto, Canada: McGraw-Hill-Ryerson Ltd.

HARTWIG, F., and B. E. DEARING (1979). *Exploratory Data Analysis*. Sage University Paper on Quantitative Applications in the Social Sciences, 07-016. Beverly Hills, CA: Sage Publications.

McGILL, R. J., J. W. TUKEY, and W. A. LARSEN (1978). Variations of Box Plots. *The American Statistician* 32, 12–16.

McNEIL, D. R. (1977). *Interactive Data Analysis*. New York, NY: John Wiley and Sons.

NIE, N. H., C. H. HALL, J. G. JENKINS, K. STEINBRENNER, and D. H. BENT (1975). *SPSS: Statistical Package for the Social Sciences,* 2nd ed. New York, NY: McGraw-Hill Book Co.

TUKEY, J. W. (1977). *Exploratory Data Analysis*. Reading, MA: Addison-Wesley Publishing Co.

# Part 2

## Solving a Forecasting Problem

CHAPTER **8**

# Forecasting with Exponential Smoothing Models

An effective forecasting technique must provide a theoretical framework: it must be able to describe the variability in the forecast data and supply a methodology for parameter estimation. Exponential smoothing models provide such a framework and are dealt with in this chapter; these are specific statistical forecasting techniques that

- Are widely used in the areas of sales, inventory, and production management as well as in quality control, process control, financial planning, and marketing planning.
- Are based on the mathematical projection of past patterns into the future, accomplished by using forecasting equations that are simple to update and require a relatively small number of calculations.
- Are analytically "naïve," but are of great practical value.
- Are especially suitable for use with desk-top computers, since they require little data storage.
- Are suitable for applications in which there are large numbers of time series, since few calculations are needed.

## WHAT IS SMOOTHING?

Most often *smoothing* refers to a procedure of taking weighted sums of data in order to "smooth out" very short term irregularities. To forecasters, smoothed data reveal information about secular trends (those of long duration) and economic cycles which need to be understood and projected by means of a set of assumptions about the future. Smoothed data are required in econometric modeling in order to have meaningful estimates of changes for many time series. A very appealing aspect of the use of smoothed data is that these can be interpreted easily. A plot of a smoothed employment series or of a smoothed industrial production series readily communicates information about the health of the economy, and percent changes based on smoothed data are understandable by lay persons and corporate managers. Percentages based on unadjusted series, on the other hand, often behave too erratically to be practically meaningful.

The smoothing of data and their subsequent decomposition into components or their expression in the form of an econometric model assists an analyst in understanding the real economic world. If the analyst finds a variation between unadjusted and smoothed data that is of particular importance, this can then be explained in quantitative (statistical) or theoretical terms; if variations are less important, through smoothing they can be removed, since they are irrelevant for the purposes of a given analysis. In macroeconomics, the seasonal component is often removed and the notions of "trend-cycle" and "turning point" come about from analyzing a smoothed version of the resulting data.

However, unadjusted data and smoothed data may at times indicate movement in opposite directions, because of a technical feature in the smoothing method. As you gain experience you will learn to be aware of these anomalies so that their meaning can be properly interpreted and adequately communicated to forecast users. It is also worth noting that certain time series models known as ARIMA models do not require smoothed data as inputs and yet can produce excellent forecasting results.

## Smoothing with Moving Averages

In order to create a smoothed time series in which the effect of seasonality and the impact of an irregular component has been reduced, you can often subject a time series to some type of *moving average* operation. In doing so, realize that too much smoothing will cause a delayed or even unnoticed change in direction in the data. Therefore, you must use discretion and match the degree of smoothing with each particular application.

The most common moving-average smoother is the *unweighted moving average*, in which each value of the data carries the same weight in the smoothing calculation. For $n$ values of a time series $y_1, \ldots, y_n$, the three-term moving average $z_t$ has the formula

$$z_t = \frac{1}{3} \sum_{i=0}^{2} y_{t-i} \qquad (t = 3, \ldots, n).$$

In general, the $p$-term moving average is written as

$$z_t = \frac{1}{p} \sum_{i=0}^{p-1} y_{t-i} \qquad (t = p, \ldots, n).$$

There are even more general ways in which a moving average can be expressed. In connection with most seasonal adjustment procedures (Chapters 18 and 19), the *weighted moving average* plays a significant role. A ($p$-term) weighted moving average has the formula

$$z_t = \sum_{i=0}^{p-1} a_i y_{t-i} \qquad (t = p, \ldots, n),$$

where

$$\sum_{i=0}^{p-1} a_i = 1.$$

The $a$'s are known as weights and ultimately they sum to unity. Should the weights be positive and not sum to unity, however, then the weighted moving average must be divided by the sum of the weights (see Table 8.1 for an example of a weighted average). Thus, for the ordinary ($p$-term) moving average, the $a$'s are all equal to $1/p$.

In discussions of ARIMA time series models, the term "moving average" occurs in a different context with a somewhat different meaning. The moving average operation discussed here is a smoothing operation.

Two major difficulties arise in considering moving averages as a smoothing procedure:

- Isolated outlying values may cause undue distortion of the smoothed series.
- Cyclical peaks and troughs are rarely followed smoothly by the procedure.

A smoothing technique based on *moving* ("running") *medians*, on the other hand, overcomes these shortcomings quite well (Mosteller and Tukey, 1977, p. 52 ff; Tukey, 1977, p. 210). Similar smoothing techniques are used in the SABL computer program, the Bell Laboratories seasonal adjustment procedure, which is treated in Chapter 19.

**Table 8.1** An example of a weighted-average calculation.

| | Observation | Weight | Observation × Weight |
|---|---|---|---|
| | 1.14 | 0.96 | 1.0944 |
| | 0.00 | 1.00 | 0.0000 |
| | 1.24 | 0.95 | 1.1780 |
| | 2.08 | 0.86 | 1.7888 |
| | 2.18 | 0.85 | 1.8530 |
| Total: | | 4.62 | 5.9142 |

$$\text{Weighted average} = \frac{5.9142}{4.62} = 1.28$$

## Single Exponential Smoothing

The exponential smoothing operation, in its simplest form, is expressed by

$$S_{t+1} = \alpha y_t + (1 - \alpha)S_t;$$

the forecast $S_{t+1}$ is expressed in terms of the *smoothing constant* $\alpha$ times a historical value $y_t$ in the current period of the data plus $(1 - \alpha)$ times $S_t$, the forecast of one period ago. The parameter $\alpha$ lies between 0 and 1, and can be estimated from past data or simply guessed at (as will be explained later).

By rewriting $S_{t+1}$ in another way as

$$S_{t+1} = S_t + \alpha(y_t - S_t),$$

it can be seen that single exponential smoothing is a procedure in which the forecast for the next period equals the forecast for the prior period adjusted by an amount that is proportional to the most recent forecast error

$$e_t = y_t - S_t.$$

This illustrates the simplest form of control whereby the current forecast error is used to modify the forecast for the next period.

The name "exponential smoothing" comes from the fact that $S_t$ can be expressed as a *weighted average* with exponentially decreasing weights. To see how this is so, substitute the expression for $S_t$ and $S_{t-1}$, namely,

$$S_t = \alpha y_{t-1} + (1 - \alpha)S_{t-1}$$

and

$$S_{t-1} = \alpha y_{t-2} + (1 - \alpha)S_{t-2},$$

in the original expression for $S_{t+1}$. Thus

$$\begin{aligned} S_{t+1} &= \alpha y_t + (1 - \alpha)[\alpha y_{t-1} + (1 - \alpha)S_{t-1}] \\ &= \alpha y_t + \alpha(1 - \alpha)y_{t-1} + \alpha(1 - \alpha)^2 y_{t-2} + (1 - \alpha)^3 S_{t-2}. \end{aligned}$$

Successive substitutions for $S_{t-k}$, where $k = 2, 3, \ldots, t$, yields

$$S_t = \alpha \sum_{k=0}^{t-1} (1 - \alpha)^k y_{t-k} + (1 - \alpha)^t S_0 \qquad (0 < \alpha < 1),$$

when $S_0$ is an initial estimate of the smoothed value.

The initial estimate $S_0$ of the smoothed value can be estimated from historical data by using a simple average of the most recent observations. Without historical data, a subjective estimate must be made. In order for the model to be responsive to changes, a larger value of $\alpha$ can be used in the first few periods to allow for a rapid adjustment.

The weights sum to unity and hence the term "average." Since the weights decrease geometrically with increasing $k$, the most recent values of $y_t$ are given the greatest weight. All the previous values of $y_t$ are included in the expression for $S_t$. Since $\alpha$ is less than unity, the values of $y_t$ most distant in the past will have the smallest weights associated with them.

The smoothing constant $\alpha$ must be determined judgmentally, depending on the sensitivity of response required by the model. The smaller the value of $\alpha$, the slower the response. Larger values of $\alpha$ cause increasingly quicker reactions in the smoothed (forecast) value. This may or may not be advantageous since forecast changes may be the result of real changes in the data or random fluctuations. High values of $\alpha$ are appropriate for smooth data but will cause excessive forecast changes for volatile data. It is often recommended that $\alpha$ should lie between 0.01 and 0.30 (Montgomery and Johnson, 1976).

### Comparing Exponential Smoothing with Moving Averages

The responsiveness of an exponential smoothing can be compared with that of a moving average. A moving average forecast $M_t$ for time $t$ averaged over $n$ periods is given by

$$M_t = \frac{1}{n} \sum_{i=t-n}^{t-1} y_i.$$

The technique of forecasting one step ahead with moving averages is represented by

$$\begin{aligned} M_{t+1} &= \frac{1}{n} \sum_{i=t-n+1}^{t} y_i \\ &= \frac{y_t - y_{t-n}}{n} + M_t. \end{aligned}$$

The moving average forecast $M_{t+1}$ is given by the preceding moving average forecast $M_t$ plus an adjustment (the average growth over the period $n$),

$$(y_t - y_{t-n})/n,$$

which generally becomes smaller for larger $n$. Thus the smoothing effect increases with larger $n$.

By approximating $y_{t-n}$ by the smoothed value $M_t$, the expression for $M_{t+1}$ can be made to look like a single exponential smoothing model:

$$M_{t+1} = \frac{1}{n} y_t + \left(1 - \frac{1}{n}\right) M_t,$$

where $\alpha = 1/n$ is the smoothing parameter.

To develop the comparison of exponential smoothing and a moving average further, it may be useful to calculate the "average age" of the data in the two methods. For an $n$-period moving average, the average age is

$$\frac{1}{n}\sum_{k=0}^{n-1} k = (n - 1)/2,$$

and for exponential smoothing, this is

$$\alpha \sum_{k=0}^{\infty} (1 - \alpha)^k k = (1 - \alpha)/\alpha.$$

Thus an exponential smoothing model that has the same average age as the $n$-period moving average would have a smoothing constant given by $\alpha = 2/(n + 1)$. It can be shown that the same result can be obtained by equating the variances of $S_t$ and $M_t$ (Montgomery and Johnson, 1976).

You can see that exponential smoothing is closely related to moving average methods. Like moving averages, single exponential smoothing models are not responsive enough to sudden changes in slope or level. While single exponential smoothing gives greater weight to the more recent observations, the subjective or *ad hoc* determination of the appropriate value of the weights is still a basic limitation of this method. On the positive side, the simplicity and low computation cost for many series have made single exponential smoothing an attractive, widely applied technique.

## An Application of Single Exponential Smoothing

In Chapter 7 we made use of data about service-order travel times. In this chapter let us use those data to illustrate a single exponential smoothing model. The data represent the times it takes an installer or repair person to travel from a service-center garage to customers' locations. The data are erratic and contain possible outliers.

Several values of $\alpha$ were used (0.5, 0.3, 0.2, 0.1, 0.05, 0.025). Recall that we indicated earlier that low values of $\alpha$ are generally better for volatile series. A criterion for selecting $\alpha$ is the minimization of the *mean square error* (MSE). Minimizing the mean square error is a technique for examining the accuracy of forecasts. The MSE is calculated by first squaring the forecast errors (actual value minus forecast) and then taking their average value. In this simulation, the MSE was minimized with $\alpha = 0.025$, though this does not represent the smallest value of $\alpha$ that could have been simulated. Figure 8.1 shows a plot of the actual and fitted travel-time values with $\alpha = 0.025$.

Other numerical examples of exponential smoothing may be found in Bowerman and O'Connell (1979, Section 3-3), Makridakis and Wheelwright (1978, Section

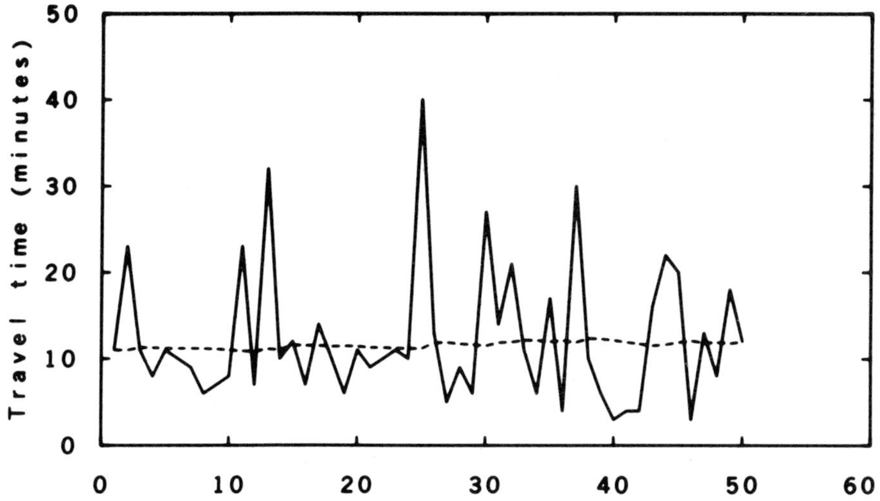


**Figure 8.1** Time plot of actual and smoothed values from a single exponential smoothing model ($\alpha = 0.025$) for travel-time data. (Actual data are plotted with solid line; fitted values are plotted with a dashed line.)

3-3), Montgomery and Johnson (1976), and Wheelwright and Makridakis (1980, Chapter 4).

Exponential smoothing was first introduced by Holt (1957) and popularized by Brown (1959, 1963). Winters (1960) introduced the seasonal exponential smoothing model. Other contributors include Trigg and Leach (1967) and Harrison (1965), who developed harmonic smoothing models.

## EXPONENTIAL SMOOTHING FOR TRENDING DATA

The single-exponential smoothing technique just described is best suited for historical data that can be regarded as *stationary* or having essentially a horizontal pattern. When dealing with trend or even seasonal patterns, it becomes necessary to introduce *higher-order exponential smoothing*.

### Double Exponential Smoothing

A *second-order* or *double* exponential smoothing is appropriate when a time series is expected to change linearly with time according to the model

$$y_{t+l} = \beta_{0,t} + l\beta_{1,t} + \varepsilon_t,$$

where $y_{t+l}$ is the forecast $l$-periods ahead, and $\varepsilon_t$ is the error term with zero mean and constant variance. The basic idea behind double exponential smoothing is to apply single exponential smoothing first to the original data. For a time series with a trend pattern, the smoothed series tends to lag or fall below the trend. Next, the exponential smoothing is applied again, but this time to the smoothed series. This results in

$$S_t^{[2]} = \alpha S_t + (1 - \alpha)S_{t-1}^{[2]},$$

where the notation $S_t^{[2]}$ implies the second-order smoothing step. An estimate of trend can be made by taking the difference between the single exponential smoothing statistic $S_t$ and the double exponential smoothing statistic $S_t^{[2]}$. Thus the intercept is estimated by

$$\begin{aligned}\hat{\beta}_{0,t} &= S_t + (S_t - S_t^{[2]})\\ &= 2S_t - S_t^{[2]}.\end{aligned}$$

The slope is estimated by

$$\hat{\beta}_{1,t} = \frac{\alpha}{1 - \alpha}(S_t - S_t^{[2]}).$$

To forecast $l$-periods ahead by using double exponential smoothing, the following forecasting equation is used:

$$\begin{aligned}y_{t+l} &= \hat{\beta}_{0,t} + l\hat{\beta}_{1,t}\\ &= (2 + \frac{\alpha l}{1 - \alpha})S_t - (1 + \frac{\alpha l}{1 - \alpha})S_t^{[2]}.\end{aligned}$$

As with single exponential smoothing, the initial smoothed statistics $S_0$ and now $S_0^{[2]}$ need to be determined. With historical data available, a straight line regression can be used to obtain estimates $\hat{\beta}_{0,0}$ and $\hat{\beta}_{1,0}$; otherwise they have to be estimated subjectively. Then

$$S_0 = \hat{\beta}_{0,0} - (\frac{1 - \alpha}{\alpha})\hat{\beta}_{1,0},$$

and

$$S_0^{[2]} = \hat{\beta}_{0,0} - 2(\frac{1 - \alpha}{\alpha})\hat{\beta}_{1,0}.$$

A seasonally adjusted version of the logarithms of airline data from Box and Jenkins (1976, Series G) shows a trending pattern for which the use of a double exponential smoothing model seems appropriate. For those data, Brown's (1963) linear exponential smoothing model with $\alpha = 0.5$ resulted in zero mean percent error or bias, a mean square error of 10.4, and a mean absolute error of 0.4 percent.

## Triple Exponential Smoothing

Higher-order (more than double) smoothing procedures arise when a higher-order polynomial is assumed as the trend model. Thus, for quadratic models, it is appropriate to use *triple* exponential smoothing. The quadratic or triple smoothing model produces forecasts that either increase or decrease in a quadratic manner according to

$$y_{t+l} = \beta_{0,t} + l\beta_{1,t} + l^2\beta_{2,t} + \varepsilon_t.$$

A third smooth is performed by using

$$S_t^{[3]} = \alpha S_t^{[2]} + (1 - \alpha)S_{t-1}^{[3]},$$

and the following equations are used to estimate the coefficients:

$$\hat{\beta}_{0,t} = 3S_t - 3S_t^{[2]} + S_t^{[3]};$$

$$\hat{\beta}_{1,t} = \frac{\alpha}{2(1 - \alpha)^2}[(6 - 5\alpha)S_t - 2(5 - 4\alpha)S_t^{[2]} + (4 - 3\alpha)S_t^{[3]}];$$

and

$$\hat{\beta}_{2,t} = \frac{\alpha^2}{(1 - \alpha)^2}S_t - 2S_t^{[2]} + S_t^{[3]}.$$

The initial conditions are

$$S_0 = \hat{\beta}_{0,0} - \frac{(1 - \alpha)}{\alpha}\hat{\beta}_{1,0} + \frac{(1 - \alpha)(2 - \alpha)\hat{\beta}_{2,0}}{4\alpha^2},$$

$$S_0^{[2]} = \hat{\beta}_{0,0} - \frac{2(1 - \alpha)}{\alpha}\hat{\beta}_{1,0} + \frac{2(1 - \alpha)(3 - 2\alpha)\hat{\beta}_{2,0}}{4\alpha^2},$$

and

$$S_0^{[3]} = \hat{\beta}_{0,0} - \frac{3(1 - \alpha)}{\alpha}\hat{\beta}_{1,0} + \frac{3(1 - \alpha)(4 - 3\alpha)\hat{\beta}_{2,0}}{4\alpha^2}.$$

Such higher-order procedures are treated in Montgomery and Johnson (1976) and Makridakis and Wheelwright (1978, Chapter 3). Bowerman and O'Connell (1979, Chapter 5) have a detailed example worked out for forecasting loan requests from a university credit union. Since the computational complexities increase with higher orders, smoothing techniques of a higher order than double exponential may not be very practical.

Another two-parameter linear-exponential trend model was proposed by Holt (1957); Brown's (1963) model is generally preferred, however, since it requires that fewer parameters be estimated. Generally, $\alpha$ lies in the 0.1 to 0.2 range.

## APPLICATION TO THE TELECOMMUNICATIONS EXAMPLE

Figures 8.2–8.5 display plots of the original (unadjusted) and seasonally adjusted time series, together with their predictions, for the telecommunications example introduced in Chapter 1 and used throughout the book as an illustrative data set. The computer program used selects the single, double, or triple exponential smoothing model on the basis of the minimum mean absolute deviation between the predictions and actual values.

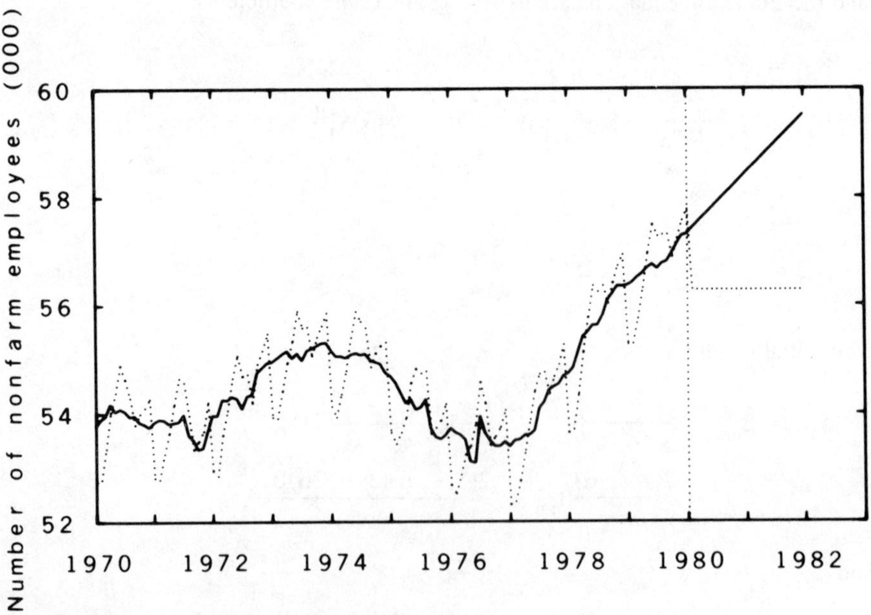


**Figure 8.2** Time plot of original and seasonally adjusted nonfarm employment data shown with "best" exponential smoothing model.

The seasonal components in the four original series are relatively small (see Chapter 9). However, the seasonality is sufficient to cause the computer program to select optimum models in each of which the unadjusted time series is smoothed to one lesser degree than the seasonally adjusted data is (e.g., single versus double). Consequently, the mean absolute deviation for seasonally adjusted data in each

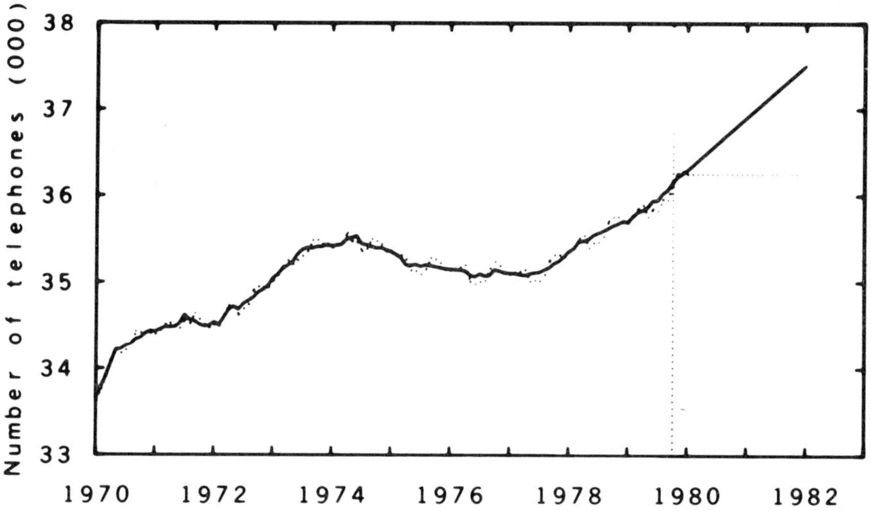


**Figure 8.3** Time plot of original and seasonally adjusted business telephones data shown with "best" exponential smoothing model.

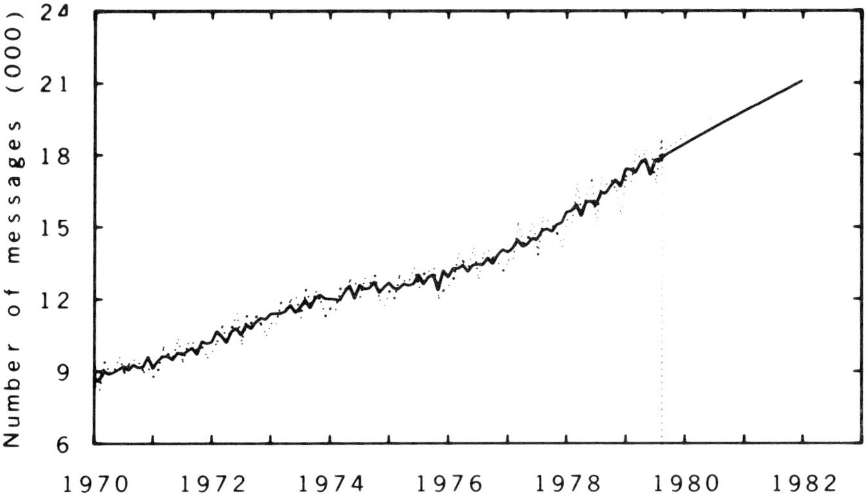


**Figure 8.4** Time plot of original and seasonally adjusted toll-message data shown with "best" exponential smoothing model.

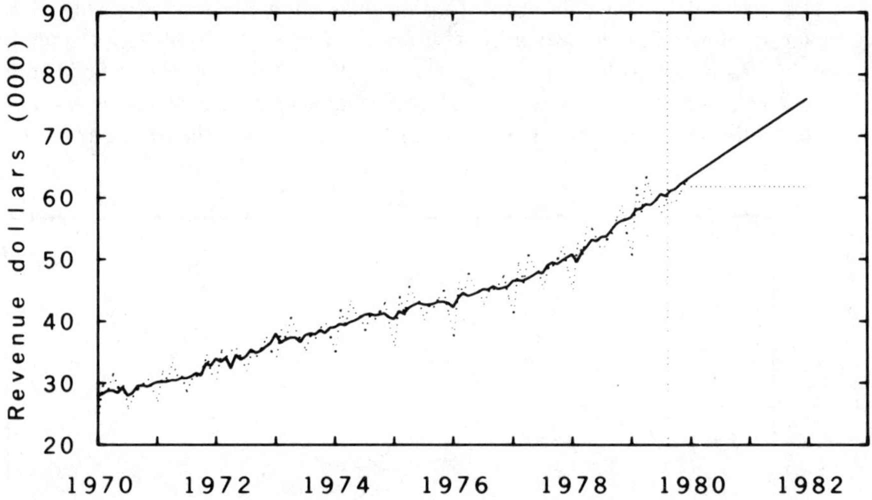


**Figure 8.5** Time plot of original and seasonally adjusted toll-revenue data shown with "best" exponential smoothing model.

model is significantly less than the deviation for the original series in each model. Table 8.2 summarizes the results of the model. Based on these results, for forecasting one might prefer to base the exponential smoothing models on seasonally adjusted data. Because the magnitude of the smoothing parameter is smaller in all models based on seasonally adjusted data, forecasts from these models will be less volatile than those based on unadjusted data.

There are at least two other approaches that can be tried as alternative ways of lessening seasonal patterns in data. The first approach is to use exponential smooth-

**Table 8.2** Comparison of exponential smoothing models for unadjusted (U) and seasonally adjusted (SA) series, showing mean absolute deviation (MAD) and the estimate of $\alpha$ ($\hat{\alpha}$).

| Time series | Model type<br>Unadjusted (U)<br>MAD | <br><br>$\hat{\alpha}$ | <br>Seasonally adjusted (SA)<br>MAD | <br><br>$\hat{\alpha}$ |
|---|---|---|---|---|
| Employment | Single<br>470 | 0.95 | Double<br>143 | 0.60 |
| Telephones | Single<br>63 | 0.95 | Double<br>26 | 0.60 |
| Messages | Double<br>288 | 0.20 | Triple<br>117 | 0.15 |
| Revenues | Single<br>481 | 0.40 | Double<br>103 | 0.20 |

ing models on year-over-year growth (the difference between the current period and one year ago). Differencing may remove linear trend as well, however, and produce a series with pronounced cyclical patterns which are rather difficult to forecast (see Chapter 11). The second approach is a somewhat complex seasonal exponential smoothing model due to Winters (1960). This model has an additional parameter that smooths the seasonal pattern. The approach is complex, however, in that it requires a trial-and-error method for selecting the three smoothing parameters (for randomness, trend, and seasonality).

## BE WARY OF "AUTOMATIC" FORECASTING METHODS AND SOFTWARE PROGRAMS

Computer programs for exponential smoothing are relatively simple to implement. Consequently, they are widely available in most time series packages. In fact, Sullivan and Claycombe (1977) provide a listing of an exponential smoothing program. Some exponential smoothing programs have built-in parameter-selection algorithms. This may work well when the data have low variability and are otherwise well behaved. However, the forecaster should always plot the data, fitted values, and forecasts to make certain that the "automatic" models do a reasonable job.

Figures 8.6 and 8.7 illustrate two examples of products in which potentially serious problems could result from blind acceptance of computer-selected forecasts, methods, and parameter estimates.

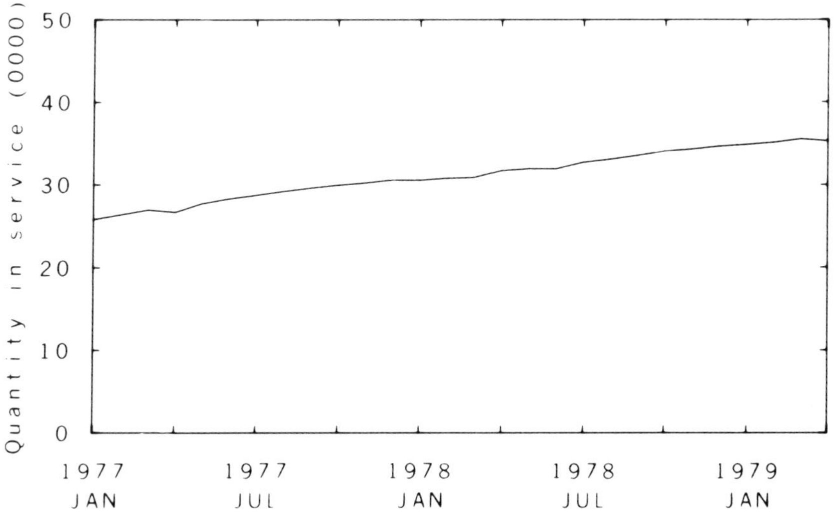


**Figure 8.6** Monthly time plot of Product A from January 1977 to April 1979.

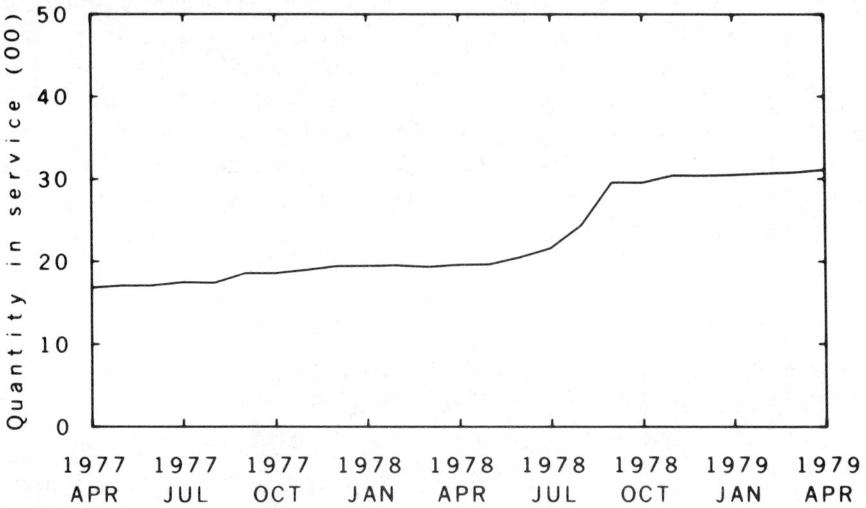


**Figure 8.7** Monthly time plot of Product C from April 1977–June 1979.

Product A—let us say it was a new kind of computer system—existed in the marketplace for a number of years; Figure 8.6 shows a plot of the quantity of the product used since 1977. In 1978 a new product (B) was introduced which had improved price-performance characteristics. The new product was promoted in late 1978 and started to take a share of the market away from Product A. Figure 8.8 shows three exponential smoothing forecasts (single, double, and triple) that were generated automatically by computer-selected parameter estimates.

The computer program selected the quadratic (triple exponential) model as the best model because it minimized the mean absolute deviation. A characteristic of the quadratic smoothing model is that it tends to produce either rapidly rising or rapidly falling forecasts. In this case a sharp drop in demand for Product A (in terms of leased systems in service) predicted by the quadratic model could not be justified by the product manager. After all, even though the new product might be superior to the old, the cost of changing from the old to the new (cost of removal and installation) made wholesale replacements seem noneconomical for people who used Product A. What the computer program could not know is that the new product would be more economical for handling growth or new service requirements (that is, would be used by people who did not use Product A). Therefore, the linear smoothing model forecasts were selected for Product A by the forecaster, and the computer program's choice of a quadratic model was overridden.

A more dramatic depiction of the potential problems with automatic computer-selected models is illustrated for Product C. In this example, six curve-fitting models were fitted to the data (linear, exponential, geometric, and three forms of the hyperbolic function). In the computer program used for this example, the computer program automatically selects the model with the highest $R$-squared statistic (the

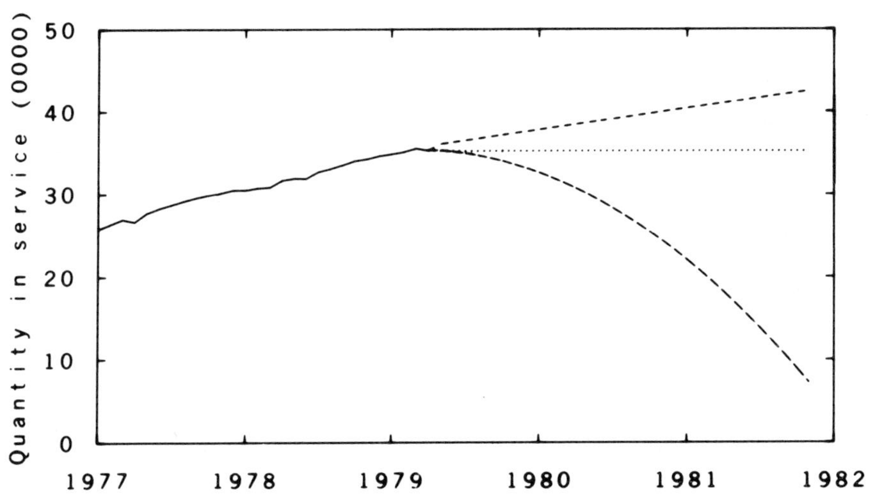


**Figure 8.8** Single (middle), double (upper), and triple (lower), exponential smoothing forecasts for Product A.

*R*-squared statistic is used as a measure of goodness-of-fit in regression, as is discussed in Chapters 12 and 13).

In this example the sharp increase in demand for 1978 caused the computer program to select one of the hyperbolic models: [$\hat{Y} = 1/(0.000667 - 0.000013 \cdot \text{Time})$]. The forecast profile of this model is shown in Figure 8.9. The peak forecast (April 1981) is almost 150,000 units larger than the quantity in service in 1979. The following month the forecast goes negative by a huge amount.

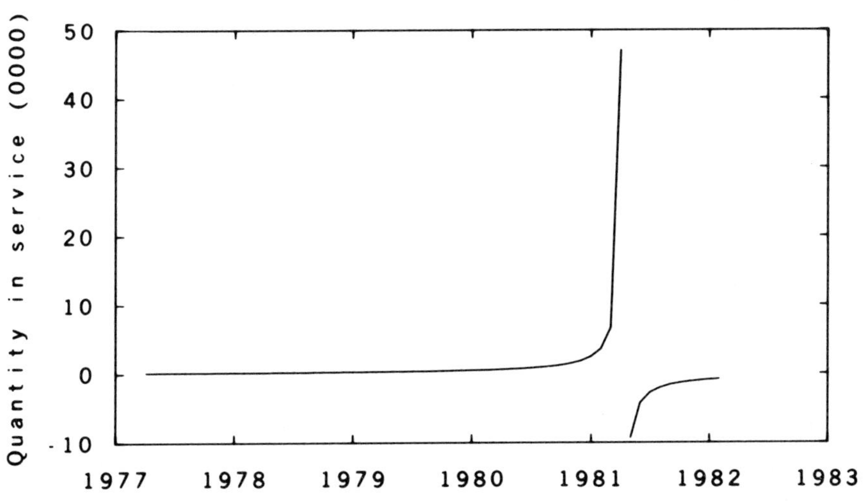


**Figure 8.9** Forecast profile for the "best" model for Product C selected by an automatic curve-fitting program.

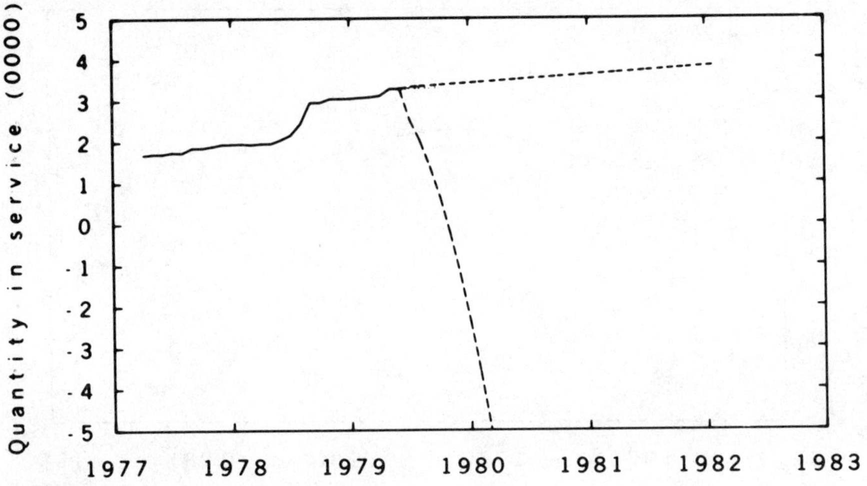


**Figure 8.10** Single (middle), double (upper), and triple (lower) exponential smoothing forecasts for Product C.

Figure 8.10 shows the forecasts from three exponential smoothing models for Product C. While the single smoothing model had the lowest mean absolute deviation (71, versus 79 for double and 129 for triple), the double exponential smoothing model forecasts were selected by the forecaster on the assumption that the market was not yet saturated.

The product forecasts for "Product A," "Product B," and "Product C" were taken from actual forecast situations for which data were limited and simple trending approaches were sought. The historical data for both series are somewhat erratic and highlight the problems that may exist in the mechanistic execution of computer programs. When the primary objective of a model is to generate forecasts, basing model selection on the maximum value for the $R$-squared statistic is highly questionable and cannot be recommended.

## SUMMARY

Exponential smoothing models have valuable characteristics that make them useful in practice:

- They are relatively simple, naïve forecasting methods.
- They can be applied with relatively little historical data and can be useful for short-term forecasting.
- The single, double, and triple exponential smoothing models are appropriate for horizontal, linear, and quadratic time series, respectively. Their forecasts

should, however, be evaluated in the economic context or market that is expected to exist.

Other significant considerations include these:

- Since the models are incapable of providing this input, the forecaster's judgment plays a primary role. Never accept a model's prediction without plotting history and forecast on the same graph, for reasonableness.
- Whenever possible, the sum of the partial forecasts should be compared to the forecast of an appropriate aggregated variable. In product demand forecasting, for example, an independently derived total sales or revenue forecast can serve this purpose. Such a check of reasonableness is even more valuable when additional forecasting methods can be applied at the aggregated level.

For time series with significant seasonality, the series can be seasonally adjusted before modeling, or other methods, such as a seasonal exponential smoothing model, or—better yet—ARIMA time series modeling should be attempted.

## USEFUL READING

BOWERMAN, B. L., and R. T. O'CONNELL (1979). *Time Series and Forecasting*. North Scituate, MA: Duxbury Press.

BOX, G. E. P., and G. M. JENKINS (1976). *Time Series Analysis—Forecasting and Control*. Rev. ed. San Francisco, CA: Holden-Day.

BROWN, R. G. (1959). *Statistical Forecasting for Inventory Control*. New York, NY: McGraw-Hill Book Co.

BROWN, R. G. (1963). *Smoothing, Forecasting and Prediction of Discrete Time Series*. Englewood Cliffs, NJ: Prentice-Hall.

HARRISON, P. J. (1965). Short-Term Sales Forecasting. *Applied Statistics* 14, 102–39.

HOLT, C. C. (1957). *Forecasting Seasonals and Trends by Exponentially Weighted Moving Averages*. Pittsburgh, PA: Carnegie Institute of Technology.

MAKRIDAKIS, S., and S. C. WHEELWRIGHT (1978). *Forecasting Methods and Applications*. New York, NY: John Wiley and Sons.

MONTGOMERY, D. C., and L. A. JOHNSON (1976). *Forecasting and Time Series Analysis*. New York, NY: McGraw-Hill Book Co.

MOSTELLER, F., and J. W. TUKEY (1977). *Data Analysis and Regression*. Reading, MA: Addison-Wesley Publishing Co.

SULLIVAN, W. G., and W. W. CLAYCOMBE (1977). *Fundamentals of Forecasting*. Reston, VA: Reston Publishing Company.

TRIGG, D. W., and A. G. LEACH (1967). Exponential Smoothing with Adaptive Response Rate. *Operational Research Quarterly* 18, 53–59.

TUKEY, J. W. (1977). *Exploratory Data Analysis*. Reading, MA: Addison-Wesley Publishing Co.

WHEELWRIGHT, S. C., and S. MAKRIDAKIS (1980). *Forecasting Methods for Management,* 3rd ed. New York, NY: John Wiley and Sons.

WINTERS, P. R. (1960). Forecasting Sales by Exponentially Weighted Moving Averages. *Management Science* 6, 324–42.

CHAPTER **9**

# A First Look at Trend and Seasonality

A basic assumption in the time series decomposition approach to forecasting is that a time series can be represented by a number of components:

- A time series may contain a long-term trend consisting of a smooth increase or decrease over time.
- Other series may have a cyclical pattern possibly related to economic factors.
- Many series have an annually recurring seasonal pattern.
- Superimposed on all of the above may be an irregular pattern often referred to as a random fluctuation or "noise."

The two-way table decomposition discussed in this chapter leads to an understanding of the relative contributions of seasonal, trend-cyclical, and irregular variations to the total variation in a time series. This will help the forecaster more effectively select the technique that is most appropriate in a given situation.

## YEAR-BY-MONTH TABLE ANALYSIS

The components of a time series that are usually the most predominant are the trend and seasonal components. In reality it is probably impossible to separate the trend and cycle components as distinctly identifiable factors. In fact, most economists speak of trend-cycle as a single source of variation in which the two factors are inseparable. However, for the discussion below it is instructive to consider trend and cycle as essentially separate components.

By removing or subtracting trend and seasonal effects from the total variation, it is possible to examine the residual variation for more subtle patterns; that is

$$\text{Residuals} = \text{Data} - \text{Trend effect} - \text{Seasonal effect.}$$

For example, does the residual variation show the effects of cyclic "downturns" consistent with empirical data or economic theory? If so, the trend-seasonal decomposition may be a reasonable first approximation to the quantification of these effects in the data. The analysis also shows whether the seasonal pattern is stable from year to year. Have school openings and closings perhaps been shifting, thereby shifting the seasonality of the data? Have pre-Christmas buying patterns of shoppers shifted, thus affecting sales data? Do nontypical observations destroy the underlying trend and/or seasonal pattern? All these questions may be reasonably answered with a preliminary analysis of variance (ANOVA).

## The ANOVA Model

The ANOVA model is a rough mechanism for quantifying row and column effects in terms of their relative contributions to the total variation in a table. Consider the display of a telephone gain series as a two-way table, such as is shown in Figure 9.1. In this display the rows represent "months" and the columns are "years." Each row shows a trending pattern, if any, for a given month. If a seasonal pattern were present, this would be exhibited by a regularity of the pattern in each column. A low-resolution display of the same data is also helpful, initially, and is shown in Figure 9.2. We shall explain details of low-resolution displays later in this chapter.

For purposes of this discussion, the ANOVA model should be thought of as an elementary descriptive tool and cannot, in practice, be used as an effective projection technique. Its value is in providing the analyst with an understanding of the relative contribution of the trend, seasonal, and cyclical-irregular variations to the total variation in the data. The time series and regression models to be discussed in later chapters are better suited for forecasting purposes.

The method by which a two-way table is decomposed is not complex, but the notation is somewhat cumbersome. By working slowly through the analysis, you should be able to understand it completely. See also Erickson and Nosanchuk (1977, Chapter 15), McNeil (1977, Chapter 5), and Tukey (1977, Chapter 10) for additional examples and interpretations.

Assuming monthly data, let $y_{ij}$ ($i$ = month, $j$ = year) be a representation of a typical observation in the table, where $i = 1, 2, \ldots, 12$, and $j = 1, 2, \ldots, J$ (number of years). This representation can also be used for quarterly data, but then $i = 1, 2, 3, 4$. A model which describes a typical observation in terms of a seasonal effect $S_i$, a trend or yearly effect $T_j$, and an error term $\varepsilon_{ij}$ is given by

$$y_{ij} = \mu + S_i + T_j + \varepsilon_{ij},$$

where $\mu$ denotes a mean effect or "typical value." Then the following symbols can be used to summarize certain totals and averages of interest in the analysis:

$$y_{\cdot j} = \sum_{i=1}^{12} y_{ij}$$

is the *total of year j,* which has been summed over 12 rows, and

$$\bar{y}_{\cdot j} = y_{\cdot j}/12$$

represents the average per month for year $j$.

Thus $\{y_{\cdot j}; j = 1, \ldots, J\}$ are *yearly totals* which are used to summarize trend over $J$ years.

Summing across columns corresponding to the number of years gives

$$y_{i\cdot} = \sum_{j=1}^{J} y_{ij},$$

which is the total of month $i$ (sum over $J$ years). Then

$$\bar{y}_{i\cdot} = y_{i\cdot}/J$$

is the *average per month of month i.*

Thus $\{\bar{y}_{i\cdot}; i = 1, \ldots, 12\}$ are *monthly averages* which are used to summarize the average seasonal pattern over $J$ years.

To get overall totals, define $y_{\cdot\cdot}$ by

$$\begin{aligned} y_{\cdot\cdot} &= \sum_{j=1}^{J} \sum_{i=1}^{12} y_{ij} \\ &= \sum_{j=1}^{J} y_{\cdot j} \\ &= \sum_{i=1}^{12} y_{i\cdot}. \end{aligned}$$

The quantity $y_{\cdot\cdot}$ is known simply as the *grand total,* and $\bar{y}_{\cdot\cdot} = y_{\cdot\cdot}/12J$ is the average per month over $J$ years, or the *grand mean.*

In Figure 9.1, it is convenient to display the yearly totals $\{y_{\cdot j}\}$ and the monthly averages $\{\bar{y}_{i\cdot}\}$ as an additional row and column, respectively. By looking at the yearly totals $\{y_{\cdot j}\}$ it is possible to detect a trend if the annual sums have been steadily increasing or decreasing. The high and low seasonal months can be readily determined from looking at the monthly averages $\{\bar{y}_{i\cdot}\}$.

It is now possible to describe the various contributions to the total variation in the data. The *total variation* (as measured from the grand mean) is given by

$$S^2 = \frac{1}{12J-1} \sum_{j=1}^{J} \sum_{i=1}^{12} (y_{ij} - \bar{y}_{\cdot\cdot})^2.$$

This is a measure of the overall variation in the data, which may be due to trend, seasonal, and irregular patterns.

| MON | YEAR 1970 | 1971 | 1972 | 1973 | 1974 | 1975 | 1976 | 1977 | 1978 | AVG | STD |
|---|---|---|---|---|---|---|---|---|---|---|---|
| JANUARY | 16838 | 13699 | 19184 | 21567 | 19113 | 10227 | 17696 | 15182 | 20006 | 17057 | 3530 |
| FEBRUARY | 14715 | 14949 | 17600 | 17177 | 14692 | 7234 | 14584 | 14103 | 18085 | 14793 | 3203 |
| MARCH | 14207 | 15214 | 23828 | 21683 | 18505 | 10422 | 17183 | 22797 | 24800 | 18738 | 4904 |
| APRIL | 15733 | 12510 | 16256 | 13789 | 11676 | 11890 | 14681 | 15162 | 21397 | 14788 | 2982 |
| MAY | 3688 | 4030 | 56 | 5278 | 2137 | 1263 | 2628 | 2058 | 1215 | 1746 | 2476 |
| JUNE | 1213 | 1407 | 5111 | 5468 | 6231 | 5403 | 2615 | 6264 | 8827 | 3563 | 4141 |
| JULY | 13469 | 1667 | 8775 | 11238 | 8148 | 10585 | 9935 | 14344 | 10643 | 9497 | 4636 |
| AUGUST | 7585 | 8697 | 17440 | 18611 | 12972 | 12883 | 9594 | 16224 | 21883 | 13988 | 4888 |
| SEPTEMBR | 32365 | 33558 | 36430 | 33470 | 27987 | 28240 | 36179 | 38116 | 37308 | 33739 | 3715 |
| OCTOBER | 21381 | 21441 | 24490 | 21502 | 18474 | 20264 | 20922 | 22576 | 22698 | 21528 | 1679 |
| NOVEMBER | 9427 | 13802 | 21132 | 17719 | 8794 | 15348 | 11258 | 21895 | 19838 | 15468 | 4989 |
| DECEMBER | 10546 | 14430 | 14554 | 6705 | 538 | 6937 | 11669 | 16274 | 17083 | 10851 | 5676 |
| SUM | 158739 | 149256 | 204856 | 194205 | 148190 | 138172 | 163713 | 200880 | 223783 | 175755 | 0 |
| STD | 8572 | 9648 | 9559 | 8254 | 8035 | 7487 | 9616 | 9702 | 9000 | 0 | 0 |

**Figure 9.1** A month-by-year table for a telephone gain series, 1970–1978.

```
VBL         15 1970            16 1971            17 1972            18 1973            19 1974            20 1975            21 1976
MIN            -12133.00          -16667.00             558.00           52778.00           -5384.00          -12626.00          -26148.00
MAX            323646.00          335576.00          364302.00          334697.00          279865.00          282402.00          361792.00

JANUARY     53 ******          43 *****           52 ******          57 ******          68 *******         38 ****            52 ******
FEBRUARY    47 *****           47 *****           48 *****           42 *****           53 ******          28 ***             44 *****
MARCH       45 *****           47 *****           65 *******         58 ******          66 *******         39 ****            51 ******
APRIL       50 ******          40 *****           44 *****           30 ****            42 *****           44 *****           44 *****
MAY         14 **              16 **               0 *                0 *                9 *                0 *               13 **
JUNE         0 *                0 *               13 **               0 *               23 ***             22 ***              0 *
JULY        43 *****            0 *               23 ***             21 ***             30 ****            40 *****           32 ****
AUGUST      26 ***             29 ***             47 *****           47 *****           47 *****           47 *****           31 ****
SEPTEMBR    99 **********      99 **********      99 **********      99 **********      99 **********      99 **********      99 **********
OCTOBER     67 *******         65 *******         67 *******         57 ******          66 *******         72 ********        60 *******
NOVEMBER    31 ****            43 *****           57 ******          44 *****           32 ****            56 ******          35 ****
DECEMBER    35 ****            45 *****           39 ****             5 *                0 *               27 ***             36 ****

VBL         22 1977            23 1978
MIN            -20584.00           12145.00
MAX            381163.00          373084.00

JANUARY     42 *****           52 ******
FEBRUARY    40 *****           46 *****
MARCH       61 *******         65 *******
APRIL       42 *****           55 ******
MAY          0 *                0 *
JUNE        20 ***             21 ***
JULY        40 *****           26 ***
AUGUST      45 *****           57 ******
SEPTEMBR    99 **********      99 **********
OCTOBER     61 *******         59 ******
NOVEMBER    59 ******          51 ******
DECEMBER    45 *****           43 *****
```

**Figure 9.2** A low-resolution, month-by-year "star-chart" display for a telephone gain series, 1970–1978.

Specific entries within each row (month) can be measured against the row mean to give a measure of variation for the given month. This variation may be due to trends and changes in the seasonal patterns as well as irregularity. Thus

$$S_i^2 = \sum_{j=1}^{J} (y_{ij} - \bar{y}_{i\cdot})^2/(J - 1).$$

Similarly,

$$S_j^2 = \sum_{i=1}^{12} (y_{ij} - \bar{y}_{\cdot j})^2/11$$

is a measure of the variation within column $J$ (year) measured from the column mean. This variation may be due to seasonal patterns and changes in trend as well as irregularity.

Since row and column means represent average seasonal and trend effects, variations of these averages reflect the respective "variation due to average seasonal pattern and trend." Thus

$$S_r^2 = \sum_{i=1}^{12} (\bar{y}_{i\cdot} - \bar{y}_{\cdot\cdot})^2/11$$

and

$$S_c^2 = \sum_{j=1}^{J} (\bar{y}_{\cdot j} - \bar{y}_{\cdot\cdot})^2/(J - 1)$$

represent variation in row ($r$, monthly) means and column ($c$, yearly) means, respectively.

### Contribution of Trend/Seasonal Effects

It is also possible to quantify the *proportion of variability due to seasonal effects, S,* by the ratio

$$R_S^2 = \frac{J \sum_{i=1}^{12} (\bar{y}_{i\cdot} - \bar{y}_{\cdot\cdot})^2}{\sum_{i=1}^{12} \sum_{j=1}^{J} (y_{ij} - \bar{y}_{\cdot\cdot})^2},$$

and the *proportion of variability due to trend effects, T,* by

$$R_T^2 = \frac{12 \sum_{j=1}^{J} (\bar{y}_{.j} - \bar{y}_{..})^2}{\sum_{i=1}^{12} \sum_{j=1}^{J} (y_{ij} - \bar{y}_{..})^2}$$

Ideally, or for an extreme case, if there were no trend in the data, the column means would equal the grand mean and the proportion of variability that is due to trend effects would equal zero.

The foregoing computations can be summarized in a form shown in Figure 9.3. That figure is an example of an *analysis of variance table* (ANOVA for short). The "Source" column lists the three effects as monthly (seasonal), yearly (trend), and residual (unexplained). These three effects sum to the total. Each "DF" column (for degrees of freedom) entry is one less than the number of items used to calculate the averages. The "SS" column figures (for sum of squares) are $11S_r^2$ for the row effect and $(J - 1)S_c^2$ for the column effect. The "MS" column figures (for mean squares) are the SS column figures divided by their corresponding DF values.

The most important column is the "%SS" column (percent sum of squares), which represents the figures $R_S^2$, $R_T^2$, and $1 - (R_T^2 + R_S^2)$, respectively, as percentages.

In Figure 9.3 the variation for the main-telephone gain data is summarized in the column denoted %SS. This shows

| Effect | Percent |
|---|---|
| Monthly | 81.3 |
| Yearly | 7.3 |
| Residual | 11.4 |
| | (Total: 100.0) |

In contrast, if you were to look at the variation for monthly toll-message data between 1970–1978 and compile a "%SS" column for that, the entries for $R_S^2$, $R_T^2$, and $1 - (R_T^2 + R_S^2)$, respectively, would be

| Effect | Percent |
|---|---|
| Monthly | 3.6 |
| Yearly | 95.7 |
| Residual | 0.7 |
| | (Total: 100.0) |

| SOURCE | DF | SS | MS | %SS | #CAT | #EFF | EFFECT |
|---|---|---|---|---|---|---|---|
| MON EFCT | 11 | 6.8920E+11 | 6.2655E+10 | 81.3 | 12 | 1 | MON |
| YEAR EFCT | 8 | 6.1952E+10 | 7.7440E+09 | 7.3 | 9 | 1 | YEAR |
| RSID | 88 | 9.6503E+10 | 1.0966E+09 | 11.4 | 108 | 0 | |
| TOTL | 107 | 8.4766E+11 | 7.9220E+09 | 100.0 | 108 | 0 | |

**Figure 9.3** An ANOVA table for main telephone gain, depicting the percent contribution of trend and seasonal effects to the total variation.

Notice that the variation is dominated by trend (yearly) rather than the seasonal (monthly) effect.

Yet another possibility, the total variation in housing-starts data, would break down as

| Effect | Percent |
|---|---|
| Monthly | 40.7 |
| Yearly | 47.7 |
| Residual | 11.6 |
| | (Total: 100.0) |

Here the seasonal and trend effects appear to be about evenly split. This type of analysis might be useful in (1) characterizing (roughly) the dominant patterns in the data, (2) identifying potential modeling problems if the residual percent is relatively large, and (3) correlating data with similar structures. These results provide an important input to the "patterns of data that can be handled" criteria for forecasting technique selection discussed in Chapter 3.

As expected, the residual effects for the main-telephone gain and housing-starts data are quite high and might be reduced through an adjustment of irregulars before modeling starts. In general, the smaller the residual percent, the better the series would lend itself to modeling.

## ANALYSIS OF RESIDUALS

Since trend and seasonal variation can generally be quantified quite well, the "percent residual" provides a relative measure of the modeling and forecasting difficulty likely to be encountered. Since the residual effect for main-telephone gain data appears relatively high, it is essential to examine the data closely before modeling can begin. The residual effect may be overstated because of the presence of outliers.

### Residual Analysis for a Two-Way Table

In order to develop the two-way table for residuals, it is necessary to introduce some more notation. First, let

$$y_{ij} - \bar{y}_{..}$$

be the deviation from the grand mean of the observation for the *i*th month and *j*th year; then

$$\bar{y}_{i\cdot} - \bar{y}_{..}$$

is the estimate of the *average seasonal effect due to month i;* and

$$\bar{y}_{\cdot j} - \bar{y}_{..}$$

is the estimate of the *average year (trend) effect due to year j;* and

$$(y_{ij} - \bar{y}_{..}) - (\bar{y}_{i\cdot} - \bar{y}_{..}) - (\bar{y}_{\cdot j} - \bar{y}_{..}) = (y_{ij} - \bar{y}_{i\cdot} - \bar{y}_{\cdot j} + \bar{y}_{..})$$

is the $(i,j)$th *residual.*

This represents the $(i,j)$th deviation from the grand mean less the *i*th month's seasonal effect and the *j*th year's trend effect. Thus the $(i,j)$th residual is the $(i,j)$th observation corrected for seasonal and trend effect in the sense of the two-way ANOVA decomposition.

Other useful quantities can be derived from the residual two-way table: the residual variance is the total variation corrected for trend and seasonal effects. This provides a measure of variation for all the residuals and has the formula

$$\sum_{j=1}^{J} \sum_{i=1}^{12} (y_{ij} - \bar{y}_{i\cdot} - \bar{y}_{\cdot j} + \bar{y}_{..})^2/11(J - 1).$$

The residual column variance $S_j^2(C)$ provides a variance measure for each column and is given by

$$S_j^2(C) = \sum_{i=1}^{12} (y_{ij} - \bar{y}_{i\cdot} - \bar{y}_{\cdot j} + \bar{y}_{..})^2/(J-1),$$

and the residual row variance $S_i^2$ (R) provides a variance measure for each row and is given by

$$S_i^2(R) = \sum_{j=1}^{J} (y_{ij} - \bar{y}_{i\cdot} - \bar{y}_{\cdot j} + \bar{y}_{..})^2/11.$$

Large differences among the $S_j(C)$'s ($j = 1, \ldots, J$) may indicate some outliers or special events in a year having a large deviation. Large differences among the $S_i(R)$'s ($i = 1, \ldots, 12$) for various months may indicate the relative difficulty of forecasting months with large variability and may also indicate the presence of outliers in certain months.

## Interpretation of the Residual Table

Figure 9.4 is a "star-chart" of residuals resulting from removal of the yearly and monthly effects from the main-telephone gain data. The scaling in this table is based on the largest residual (= 94192) in the entire series which, in this case, takes a value of positive unity. In the table the stars vary from negative one (zero stars) to positive one (ten stars). The middle range, between four and five stars, corresponds to zero and represents a small or zero-value residual. The numbers to the left of the stars are again percentages representing the range from negative one to positive one; 50 percent corresponds to five stars—a very small residual. By drawing a vertical line between the fifth and sixth asterisks, it is possible to visualize a type of residual plot. In such displays it is the absence of structure that is important.

The thirteenth or last column, labeled "Effect," in Figure 9.4 is an aid to identifying an "outlier year" after the seasonal effect has been removed. What is desirable here is to find a triangular pattern having increasing slope down the column, assuming increasing trend in the original data. The year effect has also been scaled so that it would fit with the rest of the display.

For the main telephone gain, it is evident that the residuals for July show an unusual pattern (the << character is a round-off problem, but corresponds to a single asterisk) that may require further investigation. Reviewing Figure 9.1, it can be seen that July 1971 was negative and is unrepresentative of the yearly pattern for July.

Since year and month effects have been removed, the residual patterns for most months generally reflect the 1970 and 1975 downturns in the economy. This is further supported by column 13. As a forecasting tool, it is useful to compare Figure 9.4 with an equivalent chart for housing starts (Figure 9.5), a series that is considered to be a "driver" for the main telephone gain. In both figures, the year effects in column 13 correspond quite well for corresponding years for the two series. The monthly residual patterns do not look very similar, suggesting that main telephone gain and housing starts have quite different seasonal structures, though their cyclical patterns correlate rather closely.

It will be seen later that this observation will be taken into account when modeling main telephone gain as a function of housing starts. In terms of forecasting performance, it will turn out to be better to correlate year-over-year changes (i.e., differences of order 12) between the series than actual levels. Besides considering differences it will also prove helpful to accumulate the data into quarterly series, thereby reducing the differences in the monthly patterns.

```
VBL:      1 JANUARY     2 FEBRUARY    3 MARCH       4 APRIL       5 MAY         6 JUNE        7 JULY
MIN:          -1.00         -1.00         -1.00         -1.00         -1.00         -1.00         -1.00
MAX:           1.00          1.00          1.00          1.00          1.00          1.00          1.00

1969     57 ******     54 ******     34 ****       44 *****      69 *******    40 *****      72 ********
1970     55 ******     56 ******     35 ****       63 *******    65 *******    33 ****       76 ********
1971     43 *****      62 *******    44 *****      50 ******     71 ********   36 ****       <<
1972     47 *****      51 ******     65 *******    45 *****      25 ***        46 *****      30 ****
1973     64 *******    54 ******     59 ******     37 ****       58 ******     53 ******     48 *****
1974     72 ********   61 *******    62 *******    46 *****      62 *******    77 ********   52 ******
1975     29 ***        26 ***        24 ***        51 ******     48 *****      77 ********   69 *******
1976     57 ******     53 ******     48 *****      55 ******     57 ******     23 ***        55 ******
1977     28 ***        34 ****       62 *******    41 *****      16 **         54 ******     62 *******
1978     43 *****      45 *****      62 *******    64 *******    23 ***        57 ******     32 ****

VBL:      8 AUGUST      9 SEPTEMBR   10 OCTOBER    11 NOVEMBER   12 DECEMBER   13 EFFECT
MIN:          -1.00         -1.00         -1.00         -1.00         -1.00         -1.00
MAX:           1.00          1.00          1.00          1.00          1.00          1.00

1969     24 ***        44 *****      58 ******     39 ****       59 ******     58 ******
1970     26 ***        50 ******     55 ******     26 ***        54 ******     30 ****
1971     36 ****       61 *******    60 *******    54 ******     79 ********   20 ***
1972     58 ******     51 ******     51 ******     68 *******    55 ******     79 ********
1973     69 *******    40 *****      40 *****      54 ******     18 **         68 *******
1974     59 ******     32 ****       45 *****      27 ***         0 *          19 **
1975     63 *******    38 ****       58 ******     67 *******    44 *****       9 *
1976     34 ****       68 *******    51 ******     34 ****       58 ******     36 ****
1977     53 ******     62 *******    43 *****      74 ********   66 *******    75 ********
1978     73 ********   48 *****      34 ****       53 ******     60 *******    99 **********

SCALING: RESIDUALS 1 0 = 94192 0833 . YEAR EFFECTS 1 0 - 39254 4667
```

**Figure 9.4** A two-way, low-resolution "star-chart" display of the telephone gain residuals.

```
VBL:        1 JANUARY      2 FEBRUARY     3 MARCH        4 APRIL        5 MAY          6 JUNE         7 JULY
MIN:               -1.00          -1.00          -1.00          -1.00          -1.00          -1.00          -1.00
MAX:                1.00           1.00           1.00           1.00           1.00           1.00           1.00

1970       48 *****       48 *****       42 *****       37 ****        21 ***         36 ****        53 ******
1971       39 ****        22 ***         44 *****       61 *******     45 *****       44 *****       55 ******
1972       54 ******      50 ******      56 ******      44 *****       47 *****       48 *****       40 *****
1973       80 *********   63 *******     80 *********   66 *******     86 *********   54 ******      65 *******
1974       77 ********    97 **********  62 *******     81 *********   57 ******      58 ******      46 *****
1975       62 *******     52 ******      29 ***         29 ***         36 ****        33 ****        54 ******
1976       45 *****       56 ******      36 ****        37 ****        37 ****        47 *****       38 ****
1977       13 **          40 *****       56 ******      46 *****       55 ******      54 ******      56 ******
1978       37 ****        39 ****        51 ******      56 ******      55 ******      57 ******      47 *****
1979       41 *****       29 ***         39 ****        38 ****        57 ******      64 *******     42 *****

VBL:        8 AUGUST       9 SEPTEMBR    10 OCTOBER     11 NOVEMBER    12 DECEMBER    13 EFFECT
MIN:               -1.00          -1.00          -1.00          -1.00          -1.00          -1.00
MAX:                1.00           1.00           1.00           1.00           1.00           1.00

1970       37 ****        53 ******      58 ******      70 ********    91 **********  27 ***
1971       65 *******     44 *****       43 *****       65 *******     68 *******     76 ********
1972       63 *******     48 *****       56 ******      50 ******      38 ****        99 **********
1973       57 ******      16 **           8 *           20 ***          0 *           75 ********
1974       27 ***         26 ***         17 **          21 ***         26 ***         20 ***
1975       50 ******      58 ******      64 *******     62 *******     66 *******      6 *
1976       47 *****       67 *******     56 ******      61 *******     66 *******     36 ****
1977       59 ******      54 ******      64 *******     50 ******      47 *****       71 ********
1978       47 *****       53 ******      56 ******      49 *****       49 *****       45 *****
1979       43 *****       75 ********    74 ********    47 *****       45 *****       40 *****

SCALING: RESIDUALS 1.0 = 44.7666667 ; YEAR EFFECTS 1.0 = 53.3583333
```

**Figure 9.5** A two-way, low-resolution "star-chart" display of the housing starts residuals.

### The Median Polish

A similar tool for analyzing two-way tables, though somewhat undeveloped, is the *median polish* described in Erickson and Nosanchuk (1977), McNeil (1977), and Tukey (1977). The median polish procedure is designed to replace the original table by an associated residual table for which the medians (as opposed to the means) for each row and each column are zero. This procedure for "taking out" medians is an iterative, *ad hoc* procedure in the sense that the procedure depends on whether one starts with rows or columns. However, as a complementary tool to the ANOVA approach, it should be effective in prescreening data for outliers that can severely distort the importance of underlying trend and seasonal effects.

## SUMMARY

As a preliminary data-analysis tool, an ANOVA decomposition has some very useful features:

- It is used to decompose a time series into additive "trend" and "seasonal" factors.
- The residual component is used to describe all other variation, which may include a portion ascribable to a "trend-seasonal interaction" and cycle.
- It can be used to quantify approximately the relative contributions of seasonal and trend effects to the total variation of the data. This allows one to ask how much variability may be due to trend and seasonality, respectively. The answer to the question is an important consideration in technique selection.

Modeling techniques can be very versatile. Several techniques may be combined to take into account the patterns discussed above. However, all modeling techniques have limitations and this should be recognized early. Unless identified and accounted for, changes in trend, cycle, seasonal, and irregular variations—and possibly their interactions—can cause significant modeling problems. Recognizing these characteristics is a first step to reducing their effect. Subsequent adjustments that prepare the data for modeling are discussed in the next chapter.

## USEFUL READING

ERICKSON, B. H., and T. A. NOSANCHUK (1977). *Understanding Data*. Toronto, Canada: McGraw-Hill-Ryerson Ltd.

McNEIL, D. R. (1977). *Interactive Data Analysis*. New York, NY: John Wiley and Sons.

TUKEY, J. W. (1977). *Exploratory Data Analysis*. Reading, MA: Addison-Wesley Publishing Co.

CHAPTER **10**

# Preparing the Data for Modeling

Most time series do not have patterns that permit the direct application of standard forecasting methods. Before certain forecasting techniques can be introduced, it is important

- To know how to put data in the proper form for modeling.
- To reexpress the data so that they will be consistent with the modeling assumptions of a quantitative technique.

Unfortunately, many inexperienced analysts fail to perform the analytical steps necessary to prevent the violation of modeling assumptions.

## WHY MAKE TRANSFORMATIONS?

The process of transforming data is an essential part of the data analysis process (see, for example, Erickson and Nosanchuk, 1977, Chapters 5 and 6; and Mosteller and Tukey, 1977, Chapters 5 and 6). An important reason for making transformations of data is so that linear relationships among variables can be seen. The theory of linear regression is applied in Chapter 12 to describe linear relationships among variables. Straight line relationships are the most useful and simplest patterns to visualize. They often can be identified in plots of the data, where it may be visually obvious that a particular variable is linearly related to time or to some other relevant variable. If more than one variable is assumed to be related to the variable of interest, making a transformation that closely approximates a linear relationship among these variables has certain advantages.

Aside from the desire to apply linear regression models, there are other reasons why transformations are useful. In informal data analysis, it is often possible to display transformed data in such a way that some desired characteristics, such as growth rates, become immediately apparent. Many numbers that are reported for public use and to business managers, for example, deal with profits and sales. In reporting results, current sales may be compared with sales of the past month and with the same sales month a year ago. This involves the differencing of data. Also, the expression of comparisons as percentages is consistent with the use of the logarithmic transformation, since growth rates can be viewed as absolute changes in the logarithms of the data.

In time series analysis, the benefits of selecting the appropriate transformation include:

- Applicability of *linear* time series modeling techniques.
- Determination of the approximate *normality* of the prediction error distribution. This allows the forecaster to describe confidence intervals about the forecasts.
- Determination of *constancy of the variance* of the prediction error. This is a basic assumption upon which the least-squares regression methodology is founded.

### Achieving Linearity

Although it is not always possible to find the best transformation that simultaneously fulfills all of one's needs, there are a number of simple transformations that closely approximate at least one of the above properties.

Two commonly used transformations for achieving a linear pattern of data are the *logarithmic* and *square root* transformations. For variables that display a multiplicative behavior, such as data that tend to show an approximately constant growth rate, the logarithmic transformation can be applied. The square root transformation is generally useful where data represent counts or numbers of items.

A family of transformations can be defined which include the logarithmic and square root transformations as special cases. Box and Cox (1964) considered a parametric family (depending on the parameter $\lambda$), which transforms data $y_1, \ldots, y_n$ to $y_1^{(\lambda)}, \ldots, y_n^{(\lambda)}$ by the formula

$$
\begin{aligned}
y_i^{(\lambda)} &= \frac{y_i^{\lambda} - 1}{\lambda} && (\text{if } \lambda \neq 0) \\
&= \log y && (\text{if } \lambda = 0),
\end{aligned}
$$

for $y_i > 0$ and $|\lambda| \leq 1$.

A slightly more general version was given by Box and Cox (1964) in the form

$$
\begin{aligned}
y_i^{(\lambda)} &= \frac{(y_i + \lambda_2)^{\lambda_1} - 1}{\lambda_1} && (\text{if } \lambda_1 \neq 0) \\
&= \log(y + \lambda_2) && (\text{if } \lambda_1 = 0),
\end{aligned}
$$

where $y + \lambda_2 > 0$. It is assumed that for some appropriate values of $\lambda_1$ and $\lambda_2$ the series $y_1^{(\lambda)}, \ldots, y_n^{(\lambda)}$ can be well described by a model of the type discussed in this book. There are a variety of statistical procedures, such as *maximum likelihood* and *Bayesian* estimation, that can be applied for estimating $\lambda_1$ and $\lambda_2$ in a particular application; computer programs are generally available for use by the practitioner—e.g., the P1S program in BMDP (Dixon and Brown, 1979); however, a discussion of these methodologies is beyond the scope of this book.

We shall show the results of applying the Box-Cox transformations to the four kinds of monthly data in the telecommunications example we have examined throughout the book. The data were first detrended with straight line time trends. The resulting parameter estimates, determined by a maximum likelihood method, are shown in Table 10.1.

Table 10.1 suggests that for practical purposes it may be useful to consider a cube root for revenues, square roots for messages and business telephones, and no transformation for the employment data. A logarithmic transformation ($\lambda_1 = 0$) for toll revenues could also be considered.

For the telephone-gain and housing-starts data, the transformation suggested by the Box-Cox method was close to 1.0 and 0.75 respectively. This case suggests that no transformations are required in a forecasting context. However, this should also be evaluated through the model diagnostic checks discussed in Chapter 15.

## Achieving Normality

Certain transformations that reduce the underlying data to approximate normality offer the opportunity to carry out an extensive program of statistical *significance testing* for model validity. Transformations for which the data display a constancy of variance over time or with respect to another variable are useful for another reason, since then the theory of linear regression offers a variety of theoretically attractive and practically useful conclusions (see Chapters 12–15).

Likewise, the subject of confidence intervals for forecasts is dependent on the *normal probability distribution*. Normal linear regression theory (Chapter 12) *as-*

**Table 10.1** Estimates of $(\lambda_1, \lambda_2)$ in the Box-Cox transformations for the telecommunications example.

| Series (Code) | Estimate of $\lambda_1$ | $\lambda_2$ | Transformation close to |
|---|---|---|---|
| Toll revenues (REV) | 0.36 | −21.4 | Cube root ($\lambda_1 = 0.33$) |
| Toll messages (MSG) | 0.43 | −7.5 | Square root ($\lambda_1 = 0.50$) |
| Business telephones (BMT) | 0.57 | −490.8 | Square root ($\lambda_1 = 0.50$) |
| Nonfarm employment (NFRM) | 0.93 | −6508.0 | No transformation ($\lambda_1 = 1.0$) |

*sumes* that the errors (Errors = Data − Model) are independently and identically distributed and that they follow the normal probability distribution. Residuals (Residuals = Data − Fit) from a fitted model are used to *assess* the *validity* of the normal error assumption. To achieve approximate normality in the residuals, extreme outliers may need to be replaced with more representative values, or transformations of one or both variables may be taken.

These data manipulations are intended to create approximately normally distributed residuals so that a wide variety of statistical "confirmatory" tests can be applied and estimates of the reliability of the model can be provided. The normal probability plot for the residuals is a useful graphical tool for assessing whether approximate normality has been achieved. Where residuals deviate too much from normality, the usual significance tests can no longer be applied, nor can one quote precise confidence limits about the forecasts. This does not mean that a regression model cannot be built—it can. The traditional tests cannot be employed, however; but "half a loaf may be better than no loaf at all."

## DEALING WITH OUTLIERS

If you look at residuals resulting from the transformation and modeling steps, you will often uncover outliers in data. For modeling purposes, replacement values are generally required to prevent distortions caused by the outliers. This is especially true if the method used is not resistant to outliers. Several suggestions are given below:

- If the outlier is caused by an administrative decision, the staff of the department responsible for a company's corporate books should be consulted. This type of problem is common with revenues, where a retroactive billing distorts the revenue data.
- Price (rate) changes produce another form of irregularity that requires adjustment. In this case, part of the entire series must be adjusted to put the data on a "constant rate base." Alternatively, price indexes can be constructed and used.
- If an irregular observation cannot be reconciled with a real event, it should be documented so as to indicate why it was felt to be an outlier.

Certain programs, such as the Bureau of Census X-11 seasonal adjustment program (Chapter 18), contain mechanized procedures for correcting outliers. There are interpolation programs in some time series analysis packages which can make "corrections" to data.

In general, the known irregularities and missing data values should be handled first. Then, through an iterative procedure, other outliers may be studied and corrected if this appears necessary. It should be remembered that the goal is not to eliminate all variation in the data but to remove from the data those values that:

- Are considered extreme and unlikely to recur.
- Will distort forecasts that are generated from statistical models which assume the data are well behaved.

## Differencing Data

A differencing operation gives prominence to the irregular structure in time series data, if it is there. It exposes changes that may not be apparent in the original data. In contrast, the smoothing operation discussed in Chapter 8 masks rapidly varying patterns and reveals the more slowly varying patterns in the data. Both serve a useful purpose depending on the intent of the analysis.

*Seasonal differences,* such as differences of order 12 for monthly data or differences of order 4 for quarterly data, produce year-over-year changes. The seasonal differences look at changes from January to January, February to February, and so on, between years. Thus the resulting data normally no longer exhibit seasonal variation. The cyclical and irregular variation will be highlighted, and this information may be useful in detecting outliers. A *first difference,* on the other hand, produces successive changes from January to February, February to March, and so on. This differencing operation has a tendency to remove trend in data.

For an "ideal" series with pure seasonality, differences of order 12 result in a series of zeroes. The series repeats itself indefinitely, and future values will simply equal the value twelve months prior. In reality, differences of order 12 of a seasonal series are not zeroes. Such a series may have trend, cyclical, and irregular variations as well.

Consider the main-telephone gain series, which represents monthly values of new telephone additions. The raw data were plotted in Chapter 5, Figure 5.3. Figure 10.1 shows the differences of order 12 (year-over-year changes) of these data as a monthly time series. It is immediately apparent that there are some extreme values.

The first extreme negative value corresponds to May 1968, a month in which a labor strike occurred, followed by an extreme positive value in June 1968, which was a month in which recovery from the strike was recorded. In this case, two extreme values offset one another. For the first value,

May 1968 − May 1967,

1968 is the first term in the subtraction process, while a year later this same value is the second term:

May 1969 − May 1968.

Thus a year later the same negative value for May 1968 creates a highly positive value for the differences of order 12. Notice that May and June 1969 exhibit the

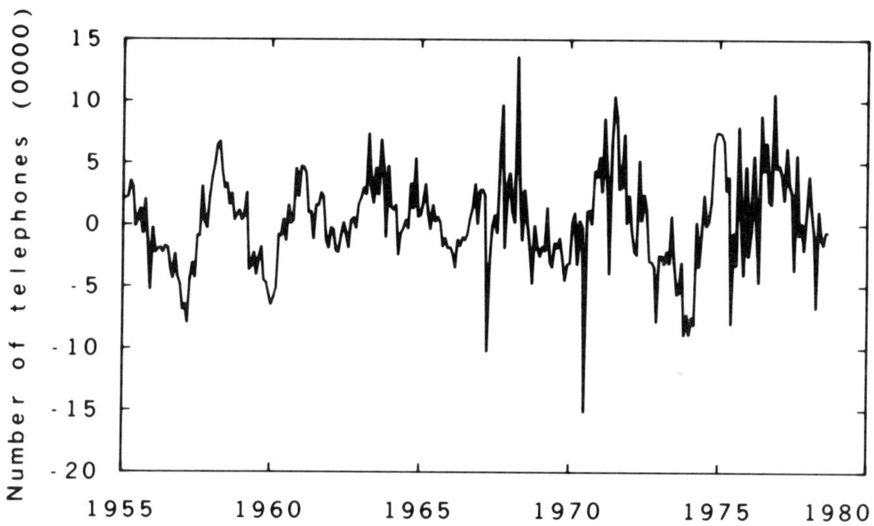


**Figure 10.1** Time plot for the differences of order 12 in the main-telephone gain series.

same behavior, though the signs are reversed from 1968. Only a single unusual event occurred, however, and that was in 1968.

A similar problem occurred three years later during the July 1971 labor strike. The loss in July was followed by an offsetting recovery value in August. Again, a reflection appears in the plot in July and August 1972. Differencing is an extremely useful tool in identifying irregular values, though it must be used with care.

It is normal practice to replace the outliers with more representative values in the following way:

- Start with the earliest data first.
- Choose a replacement value and compute new differences.
- Iterate through the remaining outliers in chronological order.

It should be noted that differencing removes seasonality and can remove trend as well. Thus, for many time series, the seasonal differencing operation reduces a trending and seasonal series to a time series with nonseasonal fluctuations about an essentially horizontal trend line. The correlogram of the differenced series in Figure 10.2 does not contain a periodic pattern in multiples of 12 (compare Figure 10.2 with the correlogram of the raw gain data in Chapter 6, Figure 6.11). An appropriate sequence of differencing operations results in time series that are termed "stationary." Stationary time series are essential in ARIMA time series modeling, where they play an important role in connection with the Box-Jenkins forecasting methodology (Box and Jenkins, 1976).

The above remarks hold for other types of seasonal data as well. Thus, for quarterly data, differences of order 4 play the same role as differences of order 12 for monthly data.

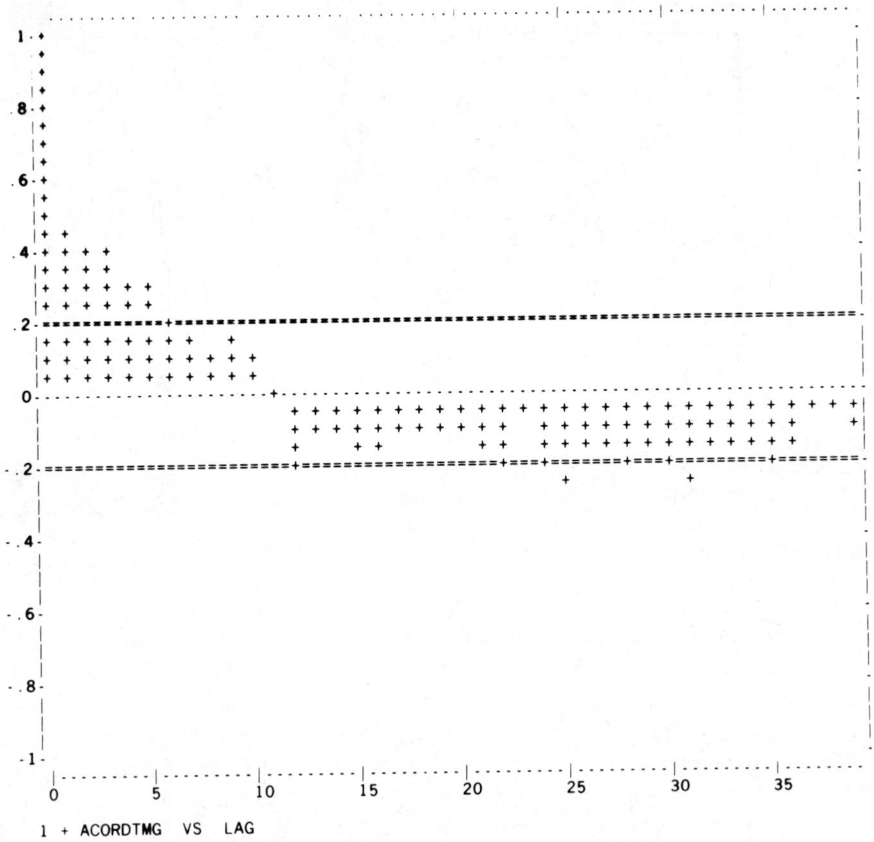


**Figure 10.2** Plot of the sample autocorrelations (correlogram) for the differenced telephone gain data.

## Changing Patterns

The discussion has focused on the analysis and adjustment of outliers, since they can have drastic effects on models. Other aspects of the data that can have serious effects on the modeling process are changing structural patterns with time. This type of change can take place in three areas:

- Trend.
- Cycle: changes in cycle can be seen from a plot of year-over-year differences. The magnitude and/or duration of the cycle may be changing. The cycle effect can also have a visual impact on a two-way table analysis when correcting for outliers.
- Seasonality: changes which should be apparent from a month-by-year table analysis. Seasonal adjustment techniques, as described in Chapters 18 and 19,

can accommodate changing seasonal patterns. When the data indicate changing patterns, the best approach may not be to adjust the data (unless the changed pattern is caused by outliers). Rather, one should consider methods and modeling approaches that are specifically designed for use with changing patterns.

## SUMMARY

In this chapter several analytical tools were introduced for the adjustment of data prior to modeling: transformations and differencing are important so that

- Underlying modeling assumptions can be approximated as closely as possible.
- Certain desired characteristics of the data, such as growth rates, can be displayed and interpreted.

Many analysts and researchers proceed by seeing how alike things are. Others proceed by trying to understand why things are different. The analysis of irregulars is consistent with the latter approach. The unusual data values may suggest relationships, transformations, or the need for a better understanding of events that may not be apparent in the bulk of the data. As discussed earlier, these unplanned findings may often yield the most interesting and important results in exploratory data analysis.

## USEFUL READING

BOX, G. E. P., and D. R. COX (1964). An Analysis of Transformations. *Journal of the Royal Statistical Society* B 26, 211–43.

BOX, G. E. P., and G. M. JENKINS (1976). *Time Series Analysis—Forecasting and Control.* Rev. ed. San Francisco, CA: Holden-Day.

DIXON, W. J., and M. B. BROWN (1979). *BMDP-79 Biomedical Computer Programs P-Series.* Los Angeles, CA: University of California Press.

ERICKSON, B. H., and T. A. NOSANCHUK (1977). *Understanding Data.* Toronto, Canada: McGraw-Hill-Ryerson Ltd.

MOSTELLER, F., and J. W. TUKEY (1977). *Data Analysis and Regression.* Reading, MA: Addison-Wesley Publishing Co.

CHAPTER **11**

# Cycle Analysis of Economic Indicators

---

The analysis of economic indicators is an important part of many forecasting activities:

- Forecasts of the levels of key economic indicators are often incorporated in quantitative models.
- Correlation studies are commonly made to assess the relative impact of expansions and contractions in the economy.
- Plots of economic indicators and their forecasts are frequently part of a presentation package for demand forecasts of business products.

Many national economic indicators are monitored on an ongoing basis by industry and government analysts.

---

## ORIGIN OF ECONOMIC INDICATORS

The origin of economic indicators dates back to the sharp business recession of 1937–1938. At that time an effort was initiated by the National Bureau of Economic Research (NBER) to devise a system that would signal the end of a recession.

Since quantitative analyses of the national economy were just beginning to receive attention within government circles, a considerable amount of data, assembled by the NBER since the 1920's, was analyzed to gain a better understanding of business cycles. These data, which included monthly, quarterly, and annual series on prices, employment, and production, resulted in a collection of twenty-one promising series that were selected on the basis of past performance and future promise as reliable indicators of business revival. Over the years this effort was greatly expanded to other public and private agencies (Shiskin and Moore, 1967; Moore and Shiskin, 1972).

A number of series, such as employment, indexes of consumer and wholesale prices, and manufacturers' orders, are published in the nation's newspapers. As indicators of the nation's economic health, they are followed very closely by professional economists and the business community at large, especially during periods of change in business activity.

## LEADING, COINCIDENT, AND LAGGING INDICATORS

For convenience of interpretation, *economic indicators* have been classified into three groups—leading, coincident, and lagging (Sobek, 1973). *Leading indicators* are those that provide advance warning of probable changes in economic activity. *Coincident indicators* are those that reflect the current performance of the economy. *Lagging indicators* are those that confirm changes previously signaled.

Coincident indicators provide a measure of current economic activity. They are the most familiar and include Gross National Product, industrial production, personal income, retail sales, and employment (see Figure 11.1).

### Use of Indicators

It would be very useful to forecasters and planners to have some advance warning of an impending change in the nation's economy. While coincident indicators are used to indicate whether the economy is currently experiencing expansion, contraction, recession, or inflation, leading indicators help forecasters to assess short-term trends in the coincident indicators. In addition, leading indicators help planners and policy makers anticipate adverse effects on the economy and examine the feasibility of corrective steps. Among the leading indicators, housing starts, new orders for durable goods, construction contracts, formation of new business enterprises, hiring rates, and average length of workweek are the most commonly quoted.

Housing starts, a key leading indicator plotted in Figure 11.2, tend to lead fluctuations in overall economic activity. The data are used throughout the text as an explanatory variable related to main telephone gain. The main reason that housing starts are a leading economic indicator (typically leading peaks in the business cycle by a year and troughs by six months) is that starts are very sensitive to fluctuations in interest rates. When interest rates rise substantially—as they generally do near the peak of an expansion—savings deposited with mortgage lenders tend to be diverted to other users of funds. Meanwhile, rising mortgage rates and stricter lending conditions curtail the demand for home loans. Thus homebuilding is squeezed from both sides—supply and demand—when interest rates rise.

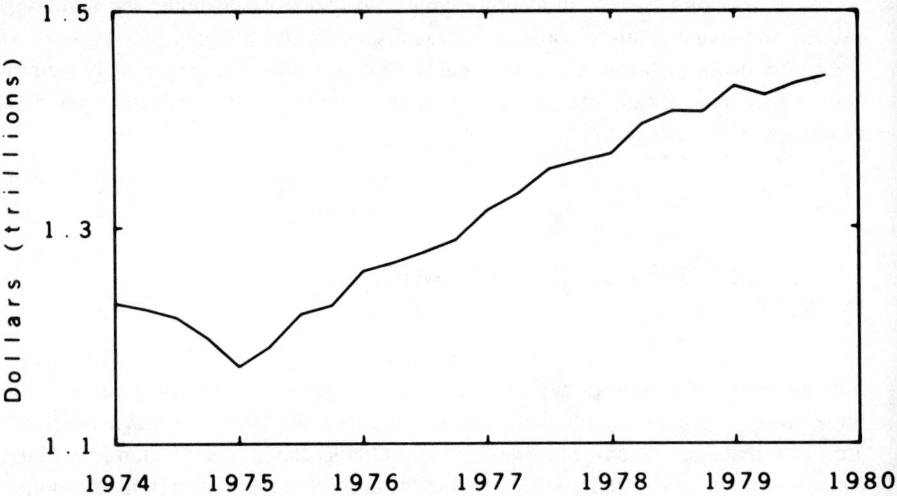


a

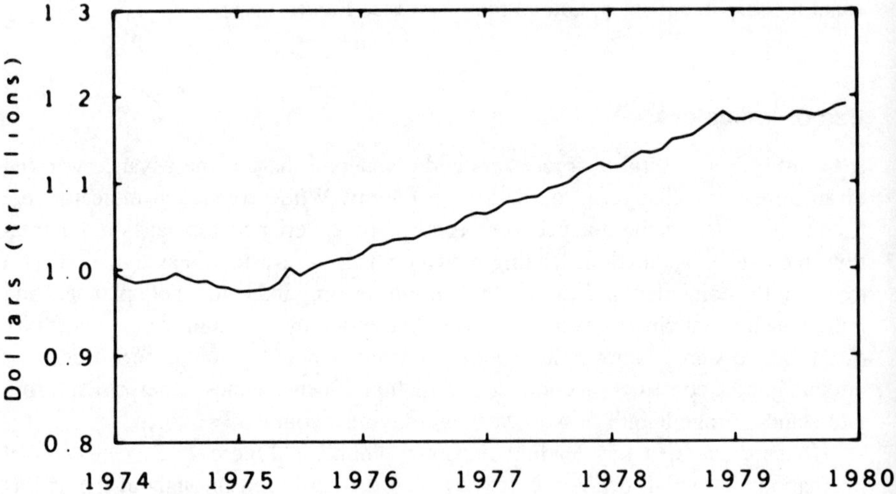


b

*Source:* U.S. Department of Commerce, Bureau of Economic Analysis for (a) and (b); U.S. Department of Commerce, Bureau of Census for (c); U.S. Department of Labor, Bureau of Labor Statistics for (d).

**Figure 11.1** Time plots of several coincident indicators of the U.S. economy: (a) Gross National Product, (b) personal income, (c) retail sales, and (d) employment.

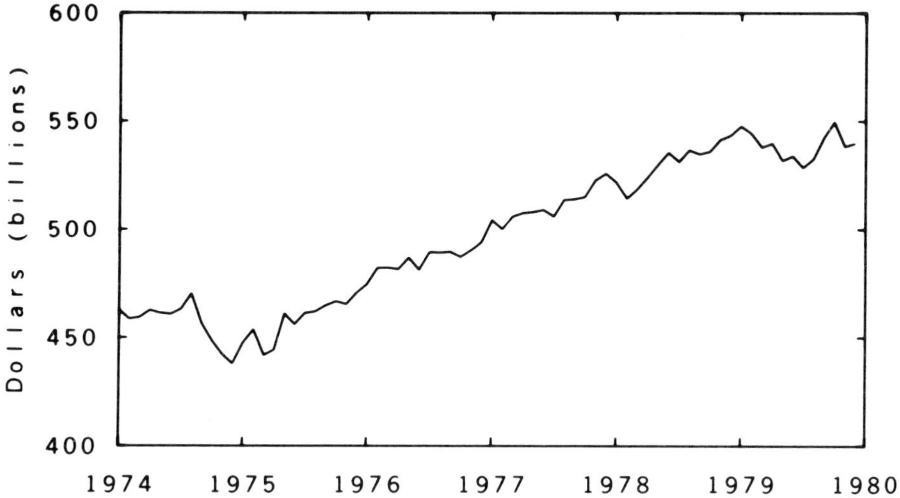


c

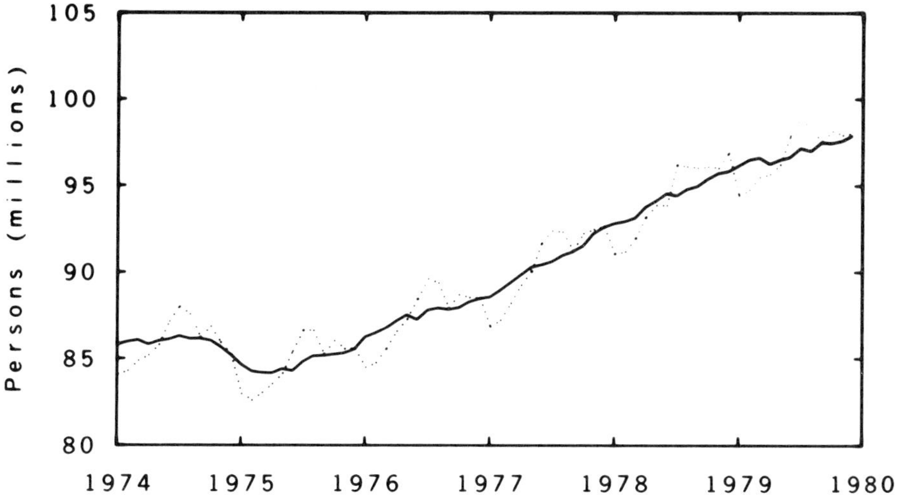


d

A useful set of indicators for revealing and explaining the economy's broad cyclical movements includes manufacturers' shipments and orders (Figure 11.3). These are comprehensive indicators of industrial activity, an especially important sector because it is the economy's most volatile component, dropping four to five times as much as the total output during business recessions.

Shipments are an indicator of current economic activity, measuring the dollar value of products sold by all manufacturing establishments. Orders, on the other

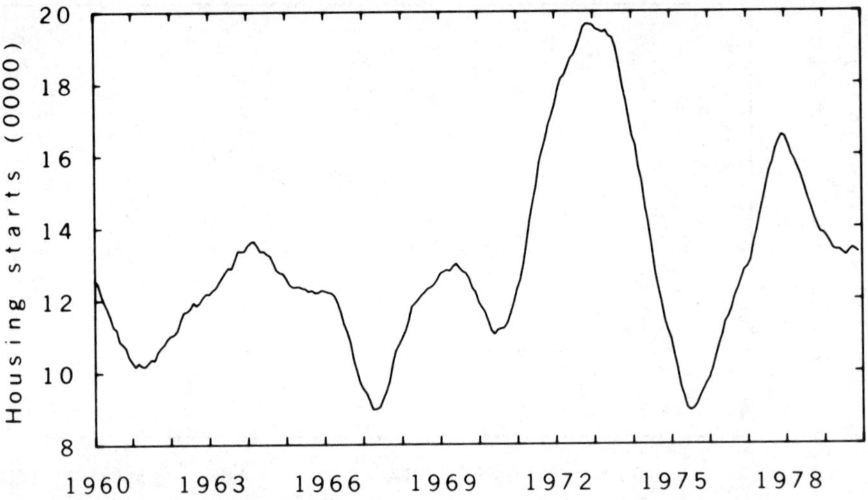


*Source:* U.S. Department of Commerce, Bureau of Census.

**Figure 11.2** Time plot of a twelve-month moving average of the housing starts (new private housing units started).

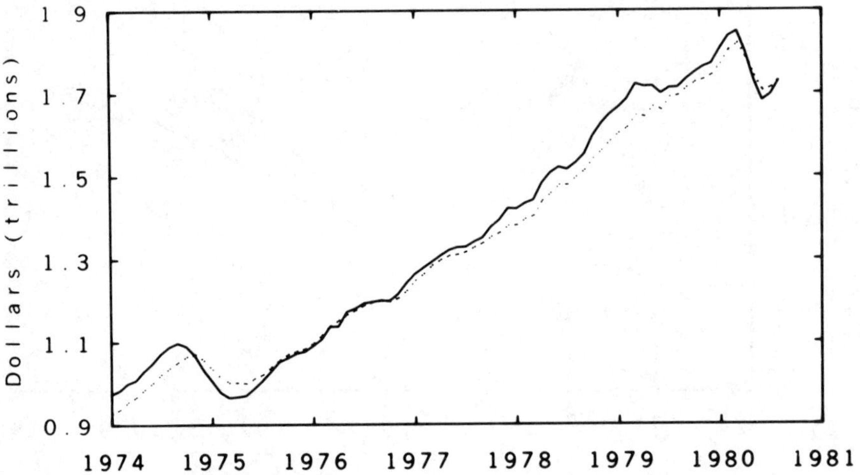


*Source:* U.S. Department of Commerce, Bureau of Census.

**Figure 11.3** Time plot of manufacturers' shipments (dotted) and orders (solid).

hand, are a valuable leading indicator. They measure the dollar value of new orders—net of order cancellations—received by all manufacturers. The two series are distorted by inflation, since there is no relevant price index to convert it to real terms. It is the difference between shipments and orders, which shows what is happening to the backlog of unfilled orders, that gives insight into the degree of sustainability of current national output.

Lagging indicators usually follow, rather than lead, the fluctuations in the coincident indicators. Examples of lagging indicators are labor cost per unit of output (Figure 11.4), long-term unemployment, and the yield on mortgage loans.

## Composite Indicators

In an attempt to reduce the number of series that must be reviewed, and at the same time not to lose a great deal of information, analysts have developed *composite indicators*. These series provide single measures of complicated economic activities that experience common fluctuations. The procedure involved includes "amplitude-adjustment" in which the month-to-month percent change of each series in the composite is standardized so that all series are expressed in comparable units. The average month-to-month change, without regard to sign, is 1.0. Each individual series is weighted by the score it receives from the scoring plan. The composite index is amplitude-adjusted so that its average month-to-month percent change is 1.0.

If an index shows an increase of 2.0 in a month, it is rising twice as fast as its average rate of change in the past. If an index increases by 0.5, it is rising only half as fast as its historical rate of increase. Composite indicators have been developed for the leading, coincident, and lagging series.

In order to have a more comprehensive coverage of the economy, the U.S. Commerce Department publishes *composite indexes* of leading and coincident indicators. These indicators are a weighted combination of individual indicators; for example, employment and real income are two components in the *index of leading indicators*.

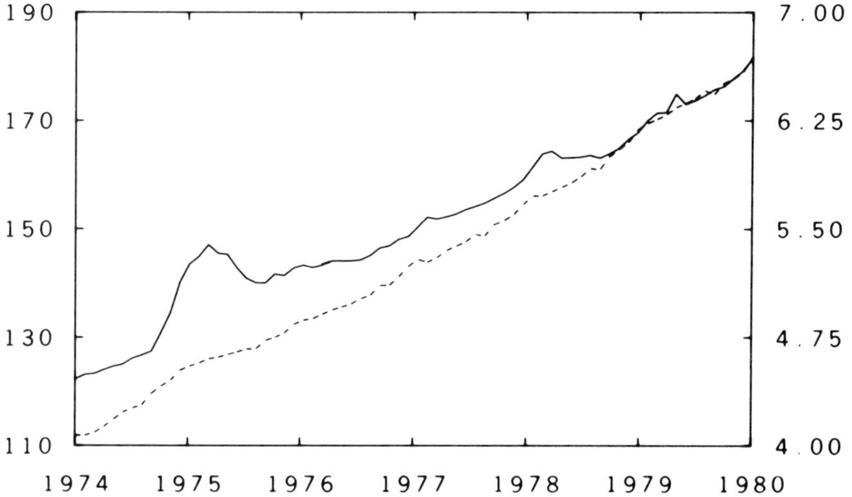


*Source:* U.S. Department of Commerce, Bureau of Economic Analysis.

**Figure 11.4** Time plots of unit labor costs (solid) and hourly earnings (dotted).

One problem with interpreting the index of leading indicators is that its month-to-month changes can be erratic. For example, the index dropped sharply in April 1980, only to recover partly during the summer, thus muddying any message about a future downturn. However, comparing movements of the index over a longer span helps to bring out the underlying cyclical movements. For example, Figure 11.5 shows the percent change in the current level of the leading index from the average level of the preceding twelve months. On that basis, the leading indicators have declined (i.e., fallen below zero) before every one of the five recessions since 1950. The two recessions during the 1970's are depicted by shaded areas.

## Reverse Trend Adjustment of the Leading Indicators

Economists have been concerned about two aspects of the leading indicators:

- The lead at the business cycle peak is much longer than the lead at the trough.
- Leading indicators do not have the long-term trend that the economy as measured by coincident indicators has.

Since the objective of forecasting is to predict current levels rather than detrended levels, the *reverse trend adjustment* procedure adds a trend to the leading indicators (rather than removing the trend from the coincident indicators). First, however, it is necessary to eliminate whatever trend already exists in the leading indicators. Then

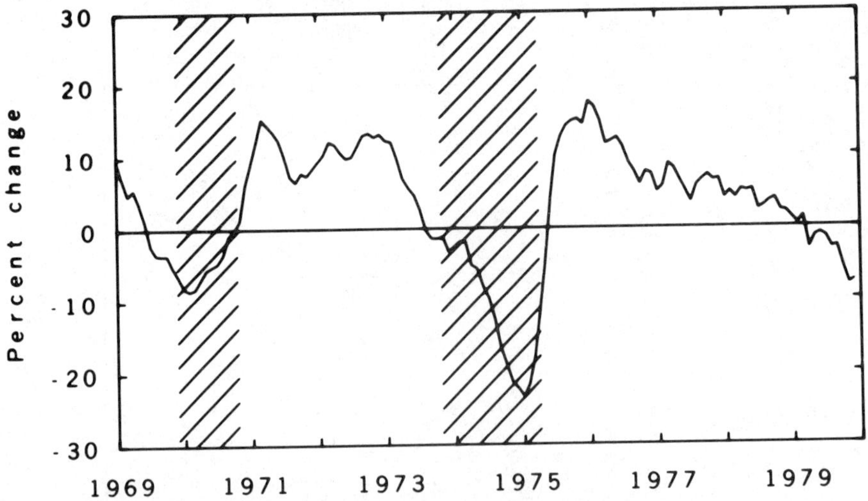


*Source:* U.S. Department of Commerce, Bureau of Economic Analysis.

**Figure 11.5** Time plot of a composite index of leading indicators; it shows the percent change in the current level of the leading index from the average level of the preceding twelve months.

the trend of the coincident indicators (based on full cycles) is added to the detrended leading indicators.

The effect of reverse trend adjustment is to shorten the lead time at business cycle peaks and increase the lead time at troughs. It also tends to reduce the number of false signals of recession that are evident when the unadjusted index turns down but a recession does not occur. Because reverse trend adjustment helps to reduce the lead time at peaks and increase the lead time at troughs, this makes the two lead times more equal. This will lessen the reaction time at the peak, however. Even with reverse trend adjustment, the lead at the peaks is about one or two months longer, on the average, than the lead at the troughs.

In forecasting with regression models, the generally *different* lead times must be reckoned with before regression models are used. Since regression models do not offer you the chance to vary lead/lag times in the explanatory variables at different periods in the cycle, the indicators will tend to average the impact of the lesser lead or lag at either the peak or the trough. It is possible to have one model in which the indicator has as its lead time the appropriate lead for a peak and a second model that has as its lead time the appropriate lead for a trough. Then, either the first or second model is used to generate forecasts, depending upon the state of the business cycle.

### Sources of Indicators

The U.S. Department of Commerce publishes a monthly booklet called *Business Conditions Digest,* which contains current data for many different indicators. The charts and graphs cover the National Income and Product accounts series, cyclical indicators, series on anticipations and intentions, analytical measures, and international comparisons. The series are usually seasonally adjusted and the NBER (National Board of Economic Research) *reference dates* for recessions and expansions are shown. It is apparent from the plots that business contractions are generally shorter than business expansions. The average peacetime cycle is slightly less than four years. Another useful reference to data sources, their description, and their use in business cycle forecasting is Silk and Curley (1970).

## SELECTING INDICATORS

Specified criteria have been applied by the NBER to hundreds of economic series from which a list of indicators could be selected. These criteria include *economic significance, statistical adequacy, historical conformity* to business cycles, *consistency of lead or lag, smoothness* of the data, and *timeliness* of the data. A score can be given for each of six criteria, and those series with the highest scores can then be retained. The scoring is subjective in many aspects.

## Economic Significance

Some aspects of criteria of *economic significance* have already been discussed—that is, the role a given economic process has in theories that purport to explain how business cycles come about or how they may be controlled or modified.

A consideration in indicator selection and scoring is the *breadth of coverage*. A "broad" indicator covers all corporate activity, total consumption, or investment. A "narrow" indicator relates to a single industry or to minor components of the "broad" series.

A broad economic indicator may continue to perform well even if some components deteriorate because of technological developments, changes in customer tastes, or rapid growth or decline of single products or industries. Therefore, a "broad" indicator receives a higher score than a "narrow" indicator.

## Statistical Adequacy

The characteristics you should consider in evaluating the *statistical adequacy* of a series include a *good reporting system* and *good coverage;* that is, the data should cover the entire period they represent, benchmarks should be available, and there should be a full account of survey methods, coverage, and data adjustments.

A *good reporting system* is one based on primary rather than indirect sources or estimates. Some important series, such as the index of industrial production, the index of net business formation, and Gross National Product, are based largely on indirect sources. Employment and retail sales are based on direct reporting from primary sources.

*Good coverage* means that if sampling is required, it should be a probability sample with stated measurement error regarding sample statistics.

Moreover, coverage means, for example, that monthly data should include all days and not be a figure based on one day or week. Also, the availability of benchmarks is important as a check on the accuracy of data. For example, the U.S. Census provides a benchmark for estimates of population.

## Conformity to Business Cycles

The National Bureau of Economic Research developed an initial index to measure how well the variations in a series *conformed to business cycle* variations. A series that rose through every business expansion and declined during every contraction received an index score of 100. This particular index did not include extra cycles, such as occurred in 1966–1967, which are not classified as recession troughs. The index did not indicate whether the lack of conformity occurred early in the data or later; and it did not take into account the amplitude of the cycles. The scoring system subsequently developed by Shiskin and Moore (1967) takes these considerations into account.

### Consistency of Timing

A number of considerations govern scoring a series on the basis of *consistency of timing*. The first is the consistency of lead or lag time relative to cycle peak or trough. The second is the variability about the average lead or lag time. A third consideration is the difference in lead time for a peak compared to the lead time for a trough. Finally, has there been any recent departure from historical relationships?

Leading indicators have a median lead time of two or more months. Lagging indicators have a median lag of two or more months. Coincident indicators have a median timing of $-1$, 0, or $+1$ months. Occasionally, median leads of $+2$ months are possible when the lead or lag is not constant over many cycles.

### Smoothness and Timeliness

The factors that are weighed in arriving at a score for *smoothness* and *timeliness* include prompt availability of data and their smoothness. It is easier to identify changes in direction in a smooth series than in an irregular series. Generally speaking, because of irregularity of data, comparisons over spans greater than one month must usually be made to detect cyclical changes. Smoothing of some irregular series may result in some delay but may still provide a longer lead time than for other series which are less irregular but have shorter lead times.

Generally speaking, leading indicators are the most erratic; lagging indicators are the smoothest. Coincident indicators have the shortest publication lag and the highest conformity scores. For example, corporate profits after taxes received an average score of 68 in the NBER index. This indicator also received fairly high scores for economic significance, statistical adequacy, conformity, and timing. However, it received a score of 60 for smoothness, because it is irregular, and only 25 for timeliness, because it is a quarterly series subject to slow reporting.

## A CYCLE FORECASTING PROCEDURE

This section describes a subjective yet useful and often appealing way to develop and present cycle forecasts. The approach is based on the decomposition of a time series into trend, cycle, and seasonal components. Each component is forecast separately, and the forecast for the series is the sum of the forecasts of the components. The approach will be illustrated by using the telephone toll-revenue series presented earlier in the book.

### A Ten-Step Procedure for Making a Turning-Point Analysis

Here is an algorithm that will guide you through this procedure:

1. Plot the time series.
2. Remove seasonality (seasonal adjustment, differencing).
3. If necessary, remove irregularity with a low-order moving average.
4. Fit a trend line to the series in Step 3 and plot deviations from trend. This is the cycle. If necessary, transform the time series so that a trend line is appropriate (i.e., no cupshaped patterns should occur).
5. Follow Steps 1–4 for other national, regional, local, or industry series for comparison of cycle patterns.

6(a). If there is a historic relationship in the cycle patterns:

- Obtain forecasts of the other variable.
- Plot these forecasts in terms of deviations from trend.
- Forecast the cycle for your series based on the cycle forecast of the economic variable. Take leading or lagging relationships into account.

(b). If there is no historical relationship, develop the cycle forecast based on a pattern analysis in which you have considered:

- Peak-to-trough or trough-to-peak historical durations (month, quarters).
- Peak-to-peak or trough-to-trough durations.
- Magnitudes (amplitudes) of peaks or troughs (amount, percent).
- Slopes of peaks or troughs (speed of recovery, decline).
- Anticipated future cyclical patterns based on economic, market, or industry information.

7. Project the trend line of Step 4 and add to it the cycle forecast from Step 6 to obtain trend-cycle forecasts.
8. To reintroduce seasonality (if desired), add the forecasts of the seasonal factors.
9. If appropriate, retransform the series (e.g., exponentiate, raise to a power) to the original scale in Step 7 or 8 if a transformation was taken in Step 4 or 2.
10. Plot the history and forecast together for reasonableness.

### Preparing a Cycle Forecast for Revenues

Let's examine results of the ten-step procedure. Figure 11.6 is a plot of the revenue series (Step 1). Figure 11.7 is a plot of the seasonally adjusted series (Step 2) for which the SABL procedure (Chapter 19) was used. A three-month moving average

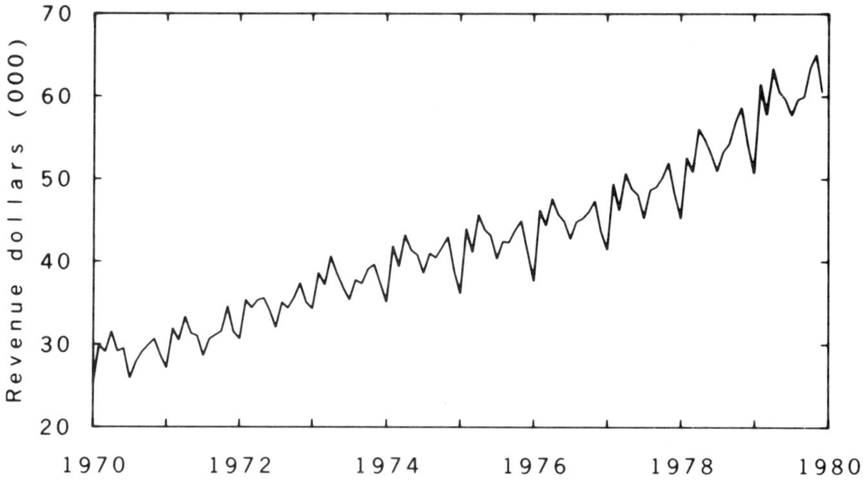


**Figure 11.6** Time plot of the original telephone toll-revenue series. The data are not seasonally adjusted.

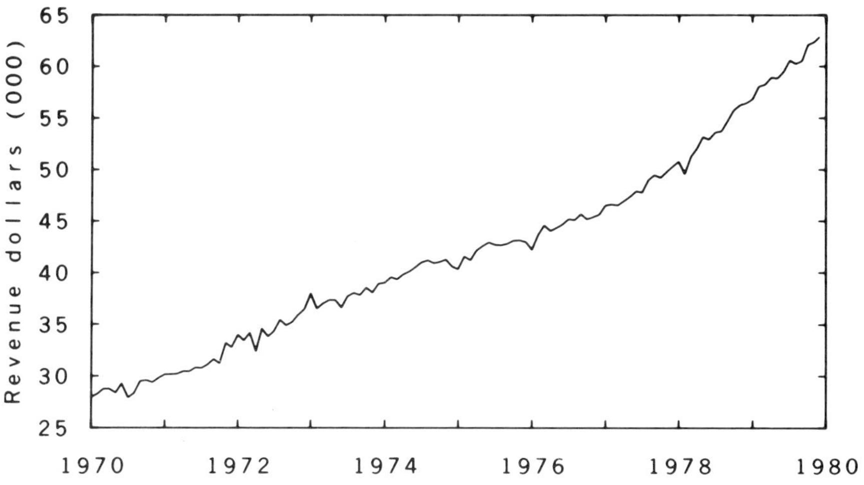


**Figure 11.7** Time plot of the seasonally adjusted telephone toll-revenue series.

of the seasonally adjusted series was performed (Step 3). This smoothed the irregular component and resulted in a smoother cycle pattern in the later stages of analysis.

Figure 11.8 shows a trend line fitted to the data from Step 3 (Step 4). The deviations from trend in Figure 11.9 show a cupshaped pattern indicating the need to transform the series. (The peak-to-trough reference dates for the 1970–1971 and 1974–1975 recessions, as determined by the National Bureau of Economic Research, are shown as shaded areas in this and subsequent figures.) A logarithmic

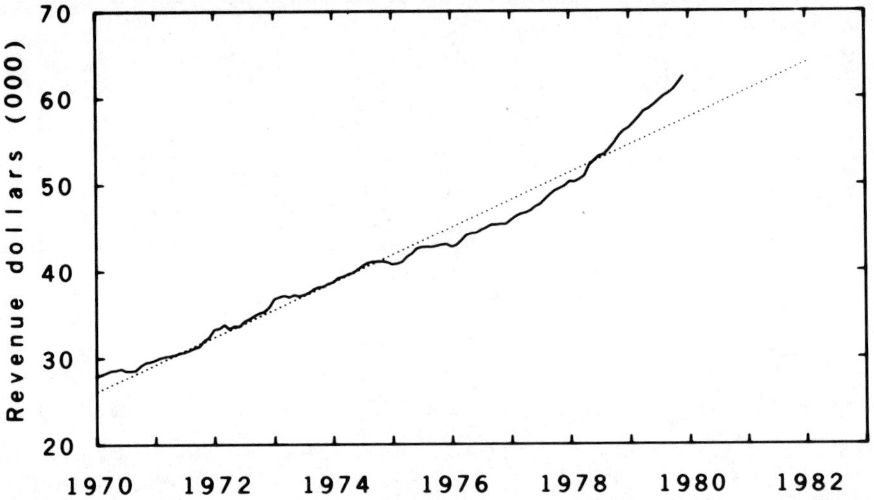


**Figure 11.8** Three-month moving average of the seasonally adjusted revenue series fitted with a straight line.

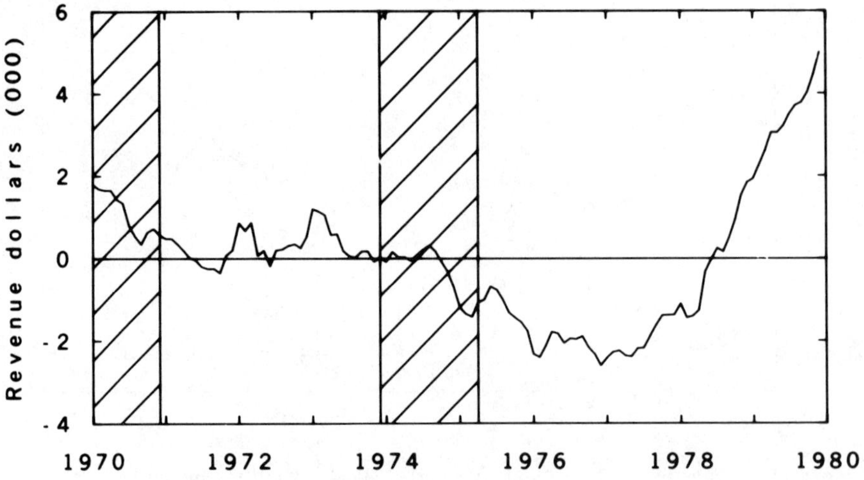


**Figure 11.9** Deviations from trend suggesting a need for a transformation. (See Figure 15.3).

transformation was then taken of the smoothed series, and a straight-line trend-line was fitted; the deviations from trend are shown as a cycle in Figure 11.10.

Similar steps were followed for an economic series (nonfarm employment), and the deviations from trend are shown in Figure 11.11 (Step 5). From the shading in Figure 11.11, it can be seen that employment in the region for which the forecast is being made peaks at approximately the same time as it does in the rest of the nation but reaches bottom a year or more after the national economy has bottomed.

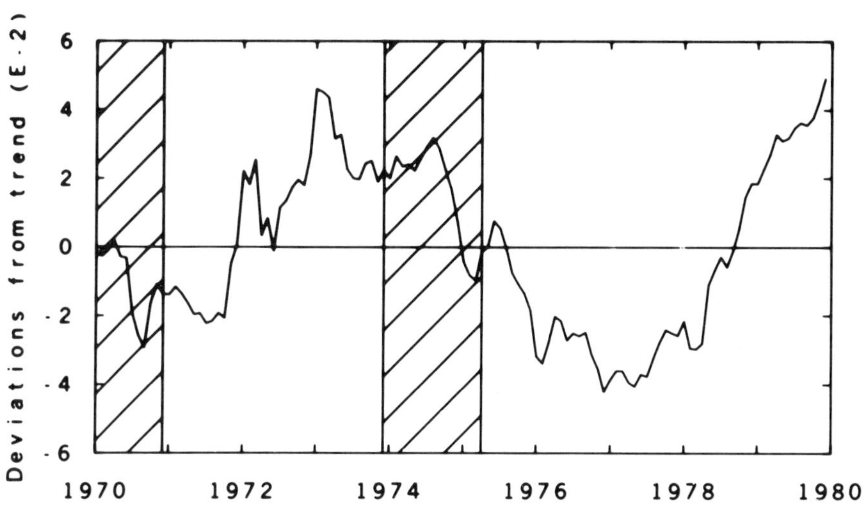


**Figure 11.10** Deviations from trend for transformed (with logarithms), smoothed (three-month moving average), and seasonally adjusted (SABL) revenue data.

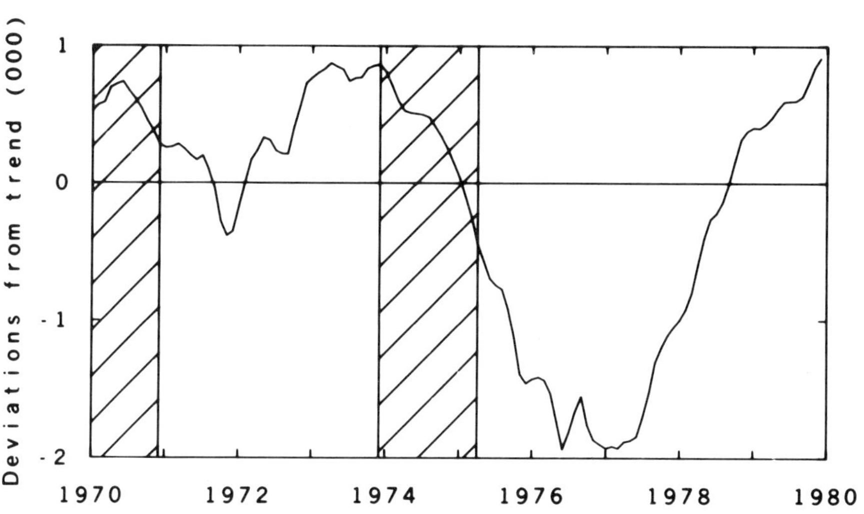


**Figure 11.11** Deviations from a straight line trend fitted to a nonfarm employment series.

A comparison of the regional employment cycle with the revenue cycle shows similar patterns—especially since 1973. A forecast of the employment series was obtained and is shown (in terms of deviation from trend) by the dotted line in Figure 11.12. With this prediction as a starting point, three scenarios were developed for the revenue cycle (optimistic, most likely, pessimistic), and these are shown in Figure 11.13. The most likely scenario approximates the relationship that existed between the two series in the past. The optimistic scenario shows a somewhat shal-

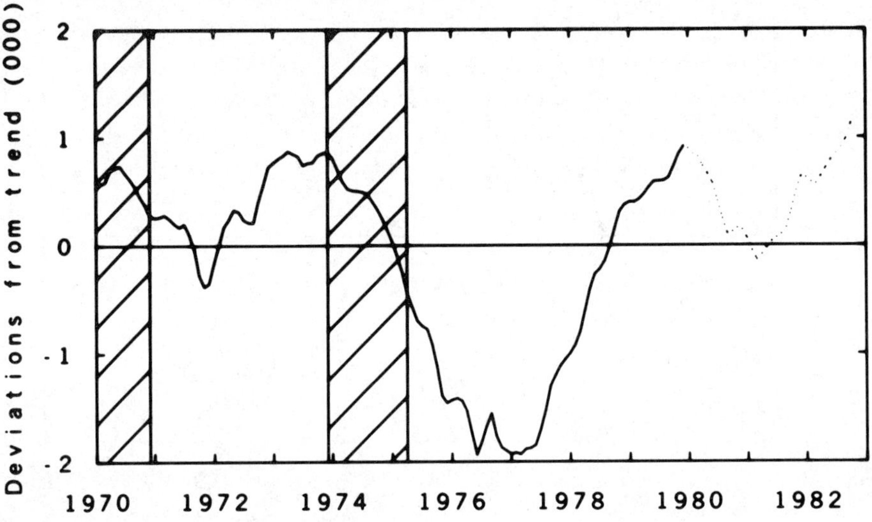


**Figure 11.12** Historical and forecast deviations from trend for a nonfarm employment series.

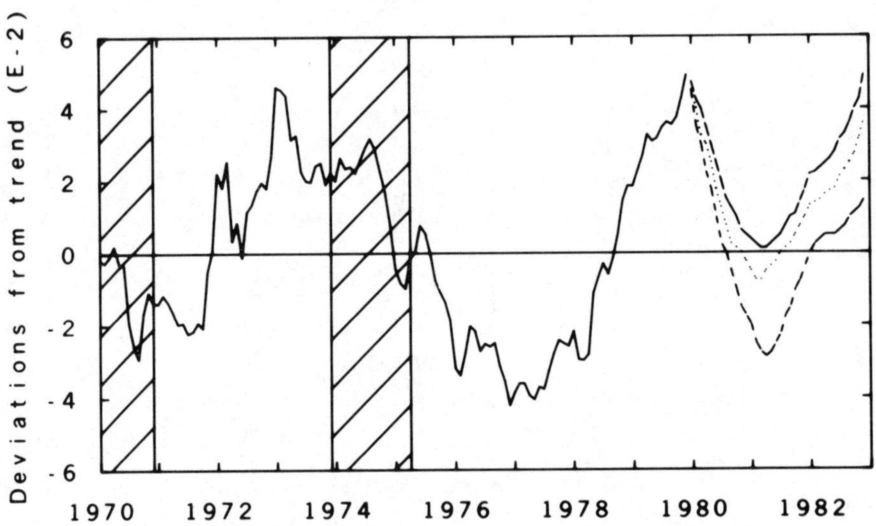


**Figure 11.13** Three forecast scenarios for the revenue series are shown above: optimistic (uppermost), pessimistic (lowest), and most likely (intermediate).

lower decline and a more rapid recovery. The pessimistic scenario projects a much sharper decline and more gradual recovery that is more similar to the 1976–1979 period. Because of the steadily worsening economic news in the first quarter 1980, the pessimistic scenario is a more probable alternative forecast than the optimistic forecast.

Figure 11.14 shows a plot of history and forecast in terms of a smoothed seasonally adjusted series. The trend line was extrapolated, the cycle forecast was added, and the result was exponentiated and plotted as the dotted line. If desired, seasonality could be reintroduced by adding the historical and projected seasonal factors. The irregular component has been smoothed over the historical period and is projected to be zero over the forecast period.

## Alternative Approaches to Turning-Point Forecasts

Strong arguments against the use of seasonally adjusted data for econometric regression models have been made (Jenkins, 1979). The objections are related, in part, to the fact that you cannot be quite sure what the statistical properties of the residuals are after you have subjected the series to a seasonal adjustment procedure. This has an impact on the inferences that can be drawn—specifically for confidence limits about the forecast (Chapter 14). In the cycle forecasting approach, illustrated in the previous telephone revenues example, the subjective nature of the forecast and the intentional omission of confidence levels recognize that this is a *highly subjective* approach.

However, an alternative to modeling seasonally adjusted data is modeling appropriately differenced data. Figure 11.15 shows a cyclical pattern in which the deviation from the trend line is measured in differences of order 12. One can also take differences of economic data, compare patterns of deviations from trend of the two series, and develop cycle forecasts. The last step is to "undifference" the series

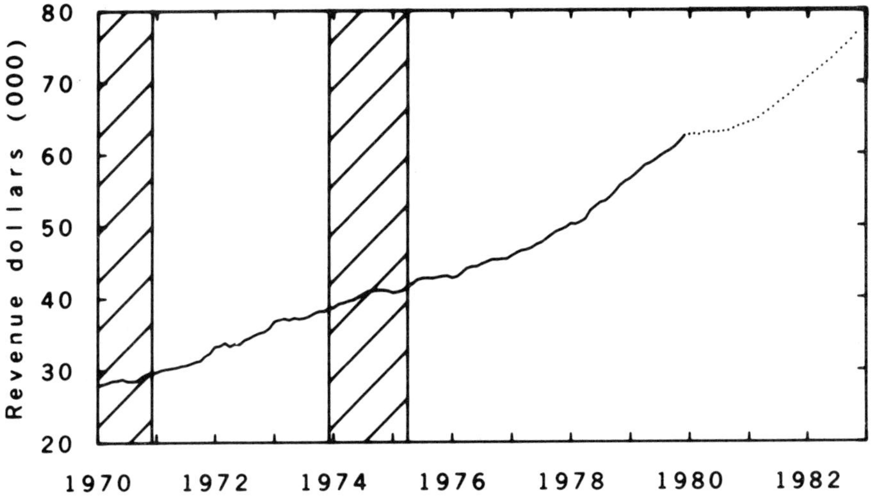


**Figure 11.14** Historical time plot and a forecast for the smoothed, seasonally adjusted revenue series. The forecast is shown as a dotted line.

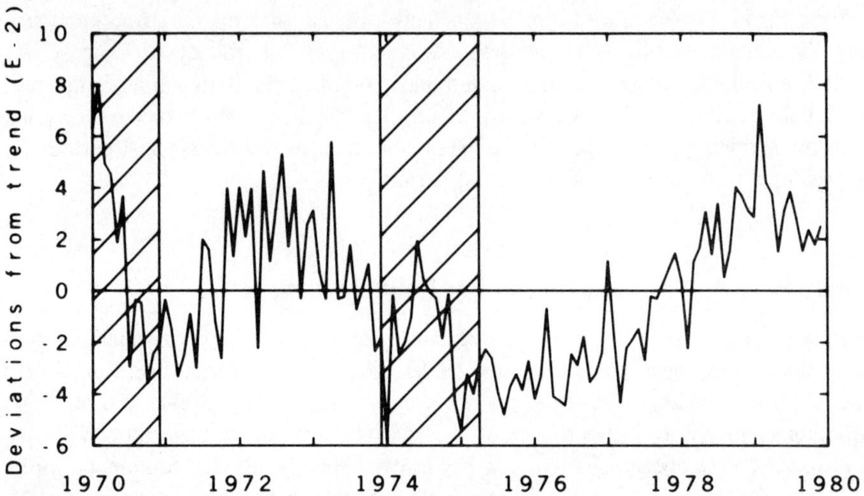


**Figure 11.15** Deviations from a straight line trend of the differences of order 12 for the monthly revenue series.

by adding the predicted differences to the appropriate actual (and later predicted) values of the revenue series.

Despite the subjective nature of the turning-point forecast, it is intuitively appealing to upper-level managers, a consideration that cannot be dismissed. Even if this approach is not used to establish the forecast values, it is an effective way of presenting the forecast to higher management. In this instance, the deviations from trend are calculated instead of subjectively projected.

## SUMMARY

In business forecasting, indicators are useful in several ways:

- They can be used to validate assumptions about the economy that are made in any forecast being presented or reviewed.
- They can help in understanding why current performance in a business or industry is weak, strong, or average.

Leading-indicator methodology is not without its problems, however. Some basic limitations of leading indicators are that

- They can produce many false signals for turning points.
- They may not be available on a timely basis; thereby their lead-advantages are reduced.

A ten-step turning-point analysis was used to prepare scenario forecasts for a revenue series. While the approach is highly subjective, it has intuitive appeal and can serve as a valuable aid in establishing credibility for a forecast among upper-level managers.

## USEFUL READING

JENKINS, G. M. (1979). *Practical Experiences with Modeling and Forecasting Time Series*. Jersey, Channel Islands: GJ&P (Overseas) Ltd.

MOORE, G. H., and J. SHISKIN (1972). *Early Warning Signals for the Economy in Statistics*. J. M. Tanur et al., eds. San Francisco, CA: Holden-Day.

SHISKIN, J., and G. H. MOORE (1967). *Indicators of Business Expansions and Contractions*. Cambridge, MA: National Bureau of Economic Research.

SILK, L. S., and M. L. CURLEY (1970). *Business Forecasting—With a Guide to Sources of Business Data*. New York, NY: Random House.

SOBEK, R. S. (1973). A Manager's Primer in Forecasting. *Harvard Business Review* 5, 1–9.

CHAPTER **12**

# Building Regression Models

- Linear regression methods are the most widely known and frequently used tools for forecasting and econometric analysis.
- These models can be used to describe a relationship between a variable of interest and one or more related variables that are assumed to have a bearing on the forecasting problem.
- The concepts and assumptions underlying ordinary least-squares regression will be explained along with forecasting examples to illustrate several key ideas.

## WHAT IS A REGRESSION MODEL?

In Chapter 6 we introduced the scatter diagram as a means of graphically displaying an underlying relationship between two variables, $X$ and $Y$. For example, in relating monthly telephone-toll revenues to toll messages, Figure 12.1 shows a very narrow cluster of points lying along a line with positive slope. This suggests a tight relationship between revenues and messages, perhaps described by a simple curve. A more complicated situation arises if one considers the relationship between quarterly main telephone gain and housing starts as depicted in Figure 12.2. Here it would be more difficult to suggest a simple forecasting relationship, because of the wider dispersion of points.

The statistical technique of quantifying such relationships among variables is known as *regression analysis*. Such relationships can be used to predict one variable, called the *dependent variable,* from knowledge of other related variables known as *independent variables*.

The term "regression" has a rather curious origin in studies by Sir Francis Galton (1822–1911) of inheritance in biology. His studies showed that while tall (or short) fathers had tall (or short) sons, the sons were on the average not as tall (or as short)

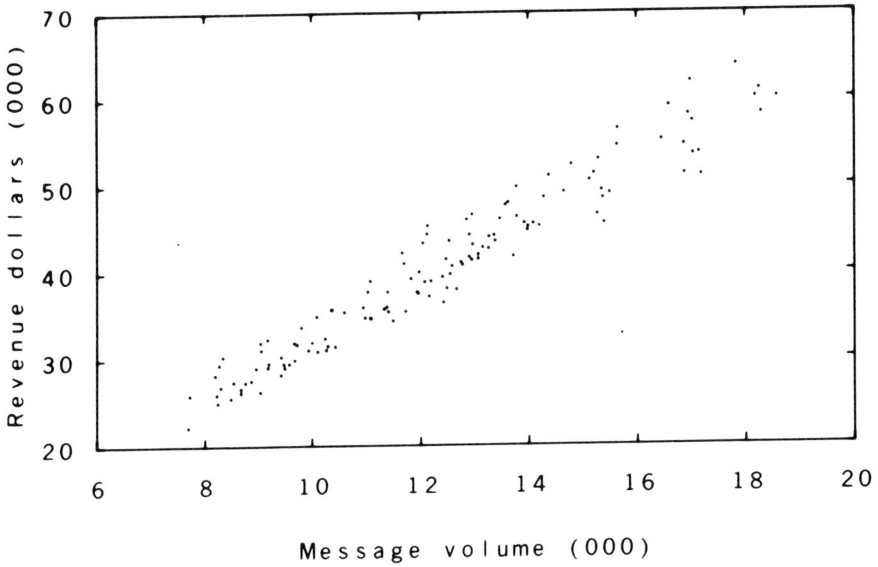


**Figure 12.1** Scatter diagram of monthly telephone toll-revenue and message volumes (January 1969–December 1978).

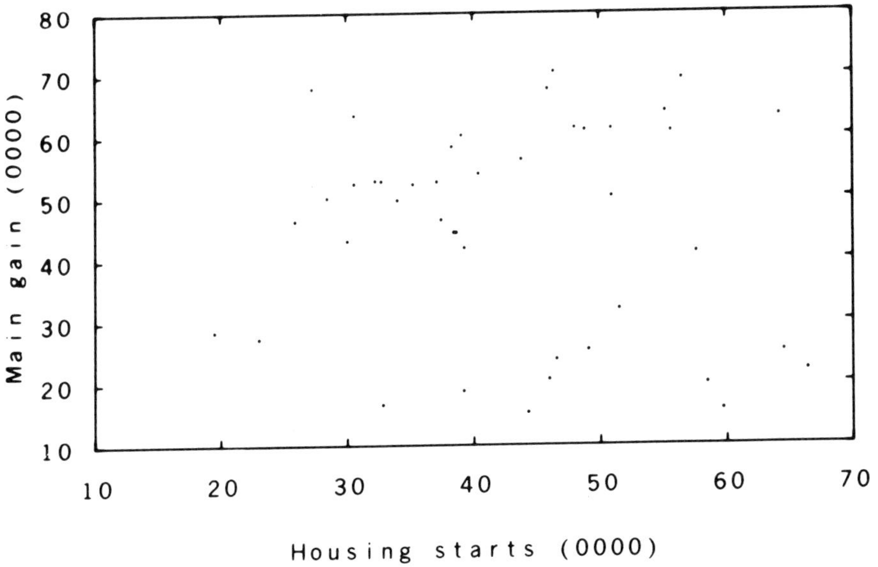


**Figure 12.2** Scatter diagram of quarterly telephone gain and housing starts (first quarter 1969–third quarter 1978).

as their fathers. Thus Galton observed that the *average* height of the sons tended to move toward the *average* height of the overall population of fathers, rather than toward reproducing the height of the parents. This "regression" toward the mean is widely observed in other examples as well, and the term has therefore found general acceptance.

## The Regression Curve

A *regression curve* (in a two-variable case) is defined as that curve which goes through the *mean value* of $Y$ (the dependent variable) for each *fixed value* of $X$ (the independent variable). If data are plentiful, a curve passing through the bulk of the data would represent the regression curve. The data are such that there is no functional relationship describing exactly one variable $Y$ as a function of $X$. For a given value of the independent variable $X$, there is a *distribution* of values of $Y$. This relationship may be approximated by determining the *average* (or median) value of $Y$ for small intervals of values of $X$.

In most practical situations, there are not enough observations to "even pretend that the resulting curve has the shape of the regression curve that would arise if we had unlimited data" (Mosteller and Tukey, 1977, p. 266). Instead, the observations result in an approximation. With only limited data, a shape for the regression curve (linear, quadratic, exponential) is assumed and the curve is fitted to the data by using a statistical method such as the *method of least squares*. This method will be explained shortly.

## A Simple Linear Model

In the telecommunications example, let's assume that a simple linear relationship exists between the toll message and revenue volumes. Suppose you wish to predict the toll revenues from the toll messages. A sample of revenue and message volumes could be collected from a billing record and plotted as a scatter diagram, in which the dependent variable (revenue) is put on the vertical axis and the independent variable (message) on the horizontal axis. Figure 12.1 is a scatter diagram for the monthly volume of toll revenues and messages in our telecommunications example.

The scatter diagram shows that, *on average,* revenues increase with increasing message volumes (and vice versa), though for a given volume of messages there is a good deal of *variability* in revenues. This simple model is only partially descriptive in that it does not take into account other factors, such as time of day, duration of call, and distance.

Since regression analysis seeks an algebraic relationship between a dependent variable $Y$ and one or more independent variables, the appropriate algebraic model describes the average value for $Y$ given a specific value of $X$:

$$\text{Model} = \text{Average } Y, \qquad \text{when } Y = f(X).$$

If it were true that revenues change the same amount for each additional message, then the data would lie along a straight line. In practice, this may be approximately true, the difference being ascribed to *random errors:*

$$\text{Data} = \text{Average } Y + \text{Random errors.}$$

The slope $\beta$ of this straight line would represent the *rate of change* in revenue with increasing message volume. The intercept $\alpha$ (revenue at "zero" message volume) would not be a meaningful quantity in this case. Thus

$$\text{Model} = \text{Average revenue} = \alpha + \beta \cdot \text{Messages.}$$

Since a "zero" message volume in this example is not meaningful, the practitioner must be cautioned that the intercept $\alpha$ cannot always be interpreted physically. Thus the regression model, as described by an equation, is only *locally* correct in the sense that it describes a meaningful relationship *within the range* of values of the data that are reasonable.

However, there is considerable variability in revenue for a given volume of messages, so that one assumption in the linear regression model is that for any value of $X$, the value of $Y$ is scattered around an *average value*. This average value is an unknown quantity which is often denoted by the Greek letter mu ($\mu$) with a subscript $Y(X)$:

$$\mu_{Y(X)} = \alpha + \beta X.$$

The intercept $\alpha$ and slope $\beta$ are known as the *regression coefficients*. The model is *linear* in $X$. Both $\alpha$ and $\beta$ are unknown parameters to be estimated from the data. As a standard statistical convention, it is useful to designate unknown parameters in models by Greek letters, to distinguish them from the corresponding estimates made from the data.

The observed values of $Y$ will not necessarily lie on a straight line in the $XY$ plane but will differ from it by some random error $\varepsilon$:

$$\text{Data} = \alpha + \beta \cdot \text{Messages} + \text{Errors.}$$

Thus the *simple linear regression model* is expressed by

$$\begin{aligned} Y &= \mu_{Y(X)} + \varepsilon \\ &= \alpha + \beta X + \varepsilon, \end{aligned}$$

where the average (expected) value of $\varepsilon$ is zero.

## THE METHOD OF LEAST SQUARES

In a particular application of the model, the forecaster has data which are assumed to have arisen as a realization of the hypothetical model. The next step is to come up with a rational procedure for estimating the parameters in the model from a given set of data:

Data = Model + Errors.

There are a number of estimation techniques in the statistical literature, of which the method of *ordinary least squares* is the most common and easiest for mathematical analyses. This is not to say that other techniques have little merit. In fact, weighted least-squares techniques of several kinds are finding increased applications in the practical world, in particular, in robust regression (Mosteller and Tukey, 1977).

### The Least-Squares Assumption

Consider now a reasonable criterion for estimating $\alpha$ and $\beta$ from data. The method of *ordinary least squares* (OLS) determines values of $\alpha$ and $\beta$ (since these will be estimated from data, we will replace $\alpha$ and $\beta$ with Latin letters $a$ and $b$) so that the sum of the squared *vertical deviations* (residuals) between the data and the fitted line,

Residuals = Data − Fit,

is less than the sum of the squared *vertical deviations* from any other straight line that could be fitted through the data:

Minimum of $\Sigma(\text{Data} - \text{Fit})^2$.

A "vertical deviation" is the vertical distance from an observed point to the line. Each deviation in the sample is squared and the least-squares line is defined to be the straight line that makes the sum of these squared deviations a minimum:

Data = $a + bX$ + Residuals.

Figure 12.3 (a) illustrates the regression relationship between two variables, $Y$ and $X$. The arithmetic mean of the observed values of $Y$ is denoted by $\bar{y}$. The vertical dashed lines represent the total deviations of each value $y$ from the mean value $\bar{y}$. Part (b) in Figure 12.3 shows a linear least-squares regression line fitted to the observed points.

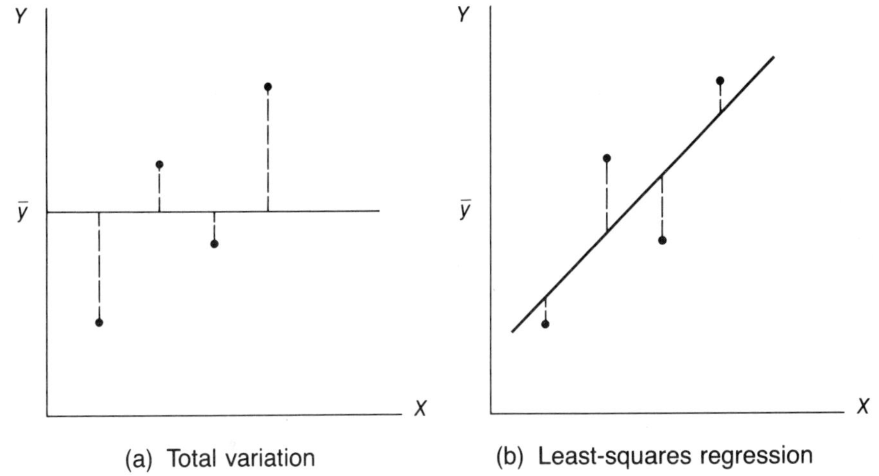


**Figure 12.3** The total variation of $Y$ and the least-squares regression between $Y$ and $X$.

The *total variation* can be expressed in terms of (1) the *variation explained by the regression* and (2) a residual portion called the *unexplained variation*. Figure 12.4 (a) shows the explained variation, which is expressed by the vertical distance between any fitted (predicted) value and the mean or $\hat{y}_i - \bar{y}$. The circumflex (ˆ) over the $y$ is used to represent fitted values determined by a model. Thus, it is also customary to write $a = \hat{\alpha}$ and $b = \hat{\beta}$. Figure 12.4 (b) shows the unexplained or residual variation—the vertical distance between the observed values and the predicted values $(y_i - \hat{y}_i)$.

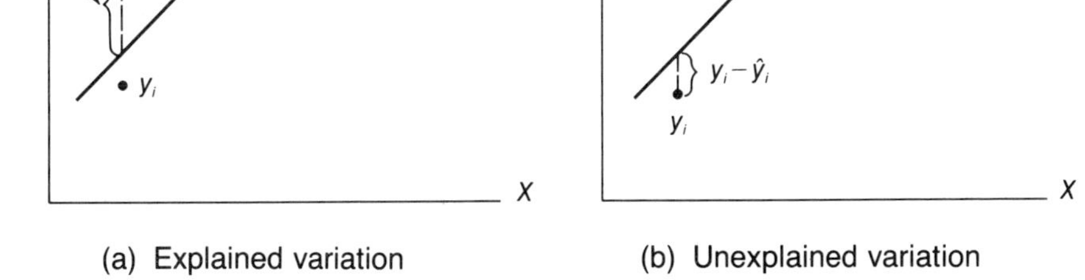

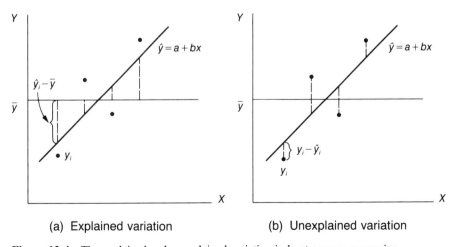

**Figure 12.4** The explained and unexplained variation in least-squares regression.

## An Algebraic Derivation

The following is an elementary algebraic derivation of the coefficients in a simple linear regression model. It is instructive in that it illustrates the nature of the calculation involved in estimating $a$ and $b$. We make temporary use of capital letters to stand for mean values: the expression $\Sigma D_i^2 = \Sigma(Y_i - a - bX_i)^2$ can be minimized and the minimizing solution will define $a$ and $b$. Consider the data pairs $(Y_i, X_i)$ for $(i = l, \ldots, n)$. Let $y_i = Y_i - \overline{Y}$ and $x_i = X_i - \overline{X}$, where $\overline{Y} = \frac{1}{n}\Sigma Y_i$ and $\overline{X} = \frac{1}{n}\Sigma X_i$. The symbol $\Sigma$ denotes the summation over $n$ values. Then

$$
\begin{aligned}
\Sigma D_i^2 &= \Sigma[(y_i + \overline{Y}) - a - b(x_i + \overline{X})]^2 \\
&= \Sigma[(y_i - bx_i) + (\overline{Y} - a - b\overline{X})]^2 \\
&= \Sigma\,(y_i - bx_i)^2 + 2(\overline{Y} - a - b\overline{X})\Sigma y_i \\
&\quad - 2b(\overline{Y} - a - b\overline{X})\Sigma x_i + n(\overline{Y} - a - b\overline{X})^2 \\
&= \Sigma(y_i - bx_i)^2 + n(\overline{Y} - a - b\overline{X})^2,
\end{aligned}
$$

since

$$\Sigma x_i = \Sigma(X_i - \overline{X}) = 0 = \Sigma y_i = \Sigma(Y_i - \overline{Y}).$$

For any value of $b$, $\Sigma D_i^2$ will be minimized by a choice of $a$ when the choice is such as to make the term $n(\overline{Y} - a - b\overline{X})^2$ zero. Hence $a = \overline{Y} - b\overline{X}$. With this choice of $a$, all terms of $\Sigma D_i^2$ except $\Sigma(y_i - bx_i)^2$ vanish, and

$$
\begin{aligned}
\Sigma D_i^2 &= \Sigma(y_i - bx_i)^2 \\
&= \Sigma y_i^2 - 2b\Sigma x_i y_i + b^2\Sigma x_i^2 \\
&= \Sigma y_i^2 + b^2\Sigma x_i^2 - 2b\Sigma x_i y_i.
\end{aligned}
$$

By completing the square for $(y_i - bx_i)$, this becomes

$$
\begin{aligned}
\Sigma D_i^2 &= \Sigma y_i^2 + \left\{\left[b\left(\Sigma x_i^2\right)^{1/2}\right]^2 - 2\left[b\left(\Sigma x_i^2\right)^{1/2}\right]\left[\frac{\Sigma x_i y_i}{(\Sigma x_i^2)^{1/2}}\right] + \right. \\
&\qquad \left.\left[\frac{\Sigma x_i y_i}{(\Sigma x_i^2)^{1/2}}\right]^2\right\} - \left[\frac{\Sigma x_i y_i}{(\Sigma x_i^2)^{1/2}}\right]^2 \\
&= \Sigma y_i^2 + \left[b\left(\Sigma x_i^2\right)^{1/2} - \frac{\Sigma x_i y_i}{(\Sigma x_i^2)^{1/2}}\right]^2 - \left[\frac{\Sigma x_i y_i}{(\Sigma x_i^2)^{1/2}}\right]^2.
\end{aligned}
$$

Since $b$ appears only in the middle squared term, $\Sigma D_i^2$ will be minimized by the choice of $b$ when this term vanishes, or

$$b = (\Sigma x_i y_i)/\Sigma x_i^2.$$

Table 12.1 shows the calculations of $a$ and $b$ for a small set of data.

## NORMAL REGRESSION ASSUMPTIONS

Next, you will want to know if the individual parameter estimates are *statistically significant* (e.g., significantly different from zero). This requires additional assumptions concerning the error term in the regression model. If it can be reasonably assumed that errors are normally distributed, then an extensive theory is applicable. Most statistics books containing chapters on statistical inference cover this area quite well (see, for example, Draper and Smith, 1981).

The normal assumption states that in a random sample of $n$ outcomes $y_1$, $y_2, \ldots, y_n$ of $Y$, the corresponding error terms $\varepsilon_1, \varepsilon_2, \ldots, \varepsilon_n$ arise independently from a common normal distribution (also called Gaussian) with mean 0 and variance $\sigma^2$. In short, the *normal linear regression model* can be expressed by

$$Y_i = \mu_{Y_i} + \varepsilon_i, \qquad \text{where } \varepsilon_i \sim N(0, \sigma^2).$$

**Table 12.1** Example illustrating the calculation of $a$ and $b$ in a simple linear regression equation.

| | $X$ | $Y$ | $y_i = (Y_i - \bar{Y})$ | $x_i = (X_i - \bar{X})$ | $y_i \cdot x_i$ | $x_i^2$ |
|---|---|---|---|---|---|---|
| | 1 | 3 | −5 | −2 | 10 | 4 |
| | 2 | 5 | −3 | −1 | 3 | 1 |
| | 3 | 7 | −1 | 0 | 0 | 0 |
| | 4 | 14 | 6 | 1 | 6 | 1 |
| | 5 | 11 | 3 | 2 | 6 | 4 |
| Sum: | 15 | 40 | | | 25 | 10 |
| Average: | $\bar{X} = 3$ | $\bar{Y} = 8$ | | | | |

$$b = \frac{\Sigma(x_i y_i)}{\Sigma x_i^2} = \frac{25}{10} = 2.5;$$

$$a = \bar{Y} - b\bar{X} = 8 - 2.5(3) = 0.5;$$

Regression equation: $Y = 0.5 + 2.5X$.

This same model can be given in an equivalent way by the assumptions:

- $Y(X)$ is normally distributed about $\mu_{Y(X)} = \alpha + \beta X$.
- The variance of $Y(X)$ is the same for all $X$.
- $n$ observed values of $Y$ are independently distributed.

The normality assumption is widely used among forecasters primarily for the following reasons:

- Observed data are often represented reasonably well by a normal distribution. This can be verified by the use of empirical frequency distributions or various normal probability plotting techniques.
- When data are not normally distributed, it is theoretically possible to find a transformation of the data that renders the distribution normal. While this may not always be practical, sometimes a very simple transformation (such as taking the logarithm or square root of the data) results in residuals that appear approximately normal.
- Practice dictates a choice between what *can* be done and *should* be done. In the absence of anything better, normality usually implies what *can* be done.
- Fortunately, the normality assumption permits you to apply a very extensive (though not always realistic), often simple, and quite elegant set of statistical tests of significance to a multitude of forecasting problems.

## COMPARING ESTIMATION TECHNIQUES

In selecting a reasonable estimator, one goal is to be able to test how the estimates differ from the true (unknown) parameters of the regression line. One set of criteria for choosing the estimates is that they possess certain theoretical properties. Among those, *unbiasedness, efficiency, consistency,* and *minimum mean-squared error* are the most often mentioned in discussions about comparative estimation techniques. While these concepts may have limited direct consequences on forecasting, they are nevertheless of great theoretical value and the practitioner does well to have a familiarity with them.

Strictly speaking, *unbiasedness, consistency,* and *asymptotic efficiency* are properties of estimators of a (real-valued) parameter. You may occasionally run into an unbiased test, a consistent estimator of a vector-valued parameter, or an asymptotically efficient ranking procedure, but they are really generalizations of the same concept when the estimation of a real-valued parameter is involved. Therefore, we will discuss only the basic forms of these concepts.

## An Estimator Is a Random Variable

A typical estimation procedure goes as follows. First, you obtain data from a random experiment. Then you construct a model that relates the data to the physical quantities of interests (parameters) through an error structure. From this model, you can apply some theory to obtain the estimators. These estimators will be expressed as some function of the original raw data. The important point is that the estimators are themselves random variables. Therefore, each estimator should have a probability distribution. The shape of the distribution of an estimator (where it is centered, how it is concentrated, and so on) essentially will tell you everything about this estimator. In a way, unbiasedness, consistency, and asymptotic efficiency can be viewed as a technical way of describing the desirable shapes of the distributions of estimators.

## Unbiasedness

In Figure 12.5, $f(x;\theta)$ describes the density function of an estimator $\delta$ of the unknown parameter $\theta$. If you place a wedge along the $x$-axis, you can see that, at some point, the wedge will "balance" the density function. This balancing point is the expected

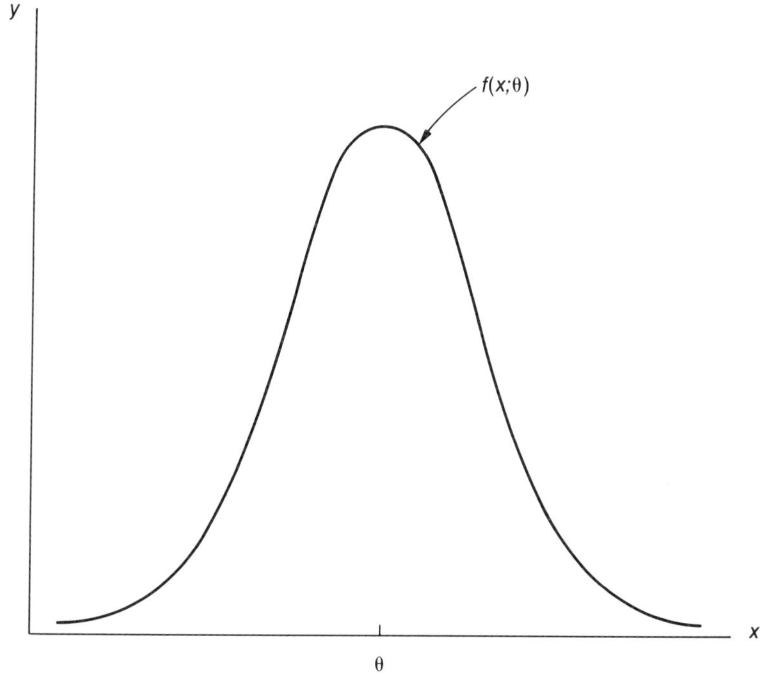


**Figure 12.5** Unbiasedness of an estimator.

value of the estimator $\delta$, denoted by $E(\delta)$. An estimator $\delta$ is an *unbiased* estimator of $\theta$ if this balancing point *happens to be* $\theta$; in symbols, $E(\delta) = \theta$.

Unbiasedness is a very restrictive property to require of an estimator. It is a convenient property to have if it comes naturally in the theory. For example, the least-squares criterion in regression leads to unbiased estimators.

### Consistency

As more and more observations are accumulated, the estimators should become better and better. Consistency is merely a formal statement of this property. Let $\delta_n$ denote the estimator of $\theta$ based on $n$ observations. Figure 12.6 shows the distribution $f_n(x;\theta)$ of $\delta_n$ for $n = 10$ and $n = 100$. If, as $n \to \infty$, $\delta_n \to \theta$ (in some formally defined way), then $\delta_n$ is said to be a *consistent* estimator of $\theta$. In Figure 12.6, this means $f_{100}(x;\theta)$ is much narrower than $f_{10}(x;\theta)$; it is a lot easier to have a typical $\delta_{100}$ close to $\theta$ than to have a typical $\delta_{10}$ close to $\theta$.

### Asymptotic Efficiency

If the density $f_n(x;\theta)$ of $\delta_n$ becomes narrower as $n$ increases, then $\delta_n$ is likely to be consistent. Some other estimator, say $d_n$, of $\theta$ may have the same property, however. How does one compare $\delta_n$ and $d_n$? Let $g_n(x;\theta)$ denote the density of $d_n$. If, for large values of $n$ at least, $f_n(x;\theta)$ is always narrower than $g_n(x;\theta)$, then $\delta_n$ is likely to be closer to $\theta$ than $d_n$. When this is so, $\delta_n$ is said to be *asymptotically* (this means as $n \to \infty$) more *efficient* than $d_n$. If an estimator $\delta_n$ beats or ties every other $d_n$ in this sense, $\delta_n$ is said to be an asymptotically efficient estimator of $\theta$. Since the spread of $f_n(x;\theta)$ is usually measured by $\text{Var}(\delta_n)$, $\delta_n$ is said to be *asymptotically efficient* if

$$\frac{\text{Var}(\delta_n)}{\text{Var}(d_n)} \leqslant 1$$

for all other $d_n$ and all large values of $n$.

In summary, an estimate or statistic is *unbiased* if its expected value is equal to the true value. An unbiased estimate is *efficient* if its variance is smaller than the variance of any other estimate. An estimate is *consistent* if it comes close in some sense to the true value of the parameter as the sample size becomes arbitrarily large.

### Robustness of Efficiency

There are a variety of instances where observed data do not satisfy the normality assumption:

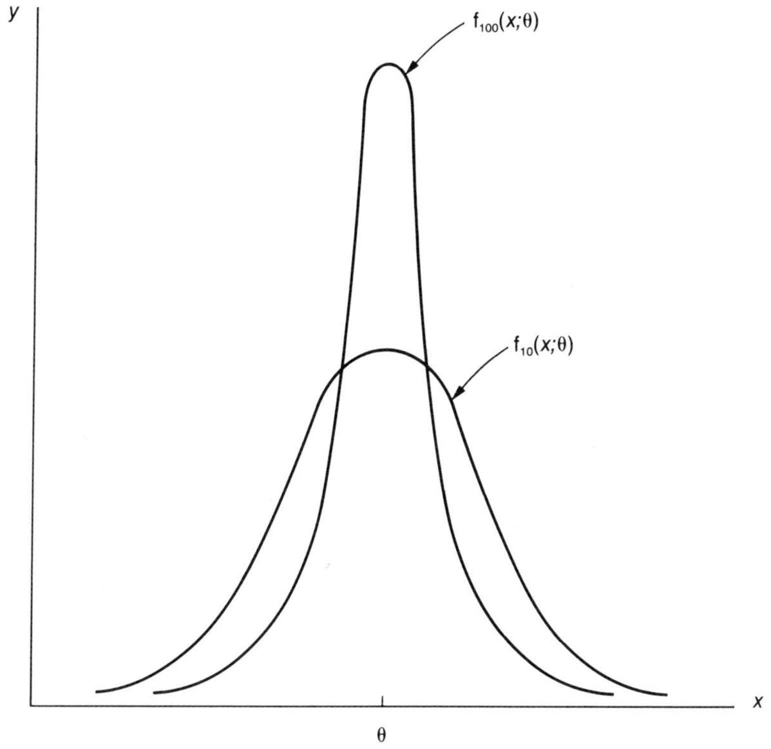


**Figure 12.6** Consistency of an estimator.

- When data arise from discrete measurements (such as stock prices quoted to the nearest ⅛) or are based on counts. Then, their range of values cannot be every number between plus and minus infinity (by "infinity" is meant an arbitrary large number).
- When data distributions are skewed or have a greater proportion of extreme values (heavier tail) than a normal population.

In such cases a statistic such as the arithmetic mean can give misleading results. In addition, confidence intervals for the mean may be stated too conservatively. What is desired, in practice, are procedures that are robust against nonnormal tails in the data distribution, in the sense that they give rise to estimates that are much better than those based on normality. When normality cannot be achieved, robust regression (Chapter 17) may offer some protection against drawing incorrect inferences about the model.

There appear to be many meanings to the word "robustness" in modern statistical literature. In the context of estimation, *robustness of efficiency* means that parameter estimates are highly efficient not only under idealized (usually normal) conditions but also under a wide class of nonstandard circumstances. The Princeton Robustness Study (Andrews et al., 1972) was an early effort to analyze systematically this concept for estimates of location. The bisquare procedure introduced in Chapter 17, for example, has high robust efficiency for the location of a symmetrical distribution. Also, estimates that have robust efficiency are often very resistant to outliers. This can be a very valuable consideration, since real-life data are frequently nonnormal and possess hard-to-detect outlying observations.

## IMPORTANT DISTRIBUTION RESULTS

References are made throughout this book to statistical significance tests based on the normal, Student's, chi-squared, and $F$-probability distributions. The following results point to why certain probability distributions result for significance tests arising from the normality assumption in regression errors.

1. If $Z_1, Z_2, \ldots, Z_n$ are normally and independently distributed random variables with mean $\mu_i$ and variance $\sigma_i^2$, then the sum $Z = \Sigma k_i Z_i$ (where the $k_i$ are constants) is also distributed normally with mean $\Sigma k_i \mu_i$ and variance $\Sigma k_i^2 \sigma_i^2$.
2. If $Z_1, Z_2, \ldots, Z_n$ are normally and independently distributed "normalized" variables with mean equal to zero and variance equal to one, then the $\Sigma Z_i^2$ follows a chi-squared distribution with $n$ degrees of freedom.
3. If $S_1, S_2$ are independently distributed random variables each following a chi-squared distribution with $k_1$ and $k_2$ degrees of freedom respectively, then

$$F = \frac{S_1/k_1}{S_2/k_2}$$

has an $F$-distribution with $(k_1, k_2)$ degrees of freedom.

Certain significance tests for summary statistics and those derived from normal regression theory utilize the above results. They may be found in any text on mathematical statistics or statistical inference, such as Draper and Smith (1981).

## SUMMARY

The discussion in this chapter will give you most of the theoretical underpinnings required for applying regression theory to forecasting problems. It is worth noting that:

- Linear regression theory is basic to forecasting.
- Regression models can be used to describe a relationship between the variable to be forecast and one (or more) related variable(s).
- The method of least squares for parameter estimation, together with normality assumptions, provides the classical statistical formulas from which many forecasting techniques are derived.

In choosing from among estimation techniques, a variety of theoretical criteria are often taken into account. The ordinary least-squares estimators in normal regression theory can be shown to have the following characteristics:

- An estimator is unbiased if its expected value is the unknown parameter.
- Consistency is the property of an estimator whereby the distribution of the estimator becomes narrower as the sample size increases.
- An estimator is efficient if its variance is less than the variance of any other estimator.

## USEFUL READING

ANDREWS, D. F., P. J. BICKEL, F. R. HAMPEL, P. J. HUBER, W. H. ROGERS, and J. W. TUKEY (1972). *Robust Estimates of Location: Survey and Advances*. Princeton, NJ: Princeton University Press.

DRAPER, N. R., and H. SMITH (1981). *Applied Regression Analysis*. 2nd ed. New York, NY: John Wiley and Sons.

MOSTELLER, F., and J. W. TUKEY (1977). *Data Analysis and Regression*. Reading, MA: Addison-Wesley Publishing Co.

CHAPTER **13**

# Interpreting Regression Output

The ordinary least-squares methodology was presented in the previous chapter for simple linear regression models with the normality assumption. In this chapter, emphasis is placed on the interpretation of the basic regression output from such models. These interpretations include:

- The standard error of the estimate as a measure of the variability about the regression function.
- The *R*-squared statistic as a measure of the goodness-of-fit.
- The *t*-statistic as a measure of the statistical significance of a regression coefficient.
- The *F*-statistic as a measure of the overall significance of the regression.
- The D-W statistic *d* for time series, to test for first-order autocorrelation.

Sample computer printouts from a regression software package will illustrate these and will be discussed. Lastly, a simple model relating the demand for business telephones to employment data will be used to illustrate its use as a forecasting tool.

## SUMMARY STATISTICS ON A COMPUTER PRINTOUT

The illustrative software package to be discussed is STATLIB, which was developed by Bell Telephone Laboratories for proprietary use within the Bell System. It is now available through Bell Laboratories (Brelsford and Relles, 1981). It contains a very extensive package of statistical and regression routines, only a few of which will be presented here. Before executing any of these programs, it is necessary to create data files (time series, a data matrix, or multidimensional tables). These files contain the observed values for the dependent and independent variables. In the examples it will be assumed that these files have already been created.

## The Printout

In Chapter 12 a scatter diagram of monthly telephone toll revenues against the number of toll messages generating those revenues was shown. Figure 13.1 is a STATLIB printout which shows the summary statistics from a simple linear regression model relating toll revenues as a function of toll messages. Whether it may be appropriate to transform the data first (such as with logarithms or the Box-Cox transformation) is not considered at this point. Let's examine some details of Figure 13.1.

The SAMPLE SIZE (= 128) refers to the *number of observations* used in the regression. In this case, the regression was performed over 128 months from January 1969 through August 1979. For a weighted regression, the SUM OF WEIGHTS may be less than the sample size, since outliers may receive less than their full weight (e.g., weight = 0.5 versus 1.0 for nonextreme observations). For ordinary least-squares regression, the SUM OF WEIGHTS equals the SAMPLE SIZE.

The ESTIMATED STD DEV (= 2.37), also called the *standard error of the estimate,* is a measure of the variability about the fitted regression function. Since

```
SAMPLE SIZE . . . . . . . . . .      128
SUM OF WEIGHTS . . . . . . . .       1.2800D+02
ESTIMATED STD DEV . . . . .          2.3683D+00
R SQUARED . . . . . . . . . .        0.9409
```

| VARIABLE | COEFFICIENT | ESTD STD DEV | T |
|---|---|---|---|
| 0 | -1.8873D+00 | 9.5882D-01 | -1.9684 |
| 2 MSG .... | 3.4244D+00 | 7.6449D-02 | 44.7940 |
| 1 REV .... | DEPENDENT VARIABLE | | |

ANALYSIS OF VARIANCE

| SOURCE | DF | SS | MS | F |
|---|---|---|---|---|
| REGRESSION | 1 | 1.1254D+04 | 1.1254D+04 | 2006.499 |
| ERROR | 126 | 7.0670D+02 | 5.6087D+00 | |
| TOTAL | 127 | 1.1961D+04 | | |

**Figure 13.1** Regression output for a simple linear regression model relating telephone toll revenues (REV) as a function of toll messages (MSG).

this statistic is related to the magnitude of the unexplained variation, a desired objective is to find a model that has the lowest estimated standard deviation of the residuals.

One note of caution is that the ESTIMATED STD DEV can only be used to compare models when the dependent variable is of the *same form*. For example, the standard deviation of the residuals of a model built on the sales of a product cannot be directly compared to the same statistic for a model built on the logarithms of the sales of the product. The latter statistic will have a different interpretation because of the transformation.

The $R$-SQUARED statistic ($= 0.94$), also called the *coefficient of determination,* is the percent of the total variation about the mean value of $Y$ that is explainable by performing a linear regression on $X$. In this case, 94 percent of the revenue variation about the mean is explained by the message data. This is known as a measure of the *goodness-of-fit* of the regression.

On the printout shown in Figure 13.1, the variable 0 represents the constant in the linear equation. The COEFFICIENT of this constant is $-1.8873D + 00$, which means that the estimated intercept is $-1.89$. The variable 2 (MSG) is the independent variable. Its coefficient is $3.4244D + 00$, which means that the regression coefficient is 3.42. The variable 1 (REV) is the dependent variable.

The column headed by ESTD STD DEV represents the estimated standard deviation of the regression coefficients. With rounding, $9.5882D - 01$ means 0.96 ($D - 01 = 10^{-1}$) and $7.6449D - 02$ means 0.08 ($D - 02 = 10^{-2}$). The ratio of coefficients to estimated standard deviations produces the $t$-statistics in the "T" column. These statistics are shown in parentheses beneath the corresponding coefficient estimates in the following equation:

$$\begin{aligned} \text{REV} = \underset{(-1.97)}{-1.89} + \underset{(44.8)}{3.42}\text{MSG} \end{aligned}$$

where "REV" is revenues and "MSG" is messages.

## The *R*-Squared Statistic

The $R$-squared statistic is derived from the analysis of variance (ANOVA) part of Figure 13.1. It has the following derivation: The "sum of squares about the mean" (TOTAL SS) can be expressed as the sum of two other terms, namely, the "sum of squares about regression" (unexplained variation—the ERROR SS entry in the table) and the "sum of squares due to regression" (explained variation—the REGRESSION SS entry). Here regression is used in the sense of the fitted equation.

The *sum of squares about the mean* is

$$\begin{aligned} \Sigma(y_i - \bar{y})^2 &= \Sigma[(y_i - \hat{y}_i) + (\hat{y}_i - \bar{y})]^2 \\ &= \Sigma(y_i - \hat{y}_i)^2 + 2\Sigma(y_i - \hat{y}_i)(\hat{y}_i - \bar{y}) + \Sigma(\hat{y}_i - \bar{y})^2. \end{aligned}$$

It is illustrative to demonstrate the decomposition for a simple linear regression. The middle term equals zero, since

$$\begin{aligned}\Sigma(y_i - \hat{y}_i)(\hat{y}_i - \bar{y}) &= \Sigma[y_i - \bar{y} - b(x_i - \bar{x})][b(x_i - \bar{x})] \\ &= b\Sigma y_i(x_i - \bar{x}) - b^2\Sigma(x_i - \bar{x})^2 \\ &= b\Sigma b(x_i - \bar{x})^2 - b^2\Sigma(x_i - \bar{x})^2 \\ &= 0.\end{aligned}$$

Hence

| | | | | |
|---|---|---|---|---|
| $\Sigma(y_i - \bar{y})^2$ | = | $\Sigma(y_i - \hat{y}_i)^2$ | + | $\Sigma(\hat{y}_i - \bar{y})^2$ |
| [TOTAL SS on $(n - 1)$ degrees of freedom] | = | [ERROR SS on $(n - 2)$ degrees of freedom] | + | [REGRESSION SS on 1 degree of freedom] |

Then

$$\begin{aligned}R^2 &= \frac{\text{Explained variation}}{\text{Total variation}} \\ &= (\text{TOTAL SS} - \text{ERROR SS})/\text{TOTAL SS}.\end{aligned}$$

In the case of *simple* linear regression, the relationship between $R$-squared and the square of the sample product moment correlation coefficient (a measure of association) is quite simple; they are the same. However, for multiple linear regression there is more than one correlation coefficient, so one doesn't know what to compare $R$-squared with.

It is not necessarily true that a high $R$-squared statistic implies that you have a good model. On the other hand, you would expect "good" models to have a reasonably high value for $R$-squared. Notice that $R$-squared can never be negative or exceed unity.

## The *t*-Statistic

A $t$-statistic measures the statistical significance of the regression coefficient for an independent variable. The $t$-ratio follows a *Student's t-distribution* that looks very similar to the bellshaped normal distribution (Figure 13.2). However, a $t$-distribution is shorter and fatter, and its variance $[= \nu/(\nu - 2)]$ is larger than that of the standard normal distribution $(= 1)$. For each positive integer $\nu$, called the degrees of freedom, there corresponds a different $t$-distribution.

With $n < 30$, the observed $t$-value should be greater than approximately 2.0 in absolute value for significance at the 95 percent level (Appendix A, Table 2). When

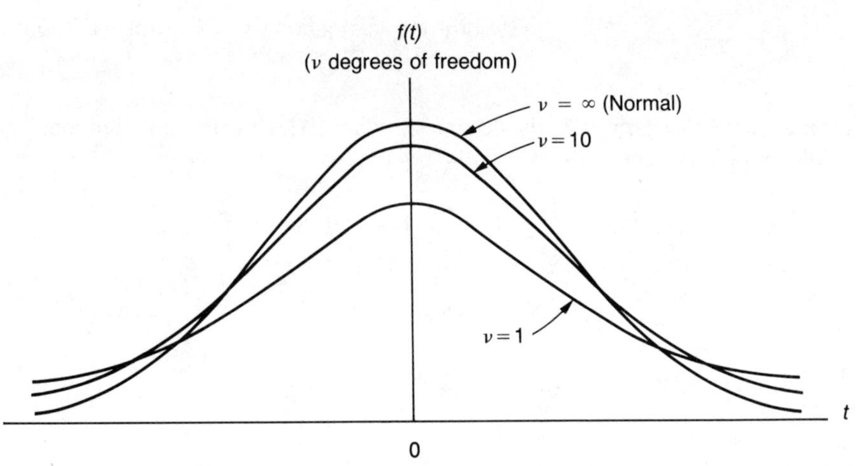


**Figure 13.2** Comparison of two $t$-distributions with a standard normal distribution ($\upsilon$ = 20).

this is the case, you can reject the null hypothesis that the regression coefficient is zero. A statistically significant value not equal to zero is said to exist for the coefficient. Thus, in Figure 13.1, both observed $t$-values in the "T" column are regarded as significant. This cannot be interpreted as proof of a cause-and-effect relationship between the dependent and independent variables, however. For example, each variable may be related to a third (possibly causally linked) factor and only coincidentally related to each other.

## The *F*-Statistic

The analysis of variance (ANOVA) table in the lower part of Figure 13.1 emphasizes a comparison of the average sum-of-squared deviations explained by the regression with the unexplained sum-of-squared deviations. This comparison forms the basis for the $F$-test:

$$F = \frac{\text{Mean square due to regression}}{\text{Mean square of errors}} = \frac{\text{MS REGRESSION entry in table}}{\text{MS ERROR entry in table}}$$
$$= 11{,}254/5.61 = 2006.$$

where

$$\text{MS REGRESSION} = \frac{\text{Sum of squares due to regression}}{\text{Degrees of freedom in regression}}$$
$$= \Sigma(\hat{y}_i - \bar{y}_i)^2/(m - 1)$$
$$= 11{,}254/1,$$

and

$$\text{MS ERROR} = \frac{\text{Sum of squares of errors}}{\text{Degrees of freedom in errors}}$$
$$= \Sigma(y_i - \hat{y}_i)^2/(n - m)$$
$$= 706.70/126 = 5.61.$$

Here $m$ = number of coefficients in the model, including the constant. All sums are from 1 to $n$.

For a simple linear regression, $m = 2$, and

$$F = \frac{\Sigma(\hat{y}_i - \bar{y})^2/1}{\Sigma(y_i - \hat{y}_i)^2/(n - 2)}.$$

If there is no relationship between $Y$ and $X$, then $\hat{y} = \bar{y}$ and $F$ equals zero.

The calculated $F$-statistic is compared to the tabular value (Appendix A, Table 4) for the appropriate degrees of freedom. For a simple linear regression, $F = t^2$, and a value of $F$ greater than approximately 4.0 indicates significance at the 95 percent confidence level. For a multiple linear regression, one must use the $F$-table to determine if the overall regression is significant.

The rationale for the $F$-test is that if there is a relationship between the dependent and independent variables, the variation of the estimated values from the observed values will be less than the variation between the estimated values and the mean value of $Y$; i.e., the $F$-ratio will be significantly different from 1.0.

## The D-W Statistic

In time series forecasting, it is not unusual to be in violation of normal regression assumptions because of *autocorrelated errors;* hence, it is important to be able to test for their presence. The Durbin-Watson (abbreviated as D-W) statistic, due to Durbin and Watson (1950, 1951), is the traditional statistic used to test for autocorrelation (*first-order only!*). The ordinary correlogram is usually more informative in assessing the nature of autocorrelation.

The D-W statistic $d$ has the formula

$$d = \sum_{t=2}^{n} (\hat{\varepsilon}_t - \hat{\varepsilon}_{t-1})^2 \Big/ \sum_{t=2}^{n} \hat{\varepsilon}_t^2.$$

If time series residuals $\{\hat{\varepsilon}_t, t = 1, \ldots, n\}$ are positively correlated, the absolute value of $\hat{\varepsilon}_t - \hat{\varepsilon}_{t-1}$ will tend to be small relative to the absolute value of $\hat{\varepsilon}_t$. If the residuals are negatively correlated, the absolute value of $\hat{\varepsilon}_t - \hat{\varepsilon}_{t-1}$ will tend to be large relative to the absolute value of $\hat{\varepsilon}_t$. Therefore $d$ will tend to be small (near 1.0) for positively correlated residuals, large (near 4.0) for negatively correlated residuals, and approximately equal to 2.0 for random residuals.

The sampling distribution of $d$ depends on the values of the independent variable $x_t$ in the sample. Therefore, the test is only able to provide upper ($d_u$) and lower ($d_l$) limits for significance testing (Appendix A, Table 5). One either accepts the null hypothesis of zero autocorrelation or rejects it in favor of *first-order* autocorrelation. If $d < d_l$, the zero correlation hypothesis is rejected in favor of *first-order* positive autocorrelation. If $d_l < d < d_u$, the test is inconclusive. If $d > 4 - d_l$, the zero autocorrelation hypothesis is rejected in favor of *first-order* negative autocorrelation.

It can be shown that $d$ is closely tied to the first autocorrelation coefficient $r_1$ of the correlogram of the residuals. In fact, $d \simeq 2(1 - r_1)$. Thus, with the use of the computer, it is just as simple to plot the correlogram of the residuals of the model and assess the overall autocorrelation structure. The patterns of the correlogram will be discussed extensively in connection with the identification of ARIMA models in *The Professional Forecaster.*

In models in which the residuals are autocorrelated, two main consequences of using ordinary least squares (OLS) are:

- Sampling variances of the regression coefficients are underestimated and invalid.
- Forecasts have variances that are too large.

In OLS estimation, the calculated acceptance regions or confidence intervals are narrower than they should be for a specified level of significance. This leads to a false conclusion that the parameter estimates are more precise than they actually are. There will be a tendency to accept a variable as significant when it is not, and this may result in a misspecified model.

There are several approaches to try to reduce the effects of autocorrelation:

- Model the first differences or the year-over-year percent changes of the time series.
- Transform the data, basing this on the assumed nature of the autocorrelated structure.
- Include an autoregressive term (the value one period back) in a multiple linear regression model.
- Build an ARIMA model on the residuals of the regression model.

The first approach will be illustrated in a forecasting application for the main gain–housing starts data in Chapter 20. The other approaches require some advanced techniques to be covered in *The Professional Forecaster.*

## A MEASURE OF ASSOCIATION

At times you may not be interested in making a forecast of a dependent variable from a forecast of an independent variable. Rather, you may be interested in simply obtaining a measure of association or correlation between two variables.

### Interchanging *X* and *Y*

It is not uncommon for beginning forecasters to think that the regression of $X$ on $Y$ and the regression of $Y$ on $X$ should give equivalent inferences about the relationships between $X$ and $Y$, and $Y$ and $X$. For example, the regression analysis for the telephone revenue-message data shows that the toll revenue $Y$ and the toll messages $X$ have a linear relationship estimated by the equation

$$\begin{aligned}\hat{Y} &= a_1 + b_1X \\ &= -1.89 + 3.42X.\end{aligned}$$

By interchanging the dependent and independent variables, and looking at the intercept and slope estimates from the least-squares fit in Figure 13.3, you can see that the regression equation for toll messages $X$ against toll revenues $Y$ becomes

$$\begin{aligned}\hat{X} &= a_2 + b_2Y \\ &= 1.24 + 0.27Y.\end{aligned}$$

The slope $b_1 = 3.42$ for the revenue equation ($\hat{Y}$) is not equal to the reciprocal of the slope $b_2 = 0.27$ for the message equation ($\hat{X}$), but why?

The reason why these two regressions give different results is that the line obtained by minimizing the sum-of-squared *vertical* deviations is different from the line derived by minimizing the sum-of-squared *horizontal* deviations (Figure 13.4).

| | |
|---|---|
| SAMPLE SIZE . . . . . . . . . . | 128 |
| SUM OF WEIGHTS . . . . . . . . | 1.2800D+02 |
| ESTIMATED STD DEV . . . . . . | 6.7084D-01 |
| R SQUARED . . . . . . . . . . | 0.9409 |

| VARIABLE | COEFFICIENT | ESTD STD DEV | T |
|---|---|---|---|
| 0 | 1.2417D+00 | 2.5258D-01 | 4.9163 |
| 2 REV . . . . | 2.7476D-01 | 6.1340D-03 | 44.7940 |
| 1 MSG . . . | DEPENDENT VARIABLE | | |

ANALYSIS OF VARIANCE

| SOURCE | DF | SS | MS | F |
|---|---|---|---|---|
| REGRESSION | 1 | 9.0297D+02 | 9.0297D+02 | 2006.499 |
| ERROR | 126 | 5.6703D+01 | 4.5002D-01 | |
| TOTAL | 127 | 9.5967D+02 | | |

**Figure 13.3** Regression output for a (unrealistic) simple linear regression model relating toll messages (MSG) as a function of toll revenues (REV).

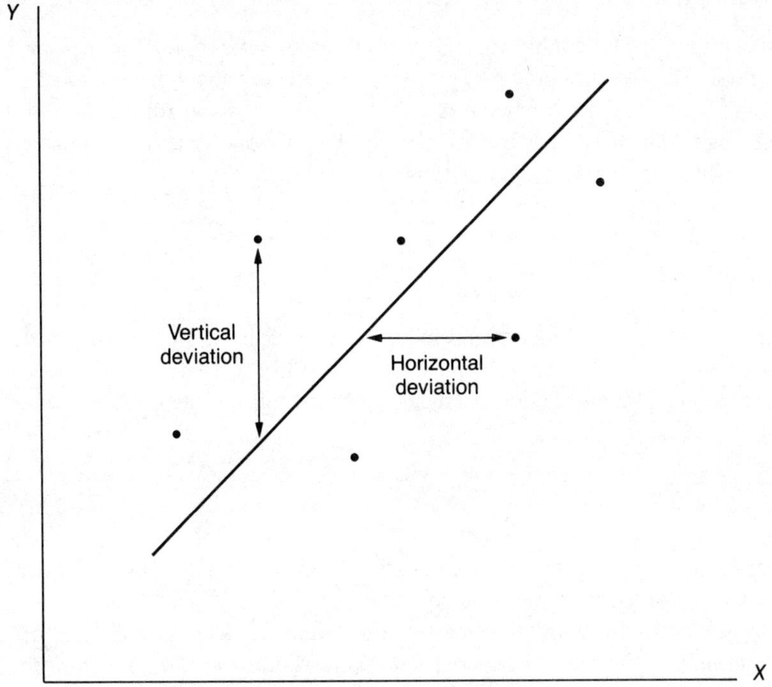


**Figure 13.4** Vertical versus horizontal deviations in ordinary least-squares regression.

This property of least squares is often misunderstood by practitioners, and this misunderstanding can lead to the misuse of regression equations.

When the variables $X$ and $Y$ are nearly independent, $b_1$ and $b_2$ are very small and the two regression lines are almost at right angles. On the other hand, when they are so closely related that the one can be taken to determine the other absolutely, the two regression lines coincide. In this case $b_1 = 1/b_2$. From this observation arises the notion of *linear correlation*.

The measure of the strength of the relationship between $X$ and $Y$ would seem to depend on the *angle* between the two regression lines. The most common measure of the strength of the relationship is the *sample product moment correlation coefficient:*

$$r = \frac{\sum_{i=1}^{n} (y_i - \bar{y})(x_i - \bar{x})}{\left[\sum_{i=1}^{n} (y_i - \bar{y})^2 \sum_{i=1}^{n} (x_i - \bar{x})^2\right]^{1/2}}.$$

Since $r^2 = b_1 b_2$, it can be seen that $r = 0$ when there is no association, and $r^2 = 1$ when one variable determines the other. The coefficient $r$ ranges from $-1$ to

+1. It is clear from the formula that $r$ is the same no matter which variable is used to predict the other.

When two series have a strong positive correlation, the scatter diagram has a scatter of points along a line of positive slope. A negative correlation shows up as a scatter of points along a line with negative slope.

## The Correlation Matrix

The *correlation matrix* gives a representation of the degree of correlation when there is more than one variable. This matrix is an array of all sample correlation coefficients between pairs of variables. Table 13.1 shows a correlation matrix for the toll revenues (REV), toll messages (MSG), business telephones (BMT), and nonfarm employment (NFRM) in the telecommunications forecasting example that has been used throughout this book.

The diagonal of a correlation matrix consists of ones, since each variable is perfectly correlated with itself. The variables are numbered 1 through 4, and each appears in a row and a column. The intersection of a row and a column is the correlation coefficient relating the row variable to the column variable. For example, the coefficient of correlation between toll revenues and toll messages is high (= 0.96). The business telephones have a positive correlation with toll messages (= 0.77) and a low correlation with nonfarm employment (= 0.015). The negative but very small correlations of the employment data with revenues and messages is not intuitively satisfying; however, their smallness suggests that this is probably not significant.

Some further analysis will enhance your understanding of the nature of the correlation among these variables. Figure 13.5 shows a low-resolution display or star-chart of the year-over-year percent changes for these four variables in the telecommunications example. For this segment of the data, the percent changes for

**Table 13.1** Correlation matrix for the four time series in the telecommunications example. REV = toll revenues, MSG = toll messages, BMT = business telephones, and NFRM = nonfarm employment.

| | 1 | 2 | 3 | 4 |
|---|---|---|---|---|
| 1 REV | 1.000 | | | |
| 2 MSG | 0.963 | 1.000 | | |
| 3 BMT | 0.765 | 0.772 | 1.000 | |
| 4 NFRM | −0.128 | −0.105 | 0.015 | 1.000 |

```
VBL:          1 PCTREV          2 PCTMSG          3 PCTBMT          4 PCTNFRM
MIN:               2.37              0.02             -1.38             -4.07
MAX:              17.34             15.46              2.27              3.14

JAN 1970  86 *********    67 *******      37 ****         76 ********
FEB 1970  99 **********   52 ******       37 ****         82 *********
MAR 1970  76 ********     99 **********   37 ****         72 ********
APR 1970  73 ********     67 *******      37 ****         68 *******
MAY 1970  53 ******       70 ********     37 ****         58 ******
JUN 1970  66 *******      76 ********     37 ****         54 ******
JUL 1970  18 **           63 *******      37 ****         46 *****
AUG 1970  37 ****         56 ******       37 ****         38 ****
SEP 1970  36 ****         61 *******      37 ****         39 ****
OCT 1970  14 **           34 ****         37 ****         25 ***
NOV 1970  22 ***          62 *******      37 ****         26 ***
DEC 1970  25 ***          48 *****        37 ****         26 ***
JAN 1971  37 ****         29 ***          99 **********   29 ***
FEB 1971  29 ***          65 *******      93 **********   24 ***
MAR 1971  16 **           43 *****        85 *********    22 ***
APR 1971  22 ***          55 ******       77 ********     18 **
MAY 1971  33 ****         37 ****         65 *******      25 ***
JUN 1971  18 **           50 ******       67 *******      24 ***
JUL 1971  54 ******       33 ****         59 ******       29 ***
AUG 1971  51 ******       58 ******       54 ******       24 ***
SEP 1971  31 ****         48 *****        53 ******       24 ***
OCT 1971  21 ***          39 ****         50 ******       32 ****
NOV 1971  69 *******      75 ********     44 *****        36 ****
DEC 1971  49 *****        35 ****         42 *****        38 ****
JAN 1972  70 ********     79 ********     47 *****        44 *****
FEB 1972  55 ******       84 *********    41 *****        44 *****
MAR 1972  69 *******      56 ******       46 *****        52 ******
APR 1972  24 ***          37 ****         49 *****        55 ******
MAY 1972  75 ********     81 *********    51 ******       57 ******
JUN 1972  48 *****        66 *******      50 ******       58 ******
JUL 1972  64 *******      51 ******       58 ******       50 ******
AUG 1972  80 *********    72 ********     66 *******      68 *******
SEP 1972  53 ******       49 *****        65 *******      70 ********
OCT 1972  70 ********     89 *********    72 ********     83 *********
NOV 1972  38 ****         60 *******      75 ********     86 *********
DEC 1972  59 ******       62 *******      76 ********     84 *********
JAN 1973  63 *******      75 ********     79 ********     78 ********
FEB 1973  45 *****        45 *****        85 *********    81 *********
MAR 1973  38 ****         58 ******       80 *********    76 ********
APR 1973  83 *********    83 *********    77 ********     76 ********
MAY 1973  38 ****         67 *******      77 ********     73 ********
JUN 1973  39 ****         37 ****         84 *********    76 ********
JUL 1973  54 ******       68 *******      82 *********    82 *********
AUG 1973  35 ****         61 *******      85 *********    77 ********
SEP 1973  41 *****        50 ******       82 *********    76 ********
OCT 1973  48 *****        58 ******       80 *********    68 *******
NOV 1973  24 ***          55 ******       79 ********     67 *******
DEC 1973  28 ***          48 *****        79 ********     63 *******
JAN 1974   0 *            37 ****         74 ********     58 ******
FEB 1974  39 ****         34 ****         71 ********     52 ******
MAR 1974  23 ***          31 ****         67 *******      49 *****
APR 1974  27 ***          46 *****        69 *******      49 *****
MAY 1974  33 ****         44 *****        64 *******      52 ******
JUN 1974  55 ******       31 ****         62 *******      51 ******
JUL 1974  44 *****        49 *****        56 ******       52 ******
AUG 1974  41 *****        23 ***          52 ******       48 *****
```

**Figure 13.5** Low-resolution display of the percent changes for toll revenues (PCTREV), toll messages (PCTMSG), business telephones (PCTBMT), and nonfarm employment (PCTNFRM).

| VBL: | 1 REV | | 2 MSG | | 3 BMT | | 4 NFRM | |
|---|---|---|---|---|---|---|---|---|
| MIN: | 25.16 | | 8.24 | | 491.20 | | 6645.00 | |
| MAX: | 63.42 | | 18.50 | | 523.94 | | 7282.00 | |
| JAN 1970 | 0 | * | 1 | * | 0 | * | 65 | ******* |
| FEB 1970 | 12 | ** | 0 | * | 5 | * | 70 | ******** |
| MAR 1970 | 10 | ** | 11 | ** | 13 | ** | 80 | ********* |
| APR 1970 | 16 | ** | 6 | * | 20 | *** | 87 | ********* |
| MAY 1970 | 10 | ** | 8 | * | 25 | *** | 90 | ********** |
| JUN 1970 | 11 | ** | 13 | ** | 23 | *** | 99 | ********** |
| JUL 1970 | 1 | * | 6 | * | 25 | *** | 85 | ********* |
| AUG 1970 | 7 | * | 10 | ** | 27 | *** | 85 | ********* |
| SEP 1970 | 10 | ** | 12 | ** | 35 | **** | 77 | ******** |
| OCT 1970 | 12 | ** | 10 | ** | 34 | **** | 72 | ******** |
| NOV 1970 | 14 | ** | 6 | * | 34 | **** | 71 | ******** |
| DEC 1970 | 9 | * | 8 | * | 34 | **** | 73 | ******** |
| JAN 1971 | 5 | * | 5 | * | 34 | **** | 44 | ***** |
| FEB 1971 | 17 | ** | 8 | * | 36 | **** | 44 | ***** |
| MAR 1971 | 13 | ** | 17 | ** | 39 | **** | 52 | ****** |
| APR 1971 | 21 | *** | 14 | ** | 43 | ***** | 56 | ****** |
| MAY 1971 | 16 | ** | 13 | ** | 41 | ***** | 64 | ******* |
| JUN 1971 | 15 | ** | 20 | *** | 40 | ***** | 73 | ******** |
| JUL 1971 | 9 | * | 11 | ** | 37 | **** | 63 | ******* |
| AUG 1971 | 14 | ** | 18 | ** | 36 | **** | 59 | ****** |
| SEP 1971 | 15 | ** | 19 | ** | 44 | ***** | 51 | ****** |
| OCT 1971 | 16 | ** | 16 | ** | 41 | ***** | 52 | ****** |
| NOV 1971 | 24 | *** | 17 | ** | 38 | **** | 55 | ****** |
| DEC 1971 | 16 | ** | 13 | ** | 37 | **** | 59 | ****** |
| JAN 1972 | 14 | ** | 15 | ** | 39 | **** | 34 | **** |
| FEB 1972 | 26 | *** | 19 | ** | 38 | **** | 35 | **** |
| MAR 1972 | 24 | *** | 25 | *** | 44 | ***** | 49 | ***** |
| APR 1972 | 26 | *** | 19 | ** | 49 | ***** | 55 | ****** |
| MAY 1972 | 27 | *** | 25 | *** | 49 | ***** | 65 | ******* |
| JUN 1972 | 23 | *** | 30 | **** | 47 | ***** | 74 | ******** |
| JUL 1972 | 18 | ** | 18 | ** | 49 | ***** | 58 | ****** |
| AUG 1972 | 25 | *** | 30 | **** | 52 | ****** | 68 | ******* |
| SEP 1972 | 24 | *** | 26 | *** | 60 | ******* | 62 | ******* |
| OCT 1972 | 27 | *** | 29 | *** | 61 | ******* | 74 | ******** |
| NOV 1972 | 31 | **** | 26 | *** | 59 | ****** | 79 | ******** |
| DEC 1972 | 25 | *** | 22 | *** | 58 | ****** | 81 | ********* |
| JAN 1973 | 23 | *** | 26 | *** | 62 | ******* | 52 | ****** |
| FEB 1973 | 35 | **** | 26 | *** | 65 | ******* | 54 | ****** |
| MAR 1973 | 31 | **** | 35 | **** | 68 | ******* | 64 | ******* |
| APR 1973 | 40 | ***** | 32 | **** | 72 | ******** | 71 | ******** |
| MAY 1973 | 34 | **** | 36 | **** | 71 | ******** | 79 | ******** |
| JUN 1973 | 30 | **** | 37 | **** | 73 | ******** | 90 | ********** |
| JUL 1973 | 26 | *** | 29 | *** | 74 | ******** | 79 | ******** |
| AUG 1973 | 32 | **** | 40 | ***** | 79 | ******** | 85 | ********* |
| SEP 1973 | 31 | **** | 35 | **** | 85 | ********* | 78 | ******** |
| OCT 1973 | 36 | **** | 39 | **** | 85 | ********* | 84 | ********* |
| NOV 1973 | 37 | **** | 35 | **** | 83 | ********* | 87 | ********* |
| DEC 1973 | 31 | **** | 29 | *** | 82 | ********* | 87 | ********* |
| JAN 1974 | 26 | *** | 33 | **** | 83 | ********* | 53 | ****** |
| FEB 1974 | 43 | ***** | 32 | **** | 84 | ********* | 51 | ****** |
| MAR 1974 | 37 | **** | 41 | ***** | 85 | ********* | 59 | ****** |
| APR 1974 | 47 | ***** | 40 | ***** | 90 | ********** | 65 | ******* |
| MAY 1974 | 42 | ***** | 44 | ***** | 86 | ********* | 76 | ******** |
| JUN 1974 | 40 | ***** | 42 | ***** | 87 | ********* | 86 | ********* |
| JUL 1974 | 35 | **** | 37 | **** | 85 | ********* | 76 | ******** |
| AUG 1974 | 41 | ***** | 44 | ***** | 88 | ********* | 79 | ******** |

**Figure 13.6** Low-resolution display of the time series for toll revenues (REV), toll messages (MSG), business telephones (BMT), and nonfarm employment (NFRM).

BMT and NFRM are very similar, unlike the corresponding patterns for the raw data (Figure 13.6). Likewise, the patterns for the percent changes of REV and MSG have strong similarities, though not as striking.

Not surprisingly, these similarities are reflected in the corresponding correlation matrices. Table 13.2 shows the correlation matrix for the percent changes of the four series. It is noteworthy that all correlations are positive. The correlation between the percent changes in the business telephone (PCTBMT) and nonfarm employment (PCTNFRM) data is higher (= 0.60) than the corresponding correlation coefficient for the raw data (= 0.015), perhaps suggesting that a linear regression model for the percent changes will have some promise. In fact, let us do further modeling between BMT and NFRM in terms of these transformed data.

It will be shown in Chapter 17 that correlations, like many other least-squares estimates, are sensitive to a few outliers (or even one). The correlations for the variables we have just examined will be reviewed again in this context, and a robust alternative will be proposed and analyzed. For now, however, let's apply the correlations from Table 13.2 to our ongoing telecommunications forecast.

## Forecasting Telephone Demand from Employment Data

Growth in the demand for business telephones is known to follow a cyclical pattern. A review of cyclical economic variables and logic suggests that the growth in nonfarm employment can be considered as an explanatory variable in a simple linear regression model.

It is further known that in an economic downturn, for example, the reduction in manufacturing employment is greater than the reduction in business telephone demand. Since most manufacturing employees do not have their own business telephones, this relationship is not surprising. This suggests that nonfarm employment *less* manufacturing employment also be considered as an explanatory variable. For modeling purposes, the monthly series can now be converted to quarterly data, also.

The year-over-year percent growths of the three quarterly series shown in Figure 13.7 suggest that it is preferable to exclude manufacturing employment from total

**Table 13.2** Correlation matrix for the percent changes of the time series in the telecommunications example.

| | 1 | 2 | 3 | 4 |
|---|---|---|---|---|
| 1 PCTREV | 1.00 | | | |
| 2 PCTMSG | 0.67 | 1.00 | | |
| 3 PCTBMT | 0.50 | 0.55 | 1.00 | |
| 4 PCTNFRM | 0.63 | 0.70 | 0.60 | 1.00 |

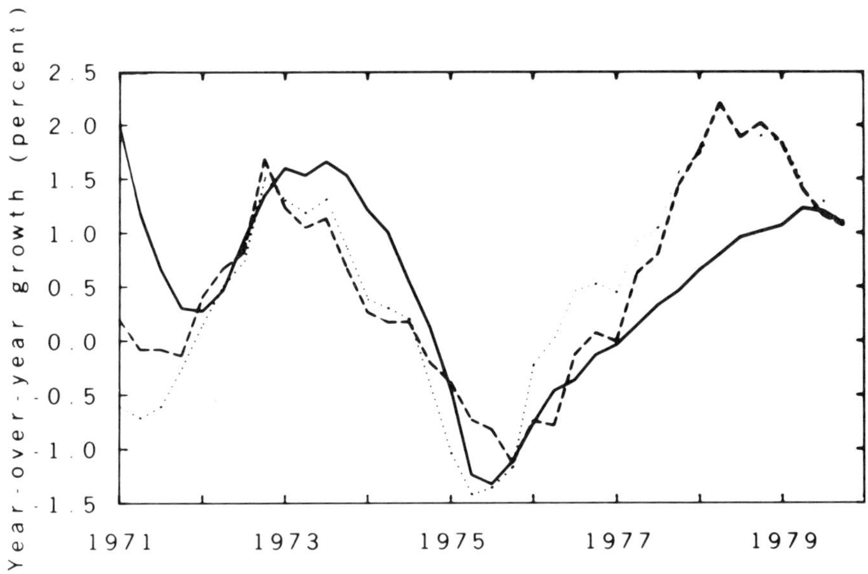


**Figure 13.7** Time plot of the year-over-year percent changes for business telephones (solid line), nonfarm employment (dashed line), and nonfarm employment less manufacturing (dotted line); First quarter 1971–Second quarter 1979.

nonfarm employment. Table 13.3 provides summary statistics for the two models; Model A utilizes percent change of nonfarm employment, and Model B has percent change of nonfarm employment less manufacturing as its independent variable. Model B has a 30 percent improvement in the *R*-squared statistic and, more importantly, provides a more accurate one-year-ahead forecast performance, on the average.

Forecast test comparisons were made in the following manner. Regressions were performed over a segment of the data, and forecasts were generated by using actual values for the independent variable over the "forecast" period. Forecast performance was evaluated by calculating the percent errors for four one-year-ahead forecasts and three two-year-ahead forecasts, using the "forecast" horizon 1976–1979. For this particular period, the forecast errors (actual minus forecast) were almost all negative (that is, the model tends to overforecast). This approach tests the relative forecasting ability of the models. In a true forecasting environment, forecast errors may also result from inaccurate forecasts of the independent variable.

If the residuals are independent of one another, have constant variance, and are normally distributed, the coefficient of the employment variable could be interpreted as follows. Assuming $\hat{\beta} = 0.4$, then, for every 10 percent increase in nonfarm less manufacturing employment, there should be an increase of 4 percent in the demand for additional business telephones.

The low value of the Durbin-Watson statistic (D-W $= 0.24$) suggests first-order positive autocorrelation in the residuals. The next step would be to attempt to reduce

**Table 13.3** Forecasting performance tests and summary statistics for the business telephones–employment models. Regression relationship expressed in terms of percent changes for the variables.

| Summary statistics | Business telephones: Versus nonfarm employment, Model A | Business telephones: Versus nonfarm employment less manufacturing, Model B |
|---|---|---|
| Number of observations | 36 | 36 |
| $R^2$ | 0.37 | 0.48 |
| $F$ | Significant | Significant |
| Standard error | 0.0069 | 0.0062 |
| $\hat{\alpha} \times 10^{-3}$ | 5.29 | 3.24 |
| (Standard error $\times 10^{-3}$) | (1.15) | (1.10) |
| $\hat{\beta}$ | 0.26 | 0.38 |
| (Standard error) | (0.06) | (0.07) |
| Durbin-Watson statistic $d$ | 0.16 | 0.24 |
| Average absolute forecast error (percent) | | |
| 1 year ahead | 0.76 | 0.63 |
| 2 years ahead | 1.68 | 1.73 |

or eliminate this problem, which generally involves adding additional variables and building multiple linear regression models. Alternatively, a number of autocorrelation correction techniques could be tried.

The result is that even a simple model of the type discussed can be a valuable forecasting tool. Since many business and governmental organizations forecast employment levels, a forecast of business telephones can be readily developed. The predictions of the model provide a good starting point in developing the forecast.

These predictions can be adjusted judgmentally to take into account the imperfections in the model and new factors which may not have existed over the regression period. It is important to notice that even a model with one or more imperfections can be useful if the forecaster takes the time to study the model and understand its strengths and weaknesses.

## SOFTWARE CONSIDERATIONS

Regression programs for doing simple linear regression are very widely available. Moore (1978) provides an elementary introduction to the use of the computer in performing statistical data analysis. Moore's book focuses on the use of BMD,

**Table 13.4** Some common statistical procedures using the SAS, SPSS, and BMD software packages.

| Procedure | Software system and name SAS | SPSS | BMD |
|---|---|---|---|
| Printout of input data | Yes | Yes | Yes |
| Perform data transformations | Yes | Yes | Yes |
| Descriptive statistics (e.g., means and standard deviations) | MEANS | CONDESCRIPTIVE | 01D |
| Frequency distributions | FREQ | FREQUENCIES | 04D |
| Histogram or plots | SCATTER | SCATTERGRAM | 05D |
| Simple correlation | CORR | PEARSON CORR | 02D |
| Multiple regression | GLM | REGRESSION | 03R |
| *t* tests | TTEST | T-TEST | 13D |
| Analysis of variance | GLM | ANOVA | 01V |

SPSS, and SAS for doing correlation coefficients, data plots, chi-squared and *t*-tests, and analyses of variance and covariance. Younger (1979) provides regression examples using these packages and shows results as they would appear on the printouts.

Table 13.4 provides a summary of some common statistical procedures in SAS, SPSS, and BMD.

Afifi and Azen (1979, Chapter 3) discuss computer packages capable of handling simple linear regression. For an evaluation of regression programs, see Velleman et al. (1977).

The SYSREG (system regression) procedure in SAS (1980) estimates coefficients in an interdependent system of equations, using a variety of least squares estimation methods. Within this procedure, the D-W option makes the procedure print the Durbin-Watson statistic $d$ and autocorrelation coefficients for residuals. Most packages for time series analysis should have this feature.

## SUMMARY

Simple linear regression models are used to describe an algebraic relationship between a dependent variable and an independent variable. This chapter treats the output from a simple linear regression model and interprets the most significant quantities.

- The $R$-squared statistic indicates the percent of the total variation about the mean value of $Y$ that is explained by performing a linear regression on $X$.
- The $t$-statistic is used to decide if the slope and intercept coefficients are significantly different from zero.

- The $F$-statistic indicates if the overall regression is statistically significant.
- The Durbin-Watson statistic $d$ is used to test for the presence of first-order autocorrelation in time series residuals. Since a consequence of autocorrelated errors is that the sampling variances of the regression coefficients are understated, there is a tendency to accept a variable as significant when it may not be.
- Correlation is a measure of linear association between two variables and is closely tied to regression.

## USEFUL READING

AFIFI, A. A., and S. P. AZEN (1979). *Statistical Analysis—A Computer Oriented Approach*, 2nd ed. New York, NY: Academic Press.

BRELSFORD, W. M., and D. A. RELLES (1981). *STATLIB—A Statistical Computing Library*. Englewood Cliffs, NJ: Prentice-Hall.

DURBIN, J., and G. S. WATSON (1950). Testing for Serial Correlation in Least Squares Regression: I. *Biometrika* 37, 409–28.

DURBIN, J., and G. S. WATSON (1951). Testing for Serial Correlation in Least Squares Regression: II. *Biometrika* 38, 159–78.

MOORE, R. W. (1978). *Introduction to the Use of Computer Packages for Statistical Analyses*. Englewood Cliffs, NJ: Prentice-Hall.

SAS (1980). *SAS/ETS User's Guide, Econometric and Time Series Library*. Cary, NC: SAS Institute, Inc.

VELLEMAN, P. F., J. SEAMAN, and J. E. ALLEN (1977). *Evaluating Package Regression Routines*. Technical Reprint 877/008-010. Ithaca, NY: New York State School of Industrial and Labor Relations, Cornell University.

YOUNGER, M. S. (1979). *Handbook for Linear Regression*. North Scituate, MA: Duxbury Press.

CHAPTER **14**

# Assessing Forecast Precision

This chapter deals with quantifying the uncertainty inherent in values predicted from a regression model. This is useful to:

- Provide the forecast user with an estimate of the accuracy of the forecast.
- Help in selecting the models for use. All other considerations equal, the forecaster places greater reliance on models that predict values with the least uncertainty.
- Track the forecasts against the actual values to determine if it is necessary to revise the forecast.

The main emphasis in this chapter is on the *accuracy* of the forecast and of estimated coefficients for simple linear regression models. "Accuracy" is, of course, not absolute but is measured in terms of limits or ranges within which a value is considered reasonably accurate. Certain confidence limits will be derived for subsequent use in Chapter 22 for tracking schemes that identify the need for forecast revision.

## HOW SHOULD CONFIDENCE INTERVALS BE CALCULATED?

As we have stated before, in the modeling process, a forecaster needs to identify an appropriate model for the data and then estimate the parameters of the model. The parameter estimation is made by using the sample data that are available, but since a "true" model cannot be known, all the forecaster can do is obtain a fitted model.

Let's assume the true model is a straight line as depicted in Figure 14.1 by a dashed line. A fitted model is shown as a solid line. The objective is to determine the slope and intercept of the hypothetical line, given that the probability distribution

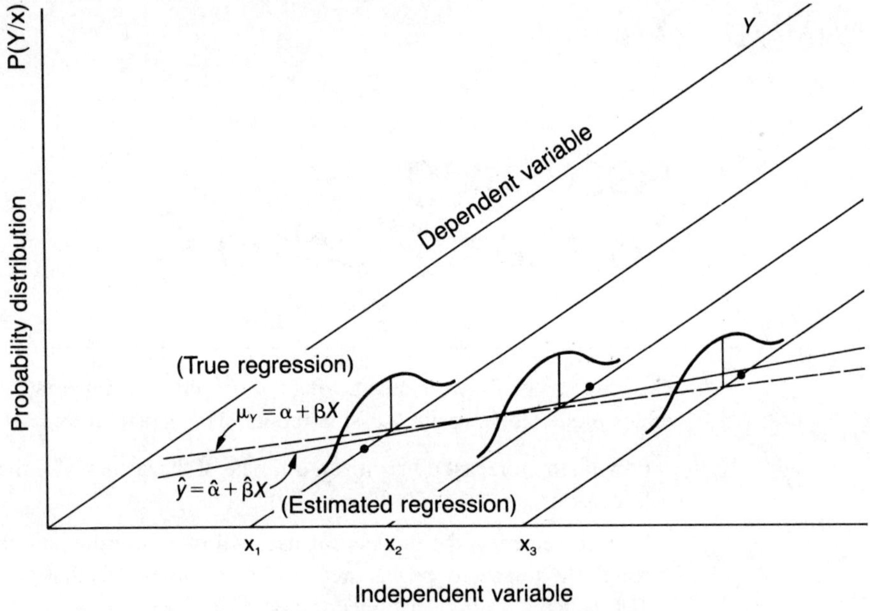


**Figure 14.1** True and fitted regression models with error distributions for given values of the independent variable.

of errors in the assumed model does not make it possible to estimate the parameters precisely. Recognizing that there will always be random errors in the observations, it is important to provide a measure of the *precision* of the parameter estimates and of the *reliability* of the fitted coefficients in the regression equation.

The three questions to be answered are:

- How *precise* will the estimate of a model coefficient be?
- What is the confidence interval for the fitted equation *within* the observed range of the independent variable *X?*
- What is the confidence interval for a *new* observation that was not part of the data used to fit the equation?

## Prediction Variances

In order to develop confidence limits on coefficients and model projections, it is necessary to derive expressions for the variances of these quantities (see, for example, Draper and Smith, 1981, and Wallis and Roberts, 1966, Chapter 17). A subsequent analysis of prediction errors in terms of the appropriate confidence intervals provides a *diagnostic function,* which is an important part of the *forecast monitoring* process.

For a simple linear regression model, the theoretical forecast equation (for a given $X = x_0$) is given by

$$\mu_{Y_0} = \alpha + \beta(x_0 - \bar{x}).$$

Here it should be noted that the independent variable $X$ is expressed as the deviation of $x_0$ from $\bar{x}$. Thus $\hat{\mu}_{Y_0} = a + b(x_0 - \bar{x})$ is the estimated regression line for a given $x_0$. In repeated samples of size $n$ from the same population, the values of $a$ and $b$ would be subject to random variation; the variances of $a$ and $b$ are, respectively,

$$\text{Var}(a) = \sigma^2/n \qquad \text{and} \qquad \text{Var}(b) = \sigma^2/\Sigma(x_i - \bar{x})^2,$$

where $\sigma^2$ is the variance of the error distribution in the model, which is assumed to be normal, in short, $N(0, \sigma^2)$.

Since $a$ and $b$ are uncorrelated, the variance of $\hat{\mu}_{Y_0}$ is

$$\text{Var}(\hat{\mu}_{Y_0}) = \sigma^2 \left[ \frac{1}{n} + \frac{(x_0 - \bar{x})^2}{\Sigma(x_i - \bar{x})^2} \right].$$

The value $x_0$ to be used in $(x_0 - \bar{x})^2$ is the particular value at which the standard deviation

$$\sigma_{\hat{y}_0} = [\text{Var}(\hat{\mu}_{y_0})]^{1/2}$$

is sought. Note that $\sigma_{\hat{y}_0}$ is smallest for $x_0 = \bar{x}$.

In addition to calculating a prediction variance for the average $\hat{\mu}_Y$, it is also of interest to derive an expression for the prediction variance of a *new* observation $y$ at $x_0$, a value of a variable which is independent of the observations used to estimate the model parameters. The variance of the difference between a *new* observation $y_0$ and the computed value $\hat{y}_0$ for the corresponding value of $x_0$ is

$$\sigma^2_{(y-\hat{y}_0)} = \sigma^2 \left[ 1 + \frac{1}{n} + \frac{(x_0 - \bar{x})^2}{\Sigma(x_i - \bar{x})^2} \right].$$

This will be larger than $\sigma_{\hat{y}_0}$ since it takes into account the variation of $Y$ about $\mu_Y$ as well as the variation associated with the unknown coefficients.

The prediction variances can be calculated once the *standard error of estimate* $\sigma$ is given. This is conventionally estimated by

$$\hat{\sigma} = \left[ \sum_{i=1}^{n} (y_i - \hat{y}_i)^2/(n - 2) \right]^{1/2}.$$

and is often denoted by $s_{y \cdot x}$, the sample estimate of the standard error of estimate.

In the telephone revenue-message example in Chapter 13, it is of interest to compare $s_{y \cdot x}$ with $s_y$, the standard deviation of the revenues when messages are disregarded. Since $s_y = 9700$ for this example, the standard deviation is reduced from 9700 for revenues irrespective of messages to 2370 for revenues at a given message volume. This is a 76 percent reduction and suggests that toll messages help a great deal in explaining toll revenues.

By using $s_{y \cdot x}$ for $\hat{\sigma}$, the estimated standard deviation for the fitted forecast equation at any point $X = x_0$ becomes

$$\hat{\sigma}_{\hat{y}} = s_{y \cdot x}\left[\frac{1}{n} + \frac{(x_0 - \bar{x})^2}{\Sigma(x_i - \bar{x})^2}\right]^{1/2}$$

and that of a new observation is

$$\hat{\sigma}_{(y - \hat{y})} = s_{y \cdot x}\left[1 + \frac{1}{n} + \frac{(x_0 - \bar{x})^2}{\Sigma(x_i - \bar{x})^2}\right]^{1/2}.$$

These estimates are used to construct confidence intervals, which is the subject of the next section.

## Confidence Limits and Intervals

Three types of confidence intervals (for the normal simple linear regression model) are considered:

- Confidence interval for the slope of the regression line.
- Confidence interval for the fitted equation.
- Confidence interval for a new observation.

If repeated samples are taken from the same normal population and corresponding regression coefficients are calculated for the regression line, what would result would be varying values of $a$ and $b$. The pattern of variability would also follow a normal distribution with mean values equal to the corresponding parameter value $\alpha$ and $\beta$. The respective standard deviations are estimated by

$$\hat{\sigma}_a = \hat{\sigma}/n \qquad \text{and} \qquad \hat{\sigma}_b = \hat{\sigma} \Big/ [\Sigma(x_i - \bar{x})^2]^{1/2},$$

where $\hat{\sigma}$ is the standard error of estimate, as before.

Observe that $\hat{\sigma}_b$ is smaller

- The smaller the variability of $Y$ for fixed values of $X$.
- The larger the sample size.
- The larger the dispersion of the independent variable.

A *confidence interval* provides a statement about the level of confidence that can be placed on an interval of values about a forecast (or coefficient) in order to be sure that the true value is within that range. For example, a 95 percent confidence interval would be the range in which the forecaster is 95 percent certain that the true value of the regression coefficient will be found.

A similar procedure can be applied to the fitted equation or a new observation. Given values of $\alpha$ and $\beta$ in the regression equation and a value of $X$ (say $x_0$) in that equation, how confident can the forecaster be that the true value $\mu_{Y_0}$ will be close to $\hat{\mu}_{Y_0}$? A confidence interval for a new observation takes the form

Lower limit < New observation < Upper limit

within which the forecaster can be, say, 95 percent sure that the new observation will lie.

The general form of a confidence interval based solely on the information provided by the data is

Point estimate $\pm$ ($t$-value)(Estimate of standard error of point estimate).

A *100(1 − α) percent confidence interval for the slope b* is, for instance,

$$b \pm t_{n-2}(\alpha/2)\hat{\sigma}_b,$$

where $t_{n-2}(\alpha)$ refers to the $(1 - \alpha)$-percentile of the Student $t$-distribution on $(n - 2)$ degrees of freedom. Usually $\alpha$ is taken as 0.05 for a 95 percent level of confidence, so $t_{n-2}(\alpha/2)$ is abbreviated by $t_{(n-2)}$ (Appendix A, Table 2).

For the revenue-message model mentioned earlier, $\hat{\sigma}_b = 0.076$ (see Figure 13.1). A 95 percent confidence interval for $b$ is

$$b \pm 1.96\hat{\sigma}_b = 3.42 \pm 0.15 = 3.27 \text{ to } 3.57.$$

Likewise, in repeated samples of size $n$ from the same normal population, the values of the intercept $a$ as well as the slope $b$ would be subject to random variation. The values of $Y$ are normally distributed around a population mean value $\mu_{Y(x)}$ of $Y$ for that $X$ with an estimated standard deviation $\hat{\sigma}_{\hat{y}}$.

A *95 percent confidence interval for the line* is

$$\hat{y} \pm t_{(n-2)}\hat{\sigma}_{\hat{y}},$$

or approximately two standard errors above and below the line for large $n$.

The *95 percent prediction interval for a new observation* is

$$\hat{y} \pm t_{(n-2)}\hat{\sigma}_{(y-\hat{y})}.$$

Increasing the sample size will tend to narrow the confidence interval for a new observation only insofar as it reduces the confidence interval for the line. Even for an infinitely large sample, the width would not be zero. Thus a lower limit on the width is set by the fact that $Y$ varies for a given value of $X$, and even complete knowledge of the population distribution for $Y$ at a given value of $X$ will not make possible exact prediction of individual values of $Y$ from $X$.

Figure 14.2 shows a plot of monthly toll revenue history, the predictions for 1980, and their 95 percent confidence limits, for the model based on the revenue-message data in the telecommunications example. The inner bands correspond to the confidence limits for each month individually. The outer bands correspond to the cumulative confidence limits. Thus, the toll revenue forecaster can be 95 percent certain that corresponding to a given message volume, the expected or true revenue would be found between the corresponding limits of the inner confidence interval.

If the forecaster wants to know the confidence interval for the sum of the monthly predictions, the outer confidence interval is used. The reason why the cumulative confidence limits are *not* simply the sums of the monthly confidence limits will be discussed in the section on confidence limits for time series.

A plot of predicted errors (Actual − Fitted values) with associated (95 percent) confidence intervals for the *regression errors* is shown in Figure 14.3. This plot can be used to identify large residuals that may correspond to potential outliers.

## A Note of Caution!

Since $X$ may take on any value within the range used in the regression, the confidence limits are relevant only over the range of the fit (sometimes called *interpolation,* because the selected value of $X$ falls within the range of $X$'s). A common application made by forecasters is to use the confidence limits for $Y$ with an $X$ value that is *outside* the range of the $X$'s over which the regression is performed. (This is *extrapolation*.)

There are several dangers in extrapolating values based on values of $X$ outside the regression interval. The first is mathematical. In the derivation of the confidence intervals, the further the values of $X$ are away from their mean $\bar{x}$, the wider the confidence intervals will be. Thus the precision that one would like to have becomes increasingly more difficult to achieve.

A second pitfall is a practical one. For example, consider a problem that farmers in the Midwest could have in determining the proper amount of fertilizer to be used to increase the yield of crops per acre. Suppose that a statistician performed a regression analysis based on the application of from 100 to 700 pounds of fertilizer per acre. It is noted that the yield in terms of bushels per acre increases linearly.

The linear model based on these data would show that the more fertilizer used, the greater the yield. The problem that the model does not take into account is that too much fertilizer will "burn out" the crop. The model is inaccurate but the statistician may not realize it. Over the regression period the relationship between yield and fertilizer is linear. However, beyond the range of fertilizer used in the regression, the more nonlinear the series becomes (Figure 14.4). In practice, one may not have

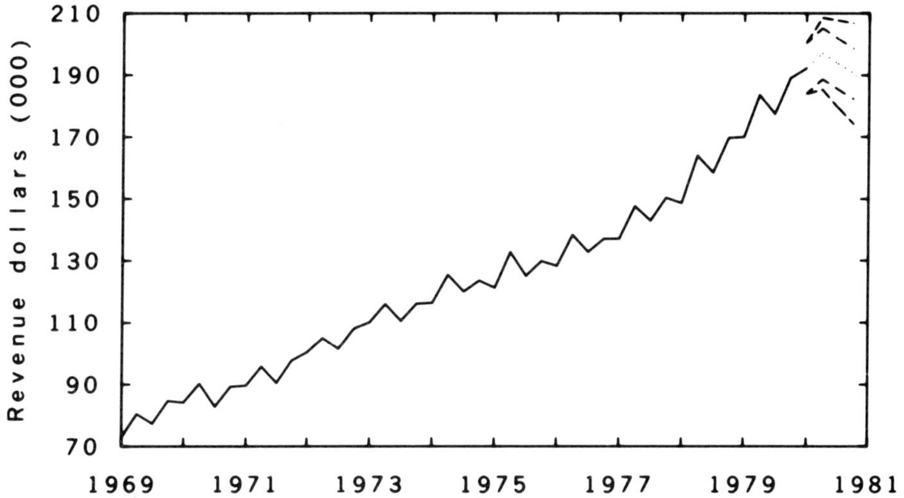


**Figure 14.2** Ninety-five percent confidence intervals for the 1980 revenue forecasts and historical values from 1969–1979, from a monthly revenue–message model. Revenue predictions are shown as dotted line.

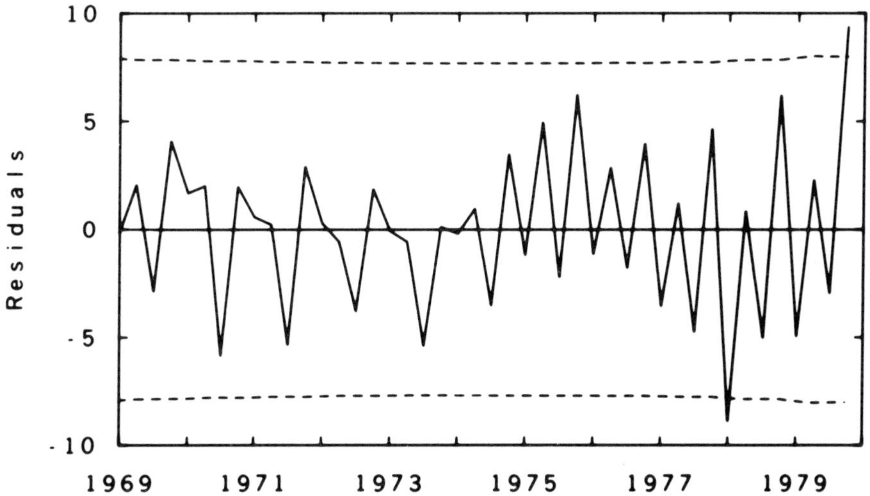


**Figure 14.3** Prediction error plot with 95 percent confidence limits for the regression errors over the fit period 1969:1–1979:12 for the revenue–message model.

models good enough to permit valid extrapolation beyond the range of the observed data. Whenever regression methods are used to assist in solving a problem, it is important to keep in mind the potential dangers of extrapolation. There may be no choice but to extrapolate, but the practical as well as mathematical problems involved should be fully recognized.

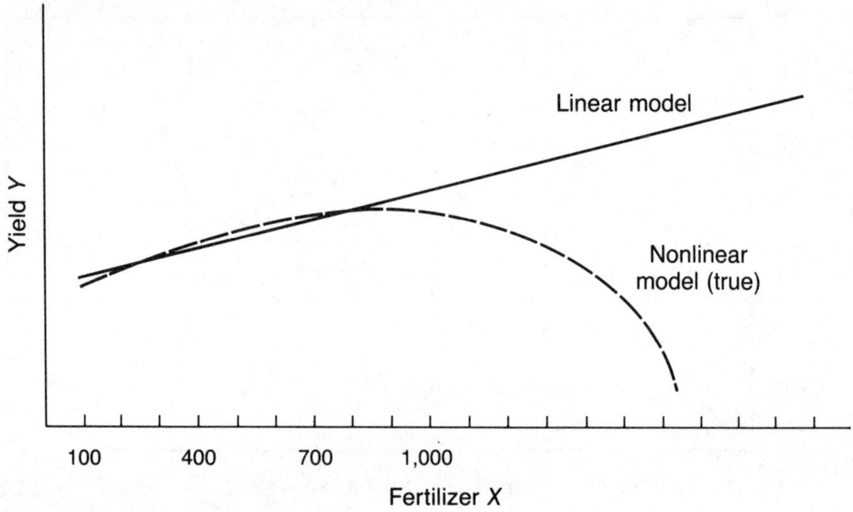


**Figure 14.4** A pitfall of extrapolating values beyond the valid range of a selected model; beyond the range of observed data, the model may actually be invalid for reasons the model does not reveal.

### What If *X* Is Not Given?

In the treatment so far, the values for the independent variable are assumed to be accurate; i.e., there is no error in the value of $X$. As one might expect, in the usual forecasting situations the values of the independent variable are obtained from an independent forecasting organization or perhaps even from another regression model. This is especially true in econometric forecasting.

In such cases, the confidence intervals described earlier are conservative. Since there is also uncertainty in $X$, more realistic confidence intervals should be wider, but how much? It is difficult to state how large they could be since one now needs to know how the uncertainty about the forecast of $X$ impacts the forecast variance for $Y$. A Monte Carlo simulation might be an appropriate technique for developing approximate confidence limits when $X$ is not known precisely.

## CONFIDENCE LIMITS FOR TIME SERIES

The confidence limits presented so far have been based on normal regression theory for simple linear regression. They are appropriate for the prediction of $Y$ at a given point in time when time is the independent variable. The forecaster often deals with aggregated data and would like to know the confidence limits about an annual forecast, which is the sum of twelve monthly (or four quarterly) predictions from a monthly (or quarterly) model. To develop the appropriate confidence limits requires that the variance for the sum of the prediction errors be calculated. This can be derived by using the variance formula

$$\mathrm{Var}(\Sigma\hat{\varepsilon}_i) = \Sigma Var(\hat{\varepsilon}_i) + 2\sum_{i \neq j}\mathrm{Cov}(\hat{\varepsilon}_i, \hat{\varepsilon}_j).$$

If the forecast errors have zero correlation—in particular, if they are independent of one another—the covariance term would equal zero and the variance of the sum would equal the sum of the prediction variances. The estimated standard error would be

$$\hat{\sigma}_{\hat{y}} = \left[\frac{\Sigma \mathrm{Var}\ \hat{\varepsilon}_i}{n - 1}\right]^{1/2}.$$

The most common form of correlation in the forecast errors of time series models is positive autocorrelation. In this case, the covariance term is positive and the confidence limits derived by using the standard deviation in the above formula would be too small.

In the case of negative covariance, the confidence limits would be too large. Rather than deal with this complexity, most computer programs assume the covariance is zero. The forecaster should recognize that, in the typical case, the confidence limits are probably too conservative.

## Relating Percent Errors to Confidence Intervals

Some executives may find a discussion of confidence intervals obtuse. In such cases, the forecaster may find greater acceptance of this technique if forecast confidence limits are expressed in terms of percentages. For example, a 95 percent confidence limit for a forecast might mean that the forecast will be within $\pm 15$ percent of the actual numerical value. The percent error associated with any confidence limit may be calculated as follows:

$$\text{Percent error} = \frac{(\text{Forecast standard deviation})(t_\nu) \times 100}{\text{Predicted value}}$$

where $t_\nu$ is the tabulated value of the Student $t$-distribution for $\nu$ degrees of freedom.

This calculation provides the percent error for any particular period. Values can be calculated for all periods—for example, for each month of the year. The median percent error could be used in place of an arithmetic average error. A plot similar to Figure 14.5 can be generated to translate confidence limits to percent errors.

The confidence limits and percent errors calculated in Figure 14.5 are for monthly or quarterly errors. Under the assumption of random errors, the cumulative percent

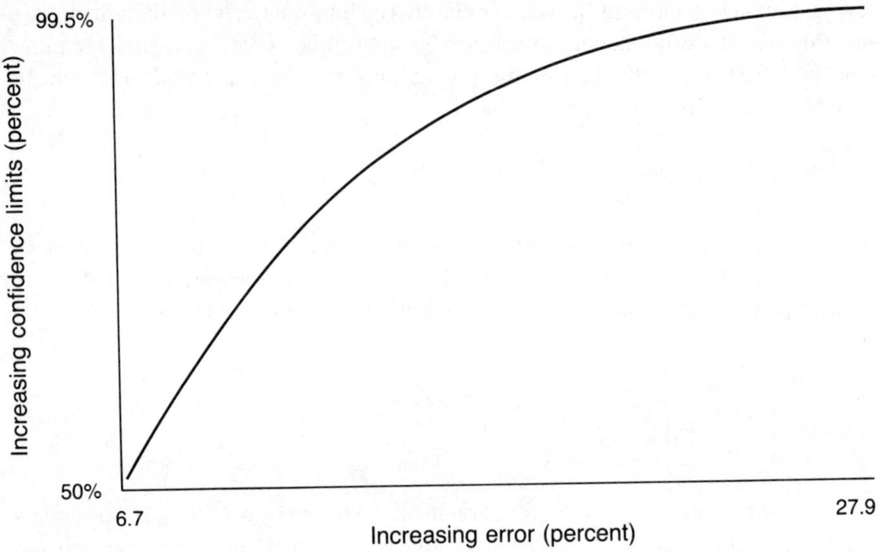


**Figure 14.5** Relating confidence limits to percent errors.

error will be less than the monthly or quarterly percent error since positive and negative residuals will cancel to some extent. As an approximate rule, the average monthly percent error can be divided by the square root of the number of months of the forecast to determine the cumulative percent error. For example, the annual percent error is calculated by dividing the average monthly percent error by $\sqrt{12}$ or the average quarterly percent error by $\sqrt{4}$ (or 2).

The formula for determining the percent error associated with given confidence limits can be transposed to calculate the confidence limits to be used to obtain a given percent error objective. Consider the situation in which accuracy objectives are provided for each time series. To determine standard error units for monthly predictions, the following formula can be used as an approximation:

$$\begin{array}{c}\text{Confidence level}\\(t\text{-statistic})\end{array} = \frac{(\text{Percent error for the period})(\text{Predicted value})}{(\text{Forecast standard deviation})(100)}.$$

In a given case, if the accuracy objective on a monthly basis were to be within 10 percent, the confidence level might only be 70 percent. To estimate the $t$-statistic for an annual forecast, the following formula would apply:

$$\begin{array}{c}\text{Confidence level}\\(t\text{-statistic})\end{array} = \frac{(\text{Percent error for the year})(\text{Annual forecast})}{(\text{Forecast standard deviation})(100)(\sqrt{4}\text{ or }\sqrt{12})}.$$

The $\sqrt{4}$ is used for quarterly data and the $\sqrt{12}$ is used for monthly data.

Quarterly data are often preferable because there is less "noise" in each observation. Tracking monthly data is difficult because of errors in recording, weather conditions, the higher volatility of the data, and similar short-term data problems.

## A Forecasting Example

Consider the toll revenue–toll message forecasting model discussed earlier. Assume that a forecast of message volumes has been prepared (perhaps with a model relating it to employment growth) for one-year-ahead by quarters. Figure 14.6 shows the most likely forecast of message volumes. Alternative optimistic and pessimistic forecasts have also been provided based upon different assumptions of factors such as inflation rates, taxes, and fiscal and monetary policies.

In this example, the sum of the quarterly revenue forecasts for the most likely view is—let us just say—$773. The 95 percent cumulative confidence limits for the annual "most likely" or "best bet" forecast are $757 to $790. The annual confidence limits are based on the assumption that the quarterly forecasts are uncorrelated. The confidence limits are based on the assumption that there is no error in the message volume forecasts.

Figure 14.7 shows another way to depict uncertainty in forecasting telephone revenues—namely, using the regression equation and the alternative message volume forecasts (shown in Figure 14.6) to generate range forecasts based on optimistic and pessimistic message volume forecasts. Although it may not be possible to determine

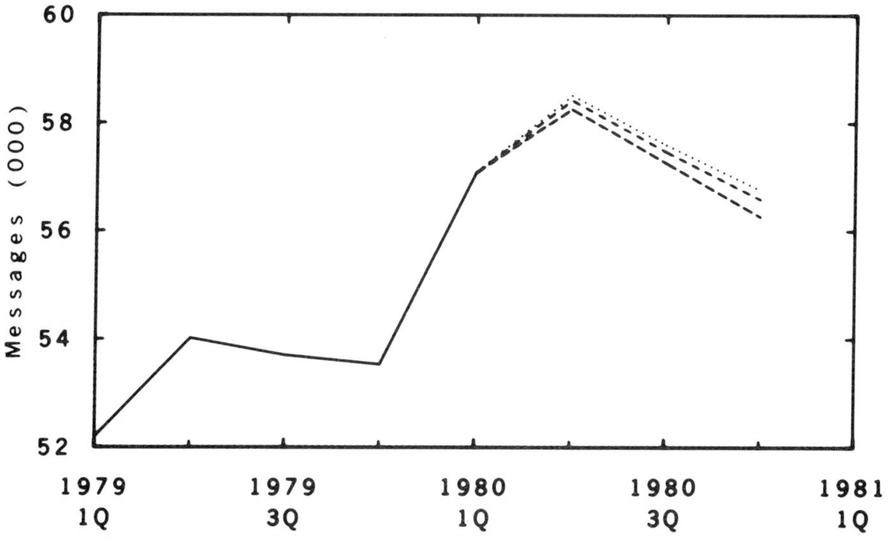


**Figure 14.6** Three scenarios (optimistic, most likely, and pessimistic), for a one-year-ahead message forecast, by quarters.

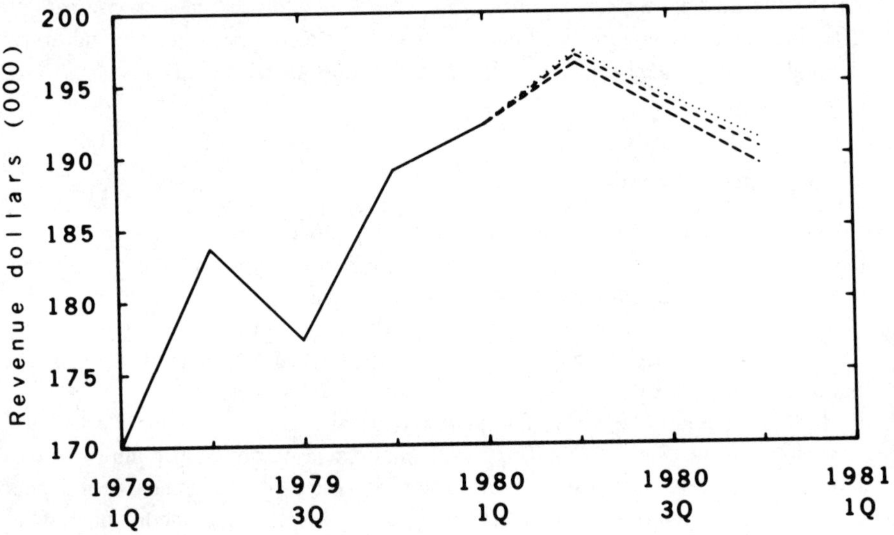


**Figure 14.7** Optimistic and pessimistic revenue forecasts compared to the "best bet" view (based on scenario views of the message volumes).

objectively the associated chances of exceeding one of the alternative forecasts, the forecast user can decide on the level of risk he or she is willing to take. These *range forecasts* can be useful when decision makers are asked to commit themselves to given levels of revenues, expenses, and earnings for future periods. *Risk analysis* requires a grounding in probability concepts, which is beyond the scope of the present treatment (see, for example, Wheelwright and Makridakis, 1980, Chapter 13).

## SUMMARY

In linear regression theory

- The predicted value of the dependent variable is the average value of $Y$ for a given value of the independent variable(s) $X$.
- Confidence limits are generated to express the probability that the average value of $Y$ will be within a specified range.
- Confidence limits about residuals provide a valuable tracking tool since they can be used to signal a need to revise a forecast. This subject is treated in depth in Chapter 22, but is dependent on the theory developed in this chapter.

In the forecasting environment, it is often necessary to extrapolate values beyond the range over which the regression was performed. Care must be exercised since nonlinear relationships may exist. It also becomes necessary to forecast values for the independent variables and this introduces additional errors in the forecast.

## USEFUL READING

DRAPER, N. R., and H. SMITH (1981). *Applied Regression Analysis,* 2nd ed. New York, NY: John Wiley and Sons.

WALLIS, W. A., and H. V. ROBERTS (1966). *Statistics, A New Approach*. New York, NY: The Free Press.

WHEELWRIGHT, S. C., and S. MAKRIDAKIS (1980). *Forecasting Methods for Management,* 3rd ed. New York, NY: John Wiley and Sons.

CHAPTER **15**

# Looking at Regression Residuals

This chapter addresses the following key topics:

- How to evaluate simple linear regression models by using residual analysis.
- Identifying outliers in residual plots.
- What the "unexplained variation" tells you about the adequacy of your model.
- How residual plots can help you to see that a transformation of the data for the dependent or independent variable is needed.

## ANALYZING REGRESSION RESIDUALS

Residual analysis in regression modeling is a process designed to reveal departures from model assumptions about the error distribution, such as normality, independence, and constant variance. Since statistical significance of parameters and confidence limits depends on the validity of assumptions about the error distribution, residual analysis is, perhaps, the single most valuable *diagnostic tool* for evaluating regression models. Fortunately, much of the residual analysis can be carried out effectively by using graphical techniques.

### Basic Residual Patterns

Five basic types of patterns are frequently seen in residual plots:

- No visible pattern.
- Cyclical pattern (positively autocorrelated residuals).
- Nonlinear relationships.

- Increasing dispersion.
- Linear trend.

A residual plot which has no visible pattern (Figure 15.1) provides no evidence against the assumption that the errors in the model are independent, have zero mean, and show constant variance. A plot in which no pattern is visible is consistent with the basic assumptions about *randomness* in a regression model. Tests will be discussed that indicate whether the randomness assumption can be supported by the data.

### A Run Test for Randomness

Some tests indicative of randomness (or lack thereof) in residuals include tests based on first differences, runs of signs, and rank correlation. The *first-differences test* assumes that if there is nonrandomness in the form of trend, the number of positive first differences (also called differences of order 1) would be large for a residual series with an upward trend and small for a residual series with a downward trend.

The *runs-of-signs test* is a simple way to test for randomness by counting runs (Roberts, 1974). A run is a string of pluses (+) or minuses (−) that accumulates

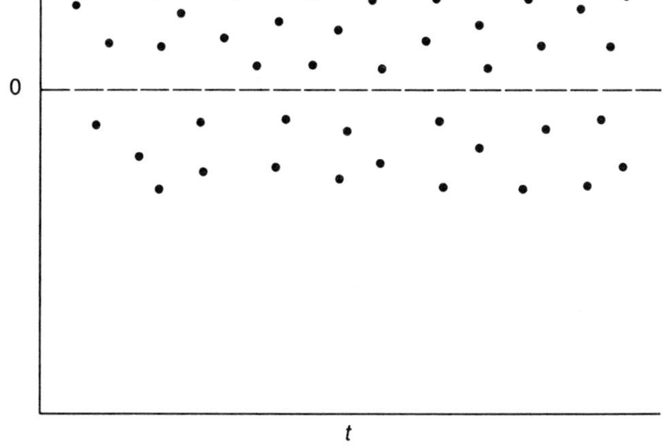


**Figure 15.1** No pattern is visible in this residual plot.

when a plus (+) value is assigned to an observation larger than the average value of the data and a minus (−) value is assigned to a value less than the average.

In counting these runs, let the number of consecutive runs of pluses be denoted by $r$ and let $n$ denote the number of data values in the sample. Then the average number of runs over all possible sequences of runs is

$$\frac{2r(n - r)}{n} + 1.$$

A measure of the expected dispersion of runs among different sequences that could have occurred is the standard error given by

$$\left[\frac{2r(n - r)[2r(n - r) - n]}{n^2(n - 1)}\right]^{1/2}.$$

Thus, if the observed number of runs is within two standard errors of the expected (average) number of runs, then there is little evidence that the series is not random. The runs measure is a measure of conformity of data to a model specification of randomness. It is often observed, for example, that changes in many stock prices behave essentially like a random series.

When signs-run counting is applied to residuals, one expects that the number of consecutive positive or negative residuals will be neither small nor large for a random residual series. A straight line trend with positive slope will have a run of negative signs followed by a run of positive signs. A wildly fluctuating series, on the other hand, will exhibit too many sign changes.

In the *rank correlation test,* residuals are ranked in order depending on size and then correlated with a straight line trend. The distribution of the test statistic is difficult to determine, so approximate tests based on the Student $t$-distribution are used. Details of these tests and similar ones may be found in Walsh (1962, Chapter 5).

## Nonrandom Patterns

If a pattern can be discerned in a residual plot, then these patterns exemplify a violation of one or more assumptions about randomness in a regression model. The identification of such patterns and some remedies will be discussed first.

The *cyclical pattern* (Figure 15.2) is often evident when fitting linear models to time series data. For example, economic booms and recessions in the business cycle become apparent in a residual plot. In the special case of time series, it makes sense to connect residuals sequentially in time to expose underlying cyclical patterns. This procedure will highlight autocorrelation in residuals. The Durbin-Watson test (Chapter 12) allows one to test for first-order autocorrelation.

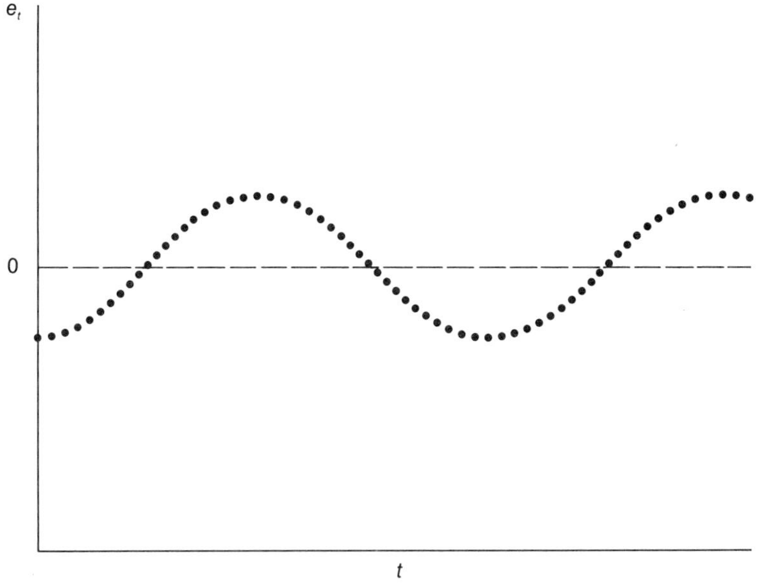


**Figure 15.2** A cyclical pattern can be seen in a residual time series plot.

When strong autocorrelation exists in the residuals, the ordinary least squares (OLS) method *understates* the variances of the regression coefficients as well as the variance of the residuals. Modeling year-over-year growth or percent changes of the variables often reduces the problem of autocorrelation considerably.

Another reason for the appearance of nonrandom patterns is that a linear model is being fit to an inherently nonlinear phenomenon. For instance, a plot of sales of a new product may show a rate of growth that is faster than linear growth. Likewise, the income tax rate on individual earnings has a nonlinear relationship with earnings. When you attempt to fit such nonlinear relationships with a linear model, the residuals will often appear to have a *cup shape* or inverted cup shape (Figure 15.3).

It often happens that the residuals for a nonlinear relationship may not look cupshaped over the entire regression period. However, if you were to make forecasts from the straight line model, the forecast errors might show *increasing dispersion* (Figure 15.4). If it did not become apparent that the data were nonlinear from analyzing residuals over the entire regression period, the pattern of over- or underforecasting would certainly exhibit nonlinearity over a long enough period.

It is important to distinguish between nonlinear growth in trend and nonlinear variations as a result of a short-term cycle. In the first case, the nonlinear relationship between two variables will continue in the same direction over a long time. In the case of a short-term cycle, the nonlinear relationship will change direction at the peaks and troughs of each cycle.

Finally, a trend, up or down, may be apparent in the residuals (Figure 15.5). This pattern is also the result of a nonlinear relationship between the variables.

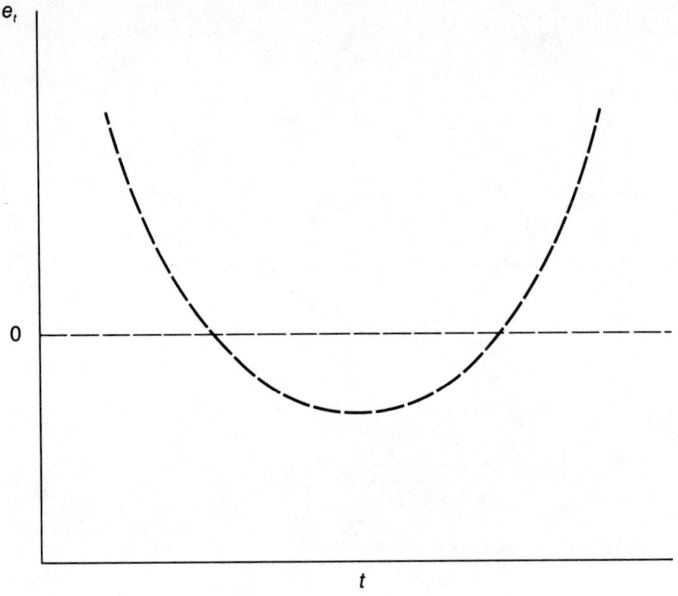


**Figure 15.3** A cupshaped residual pattern.

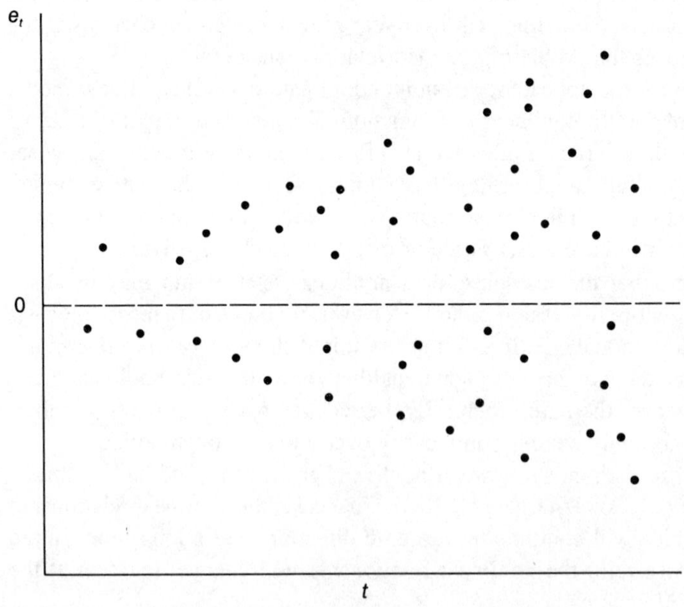


**Figure 15.4** Increasing dispersion of forecast errors.

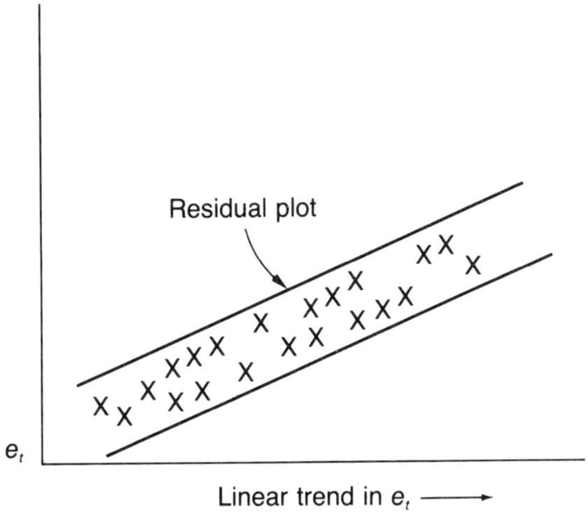


**Figure 15.5** A linear trend in the residuals.

## TRANSFORMING DATA TO IMPROVE RESIDUAL PATTERNS

In forecasting applications there are many time series that appear to grow exponentially with time. If these series are regressed against time, a pattern of increasing dispersion generally results, particularly in a comparison of forecasted values with actual data. The toll revenue and message series in the telecommunications example are two such examples.

### Logarithmic Transformation

Over the regression period, for an exponential time series, the residuals from a fitted straight line will appear to have a cupshaped pattern (Figure 15.3); after fitting a straight line, the actual values would fall above the line in the beginning and end part and would be below the line in the middle part of the regression period. The appropriate technique for improving the fit is to take a logarithmic transformation of the data. Further, substantiation that taking logarithms is the correct course will come from considering year-over-year percent changes: if the percent growth values lie in a relatively small band, near-exponential growth of the data is suggested.

A plot of the fitted (with a straight line) and actual logarithms of the toll revenue series (Figure 15.6) demonstrates that the transformation is appropriate. The residuals (Figure 15.7) are no longer cupshaped and appear more *symmetrically* distrib-

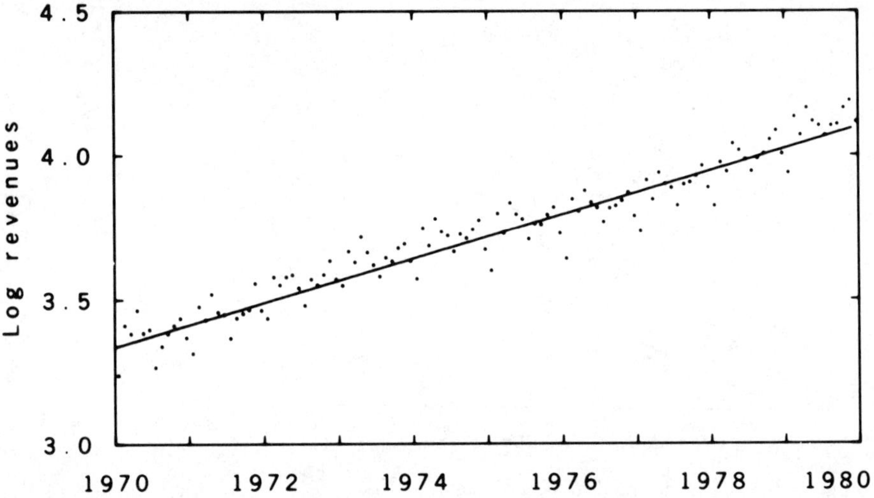


**Figure 15.6** Historical fit of the logarithms of the telephone toll revenues with a straight-line regression model.

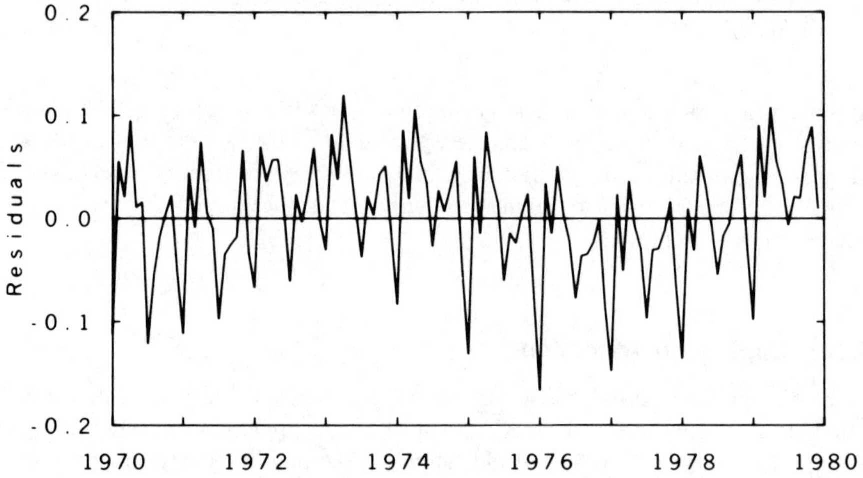


**Figure 15.7** Residuals from the straight-line regression model for telephone toll revenues in Figure 15.6.

uted. There is some evidence of a short-term cycle, but the residuals are more random than those of the straight line model.

On a rare occasion, the residuals from a straight-line regression of a log-transformed series may also show a cupshaped pattern. In this case it may be necessary to perform a logarithmic transformation on the log-transformed series, that is, a log-

log transformation. Care must be exercised in these situations since forecasts based on such transformations will grow very rapidly and likely will appear unrealistic.

Another situation where a logarithmic (or power) transformation may be appropriate occurs when data show increasing dispersion. Figure 15.8 shows data of mobile telephone units, by state, against the number of cars for each state for a recent year. It is natural to assume that numbers of mobile telephones increase with increasing numbers of cars. However, it is also apparent that the data show increasing variability with increasing numbers of cars.

Without examining residuals, a linear regression analysis could be performed with satisfactory statistical results (in terms of $R^2$, $F$, and $t$ statistics). However, the resulting residual pattern (Figure 15.9) demonstrates that faulty inference could be derived from the model. It is noteworthy that there is increasing dispersion in the residuals. California is a large residual; one might expect a large number of mobile telephone units, but the model suggests that the state has an unusually large number of mobile phones for California's total number of vehicles. The model is clearly inappropriate because of this large dispersion (indicative of nonconstant variance) in the residuals. A logarithmic transformation of the data results in equally satisfactory statistical results; but a linear regression in the logarithmic domain clearly gives a superior pattern of residuals (Figure 15.10).

Moreover, the inferences that can be made about the mobile telephone market in the different states change substantially when a log transformation is made. First of all, the residuals no longer display an unusual pattern. California no longer represents an unusual situation. Rather, Nevada and West Virginia are now the closest

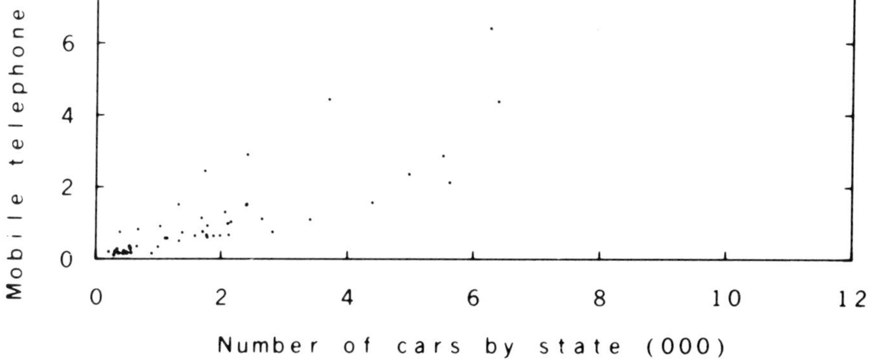

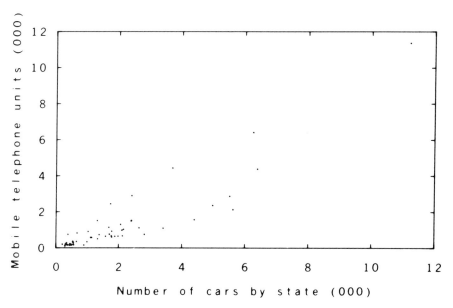

**Figure 15.8** Mobile telephone units versus number of cars by state in the United States.

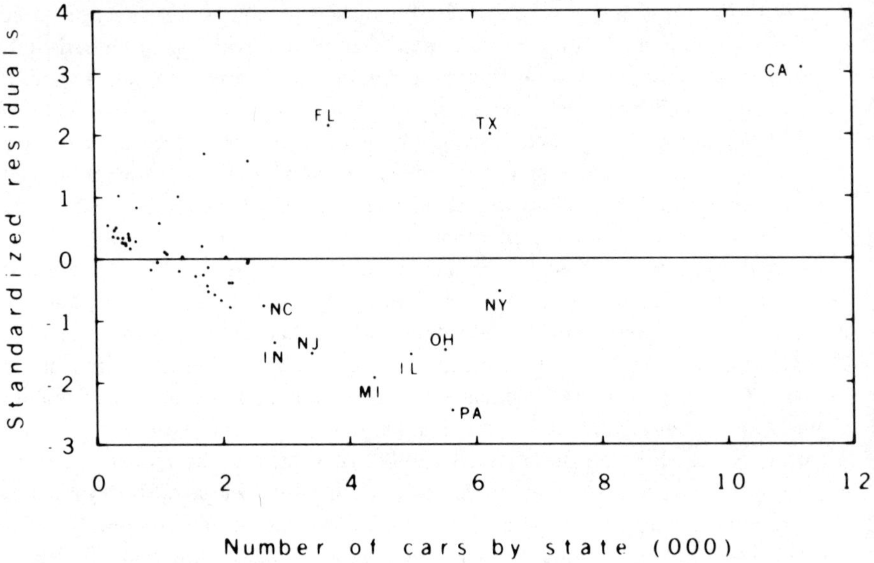


**Figure 15.9** Mobile telephone unit data: residuals after regression, showing increasing dispersion.

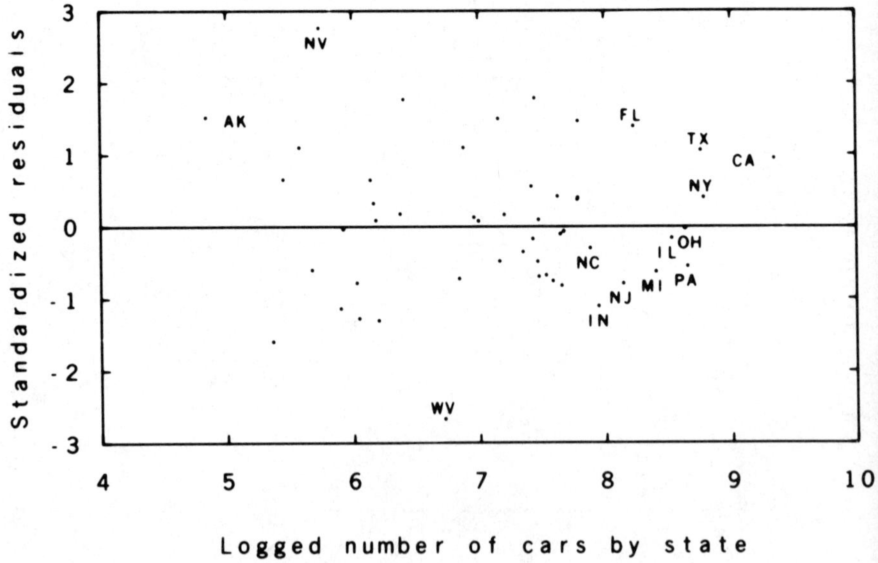


**Figure 15.10** Residuals after regression for log-transformed mobile telephone unit data.

to being viewed outliers in this regression. This observation is in fact consistent with the per capita income of the two states and the differences in the number of mobile phones relative to the number of cars.

## Square-Root Transformation

A second transformation that may be appropriately applied to data representing "counts" of items is the square-root transformation. One reason is that the square-root transformation has a *variance-stabilizing* property; i.e., variability remains constant with size.

In other situations it may be known that data behave essentially in a quadratic manner because the data describe a physical process. For example, Figure 15.11 shows a scatter diagram relating stopping distance for a car to the car's speed (Ezekiel and Fox, 1959). This plot is clearly nonlinear. Although a simple linear regression would produce acceptable summary statistics for these data, an examination of the residuals shows a distinctly nonlinear pattern (Figure 15.12). The square-root transformation of the dependent variable produced equally satisfactory summary results for the regression, and the residual pattern clearly shows a significant improvement (Figure 15.13). The residuals appear random and symmetrical with no unusual patterns or outliers.

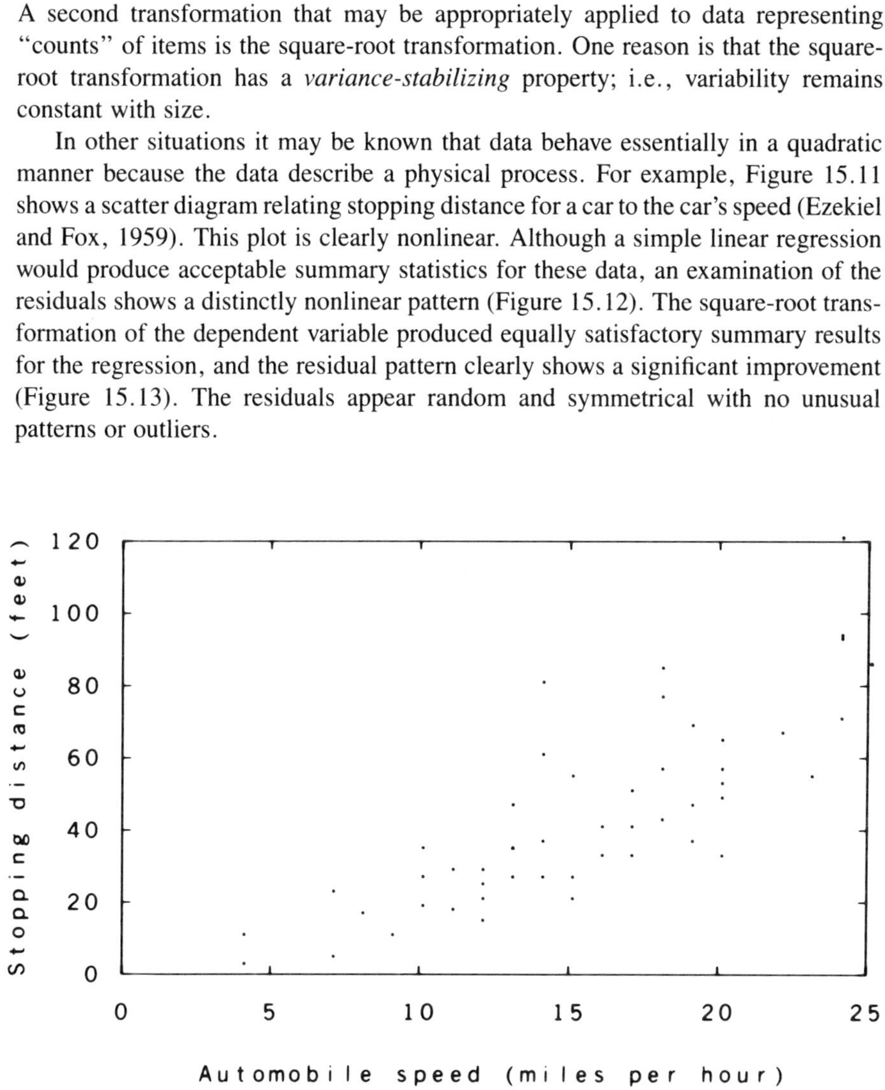


**Figure 15.11** A scatter diagram showing stopping distance versus automobile speed.

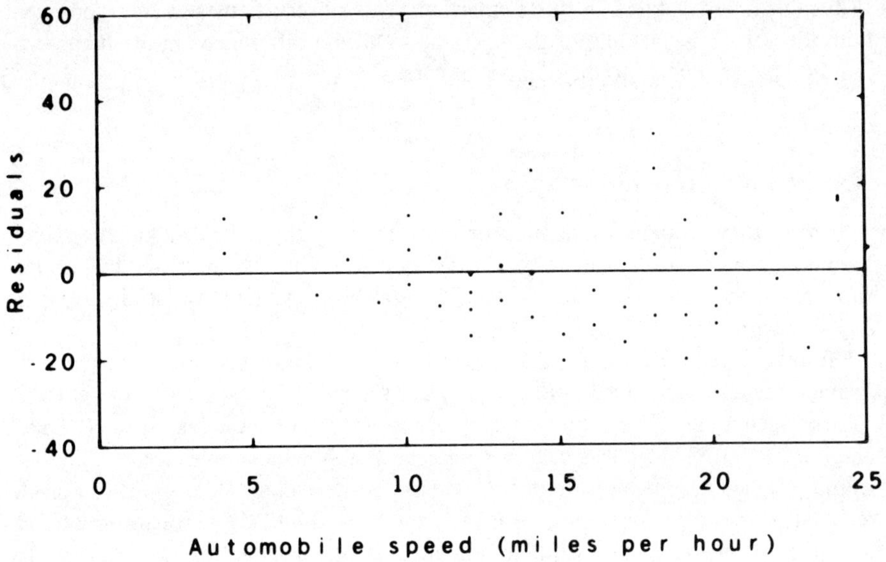


**Figure 15.12** For the data in Figure 15.11, the residuals after regression show a nonlinear pattern.

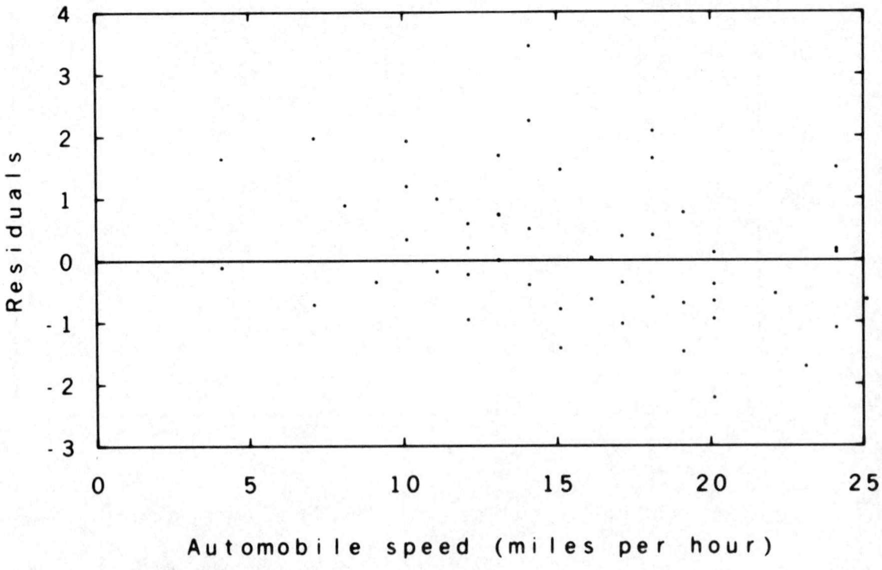


**Figure 15.13** For the data in Figure 15.11, the residuals after transformation of the dependent variable (stopping distance).

## GRAPHICAL AIDS

In addition to the visual examination of residual plots for nonrandomness, nonlinearities, and outliers, other graphical aids include the histogram, stem-and-leaf display, box plot, and quantile-quantile (Q-Q) plot (Chapters 6 and 7).

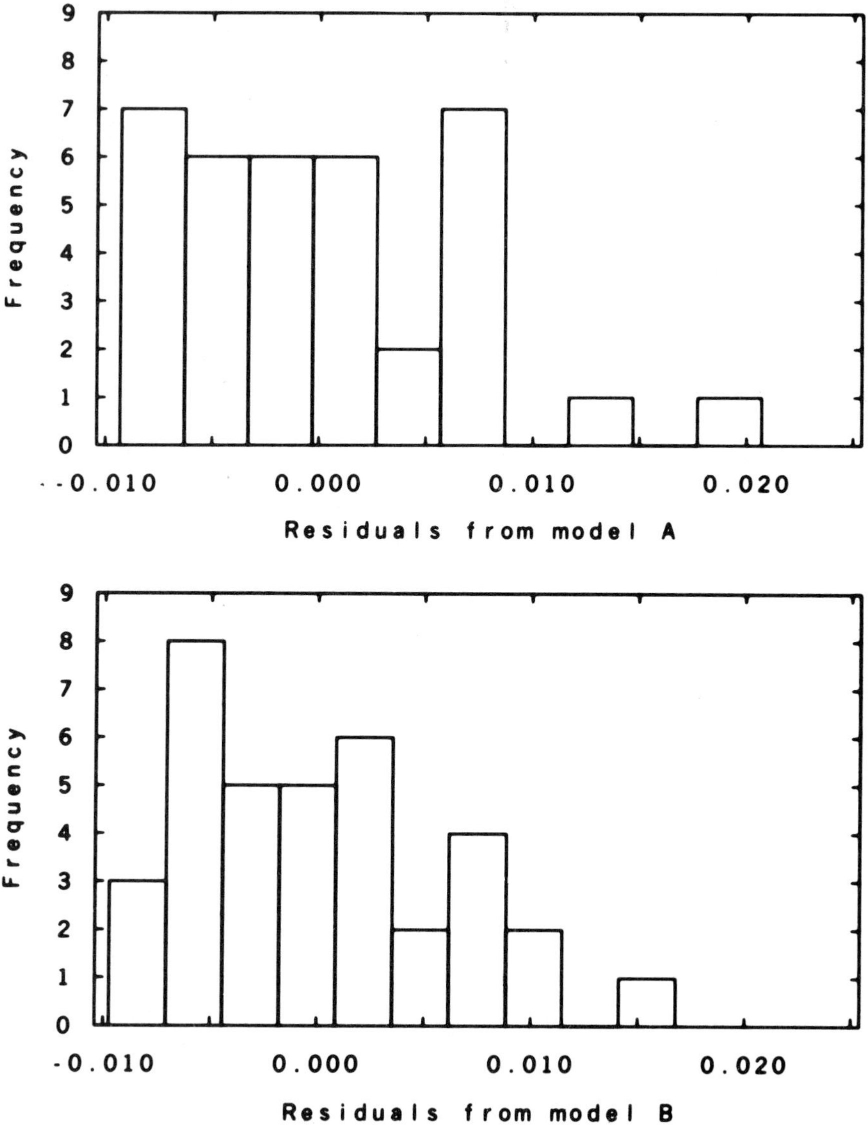


**Figure 15.14** Histograms of residuals from the business telephones example from Chapter 14.

Figure 15.14 shows a histogram of the residuals for each of the two models for business telephones from the forecasting example discussed in Chapter 13. The independent variables in the two regressions are nonfarm employment and nonfarm employment less manufacturing employment. The histograms of the residuals appear almost symmetrical, with perhaps a somewhat longer tail for positive residuals. Box plots of the residuals are shown in Figure 15.15; the figure summarizes differences in variability and shows extreme residuals for the data of Figure 15.14.

A quantile-quantile plot (quantiles of the residuals of the model versus the quantiles of a normal probability curve) is shown for comparison in Figure 15.16. This plot is linear except for some large residuals. The cause of the large residuals is related to the 1975 economic downturn and corresponding high unemployment levels. Since the presence of just one outlier can change the OLS parameter estimates and the $R$-squared statistic significantly, certain observations could be deleted or adjusted (see Chapter 10 for a discussion on data adjustment). The use of ***robust regression*** as a tool complementary to OLS will be discussed in Chapter 17.

A plot of the residuals versus the predicted values, such as is shown for the mobile phone data in Figure 15.17, is often helpful in deciding if a transformation of the dependent variable is appropriate. For example, the plot shows increasing dispersion with increasing values of the predictions; a logarithmic or square-root transformation of the dependent variable may help. The model can then be reestimated, and the plot of the residuals versus the predicted values (Figure 15.18) will then show a uniform or constant variability about the zero line.

Figure 15.19 further supports the appropriateness of taking transformations for the mobile phone unit data described earlier. The Q-Q plots represent the distribution

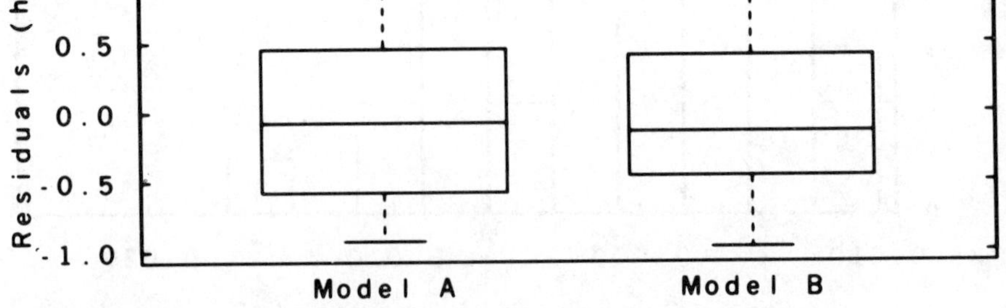

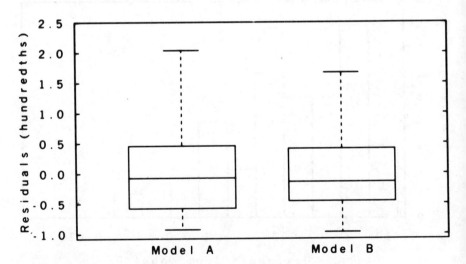

**Figure 15.15** Box plot of residuals for the business telephone data of Figure 15.14; differences in variability and potential outliers among these are highlighted.

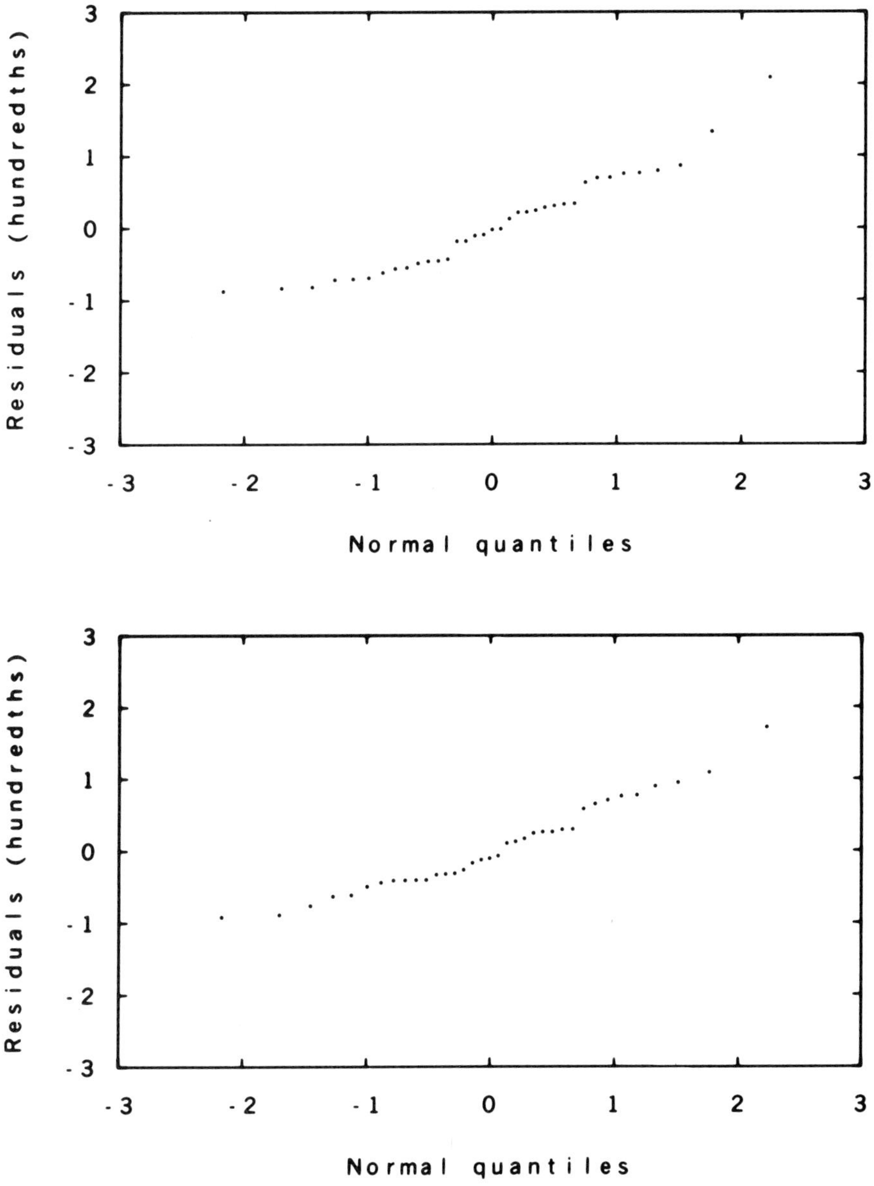


**Figure 15.16** Q-Q plot of the residuals for the business telephone data for the models A and B respectively, confirming very similar distributions for the residuals.

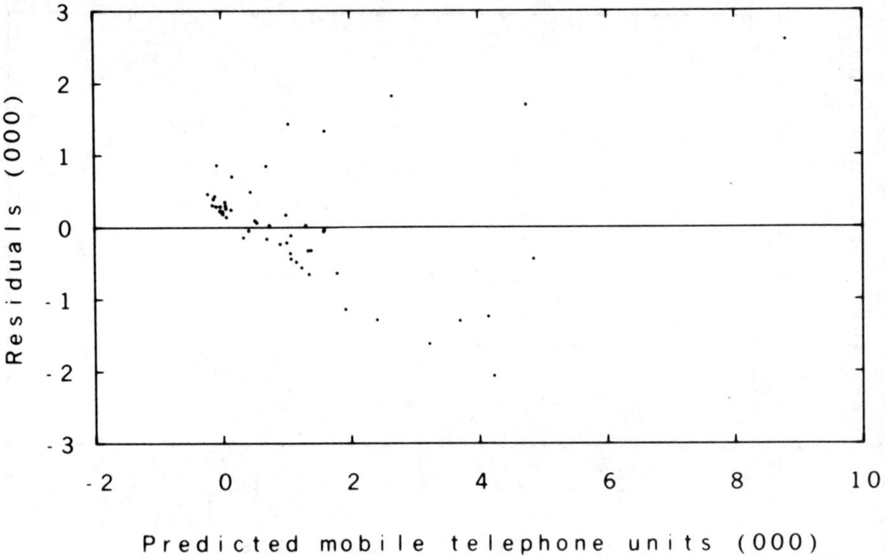


**Figure 15.17** A plot of the residuals versus the predicted values for the original mobile phone unit data in Figure 15.9.

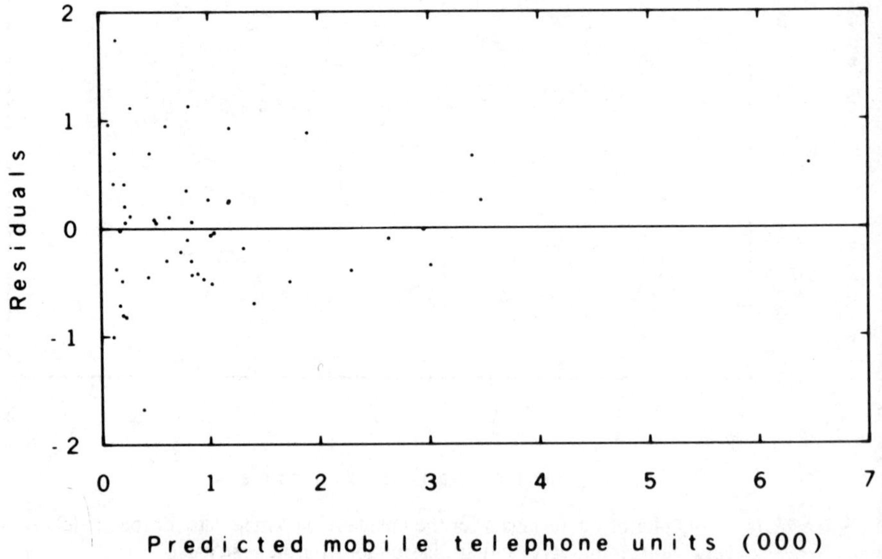


**Figure 15.18** A plot of the residuals versus the predicted values for the log-transformed mobile phone unit data in Figure 15.10.

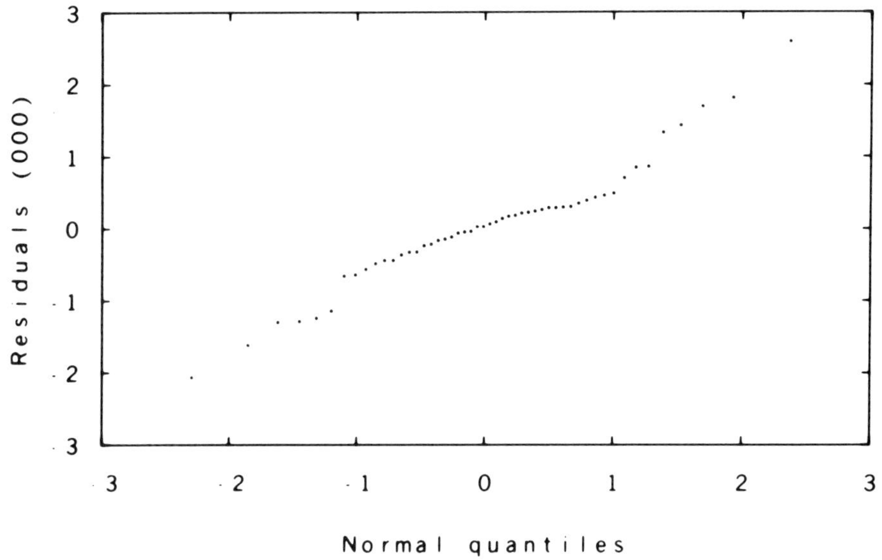


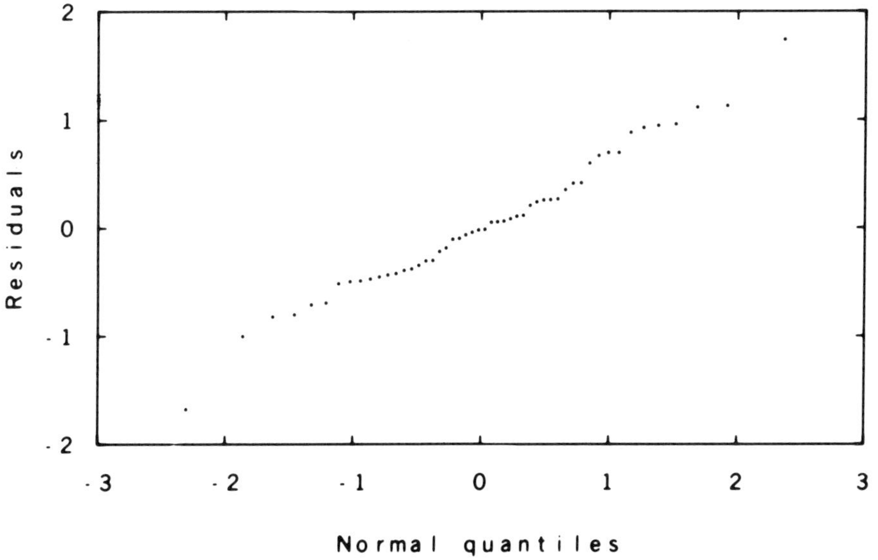


**Figure 15.19** Q-Q plots of the mobile phone unit residuals; comparison of the models for the original and transformed data shows improvement (less curvature) in the tail area of the distribution of the residuals.

of the residuals from the models for the original and log-transformed data, respectively. Evidently, the transformed model appears to be closest to the normality assumption since its Q-Q plot is the straightest.

The residuals of a model can also be plotted against the independent variable to

- Detect outliers.
- Assess nonhomogeneity of variance.
- Determine if a transformation is required.

This graphical technique is particularly useful in the early stages of modeling.

## SUMMARY

While linear regression models based on nonlinearly related data may appear to give acceptable summary statistics, the inferences drawn from such models can be erroneous and misleading. Residual analysis is an effective tool for graphically demonstrating departures from model assumptions. When looking at regression residuals, keep in mind that

- A residual plot of constant variance with no visible pattern is consistent with the basic assumptions of the linear least-squares regression model. If the residuals are also normally distributed, a variety of significance tests can be performed. Also, the run test can be applied to test for nonrandomness.
- A residual pattern of increasing dispersion may suggest the need to transform one or more variables. The logarithmic and square-root transformations are the most commonly used to solve this problem. A plot of the residuals versus the dependent variable also highlights the need for transformations.
- The normal quantile-quantile (Q-Q) plot is a convenient way to decide if the residuals are normally distributed. Also, outliers are readily detected at one or the other end of the plot.

## USEFUL READING

EZEKIEL, M., and K. A. FOX (1959). *Methods of Correlation and Regression Analysis*. New York, NY: John Wiley and Sons.

ROBERTS, H. V. (1974). *Conversational Statistics*. Hewlett-Packard University Business Series. Palo Alto, CA: The Scientific Press.

WALSH, J. E. (1962). *Handbook of Nonparametric Statistics*. Princeton, NJ: Van Nostrand Co.

CHAPTER 16

# Insuring Against Unusual Values

This chapter develops the notion of *robust estimation*—methods of insuring that an estimate will be insensitive to small departures from assumptions. In particular, this chapter describes:

- The derivation and computational procedure for two robust estimators of location of a set of data—the trimmed mean and the Huber $M$-estimator.
- Resistant smoothers for time series data, introduced here as a prelude to a robust seasonal adjustment procedure (Chapter 19).

## ROBUSTNESS DEFINED

Statistical estimation is built upon a mathematical theory that is seldom realized exactly in forecasting practice. For estimating location and scale of data, for example, the arithmetic mean and sample variance can be shown to be "best" (i.e., have optimal properties) if the data are a random sample from the normal distribution. Likewise, correlation and least squares regression generally assume a normal distribution. Least squares techniques are not only "not best," however, but can be horribly misleading when the data deviate from the normality assumption. Because of this, it is important to have estimation procedures that will be "robust" against data that would otherwise be distortive.

The need for a nontraditional approach to estimation is motivated by two facts. The first is that a forecaster never has an accurate knowledge of the true underlying distribution of the data. Second, even slight deviations from a strict parametric model can give rise to poor statistical performance for classical (associated with the method of least squares) estimation techniques. Estimators that are less sensitive to these factors are often referred to as being *robust* (Box, 1953). In particular, it is well known that outliers can distort certain estimators; a robust procedure must produce estimates that are not seriously affected by the presence of a few outliers. Thus, some robust estimators are designed to be *resistant* to unusual data values—they give less weight to observations which stray from the bulk of the data.

The importance of using robust methods is illustrated by Mallows (1979), who describes several analyses of large data sets (more than 1000 observations) in which robustness considerations have proved relevant.

## ROBUST ESTIMATES OF LOCATION

Consider an example of the effect one bad observation can have on the arithmetic mean of a group of numbers. The set of numbers {3, 4, 4, 5, 6, 6, 6, 7, 9, 10} has a mean of 6.0. But adding one observation, say 50, changes the mean to 10.0. The latter clearly does not represent the location or "center" of the bulk of the data. Depending on the use of the application, a forecaster should be cautious in using statistical measures blindly, since however well known they may be, some are possibly not well behaved.

### The Trimmed Mean

Although the arithmetic mean is a classical estimator of location with a great deal of tradition, it is often accepted uncritically by the practitioner. The above example illustrates a bad quality of the arithmetic mean, namely that one outlier can have an undue effect on the arithmetic mean and even pull an estimate of the bulk of data away from its representative value. An alternative estimator of location is the *α-trimmed mean*. Recall from Chapter 7 that a trimmed mean is calculated by deleting or "trimming" a proportion of the ordered data from each end and then calculating the arithmetic mean of the remaining numbers. The deletion of points is based on their order, but the deleted points are not necessarily extreme values.

The procedure for calculating the α-trimmed mean can be defined as follows. Let $y_{(i)}$ equal the $i$th *ordered* observation. We will need to define $a = [\alpha n]$, where $n$ is the number of observations and α denotes the trimming proportion; notice that the brackets [ ] represent the "greatest integer" function—i.e., the greatest integer equal to or less than the given number. Thus, if you trim 50 percent from each end of an ordered array of data, you will end up with the median.

The trimmed mean is equal to the sum of the untrimmed values divided by $h$, where $h = n - 2a$. Thus, the α-trimmed mean $m(\alpha)$ is defined by

$$m(\alpha) = \frac{1}{h} \sum_{i=a+1}^{n-a} y_{(i)}.$$

When using the arithmetic mean, the standard deviation is used to find an estimate of sample variability, and the standard deviation divided by $\sqrt{n}$ is an estimate of the standard error of the mean. The standard error of the trimmed mean, denoted by $s[m(\alpha)]$, can be approximated by

$$s[m(\alpha)] = [SS(\alpha)/h(h-1)]^{1/2},$$

where $SS(\alpha)$ is the sum of squares defined by

$$SS(\alpha) = \sum_{i=1}^{n} [w_i - m(\alpha)]^2.$$

The *Winsorized values* of $y_{(i)}$, denoted by $w_i$, are defined by

$$w_i = \begin{cases} y_{(a+1)} & i = 1, \ldots, a \\ y_{(i)} & i = a+1, \ldots, n-a \\ y_{(n-a)} & i = n-a+1, \ldots, n. \end{cases}$$

Notice that the trimmed values are replaced with the $(a + 1)$th value at the low end and the $(n - a)$th value at the high end.

Furthermore, Monte Carlo studies have shown that

$$[m(\alpha) - \theta]/s[m(\alpha)]$$

has an approximate $t$-distribution with $(h - 1)$ degrees of freedom. Here, $\theta$ is the location parameter for a symmetric distribution. Therefore, assuming an underlying symmetric distribution, a confidence interval for $\theta$ can be given by

$$m(\alpha) - t_{h-1}(\alpha/2)s[m(\alpha)] < \theta < m(\alpha) + t_{h-1}(\alpha/2)s[m(\alpha)],$$

where $t_{h-1}(\alpha/2)$ is the $100(1 - \alpha)$ percent significance level for a Student $t$-distribution on $h - 1$ degrees of freedom. Thus with 95 percent confidence ($\alpha = 0.05$), $\theta$ will lie between $m(\alpha) \pm t_{h-1}(0.025)s[m(\alpha)]$.

Notice that the underlying assumption of a symmetric distribution is less restrictive than the assumption of normality used in classical statistics. Estimates for the asymptotic (large sample) variance of the $\alpha$-trimmed mean of asymmetric distributions have also been studied by Andrews et al. (1972).

## *M*-Estimators

A method has been developed which will "automatically" reduce the effect of outliers by giving them a reduced weight when computing the "average" value of the data. This estimator, often called the *M-estimator,* is the "maximum likelihood estimate" (a good statistical property to assess) for the location parameter of a heavy-tailed distribution, defined by Huber (1964). Basically, the Huber distribution behaves like a normal distribution in the middle range and like an exponential distribution in the tails. Thus the bulk of the data appears normally distributed, while there is a greater chance of having extreme observations in the sample.

The steps necessary to compute the Huber $M$-estimator are:

1. Compute an initial (very "robust") estimate for $\theta$, say $\hat{\theta}$ = median, and calculate the residuals from this estimate.
2. Estimate a scale statistic $s$ by using MAD/0.6745 where MAD (median absolute deviation) is the median of

   $$|y_i - \hat{\theta}|, \qquad i = 1, 2, \ldots, n.$$
3. Compute weights $W_i^2$, using residuals and the scale estimate $s$:

   $$W_i^2 = \begin{cases} 1 & \text{if } |y_i - \hat{\theta}| \leq Ks \\ Ks/|y_i - \hat{\theta}| & \text{if } |y_i - \hat{\theta}| > Ks, \end{cases}$$

   where a constant $K$ is chosen that will obtain a desirable level of efficiency: a reasonable set of values are 1.0, 1.5, and 2.0. As $K$ becomes smaller, more points receive a weight of less than 1 (Figure 16.1). The value of $K$ depends on what percentage of the data are outliers or how much "efficiency" (see Chapter 12) you want to give up if the data are normally distributed.
4. Obtain a new estimate from

   $$\hat{\theta} = \frac{\sum_{i=1}^{n} W_i^2 y_i}{\sum_{i=1}^{n} W_i^2}.$$
5. Repeat steps 2 through 4 until convergence.

It has been shown (Huber, 1973) that the asymptotic (large sample) variance of the Huber $M$-estimator can be estimated by

$$V(\hat{\theta}) = \frac{1}{(n^*)^2} \sum_{i=1}^{n} W_i^4 (y_i - \hat{\theta})^2,$$

where $n^*$ is defined as the number of observations with $W_i = 1$.

## A Numerical Example

To get some insight into the mechanics of calculating a robust estimate of location, it may be valuable to work out an example based on a small set of (ordered) data:

$$\{-67, -48, 6, 8, 14, 16, 23, 24, 28, 29, 41, 49, 56, 60, 75\}.$$

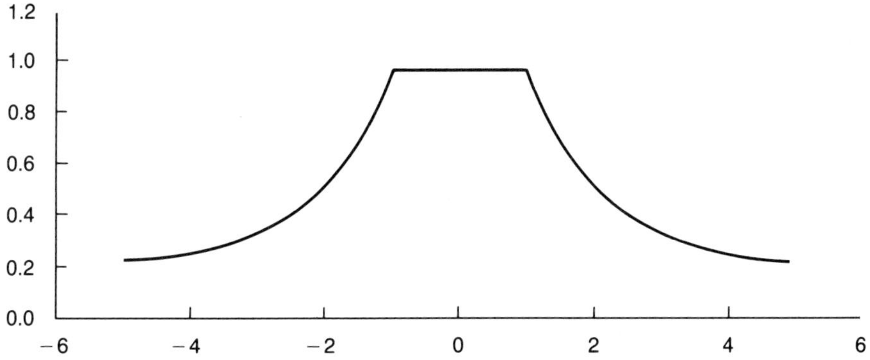


**Figure 16.1** The Huber weight function.

The first step in data analysis should be to investigate the data graphically. Reviewing the data, you would observe the extremely low values, −67 and −48. The next step might be to prepare a quantile-quantile (Q-Q) plot (Figure 16.2). If the data are normally distributed, they should lie along a straight line. The plot demonstrates that the two smallest data values are indeed extreme, indicating that the normality assumption may not be valid.

The Q-Q plot can also be used to get a "quick-and-dirty" robust estimate of the ($\mu$, $\sigma$) parameters of the normal distribution. By "eyeballing" a straight line through the *bulk* of the points on the Q-Q plot, you can determine that the $Y$-intercept at

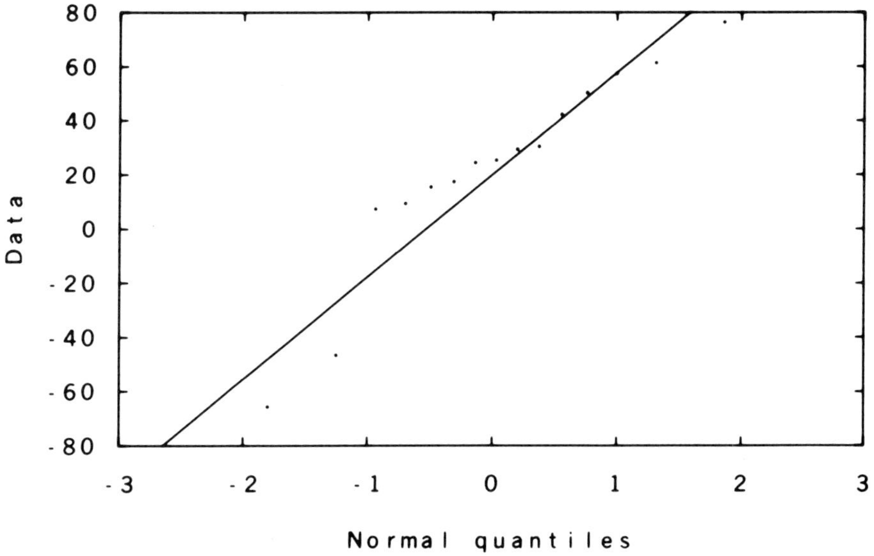


**Figure 16.2** A quantile-quantile (Q-Q) plot for a small data set.

$X = 0$ and the slope of the line correspond to estimates of $\hat{\mu}$ and $\hat{\sigma}$, respectively. On the other hand, the ordinary least squares estimates, calculated from the data, are $\hat{\mu} = 20.93$ and $\hat{\sigma} = 37.74$, which could be used to superimpose a straight line with intercept 20.93 and slope 37.74 on the Q-Q plot. As can be seen from Figure 16.2, the straight line determined from the least squares estimates doesn't represent the bulk of the data on the Q-Q plot.

Table 16.1 shows the calculations of the α-trimmed mean and *its* standard error for these data when 25 percent of the data are "trimmed." For $\alpha = 0.25$ and $n = 15$, the largest integer value of $(0.25 \times 15 = 3.75)$ is 3, and therefore three values are trimmed from each end.

Column 1 shows the ordered raw data. In Column 2, the Winsorized values of the ordered data are listed. The first three data values are replaced by the value of the fourth observation (the smallest untrimmed observation), and the last three values are replaced by the value of the twelfth observation (the largest untrimmed observation). The trimmed mean is the average of the fourth through the twelfth values

**Table 16.1** The α-trimmed mean and its standard error for the 15 numbers plotted in Figure 16.3. The trimming parameter is $\alpha = 0.25$.

| (1) $y_{(i)}$ | (2) $w_i$ | (3) $(w_i - \hat{\theta})$ | (4) $(w_i - \hat{\theta})^2$ |
|---|---|---|---|
| −67 | 8 | −17.78 | 316.13 |
| −48 | 8 | −17.78 | 316.13 |
| 6 | 8 | −17.78 | 316.13 |
| 8 | 8 | −17.78 | 316.13 |
| 14 | 14 | −11.78 | 138.77 |
| 16 | 16 | −9.78 | 95.65 |
| 23 | 23 | −2.78 | 7.73 |
| 24 | 24 | −1.78 | 3.17 |
| 28 | 28 | 2.22 | 4.93 |
| 29 | 29 | 3.22 | 10.37 |
| 41 | 41 | 15.22 | 231.67 |
| 49 | 49 | 23.22 | 539.17 |
| 56 | 49 | 23.22 | 539.17 |
| 60 | 49 | 23.22 | 539.17 |
| 75 | 49 | 23.22 | 539.17 |
| Total: | | | 3913.45 |

$\alpha = 0.25$; $n = 15$

$a = (0.25)(15) = 3.75(\text{integer } 3)$; $h = n - 2(3) = 9$

$$\hat{\theta} = m(0.25) = 1/9 \sum_{i=4}^{12} y_{(i)} = 25.78$$

$$s[m(0.25)] = [3913.45/9(8)]^{1/2} = 7.37$$

and is 232/9 = 25.78. Column 3 is the deviation between the Winsorized values and the trimmed mean. Column 4 is the square of Column 3 and is summed for use in the standard error calculation. The standard error of this trimmed mean is the square root of the sum of the squares of Column 3 divided by $(h)(h - 1)$: $(3913.45/72)^{1/2} = 7.37$.

Tables 16.2 and 16.3 show the calculations for the Huber *M*-estimator of location and its corresponding standard error for the raw data of Table 16.1. In Table 16.2, Column 1 is the ordered raw data. The median of the data is 24. Column 2 is the difference between the raw data and the median. The median absolute deviation is 17; it is the median of the absolute value of this column (the eighth largest absolute value of Column 2). An approximate unbiased scale statistic is the MAD/0.6745 = 25.2. The divisor 0.6745 is used because then MAD/0.6745 will be approximately equal to the standard deviation $\sigma$ of a normal distribution if the number of observations is large and if the data are actually a random sample from a normal distribution with variance $\sigma^2$.

By using $K = 2$ for observations whose absolute residuals are greater than two standard errors, deviations in Column 2 in excess of $Ks = (2)(25.2) = 50.4$ are downweighted. Therefore, observations 1, 2, and 15 receive less than full weight. Column 3 contains the weights $[W_{i1}^2 = 50.4/|y_i - \text{median}|]$ for those values beyond $Ks$. A weighted mean is calculated by taking the product of corresponding entries in Columns 1 and 3 and summing over the 15 products (= 357.38), then dividing this by the sum of Column 3 (= 14.24). In Table 16.3, this calculation gives $\hat{\theta}_1 = 25.13$ for this first iteration. A second iteration provides a refined estimate of $\hat{\theta}_2 = 25.17$. Thus two iterations appear sufficient for convergence.

**Table 16.2** Calculations of the Huber *M*-estimator of location, when $K = 2$ and $\hat{\theta}_0$ = median $(y_i)$ = 24.

| (1) $y_{(i)}$ | (2) $y_{(i)} - \hat{\theta}_0$ | (3) $W_{i1}^2$ | (4) $y_{(i)} - \hat{\theta}_1$ | (5) $W_{i2}^2$ |
|---|---|---|---|---|
| −67 | −91 | 50.4/91 | −92.13 | 50.8/92.13 |
| −48 | −72 | 50.4/72 | −73.13 | 50.8/73.13 |
| 6 | −18 | 1 | −19.13 | 1 |
| 8 | −16 | 1 | −17.13 | 1 |
| 14 | −10 | 1 | −11.13 | 1 |
| 16 | −8 | 1 | −9.13 | 1 |
| 23 | −1 | 1 | −2.13 | 1 |
| 24 | 0 | 1 | −1.13 | 1 |
| 28 | 4 | 1 | 2.87 | 1 |
| 29 | 5 | 1 | 3.87 | 1 |
| 41 | 17 | 1 | 15.87 | 1 |
| 49 | 25 | 1 | 23.87 | 1 |
| 56 | 32 | 1 | 30.87 | 1 |
| 60 | 36 | 1 | 34.87 | 1 |
| 75 | 51 | 50.4/51 | 49.87 | 1 |

**Table 16.3** Calculations for the Huber *M*-estimator of the standard error, when $K = 2$ and $\hat{\theta}_0 = 24$ (median).

Iteration 0: $\hat{\theta}_0 = \text{Median} = 24.$

Iteration 1:

$$s = \frac{\text{MAD}}{0.6745} = \frac{17}{0.6745} = 25.20;$$

$$Ks = 50.40;$$

$$\hat{\theta}_1 = \frac{\Sigma W_i^2 y_i}{\Sigma W_i^2} = \frac{357.38}{14.24} = 25.13.$$

Iteration 2:

$$s = \frac{\text{MAD}}{0.6745} = \frac{17.13}{0.6745} = 25.40;$$

$$Ks = 50.8;$$

$$\hat{\theta}_2 = \frac{\Sigma W_i^2 y_i}{\Sigma W_i^2} = \frac{358.72}{14.25} = 25.17;$$

$$V(\hat{\theta}) = \left[\frac{\Sigma W_i^4 (y_i - \hat{\theta}_2)^2}{(n^*)^2}\right]^{1/2} = \left[\frac{\Sigma W_i^4 (y_i - 25.17)^2}{(13)^2}\right]^{1/2} = 8.28,$$

where $n^*$ = number of observations receiving full weight.

The standard error of this estimate is obtained by multiplying the square of the weights (Column 5 of Table 16.2) by the square of the deviations between the data and the location estimate $\hat{\theta}_2$, dividing by the square of the number of observations receiving full weight, and taking the square root of the resulting number. This calculation is shown in Table 16.3.

The results for the mean, the 0.25-trimmed mean (also called the midmean), and the Huber *M*-estimator are:

| | Mean | Midmean | *M*-estimator |
|---|---|---|---|
| $\hat{\theta}$: | 20.93 | 25.78 | 25.17 |
| $V(\hat{\theta})$: | 9.74 | 7.37 | 8.28 |

Notice that $V(\hat{\theta})$ is the estimated standard deviation of the location *estimator* and not of the *sample*.

It is clear that the arithmetic mean is very sensitive to outliers or distant observations. Both the trimmed mean and Huber *M*-estimator provide estimates that are less sensitive to the extreme values. The standard error of the *M*-estimator is somewhat smaller than that for the mean. However, the standard error for the midmean is significantly less. This is somewhat expected since computations for the midmean begin by trimming and Winsorizing 40 percent of the data, the 40 percent being the most extreme values (three from each end), whereas these points still have some effect (but less than least squares) on the Huber *M*-estimator since their associated weight is not zero.

The Huber *M*-estimator is used again in Chapter 17 to downweight extreme observations so that they do not unduly distort the regression relationship determined by the bulk of the data.

## RESISTANT SMOOTHING

Resistance to outliers is also important in the smoothing of time series, where underlying trends should not be unduly distorted by extreme values in the pattern. In particular, the SABL procedure, discussed in Chapter 19, makes extensive use of resistant smoothers in the seasonal adjustment process.

It is useful, at this point, to consider the smoothing operation as sliding a *window* across data, to estimate the location or central tendency of the data within the window. To illustrate how smoothing processes are used, we have used a small section of logarithms of airline data compiled by Box and Jenkins (1976, Series G). A portion of these data is shown in Table 16.4.

The table shows monthly values for 1956 to 1959. We have arbitrarily inserted errant values for June 1957, September 1958, and July 1959 (7.0, 8.0, 3.0) to demonstrate how such extreme values can be handled (see Figure 16.3). Column 1 of Table 16.4 contains the basic data and Column 2 contains a *twelve-month moving median* of the data. To compute the medians, the data are resequenced (put in order from least to largest, twelve months at a time), and the average of the sixth and seventh values is taken in every twelve-month period. Since the period of the data is even, the median for the first twelve-month period is positioned between the sixth and seventh months. The procedure is continued through the remainder of the data.

In Column 3 of Table 16.4, a twelve-month moving mean of the medians is calculated. Again, the first entry in this column will be positioned between the sixth and seventh moving median entries, in the "December 1956" row. A three-month moving average of the means, Column 4, further smooths the data and results in a new time series with exactly one year of data missing at the beginning and end of the original data.

**Table 16.4** Monthly values of the logarithms of the airline data for 1956–1959, with three outliers.

| Year | Month | (1) Data | (2) Twelve-month moving median of (1) | (3) Twelve-month moving mean of (2) | (4) Three-month moving mean of (3) | (5) Crude trend—tapered moving mean of (4) |
|---|---|---|---|---|---|---|
| 1956 | JAN | 5.649 | | | | |
| | FEB | 5.624 | | | | |
| | MAR | 5.759 | | | | |
| | APR | 5.746 | | | | |
| | MAY | 5.762 | | | | |
| | JUN | 5.924 | | | | |
| | | | 5.753 | | | |
| | JUL | 6.023 | | | | |
| | | | 5.756 | | | |
| | AUG | 6.004 | | | | |
| | | | 5.756 | | | |
| | SEP | 5.872 | | | | |
| | | | 5.758 | | | |
| | OCT | 5.724 | | | | |
| | | | 5.807 | | | |
| | NOV | 5.602 | | | | |
| | | | 5.862 | | | |
| | DEC | 5.724 | | 5.822 | | |
| | | | 5.862 | | | |
| 1957 | JAN | 5.753 | | 5.831 | 5.831 | 5.840 |
| | | | 5.862 | | | |
| | FEB | 5.707 | | 5.840 | 5.840 | 5.844 |
| | | | 5.862 | | | |
| | MAR | 5.875 | | 5.849 | 5.849 | 5.848 |
| | | | 5.862 | | | |
| | APR | 5.852 | | 5.858 | 5.856 | 5.854 |
| | | | 5.862 | | | |
| | MAY | 5.872 | | 5.862 | 5.861 | 5.858 |
| | | | 5.862 | | | |
| (6.045)* | JUN | 7.000 | | 5.863 | 5.863 | 5.862 |
| | | | 5.862 | | | |
| | JUL | 6.146 | | 5.864 | 5.864 | 5.864 |
| | | | 5.862 | | | |
| | AUG | 6.146 | | 5.865 | 5.865 | 5.865 |
| | | | 5.862 | | | |
| | SEP | 6.001 | | 5.865 | 5.865 | 5.866 |
| | | | 5.862 | | | |
| | OCT | 5.849 | | 5.866 | 5.866 | 5.867 |
| | | | 5.862 | | | |
| | NOV | 5.720 | | 5.868 | 5.868 | 5.869 |
| | | | 5.872 | | | |
| | DEC | 5.817 | | 5.871 | 5.871 | 5.871 |
| | | | 5.872 | | | |
| 1958 | JAN | 5.829 | | 5.873 | 5.873 | 5.873 |
| | | | 5.872 | | | |
| | FEB | 5.762 | | 5.875 | 5.875 | 5.876 |
| | | | 5.872 | | | |
| | MAR | 5.892 | | 5.877 | 5.877 | 5.879 |
| | | | 5.872 | | | |
| | APR | 5.852 | | 5.880 | 5.881 | 5.883 |
| | | | 5.888 | | | |
| | MAY | 5.894 | | 5.886 | 5.887 | 5.889 |
| | | | 5.888 | | | |
| | JUN | 6.075 | | 5.896 | 5.896 | 5.896 |
| | | | 5.888 | | | |
| | JUL | 6.196 | | 5.906 | 5.904 | 5.903 |
| | | | 5.889 | | | |
| | AUG | 6.225 | | 5.911 | 5.911 | 5.910 |
| | | | 5.889 | | | |
| (6.001)* | SEP | 8.000 | | 5.917 | 5.917 | 5.917 |
| | | | 5.890 | | | |
| | OCT | 5.883 | | 5.922 | 5.923 | 5.924 |
| | | | 5.938 | | | |
| | NOV | 5.737 | | 5.931 | 5.931 | 5.932 |
| | | | 5.994 | | | |
| | DEC | 5.820 | | 5.939 | 5.940 | 5.941 |
| | | | 5.994 | | | |
| 1959 | JAN | 5.886 | | 5.949 | 5.949 | 5.950 |
| | | | 5.934 | | | |
| | FEB | 5.835 | | 5.959 | 5.959 | 5.959 |
| | | | 5.934 | | | |
| | MAR | 6.006 | | 5.969 | 5.969 | 5.969 |

*Denotes original values.

**Table 16.4** *(continued)*

| Year | Month | (1)<br>Data | (2)<br>Twelve-month moving median of (1) | (3)<br>Twelve-month moving mean of (2) | (4)<br>Three-month moving mean of (3) | (5)<br>Crude trend—tapered moving mean of (4) |
|---|---|---|---|---|---|---|
| | | | 5.934 | | | |
| | APR | 5.981 | 5.994 | 5.980 | 5.979 | 5.977 |
| | MAY | 6.040 | 5.994 | 5.988 | 5.987 | 5.985 |
| | JUN | 6.157 | 6.005 | 5.992 | 5.992 | 5.993 |
| (6.306)* | JUL | 3.000 | 6.008 | 5.995 | 5.998 | 6.001 |
| | AUG | 6.326 | 6.008 | 6.008 | 6.008 | 6.010 |
| | SEP | 6.138 | 6.021 | 6.020 | 6.020 | 6.021 |
| | OCT | 6.009 | 6.036 | 6.033 | 6.033 | 6.031 |
| | NOV | 5.892 | 6.036 | 6.045 | 6.045 | 6.039 |
| | DEC | 6.004 | 6.036 | 6.056 | 6.056 | 6.045 |
| | | . | | 6.067 | | |
| | | . | | | | |
| | | . | | | | |
| | | . | | | | |

*Denotes original values.

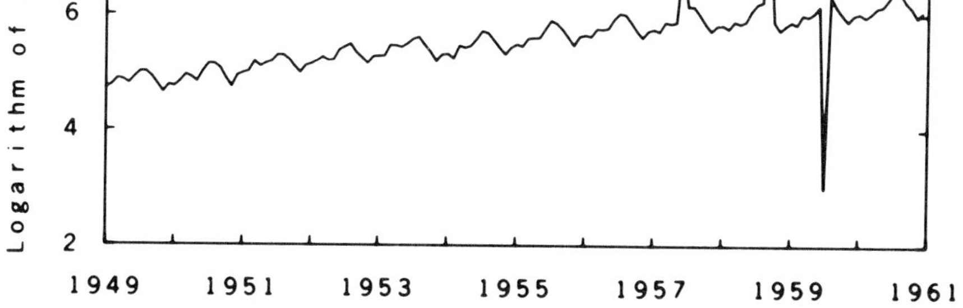

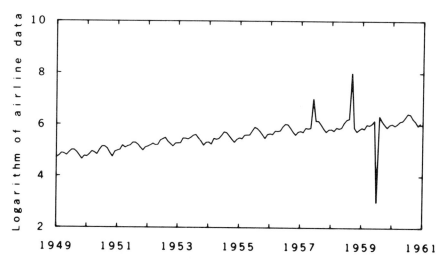

**Figure 16.3** Time plot of the logarithms of the airline data showing the three outliers. The outliers are June 1957 = 7.0, September 1958 = 8.0, and July 1959 = 3.0.

Next, a *tapered moving mean* is needed. This involves calculating weighted moving averages in which the weights diminish with distance from the month for which the calculation is being made. A scheme is used in which the weights follow a *bisquare function,* of the form

$$B(u) = \begin{cases} (1 - u^2)^2 & \text{if } |u| \leq 1 \\ 0 & \text{if } |u| > 1. \end{cases}$$

The amount of trend smoothing required is selected by the user. For a small, medium, or large amount of smoothing, the recommended smooth window is 7, 15, or 31, respectively. The calculation of the weights for a "seven-period window" bisquare weighting function is illustrated in Table 16.5.

The tapered mean is calculated by multiplying the data values by the appropriate weights, summing up the weighted values, and dividing by the sum of the weights. A sample calculation is shown in Table 16.6. Here the months of January through July in 1957 figure into the tapered mean for April 1957.

In this manner, Column 5 of Table 16.4 was compiled. Column 5 shows the tapered moving means of the values given in Column 4. The tapered mean is resistant because it is a mean of medians which are themselves resistant to the distortion of extreme values.

Table 16.4 could be extended to include additional columns. Table 16.7 shows the continuation of the calculations involved in developing a more refined trend smooth. Column 6 is simply the moving mean from Column 4 of Table 16.4 minus the tapered moving mean. This result can be viewed as a systematic noise pattern about the trend and is similar to autocorrelated residuals about a regression line. These "residual" values are smoothed (Column 7) and added to the trend approximation of Column 5 to develop the *initial trend smooth* that represents trend-cycle (Column 8).

In the SABL procedure, seasonal values are then computed. They are subtracted from the original data to yield trend plus irregular (the notation for this is $T + I$). The $T + I$ series is then smoothed to yield a resistant approximation of trend. A more detailed explanation is presented in Chapter 19.

**Table 16.5** Calculation of the weights for a seven-period bisquare weighting function.

| | |
|---|---|
| $W(t) = \mathrm{B}[t/(\mathrm{T} + 1)]$ | $t = -T, \ldots, 0, \ldots, T$ |

$W(-3) = B(-3/4) = [1 - (-3/4)^2]^2 = 0.191$
$W(-2) = B(-2/4) = [1 - (-2/4)^2]^2 = 0.563$
$W(-1) = B(-1/4) = [1 - (-1/4)^2]^2 = 0.879$
$W(0) = B(1 - 0) = (1 - 0^2)^2 = 1.0$
$W(1) = B(1/4) = 0.879$
$W(2) = B(2/4) = 0.563$
$W(3) = B(3/4) = 0.191$

**Table 16.6** Calculation for a tapered mean of log-transformed airline data for April 1957.

| Month | Data | × | Weight | = | Weighted values | Tapered moving mean* |
|---|---|---|---|---|---|---|
| JAN | 5.831 | | 0.191 | | 1.114 | |
| FEB | 5.840 | | 0.563 | | 3.288 | |
| MAR | 5.849 | | 0.879 | | 5.141 | |
| APR | 5.856 | | 1.000 | | 5.856 | 5.854 |
| MAY | 5.861 | | 0.879 | | 5.152 | |
| JUN | 5.863 | | 0.563 | | 3.301 | |
| JUL | 5.864 | | 0.191 | | 1.120 | |
| | | | 4.266 | | 24.972 | |

$$\text{Tapered mean} = \frac{24.972}{4.266} = 5.854$$

*From Column 5, Table 16.4.

**Table 16.7** Continuation of the calculation of the trend smooth.

| Year | Month | (6) (4) − (5) | (7) Tapered moving mean of (6) | (8) Initial trend smooth (7) + (5) | (9) Data − trend (1) − (8) = $S + I$ |
|---|---|---|---|---|---|
| 1956 | JAN | | | | |
| | FEB | | | | |
| | MAR | | | | |
| | . | | | | |
| | . | | | | |
| | . | | | | |
| | OCT | | | | |
| | NOV | | | | |
| | DEC | | | | |
| 1957 | JAN | −.009 | −.004 | 5.836 | −.083 |
| | FEB | −.004 | −.003 | 5.840 | −.133 |
| | MAR | .001 | −.001 | 5.847 | .026 |
| | APR | .002 | .000 | 5.854 | −.002 |
| | MAY | .003 | .001 | 5.859 | .013 |
| | JUN | .001 | .001 | 5.863 | 1.137 |
| | JUL | .000 | .001 | 5.865 | .281 |
| | AUG | .000 | .000 | 5.865 | .281 |
| | SEP | −.001 | −.001 | 5.865 | .136 |
| | OCT | −.001 | −.001 | 5.866 | −.017 |
| | NOV | −.001 | −.001 | 5.868 | −.148 |
| | DEC | .000 | −.001 | 5.870 | −.053 |

## SOFTWARE CONSIDERATIONS

The programs BMDP7D and BMDP2D (Dixon and Brown, 1979) calculate three robust estimates of location, including the Winsorized and trimmed mean. The program BMDP7D calculates robust confidence intervals and prints double asterisks (**) after the estimate of the mean with the shortest confidence interval length —i.e., after the most precise estimate of the mean. A single asterisk (*) is printed after the interval which is the next shortest. See also a software discussion by Afifi and Azen (1979, Section 2.7) for robust estimators, and McNeil (1977) and Velleman and Hoaglin (1981) for portable FORTRAN and BASIC programs for robust smoothers.

## SUMMARY

- Robust methods are a way of dealing with estimation and modeling problems in the presence of outliers and nonnormality. Trimmed means and *M*-estimates are two examples of robust procedures.
- Robust procedures are recommended as complements to the usual (least squares) procedures (Hogg, 1979). When they are in essential agreement, they should be reported together. When substantial differences exist in the two analyses, the data should be examined more thoroughly for outliers or bad data values. Even if you use robust techniques, you should still plot the data for a thorough examination of it.
- Look long and hard at data and carefully examine residuals to be certain of the conclusions drawn from a statistical analysis. Robustness highlights residuals, inasmuch as the residuals for the bulk of the data are smaller than corresponding ones from least squares, and those for outliers are larger; thus robustness makes outliers even more obvious.
- The use of resistant smoothing techniques is demonstrated in the calculation of a trend smooth. Twelve-month moving medians of a time series eliminate the influence of extreme values. These medians are then smoothed by using bisquare weights that diminish in magnitude with distance from the time point for which the calculation is made.

Resistant smoothing procedures form the basis for discussion of a resistant seasonal adjustment procedure discussed in Chapter 19. In later chapters, robust/resistant techniques will be reinforced in the selection of specific models and in the interpretation of the reasonableness of the models.

## USEFUL READING

AFIFI, A. A., and S. P. AZEN (1979). *Statistical Analysis—A Computer Oriented Approach,* 2nd ed. New York, NY: Academic Press.

ANDREWS, D. F., P. J. BICKEL, F. R. HAMPEL, P. J. HUBER, W. H. ROGERS, and J. W. TUKEY (1972). *Robust Estimates of Location: Survey and Advances*. Princeton, NJ: Princeton University Press.

BOX, G. E. P. (1953). Non-Normality and Tests on Variances. *Biometrika* 40, 318–35.

BOX, G. E. P., and G. M. JENKINS (1976). *Time Series Analysis—Forecasting and Control,* rev. ed. San Francisco, CA: Holden-Day.

DIXON, W. J., and M. B. BROWN (1979). *BMDP-79 Biomedical Computer Programs P-Series*. Los Angeles, CA: University of California Press.

HOGG, R. V. (1979). Statistical Robustness: One View of Its Use in Applications Today. *The American Statistician* 33, 108–15.

HUBER, P. J. (1964). Robust Estimation of a Location Parameter. *Annals of Mathematical Statistics* 35, 73–101.

HUBER, P. J. (1973). Robust Regression: Asymptotics, Conjectures, and Monte Carlo. *Annals of Statistics* 1, 799–821.

McNEIL, D. R. (1977). *Interactive Data Analysis*. New York, NY: John Wiley and Sons.

MALLOWS, C. L. (1979). Robust Methods—Some Examples of Their Use. *The American Statistician* 33, 179–84.

VELLEMAN, P. F., and D. C. HOAGLIN (1981). *Applications, Basics, and Computing for Exploratory Data Analysis*. North Scituate, MA: Duxbury Press.

CHAPTER **17**

# The Need for Robustness in Correlation and Regression Analysis

The method of least squares is used for doing a wide variety of statistical analyses. However, outliers or simply bad values occur with amazing frequency in many practical forecasting applications. You may reduce the effect that outlying data points and departures from the normality assumption have on your statistical analyses by using robust procedures. The treatment in this chapter will stress the need for robust methods in correlation and regression analysis by considering:

- The effects of outliers on correlation coefficients and regression parameters.
- A methodology for dealing with nonnormal situations where classical least-squares techniques often give misleading results.

## ROBUST CORRELATION

As in the case of the sample mean and variance, the uncritical use of the sample product moment correlation coefficient can be very misleading since it is extremely sensitive to outliers and data that are not normally distributed (Devlin et al., 1975).

### Influence Curves

Consider an example in which the product moment correlation coefficient is very sensitive to a single outlying point. Figure 17.1 shows a scatter plot of two economic variables for 24 chemical corporations. When all 24 points are used, the sample

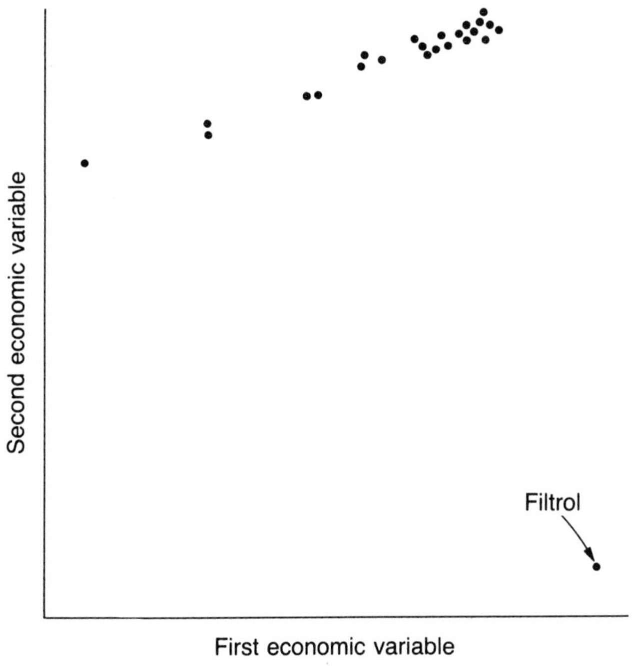


**Figure 17.1** Scatter plot of two economic variables for twenty-four corporations.

correlation coefficient is nearly zero. After eliminating the outlying point, the bulk of the data shows a very strong positive correlation; in fact, the correlation coefficient becomes 0.99. While this is an extreme example, it is important to recognize the impact outliers can have on least squares estimates.

As another example, consider a simple data analytic procedure for detecting outliers that have adverse effects on the correlation coefficient. R. A. Fisher's classical data (Fisher, 1960) on sepal lengths and widths of *Iris setosa* can be used to illustrate the use of what are called influence curves (Devlin et al., 1975). *Influence curves* are contours superimposed on a scatter plot to indicate the approximate impact of a single point on the calculation of the product moment correlation coefficient $r$. Figure 17.2 shows a scatter plot in which three of Fisher's iris data (#16, #23, #42) are labeled. Point 42 stands out both visually and in its elliptical distance from the mean. But how does this point affect the sample correlation coefficient?

Specifically, the impact of a point lying on the hyperbola marked 0.050 would be to reduce $r$ by 0.050 if that point were deleted. Similarly, a point on the contour $-0.050$ would increase $r$ by 0.050 if it were deleted. Point #23 is on the $-0.025$ contour, so its exclusion would increase $r$ by 0.025. Point #42, however, lies between two hyperbolas $\pm 0.025$, so its effect on $r$ is negligible. The contours help in the interpretation of the scatter plot and in assessing the effect of individual points distant from the bulk of the data.

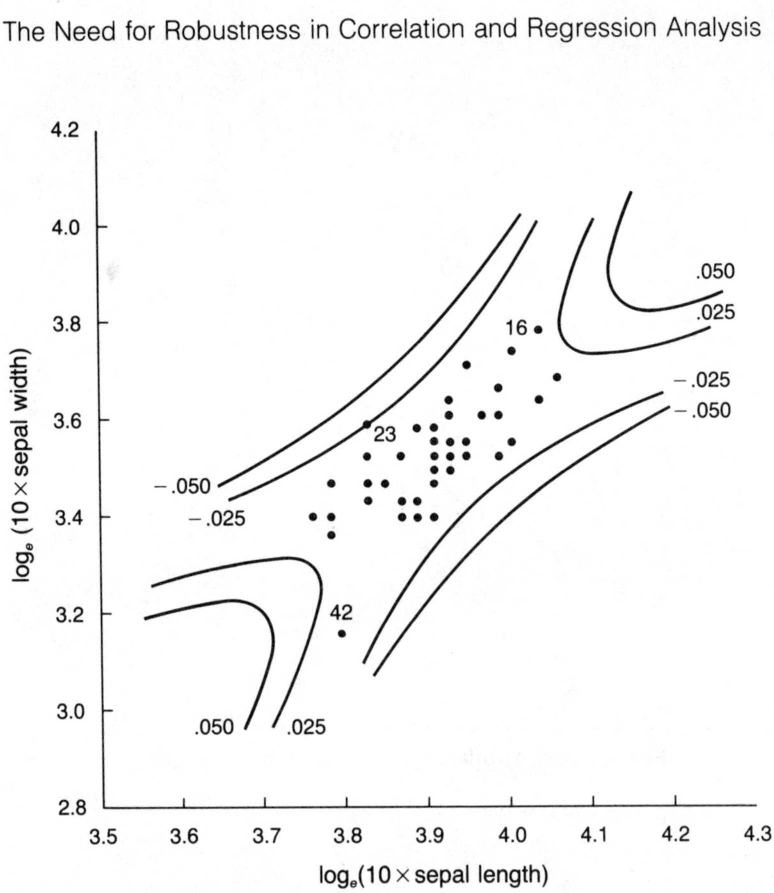


**Figure 17.2** Influence curves for the correlation coefficient (an example based on data from R. A. Fisher, 1960).

## A Robust Correlation Coefficient

For a more robust assessment, what is desired is a correlation coefficient that is less sensitive to outliers than the product moment correlation coefficient $r$. One robust estimator of the correlation coefficient, designated by SSD, is based on the standardized sums and differences of two variables—say $Y$ and $X$. The first step in obtaining SSD is to standardize both $Y$ and $X$ robustly—by constructing two new variables $\tilde{Y}$ and $\tilde{X}$,

$$\tilde{Y} = \frac{Y - \overline{Y}^*}{S^*_Y}$$

and

$$\tilde{X} = \frac{X - \overline{X}^*}{S^*_X}$$

where $\overline{Y}^*$ and $\overline{X}^*$ are robust estimates of location and $S_Y^*$ and $S_X^*$ are robust estimates of scale. Then, let $Z_1 = \tilde{Y} + \tilde{X}$ and $Z_2 = \tilde{Y} - \tilde{X}$, the sum and difference vectors, respectively. Then the robust variances of the sum vector $Z_1$ and difference vector $Z_2$ are calculated; they are denoted by $V_+^*$ and $V_-^*$, respectively. These variances are used in the calculation of the robust correlation estimate $r^*(\text{SSD})$ given by

$$r^*(\text{SSD}) = \frac{V_+^* - V_-^*}{V_+^* + V_-^*}.$$

The justification for this formula can be seen by inspecting the formula for the variance of the sum of two variables:

$$\text{Var}(Z_1) = \text{Var}(\tilde{Y}) + \text{Var}\,(\tilde{X}) + 2\text{Cov}(\tilde{Y}, \tilde{X}),$$

where Cov denotes the covariance between $\tilde{Y}$ and $\tilde{X}$.

Since $\tilde{Y}$ and $\tilde{X}$ are standardized, centered about zero, and with unit scale, the expected variance of $Z_1$ is approximately

$$\begin{aligned}\text{Var}(Z_1) &\approx 1 + 1 + 2\rho(\tilde{Y}, \tilde{X}) \\ &= 2(1 + \rho),\end{aligned}$$

where $\rho$ is the theoretical correlation between $\tilde{Y}$ and $\tilde{X}$.

Similarly, for $Z_2$,

$$\begin{aligned}\text{Var}(Z_2) &\approx \text{Var}(\tilde{Y}) + \text{Var}(\tilde{X}) - \text{Cov}(\tilde{Y}, \tilde{X}) \\ &= 1 + 1 - 2\rho(\tilde{Y}, \tilde{X}) \\ &= 2(1 - \rho).\end{aligned}$$

Notice that the expression

$$\begin{aligned}\frac{\text{Var}(Z_1) - \text{Var}(Z_2)}{\text{Var}(Z_1) + \text{Var}(Z_2)} &\approx \frac{2(1 + \rho) - 2(1 - \rho)}{2(1 + \rho) + 2(1 - \rho)} \\ &= \rho.\end{aligned}$$

Some robust estimates of the (square root of) variance, required in the formula for $r^*$, are discussed in Chapter 7; these include the MAD (median absolute deviation from the median) and the interquartile range.

## A Numerical Example

Table 17.1 shows an example of how to calculate $r^*$ with ten pairs of numbers by using the median and MAD as the robust estimates of location and scale, respectively. The calculation shows that $r^* = 0.97$, as compared to the product moment coefficient $r = 0.80$. At first sight it might appear that observation #2 for $Y$

**Table 17.1** Calculation of a robust estimate $r^*$ for ten numbers.

| $Y$ | $X$ | $\tilde{Y} = (Y - \bar{Y}^*)/S^*_y$ | $\tilde{X} = (X - \bar{X}^*)/S^*_X$ | $Z_1 = \tilde{Y} + \tilde{X}$ | $Z_2 = \tilde{Y} - \tilde{X}$ |
|---|---|---|---|---|---|
| 73 | 36 | 0.89 | 1.03 | 1.92 | −0.14 |
| −134 | −35 | −3.43 | −2.62 | −6.05 | −0.81 |
| 23 | 18 | −0.16 | 0.10 | −0.06 | −0.26 |
| 86 | 22 | 1.16 | 0.31 | 1.47 | 0.85 |
| −62 | −21 | −1.93 | −1.90 | −3.83 | −0.03 |
| 38 | 16 | 0.16 | 0.00 | 0.16 | 0.16 |
| −18 | −11 | −1.01 | −1.38 | −2.39 | 0.37 |
| −22 | −3 | −1.09 | −0.97 | −2.06 | −0.12 |
| 44 | 16 | 0.28 | 0.00 | 0.28 | 0.28 |
| 78 | 100 | 0.99 | 4.31 | 5.30 | −3.32 |

$\bar{Y}^* = \text{Median}(Y) = 30.5$; $\bar{X}^* = \text{Median}(X) = 16.0$;
$S^*_Y = \text{MAD}(Y) = 48.0$; $S^*_X = \text{MAD}(X) = 19.5$;
$\text{MAD}(Z_1) = 2.00$; $\text{MAD}(Z_2) = 0.255$;

$$\text{SSD} = \frac{2^2 - 0.255^2}{2^2 + 0.255^2} = \frac{3.935}{4.065} = 0.968 = r^*$$

(Product moment correlation coefficient $= r = 0.80$)

($y_2 = -134$) is the likely culprit. With this observation removed, $r^* = 0.95$ and $r = 0.76$. The real influential point is the last observation; when removed, the resulting nine pairs of numbers yield the same value for the product moment coefficient as for the robust estimate: $r = 0.96$ and $r^* = 0.96$. Clearly the robust estimate $r^*$ has been more representative of the bulk of the data than $r$, all along.

Table 17.2 shows correlations for the telecommunications example; the robust correlation matrix for the percent changes in the toll revenue (PCTREV), toll message (PCTMSG), the business telephones (PCTBMT), and the nonfarm employment series (PCTNFRM) can be compared with the matrix of ordinary product moment correlations shown previously in Table 13.2. For comparison, the ordinary product moment correlation coefficients are shown in parentheses underneath the corresponding robust estimates. It appears that most product moment correlation coefficients may be somewhat understated. This may possibly be due to the presence of one or more discrepant values lying along the off-diagonal (from top left to bottom right) direction in the scatter plots for the above variables.

If you will need to look at *many* pairs of correlations, it is often useful to compute each pairwise correlation in two ways—first with a sample product moment correlation coefficient $r$ and then with robust correlation coefficient $r^*$. Any large differences between these coefficients would imply the presence of outliers distorting the true estimate of correlation; in a plot of $r$ versus $r^*$, the points close to the 45-

**Table 17.2** Martix of ordinary and robust correlation coefficients for the telecommunications data. OLS correlation coefficients are shown in parentheses.

| | 1 | 2 | 3 | 4 |
|---|---|---|---|---|
| 1 PCTREV | 1.00<br>(1.00) | | | |
| 2 PCTMSG | 0.76<br>(0.67) | 1.00<br>(1.00) | | |
| 3 PCTBMT | 0.61<br>(0.50) | 0.46<br>(0.55) | 1.00<br>(1.00) | |
| 4 PCTNFRM | 0.67<br>(0.63) | 0.81<br>(0.70) | 0.64<br>(0.60) | 1.00<br>(1.00) |

degree line ($r = r^*$) would imply that there are no outliers adversely affecting $r$ in the data; on the other hand, larger deviations would suggest that you should look for outliers. These pairs of variables could then be inspected for outlier detection by using the influence curves discussed earlier.

## ROBUST REGRESSION

In least squares estimation, regression coefficients are derived by minimizing the sum of the squares of the residuals (Residual = Data − Fit). In the minimization process, all residuals are given *equal* weight. It is well known, however, that outliers can have an unusually large influence on least squares estimators. That is, the outliers pull the least squares "fit" toward them too much, and a resulting examination of residuals may be misleading because then the residuals corresponding to the outliers would look smaller than the residuals from a robust fit. They may not appear like outliers. Accordingly, robust methods have been created to modify least-squares regression procedures so that outliers have much less influence on the final estimate.

### *M*-Estimators

A family of robust estimators, called *M-estimators,* is obtained by minimizing a specified function of the residuals. Alternate forms of the function produce the various *M*-estimators. Generally, the estimates are computed by *iterated weighted least squares*.

One such function $\rho(e)$ of the residuals $e$ takes the form:

$$\rho(e) = 0.5e^2 \qquad \text{if } |e| \leq c = Ks$$
$$= c|e| - 0.5c^2 \qquad \text{if } |e| > c = Ks$$

where $s$ is a scale estimate such as UMAD, the ("unbiased") median absolute deviation of the residuals from the median, divided by 0.6745. If the data are normal and the number of observations is large, the divisor 0.6745 is used because then $s$ approximates the standard deviation of a normal distribution if the number of observations is large. Usually the sample standard deviation $\hat{\sigma}$ is not used as an $s$ value since it is influenced too much by outliers and thus is not robust. The constant $K$ is chosen to obtain a desired level of efficiency (as compared to least squares regression if the data are normal), and it is often set to between 1 and 2. If $K$ is sufficiently large, the $M$-estimates will be equivalent to ordinary least-squares estimates.

Minimizing $\rho(e)$ yields an estimate of the regression coefficients; the minimization requires Huber weights, defined by

$$W_i = \begin{cases} 1 & \text{if } |e_i| \leq Ks \\ Ks/|e_i| & \text{if } |e_i| > Ks. \end{cases}$$

The statistic $s$ approximates the standard deviation of a normal distribution, and the constant $K$ is chosen to be some number close to 1.5.

The iterative procedure involves the following steps:

1. Obtain an initial estimate of the regression coefficients. The initial estimates can be obtained in a number of ways such as by ordinary least squares.
2. Compute residuals and calculate $Ks = K \cdot$ UMAD, where UMAD is the median absolute deviation from the median divided by 0.6745.
3. Compute the weights and perform the method of weighted least squares.
4. Repeat steps 1 through 3 until convergence or a reasonable number of iterations.

To distinguish robust regression coefficients from ordinary least-squares coefficients, the robust coefficients for a simple linear regression will be denoted by $\beta_0^*$ and $\beta_1^*$. These coefficients are calculated by using the weighted least-squares formula:

$$\beta_0^* = \frac{\Sigma W_i x_i y_i - \Sigma W_i(\Sigma W_i x_i/\Sigma W_i)(\Sigma W_i y_i/\Sigma W_i)}{\Sigma W_i x_i^2 - \Sigma W_i(\Sigma W_i x_i/\Sigma W_i)^2};$$

$$\beta_1^* = (\Sigma W_i y_i/\Sigma W_i) - \beta_0^*(\Sigma W_i x_i/\Sigma W_i).$$

A second $M$-estimator, called the *bisquare estimator,* gives zero weight to data whose residuals are quite far from zero (Mosteller and Tukey, 1977). The *bisquare weighting function* was discussed in Chapter 8 and is defined by

$$W_i = \begin{cases} [1 - (e_i/Ks)^2]^2 & \text{if } |e_i| \leq Ks \\ 0 & \text{if } |e_i| > Ks. \end{cases}$$

It is worth noting that the bisquare weighting scheme is more severe than the Huber scheme. In the bisquare scheme, all data for which $|e_i| \leq Ks$ will have a weight less than 1. Data having weights greater than 0.9 are not considered extreme. Data with weights less than 0.5 are regarded as extreme, and data with zero weight are, of course, ignored.

A recommended robust regression procedure begins with OLS estimates of the parameters. This is followed by several iterations of Huber-weighted least squares followed by several iterations of bisquare-weighted least squares. To avoid the potential problem of finding local minima, which can result from "bad" initial estimates, we recommend that you start the bisquare procedure with a few iterations of the Huber scheme.

## Calculating *M*-Estimates

It is instructive to take a closer look at the weighted least-squares calculations of *M*-estimates. These estimates can be substantially different when the data contain one or more outliers. For simplicity, consider the simple time series 2.5, 4.0, 5.5, 7.0, 8.5, 10.0, 11.5, 13.0, 14.5, 3.0, which is of the form $y = 1.0 + 1.5x$ for the first nine "time points" if $x$ represents 1, 2, . . . , 10. Notice that the last point (3.0) is an outlier according to this model.

One iteration of a robust solution for these data, using Huber weights ($K = 1$), is given in Table 17.3. This is analogous to downweighting residuals that are greater than one standard error from their central measure. Notice that the initial estimates are obtained from the OLS solution: $\hat{y}_{(\text{OLS})} = 3.60 + 0.79x$.

The residuals are computed in Column 3. Column 4 shows the absolute deviations of the residuals from the median residual (= 0.595). The median value in Column 4 is the MAD statistic. Column 5 is derived by comparing Column 3 with the UMAD statistic (MAD/0.6745 = 2.64), using the definition of the Huber weight function. The weight $W$ is 1.0 if the residual in Column 3 is an absolute value less than 2.64; otherwise, the weight is 2.64 divided by the absolute value of the residual. It is evident that the last three points receive a weight less than 1 for this iteration.

The first thirteen Huber iterations using $K = 2$ are summarized in Table 17.4. The coefficients are calculated by using the weighted least-squares formula set forth in the preceding section.

It can be seen from Table 17.4 that only the last point (Column $W_{10}$) received a weighting less than 1. With each iteration the slope of the line gradually increases, as can be seen from the column under $\beta_1^*$. Notice that in this artificial example, the

**Table 17.3** One iteration of sample data, using Huber weights ($K = 1$) for fitting $y = 1 + 1.5x$.

| (1) $x$ | (2) $y$ | (3) $e_i = y_i - \hat{y}_{(OLS)}$ | (4) $\lvert e_i - e_M \rvert$ | (5) Huber weights $W$ ($K = 1$) |
|---|---|---|---|---|
| 1 | 2.5 | −1.89 | 2.49 | 1.0 |
| 2 | 4.0 | −1.18 | 1.78 | 1.0 |
| 3 | 5.5 | −0.47 | 1.07 | 1.0 |
| 4 | 7.0 | 0.24 | 0.36 | 1.0 |
| 5 | 8.5 | 0.95 | 0.36 | 1.0 |
| 6 | 10.0 | 1.66 | 1.07 | 1.0 |
| 7 | 11.5 | 2.37 | 1.78 | 1.0 |
| 8 | 13.0 | 3.08 | 2.49 | 0.86 |
| 9 | 14.5 | 3.79 | 3.20 | 0.70 |
| 10 | 3.0 | −8.50 | 9.10 | 0.31 |

$\hat{y}_{(OLS)} = 3.60 + 0.79x$;
Median residual $e_M$ (median of Column 3) = 0.595;
MAD (median of Column 4) = 1.78;
$s$ = UMAD = MAD/0.6745 = 2.64.

**Table 17.4** Thirteen iterations of the Huber ($K = 2$) solution to the fit in which the last point ($W_{10}$) is downweighted.

| | Regression coefficients | | Weights† |
|---|---|---|---|
| Iteration | $\beta_0^*$ | $\beta_1^*$ | $W_{10}$ |
| 1 | 2.85 | 1.00 | 0.62 |
| 2 | 2.26 | 1.16 | 0.38 |
| 3 | 1.83 | 1.27 | 0.24 |
| 4 | 1.54 | 1.35 | 0.15 |
| 5 | 1.34 | 1.41 | 0.09 |
| 6 | 1.21 | 1.44 | 0.06 |
| 7 | 1.13 | 1.46 | 0.03 |
| 8 | 1.08 | 1.48 | 0.02 |
| 9 | 1.05 | 1.49 | 0.01 |
| 10 | 1.03 | 1.49 | 0.01 |
| 11 | 1.02 | 1.49 | 0.00 |
| 12 | 1.01 | 1.50 | 0.00 |
| 13 | 1.01 | 1.50 | 0.00 |

†*Note:* Weights are shown only for point $W_{10}$; weights for $W_1$ through $W_9$ are 1 for all iterations. The OLS solution is $\hat{y}_{(OLS)} = 3.60 + 0.79x$.

**Table 17.5** Calculation using bisquare weights ($K$ = 4.2) for the first iteration of sample data: bisquare weights $W_i = [1 - (e_i/Ks)^2]^2$.

| | | | | | | | | | | |
|---|---|---|---|---|---|---|---|---|---|---|
| $y_i$: | 2.5 | 4.0 | 5.5 | 7.0 | 8.5 | 10.0 | 11.5 | 13.0 | 14.5 | 3.0 |
| $W_i$, ($K$ = 4.2): | 0.943 | 0.977 | 0.996 | 0.999 | 0.985 | 0.956 | 0.911 | 0.852 | 0.780 | 0.170 |

$s$ = UMAD = 2.64.

Residuals $e_i$ are given in Table 17.3, Column 3.

weight associated with the outlier becomes zero. With real data, however, the Huber weights rarely get smaller than 0.2.

In Table 17.5, a robust solution using bisquare weights ($K$ = 4.2) is shown for the first iteration. As can be seen in Table 17.6, the bisquare weighting scheme downweights all but the third ($W_3$) and fourth ($W_4$) points in the first iteration. You can see by looking at the coefficient estimates that the calculations converged after only three iterations to a final fit of the form $\hat{y}_{BS} = 1.0 + 1.5X$.

**Table 17.6** Bisquare solution to the fit in which all but the fifth and sixth values are downweighted.

| Regression coefficient (β) and weight ($W$) | OLS | Iteration 1 | 2 | 3 |
|---|---|---|---|---|
| $\beta_0^*$ | 3.60 | 1.51 | 1.00 | 1.00 |
| $\beta_1^*$ | 0.79 | 1.36 | 1.50 | 1.50 |
| $W_1$ | 1.00 | 0.94 | 0.94 | 0.83 |
| $W_2$ | 1.00 | 0.97 | 0.98 | 0.91 |
| $W_3$ | 1.00 | 1.00 | 1.00 | 0.94 |
| $W_4$ | 1.00 | 1.00 | 1.00 | 0.99 |
| $W_5$ | 1.00 | 0.98 | 0.98 | 1.00 |
| $W_6$ | 1.00 | 0.95 | 0.95 | 1.00 |
| $W_7$ | 1.00 | 0.90 | 0.90 | 0.99 |
| $W_8$ | 1.00 | 0.84 | 0.83 | 0.94 |
| $W_9$ | 1.00 | 0.76 | 0.75 | 0.91 |
| $W_{10}$ | 1.00 | 0.12 | 0.00 | 0.00 |

## A ROBUST MODEL FOR ANNUAL SALES OF A PRODUCT

Consider now a regression model for the annual sales of a Product A as a function of advertising expenditures. Figure 17.3 is a scatter plot of the annual sales of Product A and the corresponding advertising expenditures for twelve years. It is expected that the relationship between the two variables will yield a positive slope—as advertising expenditures increase, so should sales. It appears that such a relationship is true when viewing the bulk of the data; however, there was at least one year when sales were not commensurate with the advertising dollars spent.

Let us consider how OLS and a robust technique handle this situation. Figure 17.3 also shows the result of fitting the two regression lines. The outliers had a drastic effect on the OLS fit. The OLS fit does not pass through the bulk of the data. In fact, the negative slope of the least squares coefficient is distressing. Paradoxically, when there are outliers associated with extreme values for the independent variable, the least square estimate can pass through these values.

The robust estimate, however, reduces the effect of the two questionable values, and the fitted regression line passes through the bulk of the data.

Figure 17.4 shows the Q-Q plot of the robust residuals. The outliers stand out, but the remainder of the residuals lie on a reasonably straight line. Thus, the bulk of the residuals conform to the normality assumption; however, the two outliers seriously distort the results. Since OLS makes residuals appear "more normal" than perhaps they should be (Figure 17.5), the analyst is cautioned against the uncritical acceptance of "standard" techniques. The two qualities that this example highlights are that robust methods (1) are not affected by outliers, and (2) result in better residuals.

As a forecaster, you would of course want to view the data in a larger context: from a modeling perspective, the reasons for the two outliers would need to be understood and, if possible, incorporated into a more complete model. In actuality, however, a forecaster is often in a position where time constraints, lack of necessary data, lack of a sound theoretical framework, or cost-benefits trade-offs preclude a more detailed analysis. Given these constraints *and* the belief that the "typical" relationship will prevail in the forecast period, a robust fit may provide better forecasts. Simple models of the type presented above can be developed to provide reasonableness checks for the more complex econometric versions that appear in *The Professional Forecaster*.

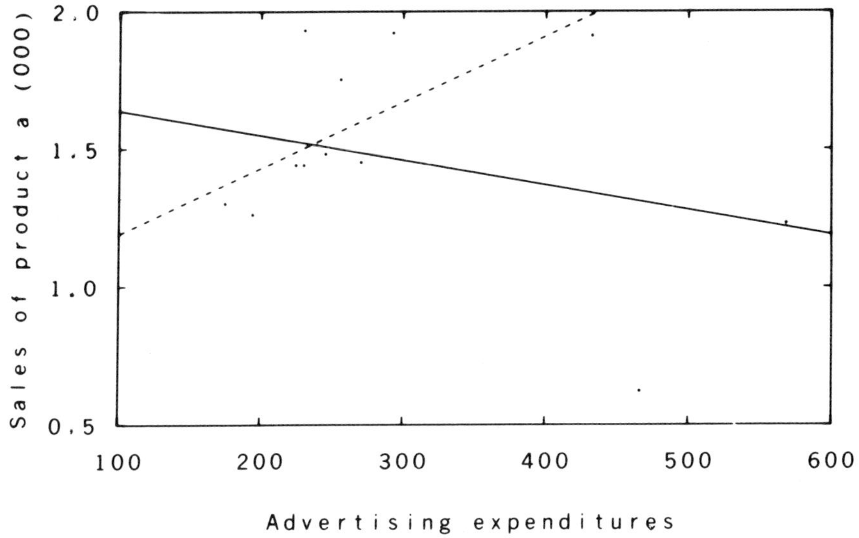


**Figure 17.3** Scatter diagram showing sales of Product A versus advertising expenditures. The solid line corresponds to the OLS fit and the dashed line is a robust fit.

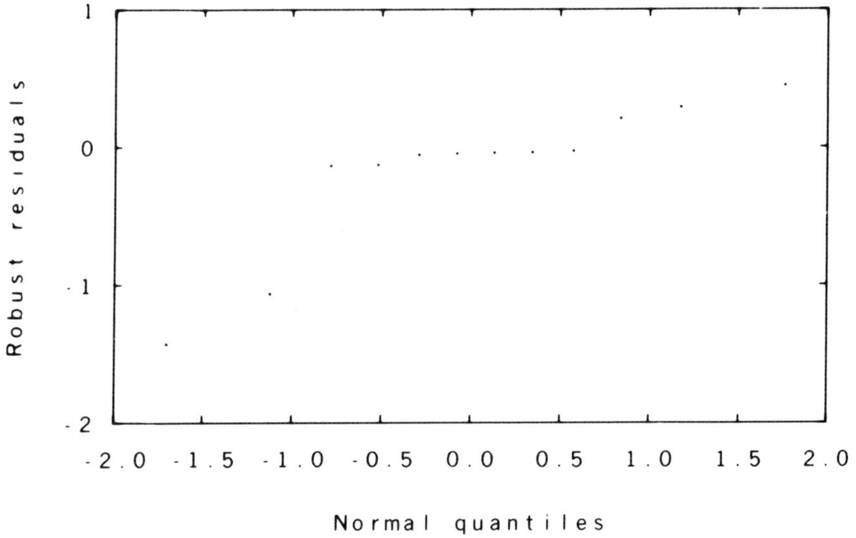


**Figure 17.4** Q-Q plot of the robust residuals in Figure 17.3 against normal quantiles. The bulk of the residuals lie along a straight line.

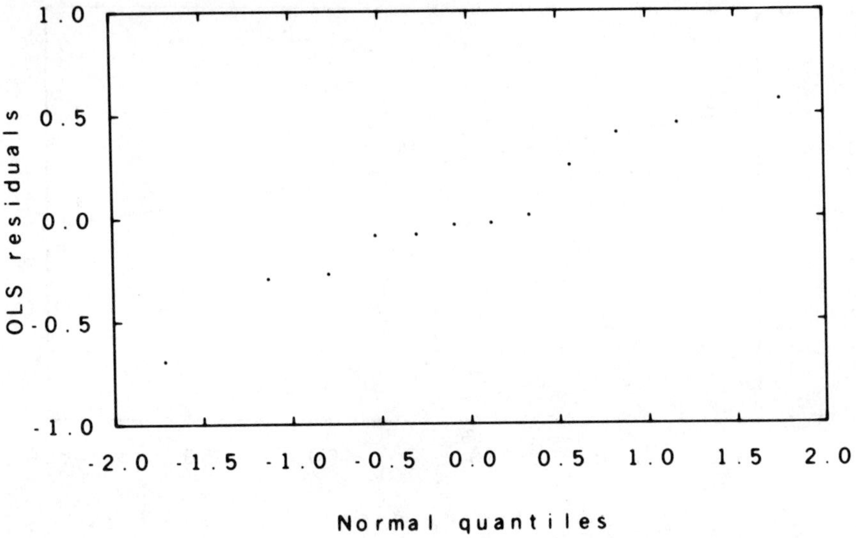


**Figure 17.5** Q-Q plot of the OLS residuals; evidence of outliers is less dramatic than in Figure 17.4.

## SUMMARY

Least squares estimation is sometimes inappropriate, since it gives equal weight to outliers, thereby distorting the fit to the bulk of the data; similarly, variables that are otherwise highly correlated may appear to have a low correlation coefficient because of the presence of outliers.

- In these circumstances, a robust correlation coefficient, $r^*$, serves as an alternative to the sample product moment correlation coefficient.
- Differences between the two kinds of coefficients imply the presence of outliers. Robust regression provides a viable alternative if unusual events occurred in the historical period. Weighted least-squares regression techniques, together with Huber or bisquare weighting schemes, provide the capability to downweight extreme values so that the regression line is not affected by them.
- If neither estimation method will yield satisfactory results, the model you have chosen is inappropriate for the expected conditions.
- If both OLS and robust methods yield similar results, you can quote OLS results with an added degree of confidence, since OLS and normality assumptions are likely to be reasonable for these data.
- If results differ significantly, you need to dig deeper into the data source or the model specification to find reasons for the difference.

## USEFUL READING

DEVLIN, S. J., R. GNANADESIKAN, and J. R. KETTENRING (1975). Robust Estimation and Outlier Detection with Correlation Coefficients. *Biometrika* 62, 531–45.

FISHER, R. A. (1960). *The Design of Experiments,* 7th ed. Edinburgh, Scotland: Oliver and Boyd.

MOSTELLER, F., and J. W. TUKEY (1977). *Data Analysis and Regression*. Reading, MA: Addison-Wesley Publishing Co.

CHAPTER **18**

# Why Make Seasonal Adjustments of Data?

Seasonally adjusted data and measures of seasonal variation have been used for over fifty years in the analysis of business and financial developments. This chapter describes several methods for adjusting time series for seasonal variation.

- In its simplest form, seasonality refers to regular periodic fluctuations which recur every year with about the same timing and intensity.
- Most procedures for seasonal analysis involve smoothing to eliminate unwanted irregular variation from patterns that are meaningful to the analyst.

## USES OF SEASONAL ADJUSTMENT

There are generally three distinct uses of seasonal adjustment:

- The historical adjustment of all available past data.
- The current adjustment of each new observation.
- The predicted seasonal factors for future adjustment.

Many economic series show seasonal variation. For example, income from a farm in the United States may rise steadily each year from early spring until fall and then drop sharply. In this case, the main use of seasonal adjustment procedures is to remove such fluctuations to expose an underlying trend-cycle.

Many industries have to deal with seasonal fluctuations. To make decisions about price and inventory policy, and the commitment of capital expenditures, the business community wants to know whether changes in business activity over a given period of time were larger or smaller than normal seasonal changes. It is important to know whether a recession has reached bottom, for example, or whether there is any pattern in the duration, amplitude, or slope of business cycle expansions or contractions (see Chapter 11).

The methods of seasonal analysis considered in this chapter are based on smoothing procedures, since the object of the procedure is to measure usual or average seasonal movements. There are a wide variety of factors that influence economic data, so it is often difficult to determine the extent to which seasonal influences dominate changes in a time series. However, most methods are based on the assumption that seasonal fluctuations can be measured and separated from underlying trend and irregular fluctuations.

In general, seasonal adjustment procedures can be categorized as either additive or multiplicative procedures. If the magnitude of the seasonal increase or decrease is assumed to be essentially constant and independent of the level of the times series, an *additive model* is used:

$$\text{Data} = \text{Trend-cycle} + \text{Seasonal} + \text{Irregular}.$$

On the other hand, when the magnitude of the seasonal increase or decrease is assumed to be proportional to the level of the time series, a *multiplicative model* is used:

$$\text{Data} = \text{Trend-cycle} \cdot \text{Seasonal factor} \cdot \text{Irregular factor}.$$

Even in this circumstance an additive model could be used if you transform the original time series. If you take logarithms, this will tend to "stabilize" the magnitude of the seasonal pattern and allow you to use the additive model on the transformed series. This is, to some extent, what is behind the SABL procedure discussed in the next chapter.

One desirable feature of a good seasonal adjustment procedure is to end up with a seasonal component that does not change over time. The choice between an additive or multiplicative model may be important here.

There are also methods that make simultaneous additive and multiplicative adjustments. Since all methods have their limitations, the practitioner needs to be aware of the advantages and disadvantages of seasonal adjustment procedures in the context of the particular application.

To illustrate how a forecaster could use seasonal factors, consider the simplified example that follows. Table 18.1 shows three rows of numbers. The first row shows

**Table 18.1** Using seasonal factors to adjust a set of data.

| | Time | | | | |
|---|---|---|---|---|---|
| Description | JAN | FEB | MAR | APR | MAY |
| 1. Actual data | 2000 | 1900 | 1700 | 1300 | 1100 |
| 2. Seasonal factors | 1000 | 900 | 600 | 0 | −400 |
| 3. Seasonally adjusted data (1 − 2) | 1000 | 1000 | 1100 | 1300 | 1500 |

the actual demand for a product during a given year. The second row shows seasonal factors that were developed, based on historical data and projected for the same year. The third row shows the seasonally adjusted data under an assumed additive model:

$$\text{Data} - \text{Seasonal factor} = \text{Trend-cycle} + \text{Irregular}.$$

In this example the actual values decline from January through May. The seasonal factors indicate that the first three months are generally strong, April has no significant seasonality, and May is generally weak. After adjusting for the seasonal effect, it can be seen that the adjusted demand grows after February. This might be a result of an economic recovery that is not apparent in the observed (first-row) values.

In Table 18.2, the same actuals are used, but a different seasonal pattern is assumed. After adjusting for the seasonal effect, the data show a flat demand pattern. In Table 18.3, the same actuals are used, but the seasonal factors have been distorted. We shall assume that the distortions are a result of severe outliers in the prior year's actuals—that is, the seasonal factors in Table 18.2 are "correct," but the method used to derive the seasonal factors in Table 18.3 has incorrectly handled outliers in the prior year. These distorted factors have then been projected into the current year. The result has been to alter the April and May seasonal factors. In this case it appears that demand is falling off when it really is not. In a subsequent comparison of traditional and resistant seasonal adjustment methods, it will be shown how this problem can be avoided by using "resistant" methods.

The examples in Tables 18.1–18.3 show how the forecaster can use seasonal factors to:

- Identify turning points that are not apparent in the raw data.
- Adjust seasonality out of the data so that forecasting techniques that cannot handle seasonally unadjusted data—e.g., simple exponential smoothing models—can be applied to the seasonally adjusted data.

Table 18.3 also highlights the importance of assuring oneself that the seasonal factors are appropriate. Otherwise, incorrect conclusions can be drawn because of incorrect

**Table 18.2** Using a different set of seasonal factors to adjust the data.

| | Time | | | | |
|---|---|---|---|---|---|
| Description | JAN | FEB | MAR | APR | MAY |
| 1. Actual data | 2000 | 1900 | 1700 | 1300 | 1100 |
| 2. Seasonal factors | 500 | 400 | 200 | −200 | −400 |
| 3. Seasonally adjusted data (1 − 2) | 1500 | 1500 | 1500 | 1500 | 1500 |

**Table 18.3** Using seasonal factors that have been impacted by outliers in the prior year's data.

| Description | JAN | FEB | MAR | APR | MAY |
|---|---|---|---|---|---|
| | Time | | | | |
| 1. Actual data | 2000 | 1900 | 1700 | 1300 | 1100 |
| 2. Seasonal factors | 500 | 400 | 200 | 0 | −100 |
| 3. Seasonally adjusted data (1 − 2) | 1500 | 1500 | 1500 | 1300 | 1200 |

seasonal adjustment. The graphical techniques discussed in the SABL procedure (Chapter 19) can be used to evaluate the adequacy of the seasonal adjustment of a time series.

## RATIO-TO-MOVING-AVERAGE METHOD

In the 1920's and early 1930's, the Federal Reserve Board and the National Bureau of Economic Research were heavily involved in the smoothing of economic time series. In 1922, Frederick R. Macauley of the National Bureau of Economic Research developed the ratio-to-moving-average method in a study done at the request of the Federal Reserve Board (Macauley, 1930).

The first step in the method is to obtain an estimate of the trend and cyclical factors by use of a $p$-month moving average, where $p$ is the length of the seasonal period. This moving average is divided into the raw data to yield a series of "seasonal-irregular" ratios—symbolically, $(TC \bullet S \bullet I)/TC = S \bullet I$, where $TC$ = trend-cycle, $S$ = seasonal, and $I$ = irregular. Smoothing these ratios for a given month over a number of years produces an estimate of the seasonal adjustment factor. The irregular factor is assumed to cancel out in the smoothing process.

Final seasonally adjusted data are obtained by dividing each monthly data value by the seasonal adjustment factor for the corresponding month. This corresponds to a multiplicative seasonal adjustment procedure. An additive procedure can be developed in an analogous manner. This simplicity of calculation was a necessity in the early days of seasonal adjustment procedures.

## BUREAU OF CENSUS SEASONAL ADJUSTMENT

In 1954 the Bureau of the Census developed a software package known as Method I for decomposing time series (Shiskin et al., 1967). The first Census program contained refinements to the ratio-to-moving-average method. Subsequent variants included moving seasonal-adjustment factors and smoother and more flexible trend-cycle curves. Adjustments for variations in the number of working days and variable holidays (such as Easter) were included in the most recent version of the program, known as the *X-11 variant*. A brief description of the Census Method II seasonal adjustment procedure is given in an appendix in Kallek (1978).

## X-11 Program

The X-11 program is a very widely used and accepted way to deseasonalize data. Literally thousands of economic and demographic time series reported by federal agencies for public use have been seasonally adjusted by these programs. There are separate programs to deal with monthly and quarterly data.

The basic goal of the X-11 program is to estimate seasonal factors from seasonal data. Then one can remove the seasonal component and produce an adjusted series which will most clearly show the trend-cycle and irregular variations. The basic strategy of the program is to remove the influence of extreme values so as to reveal the underlying movement in the data in a better way. The basic tactic is the use of iteration to achieve refinement.

The assumptions underlying the X-11 program are that a time series is composed of seasonal, trend-cycle, trading day, and irregular components. There are two versions of this program available—additive and multiplicative.

In the *multiplicative* version, the time series $Y$ (the subscript $t$ can be suppressed for convenience) is assumed to be a product of a seasonal factor $S$, trend-cycle $TC$, trading day (the number of active working or business days) $D$, and irregular component $I$:

$$Y = TC \cdot S \cdot D \cdot I.$$

The trading day adjustment is treated as a separate component since it consists of variations attributable to the composition of the calendar. The irregular component includes effects such as strikes, wars, floods, and other unusual events.

An alternative *additive* formulation is that the original time series is a summation of these components, in the form

$$Y = TC + S + D + I.$$

Generally speaking, the multiplicative model produces the best seasonal factors for most series. However, it will not work for series that have negative values and for series that are highly volatile; the additive model is more appropriate for these.

There are three major computational runs with the X-11 program. Run 1 produces a series of "B-tables," which are considered preliminary. Run 2 results in "C-tables," which are semifinal, and Run 3 results in final "D-tables" and subsequent analytical tables.

The program makes the following sequence of computations:

- The trend-cycle.
- The seasonal-irregular ratios.
- Replacement of extreme irregular ratios.
- Seasonal factors.
- Seasonally adjusted series.

Since a seasonally adjusted series consists of trend-cycle and irregular components, it is sometimes desirable to remove the irregular component and look at trend-cycle alone. This can be done by smoothing operations. The X-11 program creates two different series—the MCD series and Henderson curves.

The MCD stands for *Months for Cyclical Dominance,* which indicates the minimum period over which the average absolute change can be attributed to cyclical change rather than unexplained fluctuations. It is an unweighted moving average of, at most, six months. The irregular component is divided by the trend-cycle. The number of months that must be added together before that ratio is less than one becomes the "months for cyclical dominance." If the months for cyclical dominance exceed six, then six months is used as the maximum term in the smoothing.

The reason for using the MCD series is to have *current* values. Using a smoothing operation in which more than six terms are needed would introduce a significant lag in the data and many months would be lost at both ends of the data. Clearly the MCD series is particularly important when the most current data are of interest. Table F-2 of the X-11 program contains the MCD series.

A Henderson curve is a 9-, 13-, or 26-term weighted moving average; this is particularly useful for series with strong cyclical patterns. In the Henderson calculations, an attempt is made to overcome the lag introduced by long-term moving-average operations, by applying different weights to the varying months. Estimates are also made of what the last $(n - 1)/2$ months would be if future data were available, since with any centered moving average the end values are lost.

To determine the reasonableness of the estimates of the current months, an analyst compares the MCD curve with the Henderson curve. If the MCD curve moves in a different direction than the Henderson curve, the Henderson estimates for the last $(n - 1)/2$ months should not be used, or at least the estimates should be modified to conform to the most recent actual data. Table D-12 of the X-11 program contains data for Henderson curves.

### Computational Procedure

It is important to be aware of the kinds of data manipulations that are made when adjusting data by means of the X-11 seasonal adjustment program. As an example, we shall use logarithms of airline data from Box and Jenkins (1976, Series G) to illustrate the X-11 (multiplicative) computational procedure. Special end-point treatments will not be discussed in the interest of understanding the basic methodology (for a complete description, see Shiskin et al., 1967).

- First, a twelve-month smoothing (unweighted moving average) of the data is calculated and centered in the middle of the period (June 15 for data beginning in January and ending in December).
- Second, two-month smoothing of the twelve-month moving totals is done. This centers the data for the next month (July for year 1) and "lines up" the data again. This produces the initial trend-cycle.
- The seasonal-irregular ratios are then defined by finding the ratio of the original data to the trend-cycle.

The procedure for identifying and adjusting for irregular values is as follows:

- First, a preliminary seasonal component is determined. Smooth the seasonal-irregular (*SI*) ratios for each month separately, using a weighted five-term moving average (see Table 18.4). This provides preliminary seasonal factors.
- Compute centered twelve-month moving averages of the preliminary seasonal factors [(Jan + Feb + ··· + Dec)/12] for the entire series. Adjust the factors to sum to 12.0 over any twelve-month period.
- Divide the seasonal factor estimates into the seasonal-irregular ratios to obtain estimates of the irregular component. For January 1974 this gives $I = SI/S = 0.952/0.929 = 1.025$.
- Compute a moving standard deviation ($\sigma$) of the irregulars for five years (60 months) of data at a time.

**Table 18.4** Smoothing monthly *SI* values to estimate a preliminary seasonal factor for January 1974.

| Year | January *SI* | × 5-term weights = | Weighted *SI* values | January 1974 seasonal factor |
|---|---|---|---|---|
| 1972 | 1.002 | 0.111 | 0.111 | |
| 1973 | 0.925 | 0.222 | 0.205 | |
| 1974 | 0.952 | 0.333 | 0.317 | 0.929 |
| 1975 | 0.896 | 0.222 | 0.199 | |
| 1976 | 0.864 | 0.111 | 0.096 | |
| 1977 | 0.899 | | | |
| 1978 | 0.900 | | | |
| | | 0.999 | 0.928 | |

$$\text{January 1974 seasonal factor} = \frac{\Sigma W_i(SI)_i}{\Sigma W_i} = \frac{0.928}{0.999} = 0.929$$

- Remove any irregulars greater than $2.5\sigma$ in the central (middle) year and recompute the moving five-year standard deviation.
- Irregulars in the central year beyond $2.5\sigma$ receive a zero weight. Irregulars less than $1.5\sigma$ receive full weight (1.0). Irregulars between 1.5 and $2.5\sigma$ receive a linear weighting; the weights decline linearly from a value of one at $1.5\sigma$ to a value of zero at $2.5\sigma$.
- For irregular values receiving less than full weight, replace the corresponding *SI* ratios with the average of the weight times the ratio; and the two nearest preceding and two nearest following *SI* ratios receive *full weight* for that month (see Table 18.5). This yields a new set of *SI* ratios for which the effects of extreme outliers have been removed.
- To obtain preliminary seasonal factors, the first two steps are repeated with the new *SI* ratios.

Several stages of iteration follow these initial steps. A refined trend-cycle is calculated, using Henderson weights. This leads to a refined seasonal where the individual months are now smoothed with a seven-term weighted average. A new irregular is calculated and weights are estimated as before.

The irregular component is reduced where appropriate by its weight. The above steps are repeated with the new series ($TC \cdot S \cdot I^*$), where $I^*$ is a weighted irregular series. A revised trend-cycle is calculated and applied once again to estimate a refined seasonal and irregular. The process is repeated once again to arrive at final seasonal factors.

**Table 18.5** Calculating a revised seasonal factor.

| | (1) | (2) | (3 ) | (4) | (3) × (4) | |
|---|---|---|---|---|---|---|
| Year | Weights for irregular component | Corresponding *SI* value | Revised *SI* values | 5-term weights | | Revised seasonal factor |
| 1972 | 1.0 | 1.002 | 1.002 | 0.111 | 0.111 | |
| 1973 | 1.0 | 0.925 | 0.925 | 0.222 | 0.205 | |
| 1974 | 1.0 | 0.952 | 0.952 | 0.333 | 0.317 | 0.938 |
| 1975 | 0.85 | 0.896 | 0.915* | 0.222 | 0.203 | |
| 1976 | 0.60 | 0.864 | 0.912** | 0.111 | 0.101 | |
| 1977 | 1.0 | 0.899 | 0.899 | | | |
| 1978 | 1.0 | 0.900 | 0.900 | | | |
| | | | | 0.999 | 0.937 | |

*Revised January 1975 *SI* = [(0.85)(0.896) + 0.952 + 0.925 + 0.899 + 0.900]/4.85 = 0.915

**Revised January 1976 *SI* = [(0.60)(0.864) + 0.952 + 0.925 + 0.899 + 0.900]/4.60 = 0.912

Table D-10 in the X-11 program provides the final seasonal factors to be used for deseasonalizing the data (Figure 18.1).

These factors are used to create the final seasonally adjusted series $(TC \cdot S \cdot I)/S = TC \cdot I)$ in Table D-11 of the X-11 output. The seasonally adjusted series can be used to identify cyclical patterns in historical data since the variation due to seasonality has been removed. To identify cyclical patterns or turning points in the *current* year, one adjusts the current actuals by dividing (or subtracting in the additive case) by the seasonal factors from Table D-10. The prior year's seasonal factors or the median seasonal factor could be used. If the seasonal pattern is changing over time, projected seasonal factors are required.

The X-11 scheme for projecting seasonal factors is to take 1/2 of the difference between the last two years' seasonal factors for a month and add this value to the last year's seasonal factor.

Table D-11 provides the final seasonally adjusted series (Figure 18.2), which can be used in modeling or correlation studies with economic indicators.

### Why Use the X-11 Program?

There are times when seasonally adjusted data may be the only data readily available. For instance, computerized data banks are available commercially which contain a wide variety of seasonally adjusted economic data. It often makes sense to use these commercially available sources, rather than to adjust many of these series yourself.

The methods of seasonal adjustment in the X-11 program isolate the seasonal and irregular factors, leaving a composite trend and cycle component in the form of a long-term (Spencer or Henderson) weighted moving average. An MCD (Months for Cyclical Dominance) moving average is a short-term alternative for this trend-cycle component.

It is also advisable to compare forecasting results that are obtained from seasonally adjusted data with those from unadjusted series (Plosser, 1979). The adjusted series still contain trend-cycle components that need to be modeled.

A recent development in the time series literature combines the ARIMA modeling approach with the X-11 seasonal adjustment procedure to produce future seasonal factors (Dagum, 1976). The technique shows considerable promise and is being tested extensively (Dagum, 1978).

## SUMMARY

Seasonal adjustment is a useful procedure that helps identify turning points in the economy or the demand for products and services. Knowledge of the seasonal pattern also helps in planning employee workloads and inventory levels.

OCT. 24, 1978 LOGS OF AIRLINE PASSENGERS - W/O/ OUTLIERS - ADDIT.

D10. FINAL SEASONAL FACTORS

P. 5, SERIES MOGS

| YEAR | JAN | FEB | MAR | APR | MAY | JUN | JUL | AUG | SEP | OCT | NOV | DEC | AVGE |
|---|---|---|---|---|---|---|---|---|---|---|---|---|---|
| 1949 | −91. | −56. | 65. | −0. | −23. | 70. | 171. | 167. | 67. | −81. | −202. | −86. | 0. |
| 1950 | −89. | −61. | 64. | −2. | −21. | 71. | 172. | 171. | 66. | −78. | −202. | −86. | 0. |
| 1951 | −87. | −70. | 61. | −6. | −17. | 74. | 177. | 176. | 63. | −76. | −201. | −89. | 0. |
| 1952 | −84. | −84. | 55. | −10. | −12. | 80. | 186. | 181. | 62. | −73. | −202. | −91. | 1. |
| 1953 | −82. | −98. | 44. | −14. | −10. | 91. | 196. | 188. | 61. | −71. | −204. | −94. | 1. |
| 1954 | −81. | −112. | 31. | −16. | −10. | 104. | 208. | 195. | 63. | −71. | −206. | −97. | 1. |
| 1955 | −83. | −123. | 17. | −19. | −12. | 118. | 221. | 203. | 66. | −72. | −208. | −99. | 1. |
| 1956 | −84. | −132. | 7. | −24. | −13. | 128. | 232. | 210. | 68. | −73. | −210. | −101. | 1. |
| 1957 | −85. | −140. | −1. | −29. | −13. | 134. | 241. | 219. | 68. | −74. | −210. | −103. | 1. |
| 1958 | −87. | −148. | −4. | −34. | −10. | 134. | 248. | 226. | 67. | −73. | −210. | −105. | 0. |
| 1959 | −88. | −152. | −6. | −38. | −7. | 133. | 254. | 231. | 64. | −72. | −210. | −107. | 0. |
| 1960 | −88. | −154. | −7. | −39. | −6. | 132. | 256. | 233. | 63. | −72. | −210. | −107. | 0. |

TABLE TOTAL—61. MEAN—0. STD. DEVIATION—124.

D10A. SEASONAL FACTORS, ONE YEAR AHEAD

| YEAR | JAN | FEB | MAR | APR | MAY | JUN | JUL | AUG | SEP | OCT | NOV | DEC | AVGE |
|---|---|---|---|---|---|---|---|---|---|---|---|---|---|
| 1961 | −89. | −155. | −7. | −40. | −5. | 131. | 258. | 234. | 62. | −71. | −210. | −108. | −0. |

**Figure 18.1** The D-10 table from the Bureau of Census X-11 program provides final seasonal factors for the airline data.

OCT 24, 1978 LOGS OF AIRLINE PASSENGERS - W/O/ OUTLIERS - ADDIT.

D11. FINAL SEASONALLY ADJUSTED SERIES P. 6, SERIES MOGS

| YEAR | JAN | FEB | MAR | APR | MAY | JUN | JUL | AUG | SEP | OCT | NOV | DEC | TOT |
|---|---|---|---|---|---|---|---|---|---|---|---|---|---|
| 1949 | 4809. | 4827. | 4818. | 4860. | 4819. | 4835. | 4826. | 4830. | 4846. | 4860. | 4846. | 4857. | 58033. |
| 1950 | 4834. | 4897. | 4885. | 4907. | 4849. | 4933. | 4964. | 4965. | 4997. | 4968. | 4938. | 5028. | 59166. |
| 1951 | 5064. | 5081. | 5121. | 5100. | 5164. | 5108. | 5116. | 5117. | 5152. | 5164. | 5185. | 5201. | 61573. |
| 1952 | 5226. | 5277. | 5208. | 5209. | 5221. | 5304. | 5252. | 5308. | 5280. | 5325. | 5349. | 5359. | 63319. |
| 1953 | 5360. | 5376. | 5420. | 5474. | 5444. | 5402. | 5380. | 5418. | 5407. | 5423. | 5397. | 5397. | 64897. |
| 1954 | 5399. | 5349. | 5429. | 5441. | 5465. | 5472. | 5502. | 5485. | 5494. | 5505. | 5519. | 5531. | 65589. |
| 1955 | 5572. | 5574. | 5570. | 5614. | 5610. | 5635. | 5676. | 5646. | 5677. | 5685. | 5676. | 5727. | 67663. |
| 1956 | 5733. | 5756. | 5752. | 5770. | 5775. | 5796. | 5791. | 5794. | 5804. | 5797. | 5812. | 5825. | 69406. |
| 1957 | 5838. | 5847. | 5876. | 5881. | 5885. | 5911. | 5905. | 5927. | 5933. | 5923. | 5930. | 5920. | 70777. |
| 1958 | 5916. | 5910. | 5896. | 5886. | 5904. | 5941. | 5948. | 5999. | 5934. | 5956. | 5947. | 5925. | 71162. |
| 1959 | 5974. | 5987. | 6012. | 6019. | 6047. | 6024. | 6052. | 6095. | 6074. | 6081. | 6102. | 6111. | 72578. |
| 1960 | 6121. | 6123. | 6045. | 6172. | 6163. | 6150. | 6177. | 6174. | 6167. | 6205. | 6176. | 6175. | 73849. |
| AVGE | 5487. | 5500. | 5503. | 5528. | 5529. | 5543. | 5549. | 5563. | 5564. | 5574. | 5573. | 5588. | |

TABLE TOTAL—798008. MEAN—5542. STD. DEVIATION—422.

**Figure 18.2** The D-11 table from the X-11 program provides the final seasonally adjusted airline data.

If you can remove seasonality from a time series, you can apply a number of forecasting techniques that otherwise would not handle seasonal data to these seasonally adjusted data—e.g., the simpler exponential smoothing techniques discussed in Chapter 8.

The Bureau of Census X-11 seasonal adjustment program is widely used to deseasonalize data in government and business.

- The program is capable of mass-processing data and producing detailed analyses of seasonal factors, and trend-cycle and irregular variations.
- It can be run in an additive or multiplicative form for quarterly or monthly data.

## USEFUL READING

BOX, G. E. P., and G. M. JENKINS (1976). *Time Series Analysis—Forecasting and Control,* rev. ed. San Francisco, CA: Holden-Day.

DAGUM, E. B. (1976). Seasonal Factor Forecasts from ARIMA Models. *Proceedings of the International Statistical Institute, 40th Session, Warsaw, 1975*. Warsaw: International Statistical Institute, 206–19.

DAGUM, E. B. (1978). Modeling, Forecasting, and Seasonally Adjusting Economic Time Series with the X-11 ARIMA Method. *The Statistician* 27, 203–16.

KALLEK, S. (1978). An Overview of the Objectives and Framework of Seasonal Adjustment, in *Seasonal Analysis of Economic Time Series,* A. Zellner, ed. Washington, DC: U.S. Government Printing Office.

MACAULEY, F. R. (1930). *The Smoothing of Time Series*. Cambridge, MA: National Bureau of Economic Research.

PLOSSER, C. I. (1979). Short-Term Forecasting and Seasonal Adjustment. *Journal of the American Statistical Association* 74, 15–24.

SHISKIN, J., A. H. YOUNG, and J. C. MUSGRAVE (1967). *The X-11 Variant of Census Method II Seasonal Adjustment Program*. Technical Paper No. 15, U.S. Department of Commerce, Bureau of the Census. Washington, DC: U.S. Government Printing Office.

CHAPTER **19**

# Seasonal Adjustment with Resistant Smoothers

A recently developed procedure for adjusting seasonal time series decomposes raw data or transformed raw data into additive trend, seasonal, and irregular components by using resistant, linear, and nonlinear smoothing techniques. Resistance in this context is the property of being insensitive to gross perturbations of a small part of the data.

- Known as SABL (Seasonal Adjustment–Bell Laboratories), the procedure uses a smoothing process which consists of moving medians, tapered medians and means, and bisquare estimates.
- While SABL is applicable to any time series, the present discussion will be limited to monthly time series.

To assess the nature and adequacy of time series decomposition, we have included a set of SABL graphical displays; these include time plots of the three components, a variety of plots based on raw and smoothed seasonal values, and distributional displays of the irregular values.

## A COMPARISON OF SABL WITH X-11

The Census X-11 method (Chapter 18) and SABL (Cleveland, Dunn, and Terpenning, 1978, 1979) are similar procedures in that both attempt to express a time series in terms of its basic components. Both use smoothing operations to achieve this decomposition. However, the methods differ fundamentally in the way they carry out, summarize, and display decomposition. For example, SABL utilizes *resistant filters* which are not unduly affected by a small number of outliers. X-11, on the other hand, utilizes a more complex approach—iterating between "nonresistant" averaging procedures, and downweighting irregulars. The SABL approach also offers some additional flexibilities over X-11 by allowing a wider variety of transformations of the data.

To illustrate the differences between the two approaches, we analyzed airline data (Box and Jenkins, 1976, Series G) by both the X-11 and SABL methodologies. You will recall that these data were referred to in Chapter 18, too. Logarithms of the data were used so that the seasonal factors from the additive X-11 model could be directly compared to those from the SABL model. Figure 19.1 shows the loga-

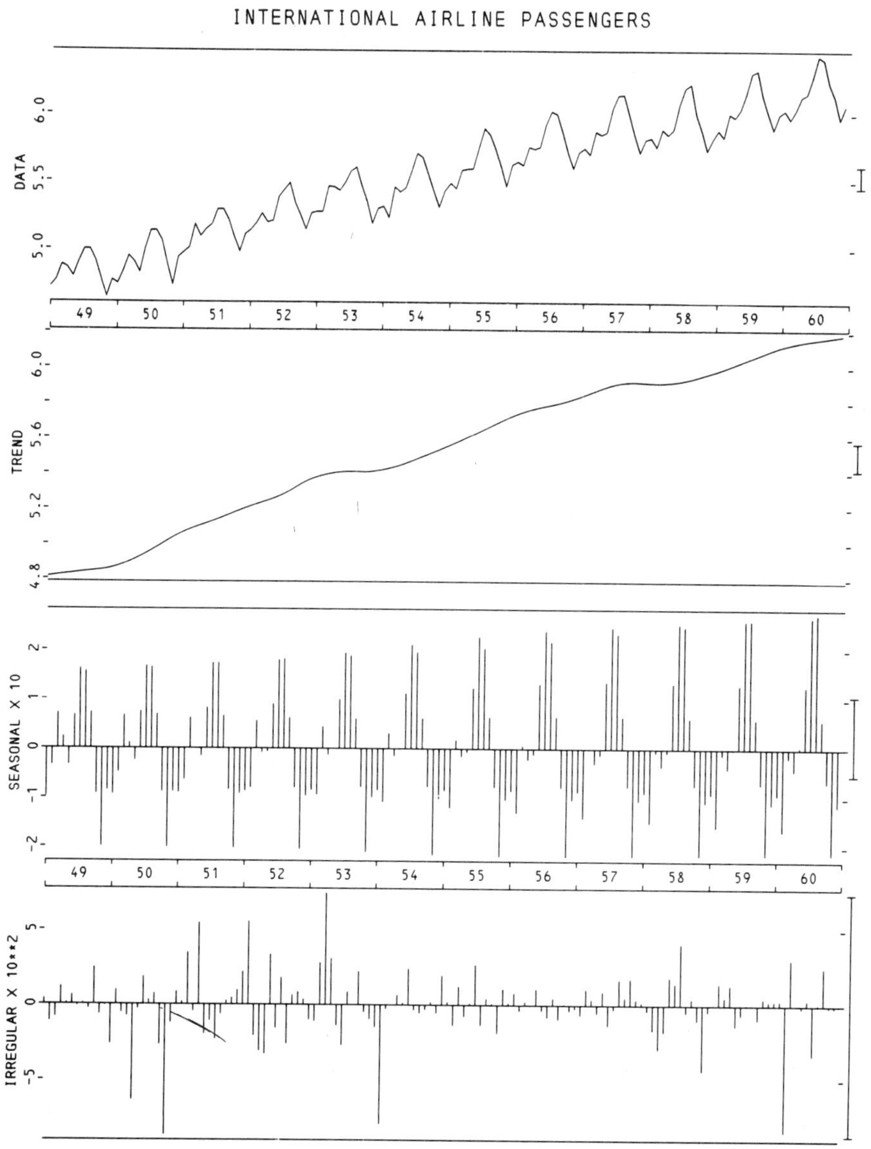


**Figure 19.1** SABL decomposition of the Box and Jenkins airline data (logarithmically transformed): monthly values from 1949–1960.

rithms of the airline data and the trend, seasonal, and irregular components as calculated in the SABL procedure. Figure 19.2 shows another SABL analysis in which three extreme outliers have been included (June 1957 = 7.0; September 1958 = 8.0; and July 1959 = 3.0). The seasonal component increases slightly in both models. In these figures, the "I-bars" at the right of each frame are used to show proportional size for comparison purposes. The top frame is the numerical sum of the corresponding values in the remaining frames. In order to keep the relatively small irregular values visible, for example, the scale of the irregulars is scaled up in proportion, as indicated by the length of the "I-bar."

Figure 19.3 shows a plot of the differences between X-11 and SABL computations of seasonal factors when no extreme outliers are present. Most differences are in absolute value less than 0.01; the two systems handle March data with the greatest difference, however. Figure 19.4 shows a plot of these differences when the large outliers are present. In this case, all months show significant differences in seasonal factors. Those differences are most pronounced in the last five years, where the outliers are concentrated. The scales in Figures 19.3 and 19.4 are kept the same to dramatize the impact of the outliers in the two procedures.

Figure 19.5 compares the seasonal factors as computed by SABL—it shows differences between the analysis with outliers and the analysis without outliers. There is very little difference. In other words, the resistant SABL procedure fits the bulk of the data and essentially ignores the severe outliers.

This is not the case with the X-11 program. Figure 19.6 compares the X-11 seasonal factors with and without outliers. It is apparent that significant differences exist, particularly in the last five years. The reason for these differences can be seen by reviewing the changes in the weights given by X-11 to the irregular components after the outliers are introduced.

Table 19.1 shows that in the X-11 program, the weights for the irregular component for the series containing the three months with large outliers (those introduced for illustrative purposes and highlighted by rectangles) dropped from 100 percent to 0 percent as expected; in other words, the irregulars were given full weight (100 percent) when the extreme outliers were absent and no weight (0 percent) when the outliers were present. However, the weights for several other months also changed by 100 percent. These were months in which the irregular components were previously considered extreme (weight = 0), but were no longer considered extreme once the three large outliers were introduced (weight = 100). These values are circled in Table 19.1.

The X-11 procedure considers five years (sixty consecutive months) of data at a time, when estimating the standard deviation of the irregular component. Table 19.2 shows that the standard deviation increases more than tenfold because of the three outliers. Since this standard deviation is applied across all months in a given year, an outlier in June can impact the weights given to all other months. Months with small variations in the irregular component will have fewer extreme values downweighted because the standard deviation that is applied to all months is inflated

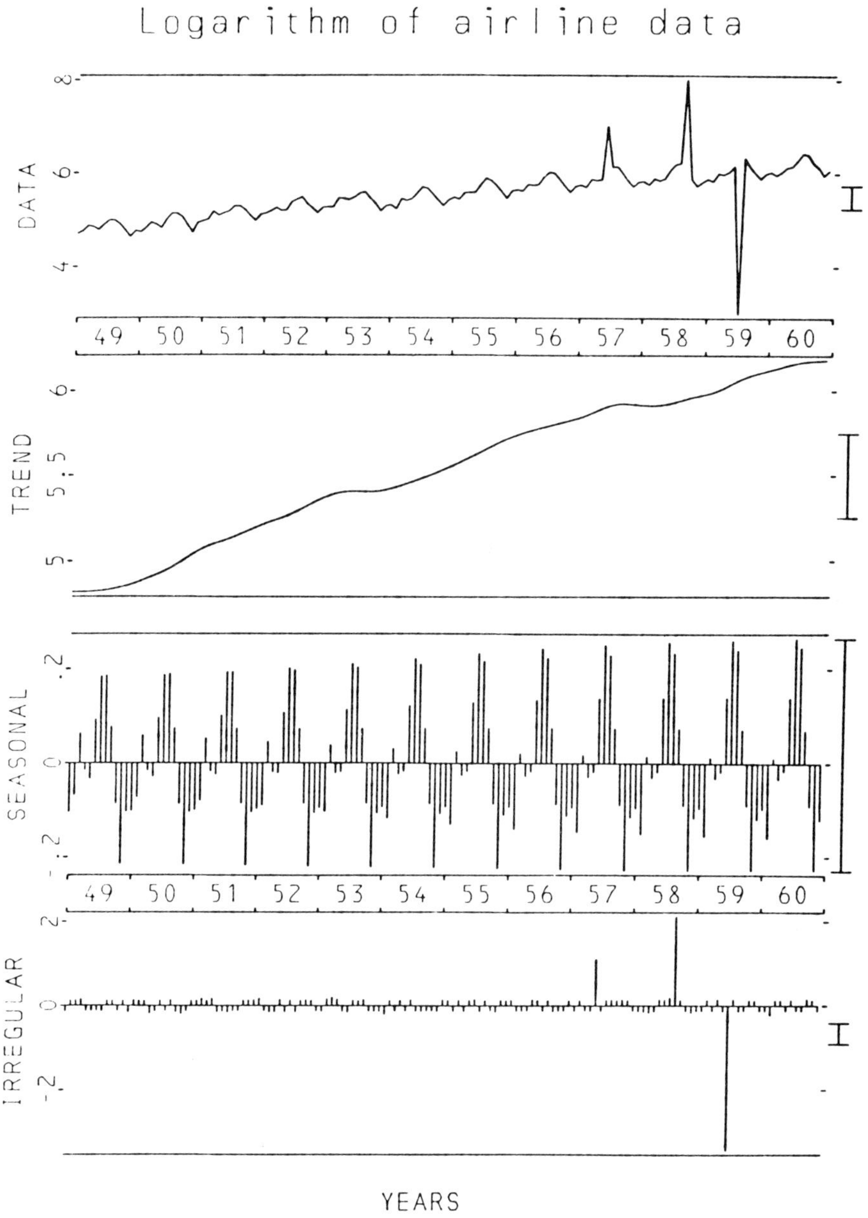


**Figure 19.2** SABL decomposition of the airline data (monthly values from 1949–1960) when three outliers are introduced. The outliers are June 1957 = 7.0; September 1958 = 8.0; and July 1959 = 3.0.

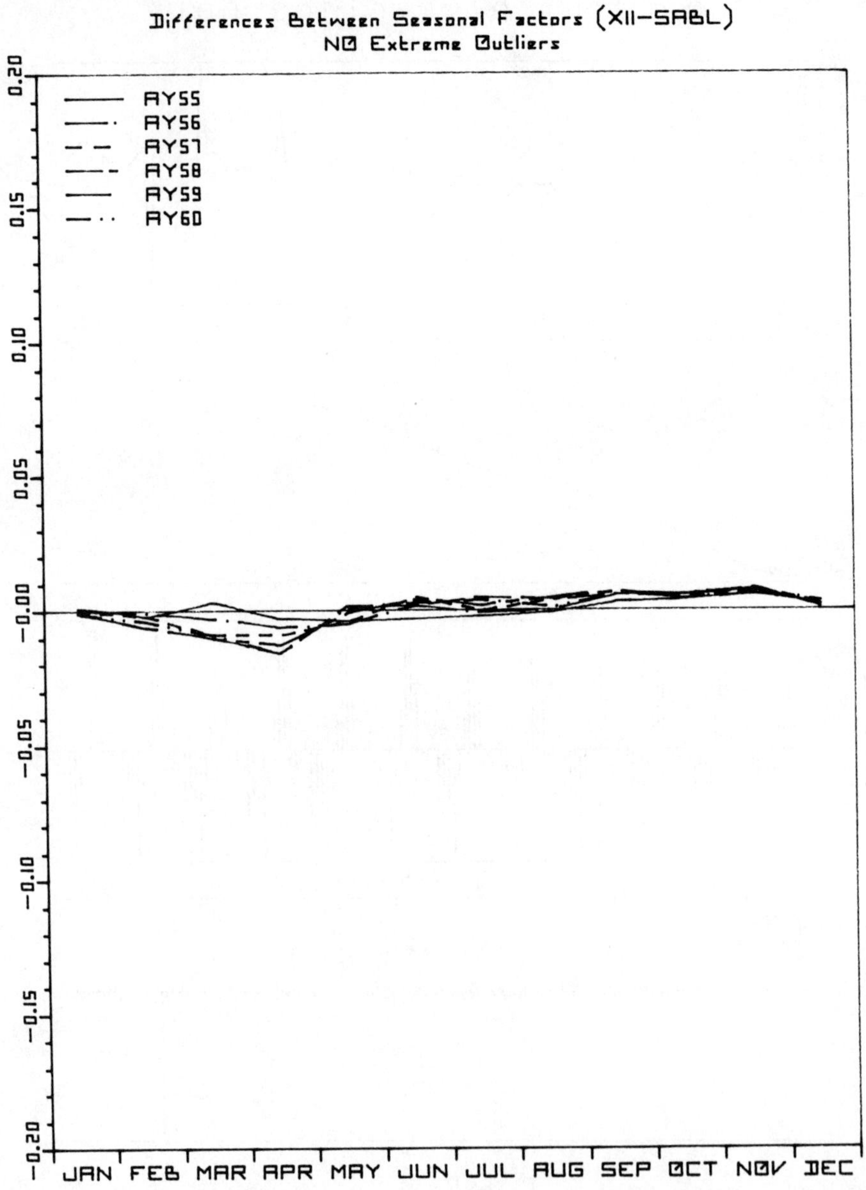


**Figure 19.3** Plot of differences between the X-11 and SABL seasonal factors (without outliers).

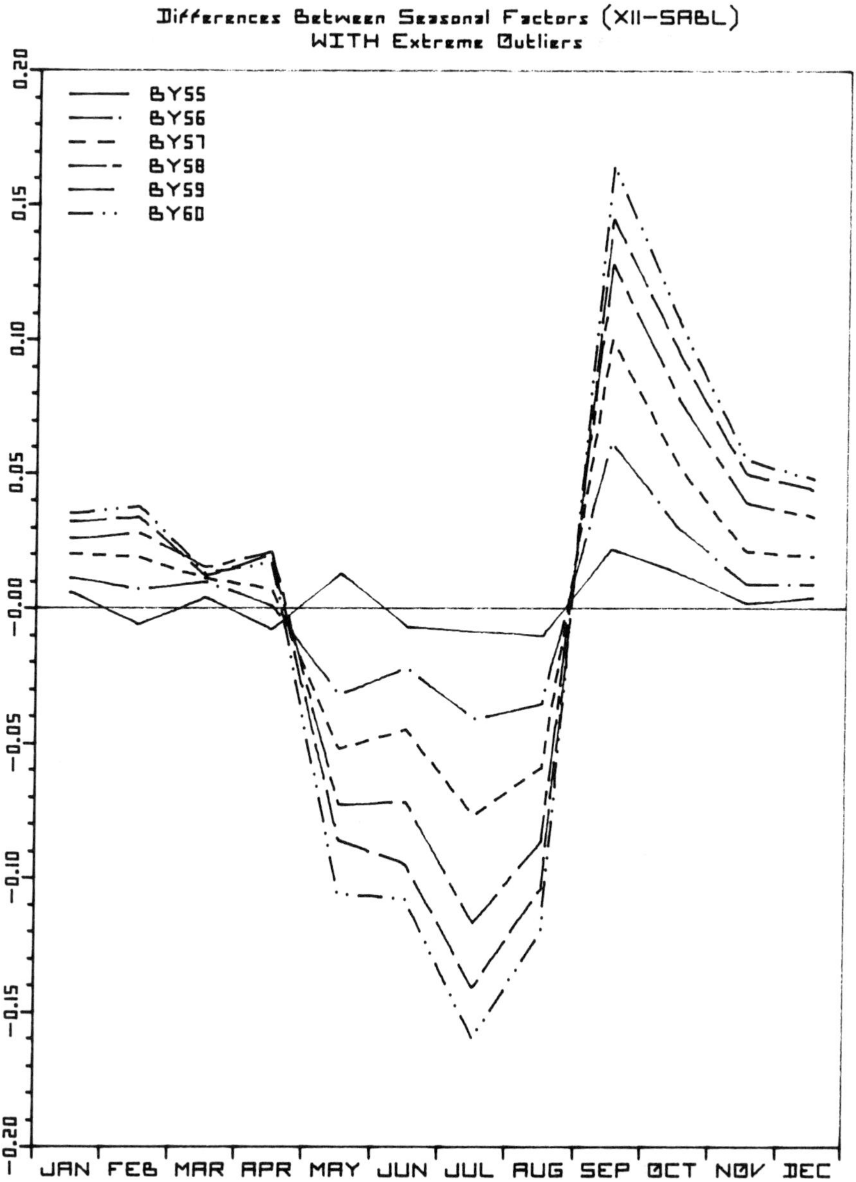


**Figure 19.4** Plot of differences between the X-11 and SABL seasonal factors (with outliers).

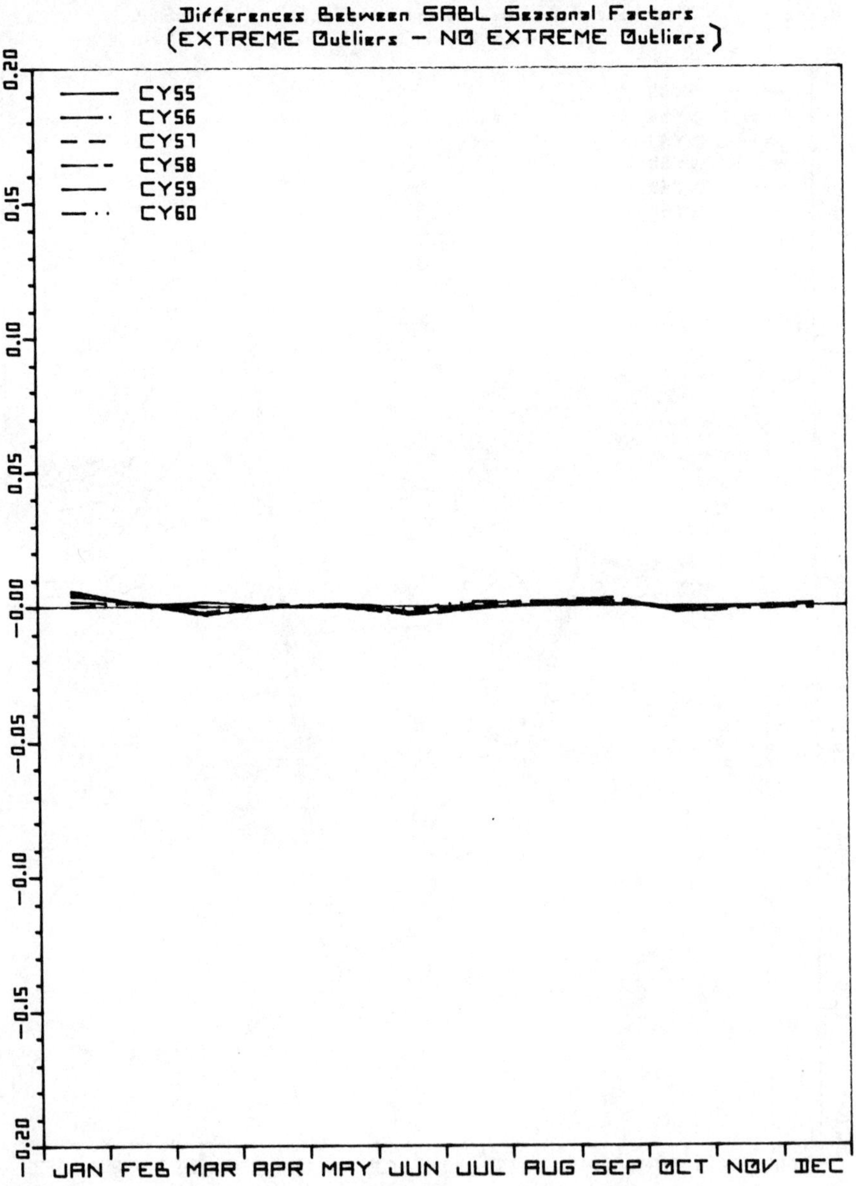


**Figure 19.5** SABL seasonal factors showing differences attributable to outliers.

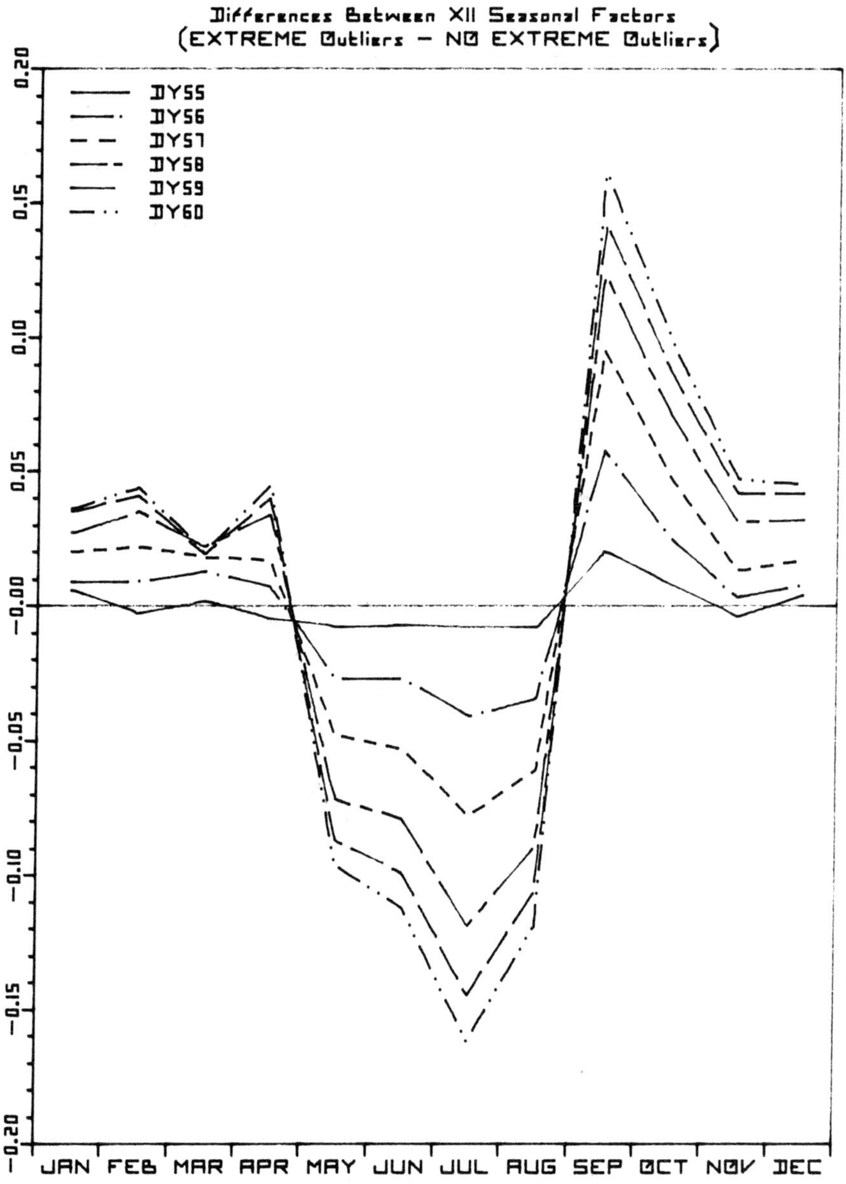


**Figure 19.6** X-11 seasonal factors showing differences attributable to outliers.

**Table 19.1** Weights from the X-11 program for the irregular component for the series containing the three months with the large outliers.

| Year | Jan. | Feb. | Mar. | Apr. | May | June | July | Aug. | Sept. | Oct. | Nov. | Dec. |
|---|---|---|---|---|---|---|---|---|---|---|---|---|
| 1949 | — | — | — | 12.0 | — | — | — | — | — | — | — | — |
| 1950 | 12.8 | 3.9 | — | — | — | — | — | — | — | 9.9 | — | — |
| 1951 | — | — | 7.9 | — | — | — | — | — | — | — | — | — |
| 1952 | 4.2 | — | — | — | — | — | — | — | 22.2 | — | — | — |
| 1953 | — | — | — | — | 23.2 | — | 63.0 | — | — | — | — | — |
| 1954 | — | 54.2 | — | — | — | — | 39.8 | — | — | — | — | — |
| 1955 | 0.3 | — | 10.9 | — | — | — | 100.0† | — | — | — | 100.0† | — |
| 1956 | — | — | — | — | — | — | — | — | — | — | — | — |
| 1957 | — | — | — | — | — | −100.0* | — | — | — | — | — | — |
| 1958 | — | — | — | 60.1 | — | — | — | 100.0† | −100.0* | 55.5 | — | 100.0† |
| 1959 | — | — | — | — | −100.0† | −76.0 | −100.0* | −0.8 | — | — | — | — |
| 1960 | — | — | 100.0† | 100.0† | — | — | — | — | — | 100.0† | — | — |

*Months with extreme outliers.
†Months with 100 percent change in weights but no extreme outliers.

**Table 19.2** Standard deviation of the irregular component in the X-11 program.

| Year | Without extreme outliers | With extreme outliers |
|---|---|---|
| 1949 | 15.4 | 16.7 |
| 1950 | 15.4 | 16.7 |
| 1951 | 15.4 | 16.7 |
| 1952 | 14.0 | 17.1* |
| 1953 | 13.3 | 17.1 |
| 1954 | 11.4 | 24.3 |
| 1955 | 9.7 | 123.6† |
| 1956 | 10.0 | 133.3† |
| 1957 | 10.5 | 187.6† |
| 1958 | 11.5 | 151.3† |
| 1959 | 11.5 | 151.3† |
| 1960 | 11.5 | 151.3† |

*Standard deviation for five years of irregulars for which this is the center year.
†The inflated standard deviation is applied to *all* months in the year rather than only months containing extreme outliers.

by highly variable months. Similarly, highly variable months may have some of their values too severely downweighted because the standard deviation understates the variability of these months.

The SABL procedure, in contrast, treats each month individually and is less subject to this problem. Figure 19.7 displays the box plots of the monthly irregulars; the first three months of the year are repeated so that you can analyze the annual variation better visually. The outside values, depicted by numbers (50 = 1950), are the most extreme irregulars. The midmeans, representing the mean of the middle 50 percent of the variation (by month), are shown as horizontal lines dividing the boxes. These midmeans show that the irregular variation is close to zero; a trend in these midmeans would suggest some leakage from the trend component into the irregulars. The figure also shows that November has considerably less variation than January.

In this example, the artificial outliers that were introduced were quite extreme and substantially affected the values for the seasonal factors computed by the X-11 method. The original data, however, were "well behaved," and the two methodologies produced results which were reasonably similar. In general, if the data are free of outliers, classical methods and resistant methods should yield similar results. When the data have a few extreme values, resistant methods yield better results when the objective is to provide measures which are representative of the bulk of the data.

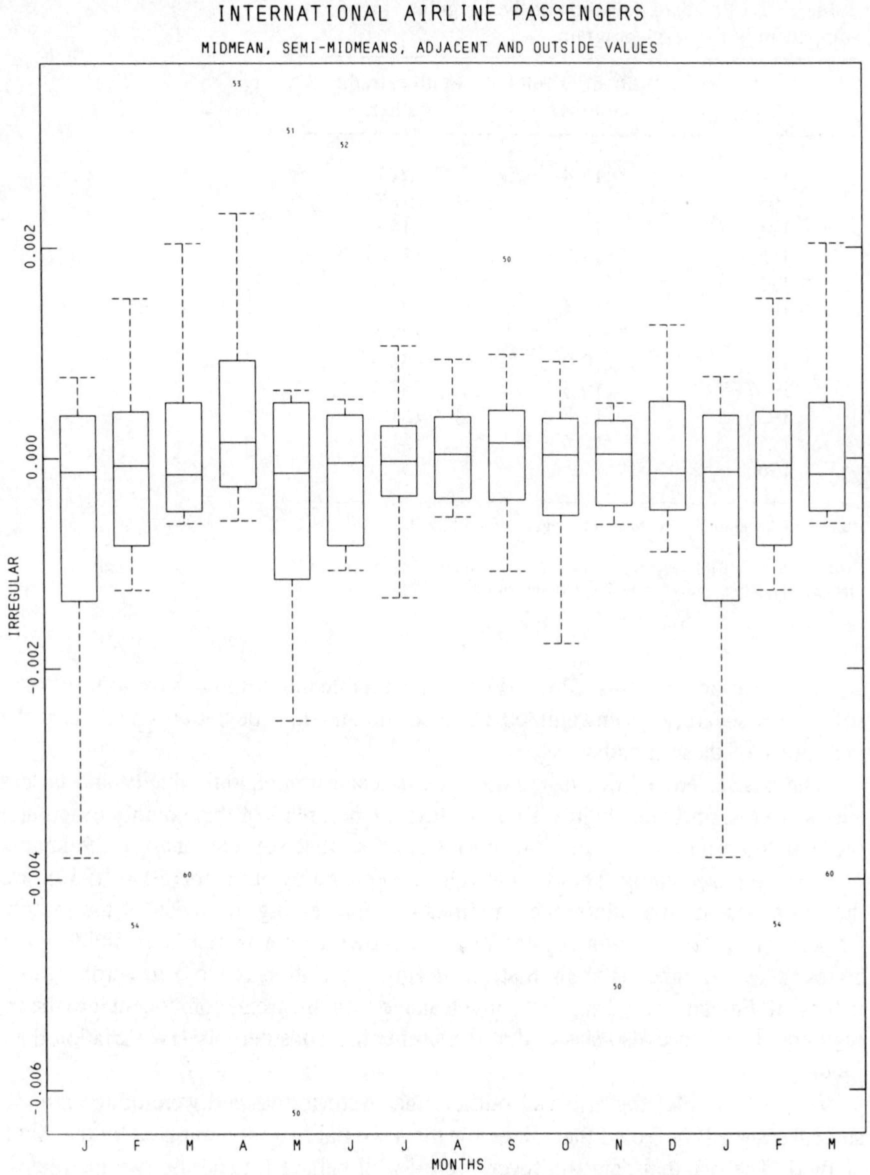


**Figure 19.7** SABL box plot showing December to have less variation than March.

## THE SABL DECOMPOSITION PROCEDURE

The decomposition of a time series is assumed to have the form

$$Y = T + S + I,$$

where $T$ represents the long-term trend, $S$ represents the seasonal component, and $I$ represents the irregular or noise component. It is implicitly assumed that $Y$ is either the raw data or the data transformed exponentially in the manner that will be described shortly.

SABL, like the Census X-11 program, is an iterative approach which sequentially estimates the seasonal and trend components at each iteration. It is designed to keep seasonality from entering trend and trend from entering seasonality. Specifically, the goals of the process are:

- Trend ($T$) should reflect the low-frequency cycle or trendlike behavior of the series.
- Seasonality ($S$) should reflect the relatively stable behavior which repeats every twelve months.
- Irregularity ($I$) should contain all behavior which is not seasonal or trendlike.
- There must be as little leakage as possible from one component into another.
- Extreme or unusual values should not distort $T$ or $S$.
- Estimates of $T$ and $S$ should be as responsive as possible to changes in their structures.

The SABL program allows one to transform the data to eliminate the large changes that often occur in the amplitudes of the seasonal component. The resulting stabilization

- Minimizes the dependence of the seasonal amplitudes on the level of the trend component.
- Often makes the task of seasonal adjustment simpler.
- Allows the results to rest on a firmer foundation.
- Makes the decomposition (into trend-cycle, seasonal, and irregular) more nearly additive.

The first part of the SABL program is a procedure for choosing a transformation $Y_t^p$ *where* $p$ is one of the values $-1.0$, $-0.5$, $-0.25$, 0, 0.25, 0.5, or 1.0, such that an additive model can be assumed.

The transformation (for nonnegative data) takes the form

| | |
|---|---|
| $(\text{Raw data})^p$ | for $p > 0$; |
| $\log_{10}$ (Raw data) | for $p = 0$; |
| $-(\text{Raw data})^p$ | for $p < 0$. |

To illustrate the SABL procedure, we shall continue to use logarithms ( $p = 0$) of the airline data (Box and Jenkins 1976, Series G), in which the seasonality is approximately proportional to the level of the data.

A smoothing procedure is first applied to the data (Data = Trend + Seasonal + Irregular) to calculate an initial resistant smooth trend. The smoothed trend is subtracted from the data to yield a seasonal/irregular series $S + I$ (Data − Trend = Seasonal + Irregular). This is followed by determining tapered medians and means of the $(S + I)$ values, to yield an initial set of resistant seasonal components.

After subtracting the initial set of seasonal components from the original data, a second resistant trend smoothing is calculated. Next, irregular values are computed (Data − Seasonal − Trend). A resistant weighting scheme involving the tapered median absolute values of the irregular values is used to develop resistant weights to be applied to the $(S + I)$ values to yield a refined, resistant seasonal component.

## Smoothing Seasonal Plus Irregular Values to Obtain Rough Seasonal Factors

Preliminary seasonal plus irregular values $(S + I)$ are obtained by subtracting an initial trend value from the original data. The procedure used to calculate the initial trend value is the one described in Chapter 16 as ''Resistant Smoothing.'' Then, the next series of steps is undertaken to smooth the seasonal plus irregular component to yield the seasonal component.

Table 19.3 shows the calculations used to derive the seasonal factors for September in the SABL procedure. The seasonal calculations are performed over each of the twelve monthly subseries (all Januarys, all Februarys, etc.). The steps taken for September are followed for all of the other remaining months, too. A tapered moving median of window length *nss* (here 7 was used and it represents the window length of the seasonal smooth) is calculated for the $(S + I)$ values of Column 1. The amount of seasonal smoothing is selected by the user; for a small, medium, or large amount of smoothing, the recommended values for the window length are 5, 11, or 23 respectively. Next, a tapered mean of window length *nss* (= 7) is taken of the values in Column 2 to yield the initial or first seasonal smoothing (Column 3).

An example of how the calculation of the tapered median for September 1960 is done for Table 19.3 is shown in Table 19.4. A bisquare weighting is associated with the $(S + I)$ values (Columns 1 and 2 of Table 19.4). September 1960 receives a weight of 1.000, and the weights for the September values in the other years diminish as the distance from 1960 increases. In this instance, however, the weights are not multiplied by the $(S + I)$ values. Rather, the $(S + I)$ values are reranked from lowest to highest and their weights move with them (Columns 3 and 4). The weights are summed (= 4.266) and divided by two to determine the median weight (= 2.133). The tapered median is the $(S + I)$ value that corresponds to the median weight. The cumulative bisquare weight in Column 5 exceeds 2.133 where the value

**Table 19.3** Calculations used to derive seasonal factors for September in the SABL procedure.

| Year | (1) $S + I$* | (2) Tapered median of $S + I$ | (3) First seasonal = tapered mean of (2) | (4) $I_t$, Initial irregular = (1) − (3) | (5) Absolute value of $\lvert I_t \rvert$ | (6) $M_t$, Tapered median of $\lvert I_t \rvert$ | (7) $R_t = B\left(\frac{I_t}{6M_t}\right)$ | (8) Resistant tapered moving mean,[†] $\frac{\Sigma R_t W_t (S + I)_t}{\Sigma R_t W_t}$ |
|---|---|---|---|---|---|---|---|---|
| 1957 | 0.136 | 0.136 | 0.134 | 0.002 | 0.002 | 0.011 | 0.998 | 0.128 |
| 1958 | 2.083 | 0.136 | 0.133 | 1.950 | 1.950 | 0.011 | 0.000 | 0.126 |
| 1959 | 0.116 | 0.130 | 0.132 | −0.016 | 0.016 | 0.011 | 0.886 | 0.126 |
| 1960 | 0.120 | 0.130 | 0.131 | −0.011 | 0.011 | 0.011 | 0.945 | 0.126 |
| 1961 | 0.140 | 0.130 | 0.130 | 0.010 | 0.010 | 0.010 | 0.945 | 0.126 |
| 1962 | 0.130 | 0.130 | 0.129 | 0.001 | 0.001 | 0.010 | 1.000 | 0.127 |
| 1963 | 0.110 | 0.130 | 0.128 | −0.018 | 0.018 | 0.010 | 0.828 | 0.127 |
| 1964 | 0.135 | 0.125 | 0.127 | 0.008 | 0.008 | 0.008 | 0.945 | 0.126 |
| 1965 | 0.125 | 0.125 | 0.126 | −0.001 | 0.001 | 0.008 | 1.000 | 0.126 |

*Values for 1960–1965 are assumed.
[†] $W_t$ is the bisquare weight (window length $= 2 \cdot nss + 1 = 15$).

**Table 19.4** Calculation of the tapered median for September 1960 in the SABL procedure ($nss = 7$)

| Year | (1)<br>$(S + I)_t$ | (2)<br>Bisquare weight<br>$(W_t)$ | (3)<br>Reranked<br>$(S + I)$ | (4)<br>Bisquare weight<br>$(W_t)$ | (5)<br>Cumulative weight<br>$= \Sigma W_t$ | (6)<br>Cumulative weight exceeds 2.133? |
|---|---|---|---|---|---|---|
| 1957 | 0.136 | 0.191 | 0.110 | 0.191 | 0.191 | No |
| 1958 | 2.083 | 0.563 | 0.116 | 0.879 | 1.070 | No |
| 1959 | 0.116 | 0.879 | 0.120 | 1.000 | 2.070 | No |
| 1960 | 0.120 | 1.000 | 0.130* | 0.563 | 2.633 | Yes |
| 1961 | 0.140 | 0.879 | 0.136 | 0.191 | | |
| 1962 | 0.130 | 0.563 | 0.140 | 0.879 | | |
| 1963 | 0.110 | 0.191 | 2.083 | 0.563 | | |
| 1964 | 0.135 | 0.000 | | | | |
| 1965 | 0.125 | 0.000 | | | | |

Total bisquare weight $= \Sigma W_t = 4.266$
Median weight $= \Sigma W_t/2 = 2.133$

*Tapered median $(S + I) = 0.130$. The tapered median is the value for $(S + I)$ where the cumulative bisquare weight as a percent of the total weight exceeds 0.5 (the value where $\Sigma W_t/2$ is exceeded).

of reranked $(S + I)$ (in Column 3) equals 0.130. The process is repeated for all the years. At each end point the sum of the weights will be less than 4.266 and the median weight will be less than 2.133.

## Deriving Missing Seasonal Factors

The missing seasonal values for the first and last year are derived by using a one-step-ahead and one-step-backward prediction routine. If *nss* equals 3, the one-step-ahead predictions are the seasonal values for the last available year. When *nss* is set above 3, the initial and final year seasonal values are determined by using a weighted least-squares estimation procedure. The weights are bisquare and are defined over the last $k$ years by

$$W_t = B[(n + 1 - t)/(k + 1)].$$

A sample of the weighting function scheme for *nss* equals 11, where the number of $(S + I)$ values equals 10, is shown in Table 19.5. In this case, only the seasonal values for the last five years are used to project the seasonal value for the year $(n + 1)$. This regression is performed for each month, and

$$S(n + 1) = a + b \cdot (n + 1).$$

**Table 19.5** Calculation of seasonal values by using the bisquare weighting function ($nss = 11$, $n = 10$).

$W_t = B[(n + 1 - t)/(k + 1)]$

Example:

$nss = 11; k = 5$

$n = 10$ (number of $S + I$ values)

$W_1, W_2, \ldots, W_5 = 0$

$W_6 = B[(10 + 1 - 6)/6] = B(5/6) = 0.093$

. .

. .

. .

$W_{10} = B[(10 + 1 - 10)/6] = B(1/6) = 0.945$

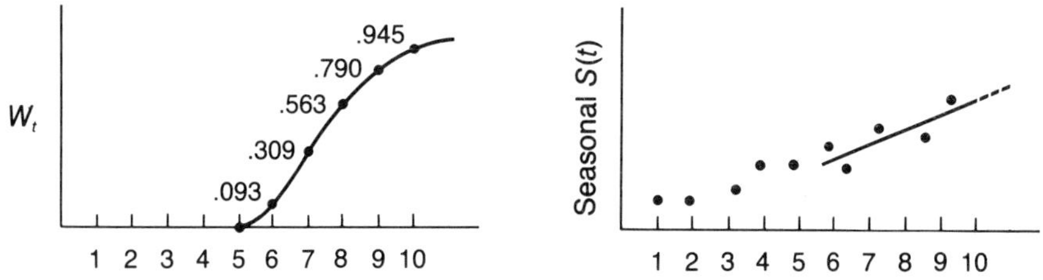


An illustration of this procedure is shown in the lower part of Table 19.5. The seasonal value for the first year is derived in a similar manner. The twelve monthly subseries form the first seasonal component. These extend over the entire time period as a result of the one-step-ahead and one-step-backward prediction routine.

## Calculating a Refined Estimate of Trend (Second Trend Smoothing)

The first seasonal component is subtracted from the original data to yield $(T + I)$. A second (refined) trend smoothing is next calculated by using tapered medians and tapered means so that no data are lost at either end. A tapered median of window length *nts* (= window length of trend smoothing) for the $(T + I)$ values is calculated; then a tapered mean is calculated to obtain a rough trend. The trend is subtracted from $(T + I)$ to yield an irregular. A tapered median irregular is calculated and smoothed (by a tapered moving mean). The smoothed irregular is added to the rough trend to yield a second trend smoothing (Trend + Cycle). These steps were skipped in the example.

## Downweighting Extremes

At the next stage of seasonal adjustment, resistant weights are calculated and used to downweight the influence of extreme values in determining the seasonal component. A resistant estimate of variation $M_t$ is computed for the irregular component. The size of the monthly irregular value, relative to $M_t$, determines the weight to be assigned to each monthly data value.

The current trend and seasonal values are subtracted from the original data to yield the initial irregular values (Column 4 of Table 19.3). Absolute values are taken. Table 19.6 shows the calculations used to estimate $M_t$. The window length is extended to 15 ($2nss + 1$).

A tapered moving median of the absolute values of the irregular values is computed in the same manner as described in Table 19.4. Since each month is treated separately, months with high variability do not distort the determination of $M_t$ for months with little variability.

The resistant weights $R_t$ are calculated by using a bisquare weighting function,

$$R_t = B(I_t/6M_t),$$

where $I_t$ is the irregular value for each month and $M_t$ is the resistant estimate of scale. Table 19.7 shows the calculation of the resistant weights for September 1957, 1958, and 1964.

**Table 19.6** Initial irregular values and a resistant estimate of variation $M_t$ for the SABL procedure.

| Year | $\|I_t\|$ | Bisquare weight $W_t$ | Reranked $\|I_t\|$ | Bisquare weight $W_t$ | Cumulative weight $\Sigma W_t$ | Cumulative weight exceeds 2.868? |
|---|---|---|---|---|---|---|
| 1957 | 0.002 | 0.969 | 0.001 | 0.563 | 0.563 | No |
| 1958 | 1.950 | 1.000 | 0.001 | 0.055 | 0.618 | No |
| 1959 | 0.016 | 0.969 | 0.002 | 0.969 | 1.587 | No |
| 1960 | 0.011 | 0.879 | 0.008 | 0.191 | 1.778 | No |
| 1961 | 0.010 | 0.738 | 0.010 | 0.738 | 2.516 | No |
| 1962 | 0.001 | 0.563 | 0.011* | 0.879 | 3.395 | Yes |
| 1963 | 0.018 | 0.371 | | | | |
| 1964 | 0.008 | 0.191 | | | | |
| 1965 | 0.001 | 0.055 | | | | |
| | | 5.735 | | | | |

Bisquare window = $2nss + 1 = 2(7) + 1 = 15$

Total bisquare weight = 5.735

Median weight = 2.868

*$M_t$ = Tapered median irregular = 0.011.

**Table 19.7** SABL calculation of the resistant weights of the irregular component. Resistant (bisquare) weight $R_t = B(I_t/6M_t)$.

| $t$ | $I_t$ | $M_t$ | $I_t/6M_t$ | $R_t$ |
|---|---|---|---|---|
| September 1957 | 0.002 | 0.011 | 0.030 | 0.998 |
| September 1958 | 1.950 | 0.011 | 29.5 | 0.000 |
| September 1964 | 0.008 | 0.008 | 0.167 | 0.945 |

Bisquare function $B(u) = (1 - u^2)^2$ if $|u| \leq 1$;
$= 0$ if $|u| > 1$.

*Note:* $M_t$ values are obtained from Table 19.3, Column 6.

## Calculating Resistant Seasonal Factors

The resistant weights $R_t$ are then used in the calculation of resistant tapered means of the seasonal plus irregular values:

$$\frac{\sum_{-k}^{k} R_t W_t (S + I)_t}{\sum_{-k}^{k} R_t W_t}.$$

Each $(S + I)$ value is multiplied by a resistant weight $R_t$ which is data dependent and a bisquare weight $W_t$ which is location dependent. The calculation of the resistant tapered mean for September 1957 is shown in Table 19.8. Column 8 of Table 19.3 shows these values for all months.

**Table 19.8** SABL calculation of the resistant tapered mean of $(S + I)$ for September 1957.

$$\text{Mean} = \frac{\Sigma R_t W_t (S + I)_t}{\Sigma R_t W_t};$$

and

$$\text{Mean} = \frac{(0.998)(1.000)(0.136) + (0.000)(0.879)(2.083) + (0.886)(0.563)(0.116) + (0.945)(0.191)(0.120)}{(0.998)(1.000) + (0.000)(0.879) + (0.886)(0.563) + (0.945)(0.191)}$$

$$= \frac{0.215}{1.677} = 0.128,$$

where

$R_t$ = Resistance weight for each value;
$W_t$ = Bisquare weight with $nss = 7$.

### Removing Trend from the Seasonal Factors

Next, the one-step prediction routine is used on each monthly subseries to create seasonal factors for the year before the data started and for the future year. These factors will be utilized as part of the remaining process to remove any trend from the seasonal factors.

The factors are reformatted into a time series (January, February, March, and so on), and a twelve-month moving average is taken to obtain the initial trend in the seasonal factors (if any). A two-month moving average is taken to recenter the data, and a tapered moving mean of the length of the trend smooth is taken. This results in a smoothed trend of the seasonal factors. The smoothed trend is subtracted from the seasonal factors to yield final seasonal factors for all the months.

The process is iterative. The calculation of the seasonal smooth with resistant weights and the calculation of a final trend smooth with resistant weights are carried out a total of $n$-step times. Seasonal predictions for year $n + 1$ are computed by using the one-step-ahead prediction procedure described earlier.

## SABL GRAPHICS

The SABL package provides a variety of graphical displays that are very helpful in analyzing the adequacy of the seasonal decomposition. Consider the way a SABL decomposition ($p = 1$) of the airline data from Box and Jenkins (1976, Series G) can be presented with graphical displays.

Figures 19.1 and 19.8 show two decompositions of the trend, seasonal, and irregular components. Figure 19.8 shows the decomposition for the raw series ($p = 1$), and Figure 19.1 represents the decomposition for the logarithms ($p = 0$) of the raw series. It is apparent that a more stable seasonal pattern is evident when a logarithmic transformation of the data is made.

Figure 19.9 shows a box plot of the irregular values ($p = 1$) for each month. The midmeans are approximately zero. If the midmeans change greatly from month to month, the seasonal component $S$ has crept into the irregular component $I$. Extreme outliers become evident in a figure such as this, as well as the difference in variability among the months. This figure can be compared with Figure 19.7, which shows the distribution of the irregular in the airline data ($p = 0$).

Another useful SABL graphic is the seasonal-by-month plot. The plot is created by taking the seasonal component time series and creating twelve new monthly subseries; that is, a series for all January seasonal components, a series for all February components, and so on. Then the midmean (average of the middle 50 percent of the ordered values) of the seasonal components for each subseries is computed.

Figure 19.10 depicts the monthly seasonal factors as deviations from the monthly midmeans. For the twelve months the midmeans are shown as horizontal lines. The

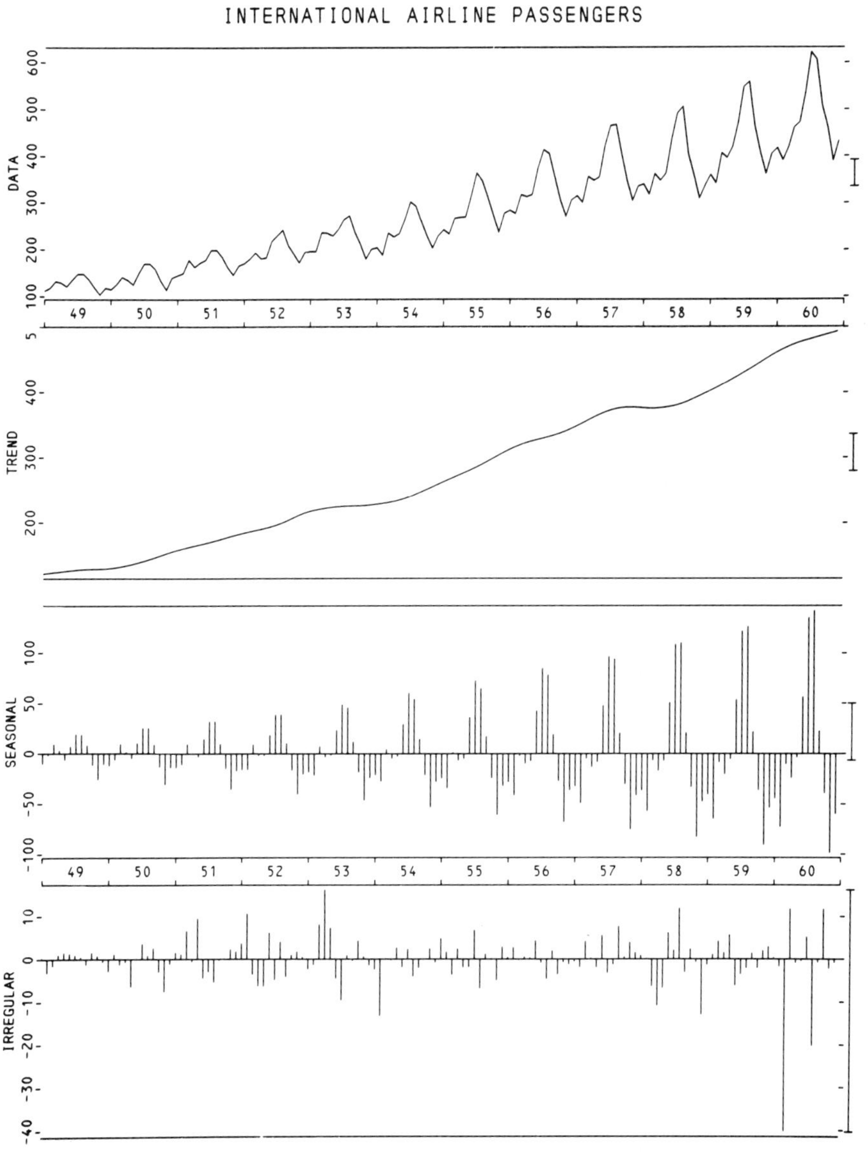


**Figure 19.8** SABL decomposition of the airline data (untransformed, $p = 1$).

deviations from the respective midmeans are depicted as vertical lines. The factors for the forecasted year are depicted as vertical dashed lines. This chart helps to compare

- Relative variation in seasonal factors (compare October to November; May to July or August).

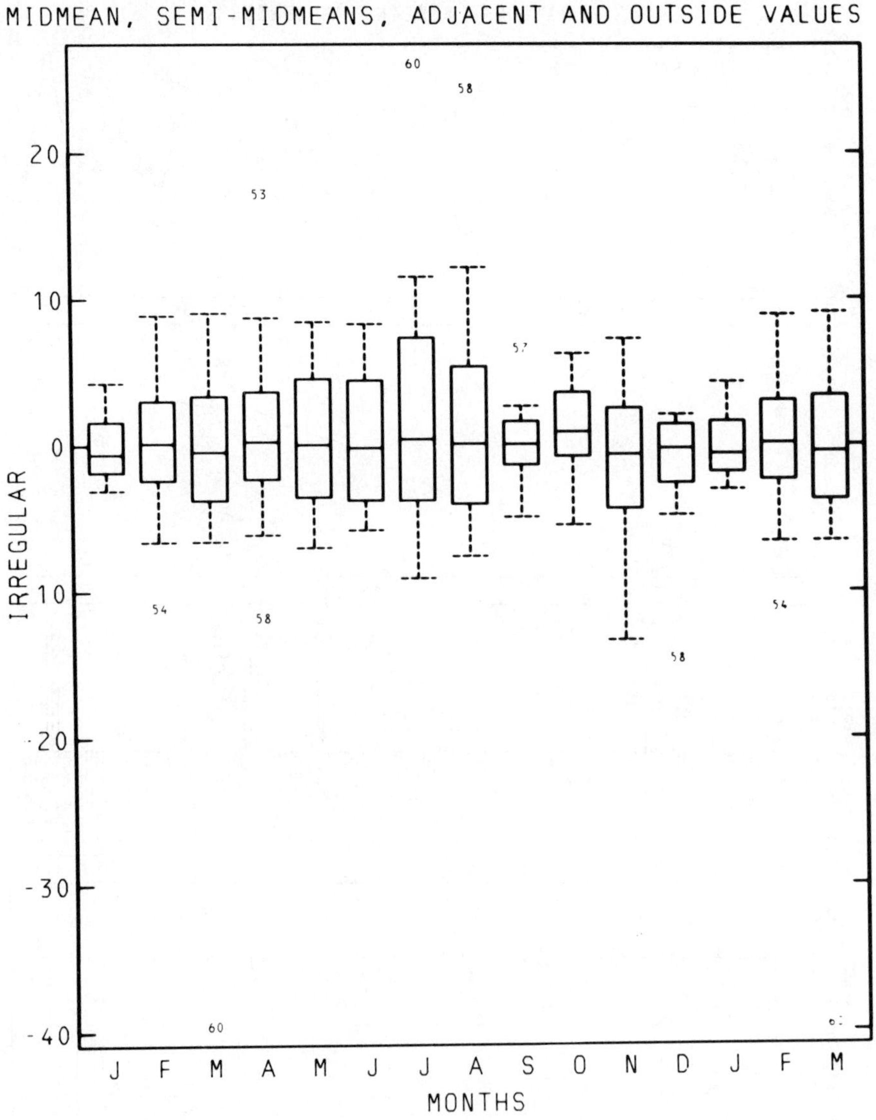


**Figure 19.9** Monthly variation in the irregular for the airline data, shown as box plots; midmeans divide the boxes, semi-midmeans define the upper and lower portions of the boxes, adjacent values are depicted with dashed-line "whiskers," and an outside value is given in terms of the last two digits of its year-value.

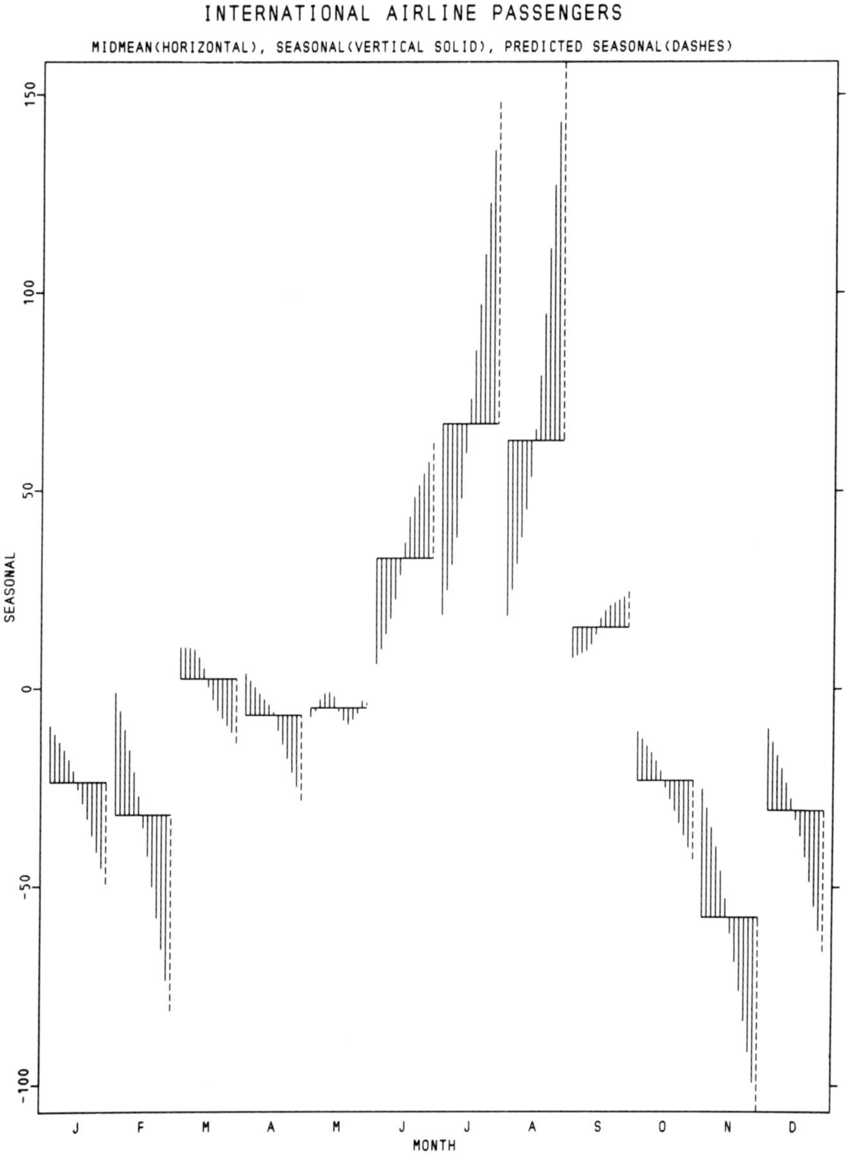


**Figure 19.10** Seasonal component-by-month plot showing monthly seasonal factors as deviations from the monthly midmeans in a SABL decomposition of the airline data ($p = 1$).

- Changing patterns in seasonality (e.g., February, March, June, . . .).
- The level of the monthly midmean as a means of assessing the impact of calendar effects. Are 31-day months high relative to 30-day months or vice versa? (Calendar effects are not obvious in this example.)

Still another SABL plot is used to check on the choice of the $p$ value in the transformation. With the inappropriate choice of $p$ there may be some interaction between the trend and seasonal components. The plot helps to isolate this problem.

To obtain the information for the plot, a *moving range* of the seasonal component (with a length equal to the period of the seasonality) is calculated first. Then a moving average of the *absolute* values of the seasonal component (also with length equal to the period of the seasonality) is calculated. Both these measures are plotted in Figure 19.11 for the airline data ($p = 1$; $nts = 15$; $nss = 7$). The upper curve is the twelve-month moving range and the lower curve is the twelve-month moving average. When the upper curve keeps increasing, then there is some evidence that the trend component has leaked into the seasonal component.

One way to reduce this effect is to take a transformation of the data. Indeed, by taking logarithms before decomposition ($p = 0$) there is some improvement in the moving-range curve (Figure 19.12).

A final SABL plot is constructed to check on the appropriate length of the seasonal smooth ($nss$). This set of frames shows for each month the seasonal component and the data minus the trend over the entire time frame. For example, Figure 19.13 shows the seasonal and data-minus-trend plot for the transformed ($p = 0$) airline data and smoothing parameters for trend ($nts = 15$) and seasonal ($nss = 7$).

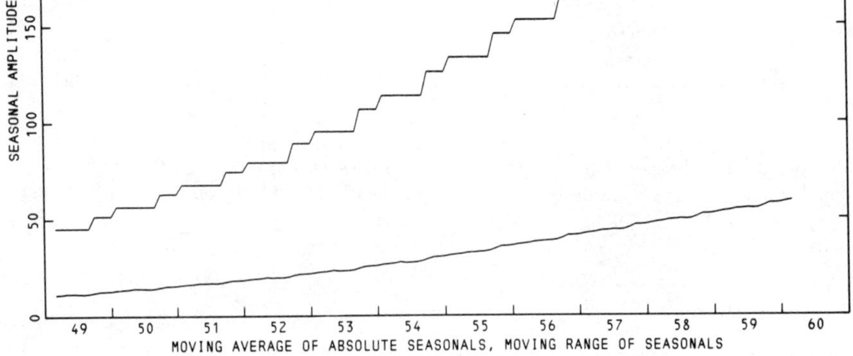

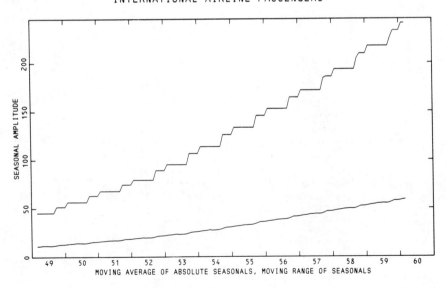

**Figure 19.11** Seasonal amplitude plot for the airline data ($p = 1$; $nts = 15$, $nss = 7$).

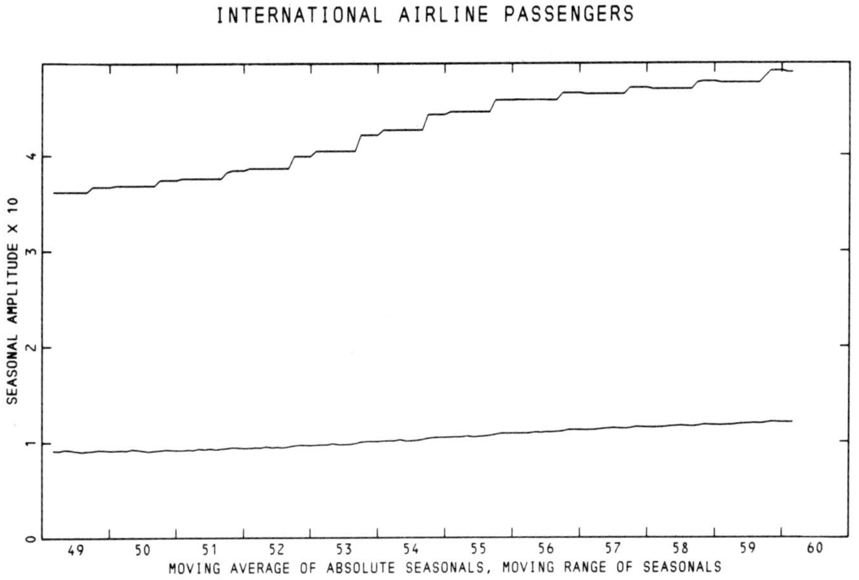


**Figure 19.12** Seasonal amplitude plot for the transformed airline data ($p = 0$; $nts = 15$; $nss = 7$), showing an improvement in the moving range curve over Figure 19.11.

The solid line (or seasonal) is a smoothing of the zeros (or data minus trend). If the solid line still appears to follow the points too much, a higher smoothing parameter can be tried.

Figure 19.14 shows what happens when the seasonal smoothing parameter is changed from $nss = 7$ to $nss = 15$. The seasonal component appears a lot smoother (perhaps too much) and is stabler over the historical period than before. The predicted seasonal (one year ahead) is depicted as a plus (+). The selection of the appropriate smoothing parameter is somewhat subjective, of course; however, the graphical tools certainly help to make this assessment relatively easy with some experimentation. We feel, on the basis of this analysis, that the airline data requires

- A logarithmic transformation ($p = 0$).
- A trend smooth ($nts = 15$).
- A seasonal smooth ($nss = 7$).

## SUMMARY

In this chapter the SABL seasonal adjustment tool was presented and compared with the X-11 procedure (Chapter 18).

- The X-11 represents an accepted, widely used procedure for systematically analyzing and adjusting a large class of seasonal data.

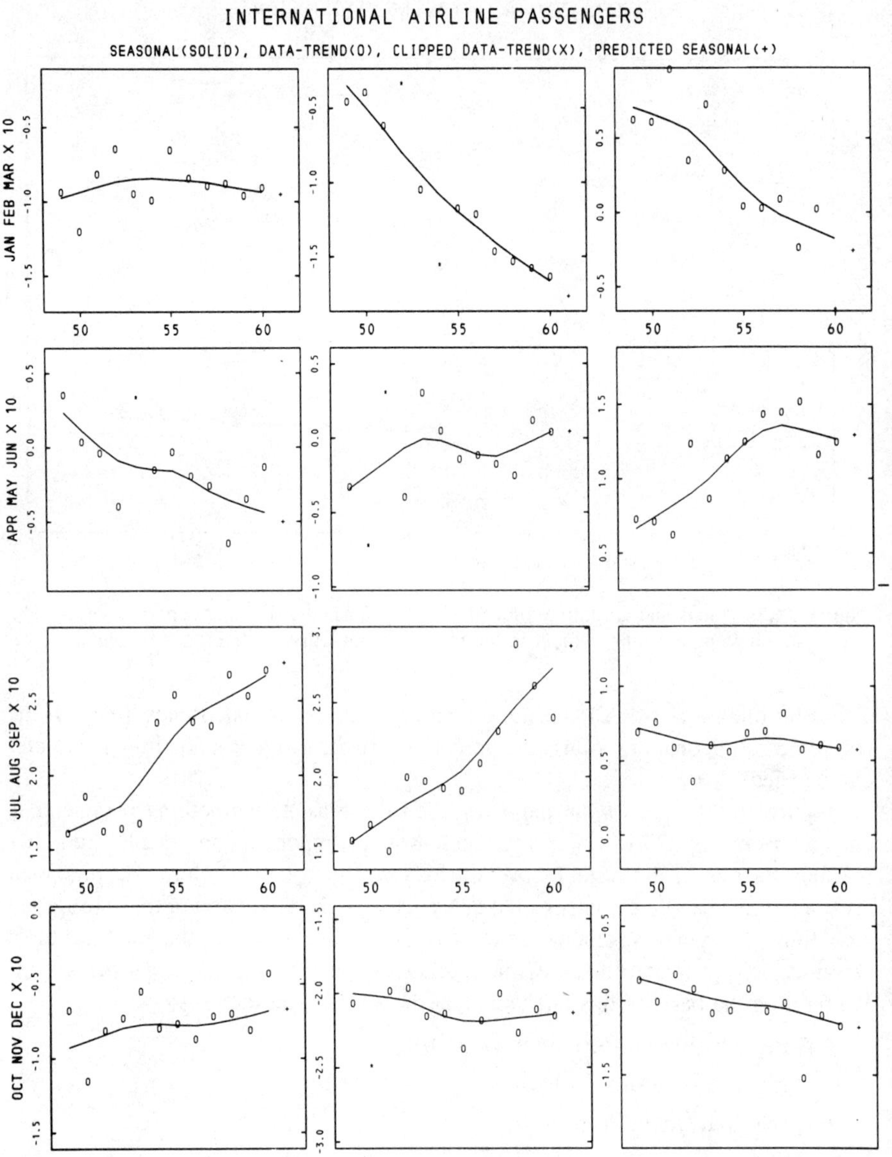


**Figure 19.13** Seasonal and data-minus-trend plot for the transformed airline data ($p = 0$; $nts = 15$; $nss = 7$).

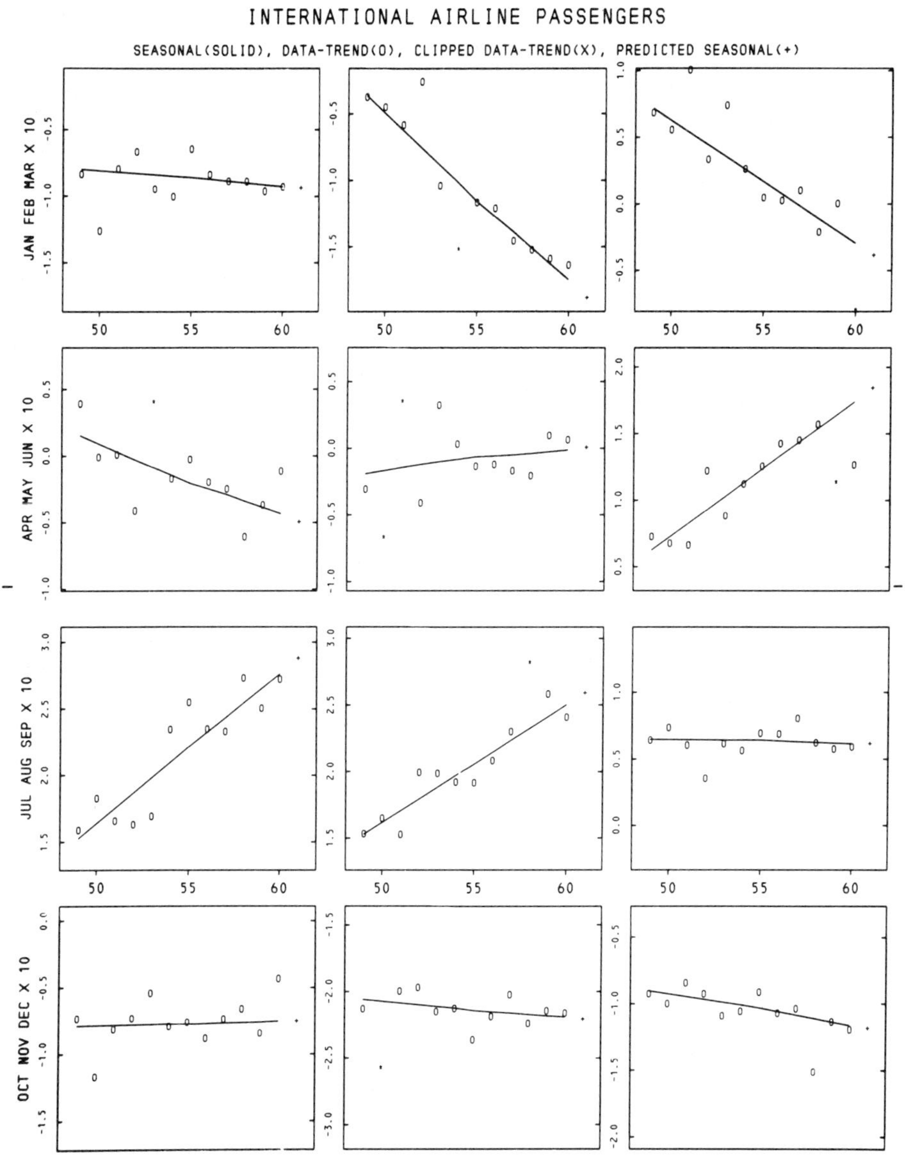


**Figure 19.14** Seasonal and data-minus-trend plot for the transformed airline data ($p = 0$; $nts = 15$; $nss = 15$).

- SABL is a lesser known but very promising new approach that relies heavily on resistant smoothing and graphical means for decomposing seasonal data.
- These two approaches complement each other in that both procedures utilize smoothing mechanisms ("filters") which are substantially different but yield comparable results when the seasonal data are stable and which provide much insight if the seasonal structures show unusual differences.

Desirable features of the SABL procedure:

- The downweighting of extreme values is based on the irregular variation of all Januarys, Februarys, and so on, taken separately.
- Months with high irregular variation do not influence the calculation of the scale statistic used to calculate resistant weights for months with low variation.
- SABL provides a variety of graphical plots that can be analyzed to determine the reasonableness of the seasonal adjustment process, and to detect the presence of calendar effects (Cleveland and Devlin, 1980).

A method alternative to both X-11 and SABL programs is to fit specific models to individual series (Granger and Newbold, 1977). Optimal seasonal adjustment procedures can be developed by using regression and time series models for specific time series. However, such parametric modeling approaches have the drawback that they may not be flexible enough nor are they as well understood by most practitioners.

## USEFUL READING

BOX, G. E. P., and G. M. JENKINS (1976). *Time Series Analysis—Forecasting and Control*, 3rd ed. San Francisco, CA: Holden-Day.

CLEVELAND, W. S., D. M. DUNN, and I. J. TERPENNING (1978). *The SABL Seasonal Analysis Package—Statistical and Graphical Procedures*. Computing Information Service, Bell Laboratories, 600 Mountain Ave., Murray Hill, NJ 07974.

CLEVELAND, W. S., D. M. DUNN, and I. J. TERPENNING (1979). SABL—A Resistant Seasonal Adjustment Procedure with Graphical Methods for Interpretation and Diagnosis, in *Seasonal Analysis of Economic Time Series*, A. Zellner, ed. Washington, DC: U.S. Government Printing Office.

CLEVELAND, W. S., and S. J. DEVLIN (1980). Calendar Effects in Monthly Time Series; Detection by Spectrum. *Journal of the American Statistical Association* 75, 489–96.

GRANGER, C. W. J., and P. NEWBOLD (1977). *Forecasting Economic Time Series*. New York, NY: Academic Press.

CHAPTER **20**

# Forecasting with Regression Models: Two Case Studies

This chapter treats two forecasting case studies with simple linear regression methods for time series and cross-sectional data.

- The first study develops (quarterly) regression models for forecasting the gain in total main telephones and to evaluate the one- and two-year-ahead forecasting performances of those models.
- The second study deals with the relationship between the development of extension telephones within residences—residence extensions (as a function of main telephones)—and several demographic variables for a number of central offices serving a geographical area. The intent of the study is to forecast the potential improvement possible in certain central offices that are below average in their present performance. Such a study permits a marketing group to focus extra sales effort in order to increase sales of extension telephones in relatively undeveloped areas.

## REGRESSION MODELS FOR FORECASTING QUARTERLY TELEPHONE GAIN

Accurate forecasts of demand volumes are important to businesses because of their relationship to revenue projections and money outlays. For example, in the telephone business, the forecast of total main-telephone gain (net demand for telephone main stations) is a crucial factor, where accuracy is of utmost importance. In addition, the forecast of main gain by market segments (residence versus business) is required for the operation of the business; it affects construction plans, departmental budgets, work force requirements, and many other related areas.

Throughout the book, we have analyzed the main gain series as an important factor in forecasting telephone demand. Likewise, we analyzed the housing starts series as a variable with a potential relationship to the main gain data. The purpose of the first case study in this chapter is to formalize the relationship with regression models and evaluate the forecasting performance one, two, and three years ahead.

The study results in six plausible models by considering equations for the original data, differenced data, and differenced data with a lag or shift in time for the independent variable (housing starts). The comparisons are made strictly on a forecast test basis by using both ordinary least squares (OLS) and weighted (robust) least squares. The emphasis on forecasting performance rather than good "fitting" stems from the fact that good forecasting models usually have satisfactory statistical properties, while the model with the best statistical fit is not necessarily a satisfactory forecasting model. This fact is often overlooked by the practitioner who feels intuitively that fitting and forecasting are essentially the same.

## Description of Data and a Rationale for Using the Data

As we defined it early in the book, a main telephone is a telephone connected directly with the central office, whether on an individual or party line. Only one telephone for each subscriber on each line is considered as a main telephone. The series for quarterly total main gain (denoted by QTMG) is plotted in Figure 20.1.

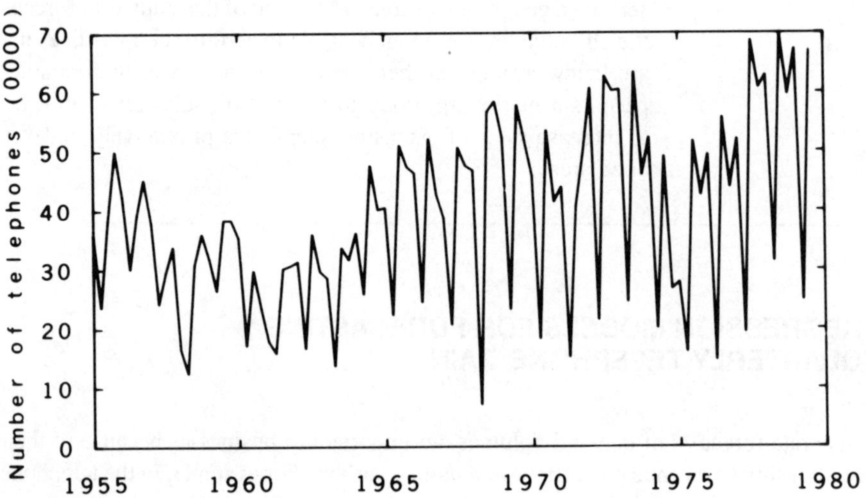


**Figure 20.1** Plot of main telephone gain—quarterly, 1954–1979.

The independent variable is HOUS, the housing starts series that has been analyzed throughout the book as an explanatory variable for main gain. Since the housing industry tends to lead fluctuations in overall business activity, it is a good starting point for the analysis and forecasting of telephone demand. Moreover, housing has always borne a disproportionately large share of cyclical declines. Indeed, the drop in residential construction in the six post-World War II recessions in the United States has equaled, on average, one-half of the total cyclical decline in real GNP itself, despite the fact that residential construction expenditures account for only 4 percent of total activity.

One of the most closely watched indicators of homebuilding is the monthly accounting of private housing starts, plotted earlier in this book in Figure 5.8. Housing starts include all housekeeping units, both single- and multi-family, begun in all fifty states in the United States, including vacation and second homes. However, they exclude mobile homes, and such nonhousekeeping units as dormitories, hotels, motels, and so on.

All units in a multi-family building are considered as started when excavation for the building that will contain them is begun, but the economic impact of homebuilding on telephone demand is not so instantaneous. For example, only about 60 percent of the final value of a single-family housing unit is recorded in construction expenditures within three months of the associated housing start, with another 30 percent being recorded in the next three months. This "lag" effect is taken into account in one of the models considered in the study.

The main reason that housing starts are a leading economic indicator (typically leading peaks in the business cycle by a year and troughs by six months) is that starts are very sensitive to fluctuations in interest rates. When interest rates rise substantially, as they generally do near the peak of an expansion, savings deposited with mortgage lenders tend to be diverted to other users of funds. Meanwhile, rising mortgage rates and stricter lending conditions curtail the demand for home loans. Thus, both the supply of new housing and the demand for new housing are reduced when interest rates rise.

The process is clearly a complex one, which cannot be completely described by a single equation and one independent variable. Nevertheless, it turns out that very meaningful and useful forecasting results can be achieved with simple models. It should also be recognized that the quality of the model is very directly related to the quality of the data and forecasts that can be obtained for it. Therefore, simple models may have some very important advantages in helping to understand the nature of the forecasting process.

### Model Building

A preliminary analysis of the data is always recommended to determine the nature and extent of the variation in trend, cycle, seasonality, and irregularity. Much of it has been done already in earlier chapters for the main gain and housing starts. It was shown in Chapter 9, for example, that seasonality contributed about 81 percent to the total variation in the monthly main-telephone gain and 41 percent to the total variation in the housing starts series. If the seasonality is high, a model based on differenced data (order 12 for monthly data) may be a promising alternative.

The residual variation is about the same (12 percent) for the two series, which provides an indication of how problematic outliers or unusual events can become in the modeling effort. When residual variation is great, the use of robust regression is highly recommended as a complementary tool. In this case, it is clear that differencing, lagging (in terms of economic considerations), and robust/resistant fitting should all be considered. To reduce the impact of reporting anomalies in adjacent months, quarterly rather than monthly models were built in this study.

Six models were considered, three fitted by OLS and three by weighted (robust) regression. Model A was simply a regression of main telephone gain on housing starts, fitted by OLS. The remaining models all used differenced data. Models B and C considered differences of order 4 for each series, where the housing starts were contemporaneous in Model B and the differenced housing starts were shifted by two quarters in Model C. Models D and E were robust versions of Models B and C, respectively. Model F was a robust version of Model B with a three-quarter lag, instead. Figure 20.2 shows the data and regressions fitted for Models C and E. Notice that the outliers impact the slopes of the two lines. In summary, Table 20.1 shows the models and their specifications.

## Comparison of Forecasting Results

Model A, which represents the regression of the quarterly main telephone gain on the quarterly housing starts did not yield statistically significant results (i.e., $R^2 = 0.002$ and a nonsignificant $F$-statistic). On a differenced basis, however, regression results for Models B through F were statistically significant. The forecasting models were tested primarily for their ability to predict year-end levels four and eight quarters from the forecasting origin. The latest actual observation used in the regression was the last quarter of the year. Model predictions were generated for the models by using a constant six-year base of data. This was done to make statistical results for model fits somewhat comparable. It also reduced early influences in the data that could have a persistent influence on the fit of the model parameters.

By starting with the first quarter of 1961 (for the differenced data), it was possible to generate thirteen one-year-ahead forecasts and twelve two-year-ahead forecasts with each model, for comparison. Table 20.2 shows a comparison of the models. The criterion used was average absolute percent error—the percent difference between projected main telephone gain *(undifferenced)* and actual gain using historical values for the housing starts in the forecast period. This is known as *ex post* forecasting.

Here

$$\text{Percent error} = (\text{Actual} - \text{Forecast})/\text{Actual}$$

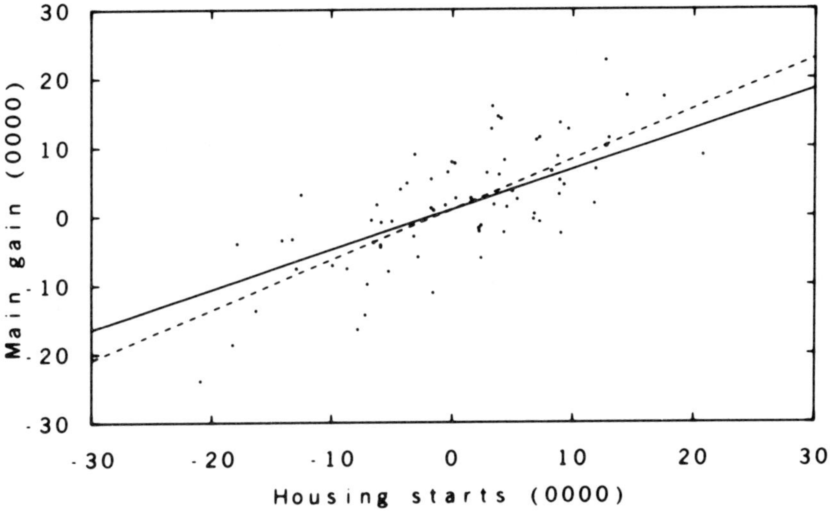


**Figure 20.2** Actual and fitted values of Model C (OLS)—solid line and Model E (robust)—dotted line.

**Table 20.1** Specifications for the quarterly main-telephone-gain models.

| Model | Differences of order 4 | Lag (quarter) | Fit |
|---|---|---|---|
| A | No | — | OLS |
| B | Yes | — | OLS |
| C | Yes | 2 | OLS |
| D | Yes | — | Robust |
| E | Yes | 2 | Robust |
| F | Yes | 3 | Robust |

**Table 20.2** Comparison of average absolute percent error for the five main-telephone-gain models.

| Model | Lead time (years) 1 | 2 | 3 |
|---|---|---|---|
| A | 19.5 | 24.6 | 27.2 |
| B | 11.5 | 19.0 | 18.3 |
| C | 10.7 | 18.9 | 20.2 |
| D | 10.3 | 16.1 | 16.1 |
| E | 8.8 | 12.4 | 14.1 |
| F | 11.9 | 21.8 | 25.3 |

*Note:* Number of percent errors used equals 14 minus the lead time. Models D, E, and F were fitted with robust regression. It can be seen that Model E is best.

for each year-by-year comparison. It is clear that Model E, the robust fit with the two-quarter lag in differenced housing starts, outperforms the other models for all three lead times. Of course, the idealized accuracy results cannot be repeated in actual practice. However, it does allow the forecaster to assess some of the limitations of the fitting procedure apart from the problem of forecasting the independent variable.

Forecast performance can also be looked at in terms of $l$-step-ahead forecast errors—namely, forecasts by quarter from a given forecast origin. The forecast errors, expressed in terms of the original domain of the main telephone gain variable, were summarized by using the root mean square error (RMSE) criterion defined by

$$\text{RMSE} = \left[\frac{1}{l}\sum_{i=1}^{l}(A_i - F_i)^2\right]^{1/2},$$

where

$A_i$ = actual quarterly value of main telephone gain,

$F_i$ = predicted value from the model,

$l$ = number of forecast steps from a given time origin.

Table 20.3 summarizes the RMSE's for several $l$-step-ahead forecasts ($l = 1, 4, 8, 12$), time origins (70:1, 73:1, and 76:1, where 70:1 denotes first quarter of 1970, and so on), and model types (B, C, E, and F). Again, regressions were performed for fixed twenty-four-quarter periods. The models are fairly comparable in forecasting quarters; at least no one model consistently outperforms any other. It is also noteworthy that the economic conditions prevalent during the forecast period can have an impact on the results. Of those shown, the later periods certainly have been more volatile for business, further complicating the forecaster's best efforts to come up with stable model results.

It is also of interest to make a comparison between models for different forecast years. This helps to determine the forecasting consistency among similar models and also to evaluate the responsiveness of the models during changing economic periods (recessions, for example).

The model runs include both the 1970–1971 and 1974–1975 recessions. As expected, the models tended to overforecast the annual main gain for the recession years, but by how much? Figure 20.3 shows a comparison of the percent of error in one-year-ahead forecasts of annual main gain, as predicted by the OLS Models A, B, and C. Model A is clearly inferior to the differenced versions, and Model C is generally somewhat better than Model B, but not in a uniform manner. This may be due to the observation made earlier that there is a three- to six-month lag between housing start and the recording of construction expenditure.

The fact that the models tended to overforecast the annual levels by about 20–25 percent during recessions could be used to adjust ("add-factor") model predictions

**Table 20.3** Root mean square errors for Models B, C, E, and F determined from forecasts made for lead times of 1, 4, 8, and 12 quarters originating in the first quarter of 1970, 1973, and 1976.

| Model | Time of origin | Lead time (quarters) 1 | 4 | 8 | 12 |
|---|---|---|---|---|---|
| | | $\times 10^4$ | $\times 10^4$ | $\times 10^4$ | $\times 10^4$ |
| B | 70:1 | 8.4 | 10.3 | 15.5 | 14.0 |
| | 73:1 | 0.6 | 6.1 | 11.9 | 13.8 |
| | 76:1 | 18.6 | 9.7 | 11.2 | 15.3 |
| C | 70:1 | 8.2 | 7.7 | 13.3 | 12.5 |
| | 73:1 | 4.3 | 7.0 | 9.6 | 10.4 |
| | 76:1 | 20.5 | 11.0 | 10.6 | 11.1 |
| E | 70:1 | 5.2 | 4.1 | 11.4 | 11.2 |
| | 73:1 | 6.0 | 7.6 | 9.8 | 10.6 |
| | 76:1 | 19.7 | 11.4 | 10.3 | 9.9 |
| F | 70:1 | 10.0 | 8.5 | 12.6 | 11.7 |
| | 73:1 | 3.8 | 6.6 | 9.7 | 11.0 |
| | 76:1 | 33.1 | 16.7 | 16.8 | 17.8 |

*Note:* All forecasts based on fixed twenty-four-quarter regressions to the time of origin.

by that amount at the appropriate time. It is usually clear whether or not the housing industry is in a recession year or not.

It is also useful to make a scatter diagram of the percent of errors forecast by two models to ascertain how similar or dissimilar their forecasting behavior is (see Figure 20.4). The 45-degree line represents the "line of identical forecasts." If two models show a narrow scatter, perhaps both are not needed—perhaps one will do. On the other hand, it is useful to compare the relative performance of OLS and robust versions this way in order to have a sense of the impact of outliers or other unusual variations in different periods. Figure 20.4 summarizes the forecast performance of Model E (the best model) and Model C (the OLS alternative) for one-, two-, and three-year-ahead performances. Gross departures from the line of identical forecasts should be investigated for insight into data problems or differences in model behavior.

In summary, Models C and E seem to have practical value, but additional variables may improve the accuracy with which main telephone gain is forecast and add to the economic and demographic explanation of changes in telephone demand. It is also appropriate to adjust the data for strike effects. All these considerations are handled further in *The Professional Forecaster.*

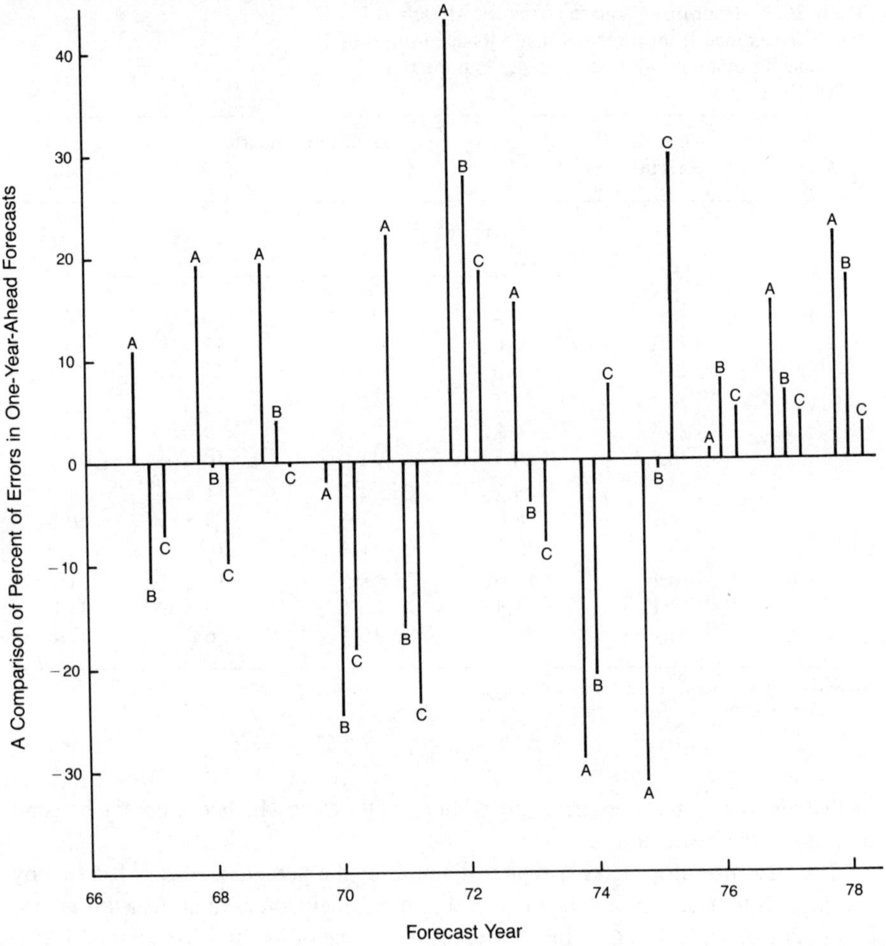


**Figure 20.3** Comparison of the one-year-ahead errors (percent) for OLS Models A, B, and C.

## A CROSS-SECTION MODEL FOR PREDICTING RESIDENCE EXTENSION DEVELOPMENT

The purpose of the second case study was to help marketing managers identify and forecast the sales potential for residential extension telephones within a geographic area. In particular, the analysis pointed to the ten "wire" centers (representing geographic regions) with the greatest potential for inclusion in a campaign to stimulate installation of extension telephones.

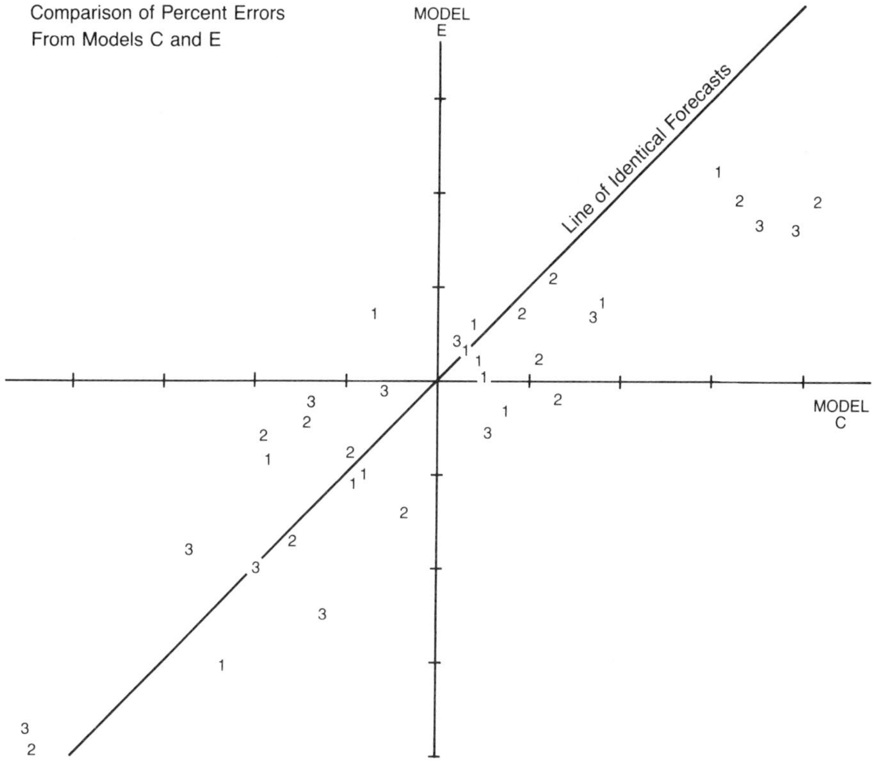


**Figure 20.4** Prediction-realization diagram for Models C and E. Numbers indicate data one, two, and three years ahead.

Among the issues to be answered by the study were

- What drives extension development?
- Can this phenomenon be quantified?
- What patterns are in evidence?
- What are the implications for the sales force?

## Preliminary Analysis

The dependent variable was the ratio of the numbers of extension telephones to main telephones in service and was the wire center's current measure of extension telephone service. A number of relevant explanatory variables were gathered on the basis of theoretical and statistical considerations. These included median family income, ADJINC (adjusted for cost-of-living differences among the areas); percent of white collar employment, %WHTCLR; percent of the households with more than one automobile, %1AUTO; the number of total housing units, UNITS; and the median housing value, HOUSVAL.

The distribution of the dependent variable was displayed as a box plot of the residence extension development (EXTDEV) for the sixty wire centers in the sample. The dependent variable ranged between a minimum of 0 percent and a maximum of 115 percent. After going back to the source of the data, it turned out that one value in the data set had a zero value, a clerical transcription error. The zero value was removed and a new box plot (Figure 20.5) was generated for the remaining fifty-nine values. The average is 57 percent and the first and third quartiles are 43 percent and 72 percent, respectively.

It makes statistical and intuitive sense to consider HOUSVAL as an independent variable. Therefore, for purposes of the study, the median housing value was considered as the independent variable in the regression model. In *The Professional Forecaster,* these data will be analyzed again in greater detail and several more complex models will be developed.

The scatter diagram between EXTDEV and HOUSVAL is shown in Figure 20.6. The plot shows a flattening curvature for the larger values of HOUSVAL. This suggests a logarithmic transformation of the independent variable to improve the linear relationship between the two variables.

Figure 20.7 shows a significant improvement in the scatter when EXTDEV is

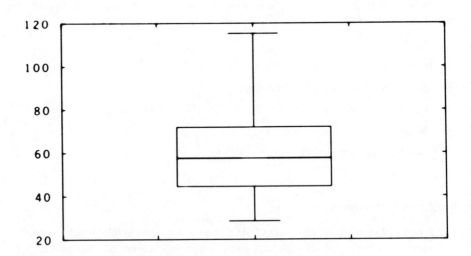

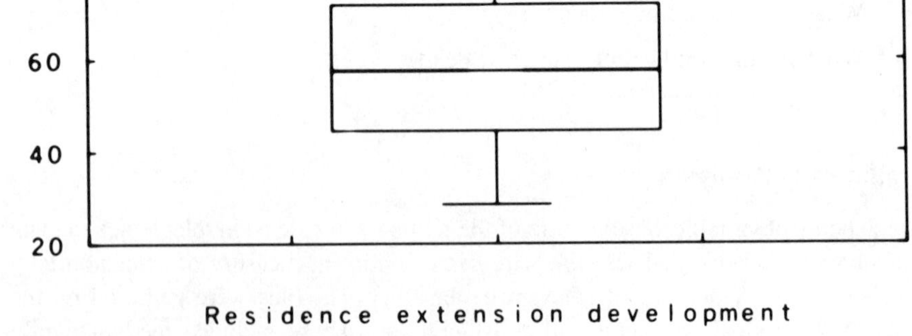


**Figure 20.5** Box plot of residence extension development.

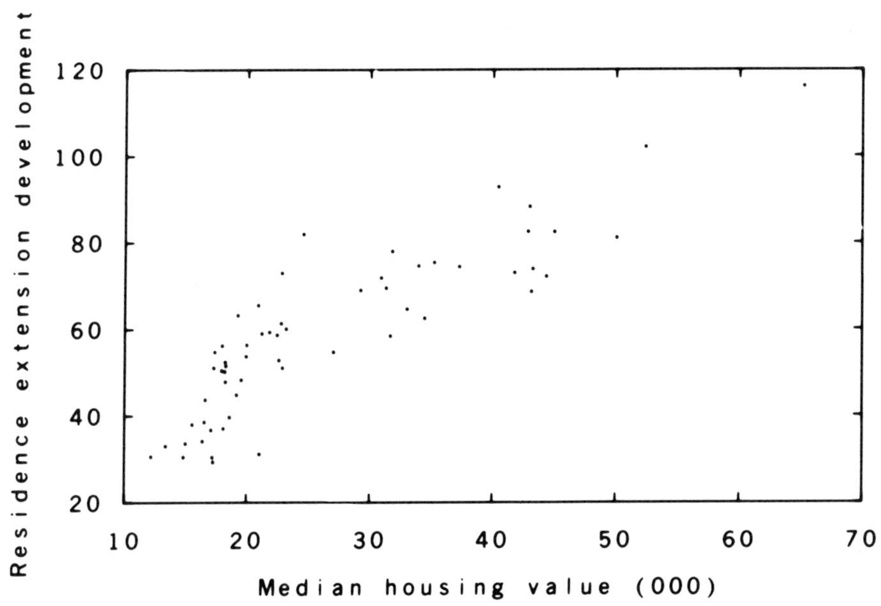


**Figure 20.6** Scatter diagram of residence extension development (EXTDEV) with median housing value (HOUSVAL).

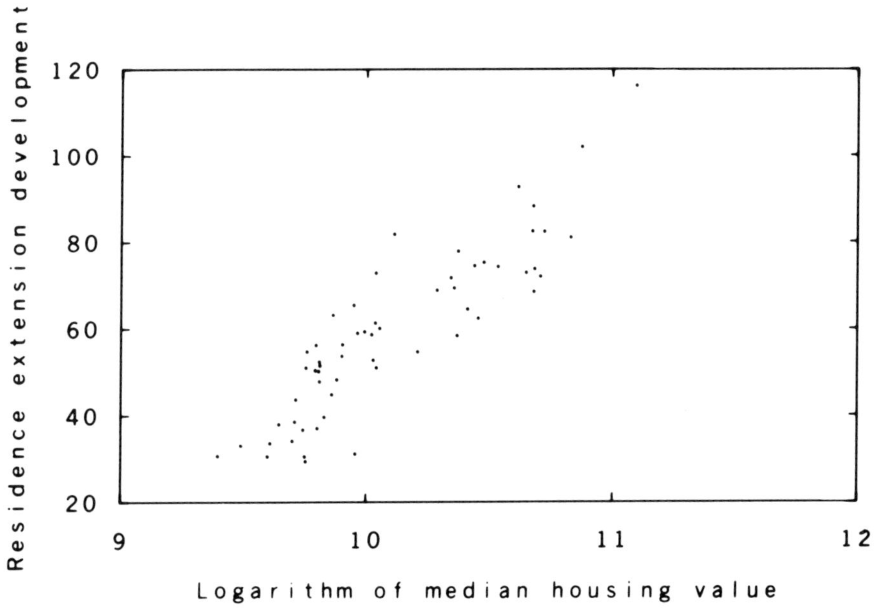


**Figure 20.7** Scatter diagram of residence extension development (EXTDEV) with the logarithms of HOUSVAL (LGHSVAL).

plotted against the logarithm of HOUSVAL, here labeled LGHSVAL. The model suggested by this relationship is

$$\text{EXTDEV} = \beta_0 + \beta_1 \text{ LGHSVAL} + \varepsilon.$$

## Model Results

Extension development (EXTDEV) was regressed on the logarithms of housing value (LGHSVAL) for the fifty-nine wire centers. The $R$-squared statistic was 79 percent (same as the square of the product moment correlation coefficient, in this case); the $t$-statistics for the coefficients and the $F$-statistic for overall regression were significant. The fitted values were $\hat{\beta}_0 = -364.5$ and $\hat{\beta}_1 = 41.9$. The coefficients are difficult to interpret directly because the independent variable (LGHSVAL) is expressed as logarithms. But, for each one-tenth of a unit increase in LGHSVAL, the residence extension development can be expected to increase by about 4.2 percent, on average.

The fit had positive slope, as expected (Figure 20.8). This figure also shows the 95 percent confidence limits about the line. Two out of the fifty-nine wire centers lie outside the limits, one at about 80 percent development, and the other at about 30 percent. The latter is an obvious candidate for further investigation and possible advertising stimulation. There may be other factors causing certain wire centers to

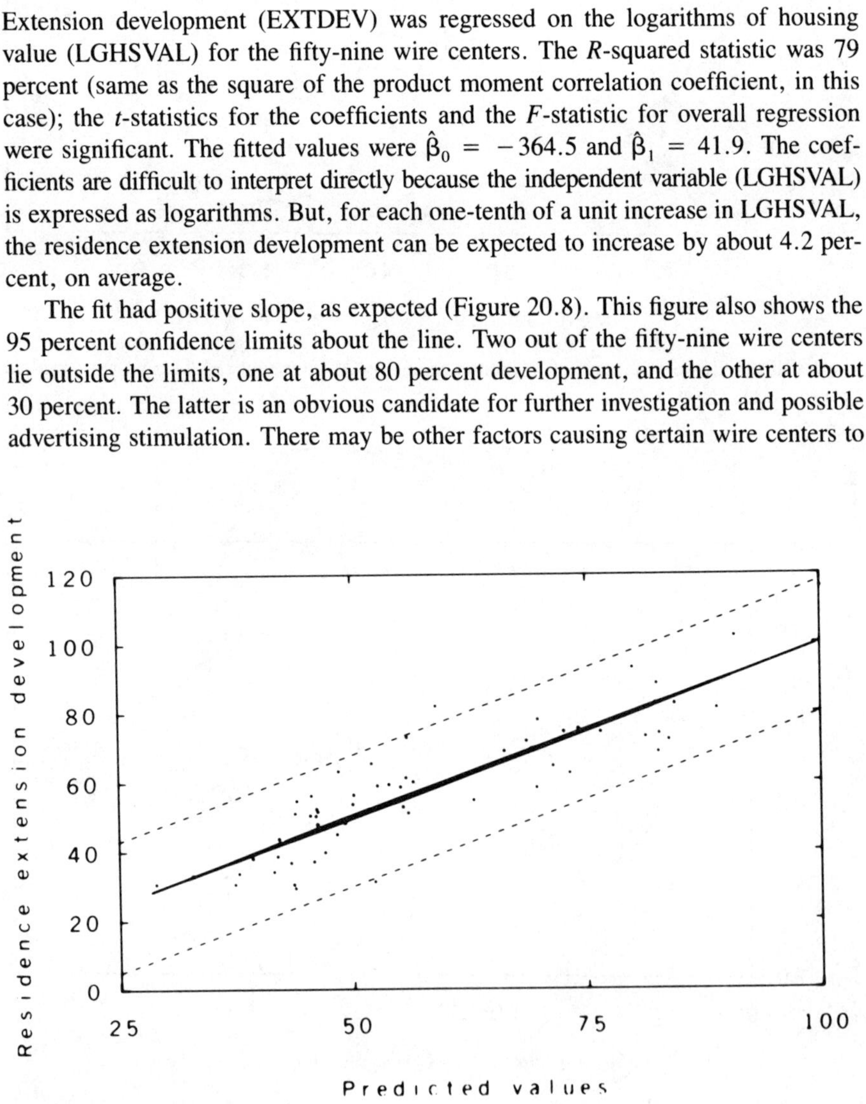


**Figure 20.8** OLS fit and 95 percent confidence limits for fitted values of EXTDEV.

deviate significantly from the fitted model—these should be investigated in light of other demographic and economic variables not treated in the model. For example, the wire center could have a large community of trailer (or "mobile") homes in a relatively low income area which might not hold too much potential for extension development.

It was important to analyze residuals to validate OLS model assumptions and to uncover additional information suggesting possible corrective action. The residuals versus the predicted values, depicted in Figure 20.9, showed nothing peculiar (outliers, residual patterns, etc.). A normal probability plot was also made (Figure 20.10), to check for nonnormality (heavy tail areas and skewness). The plot looked quite reasonable for a first pass at the model.

As a final diagnostic check, the model was run with a robust (Huber) option. The coefficients from the robust fit to the data were $\hat{\beta}_0^* = -363.8$ and $\hat{\beta}_1^* = 41.8$. These were very close to the OLS values quoted previously, so unusual data values were not distorting the results. Of course, if the original zero value had been left in the data, the robust and OLS results would have differed considerably, pointing to a problem with the model.

The residual pattern was also useful for identifying those wire centers that have "below-average" residence extension development; the ten lowest values could be identified as wire centers with a high potential for inclusion in a program to stimulate development. By identifying the fitted values corresponding to these "high potential" wire centers in the regression, a sales objective could be established. There were,

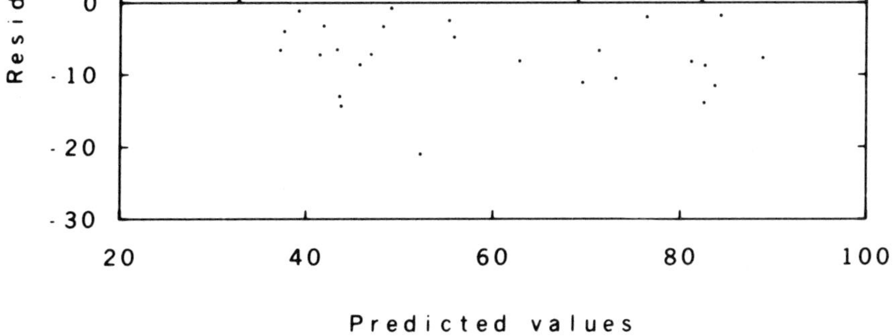

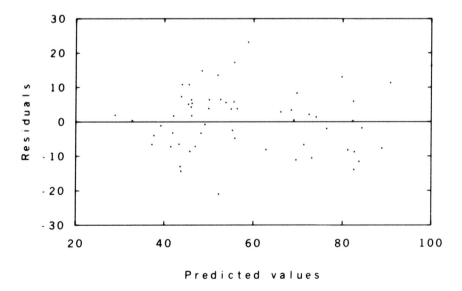

**Figure 20.9** Residuals versus predicted values for the residence extension development model.

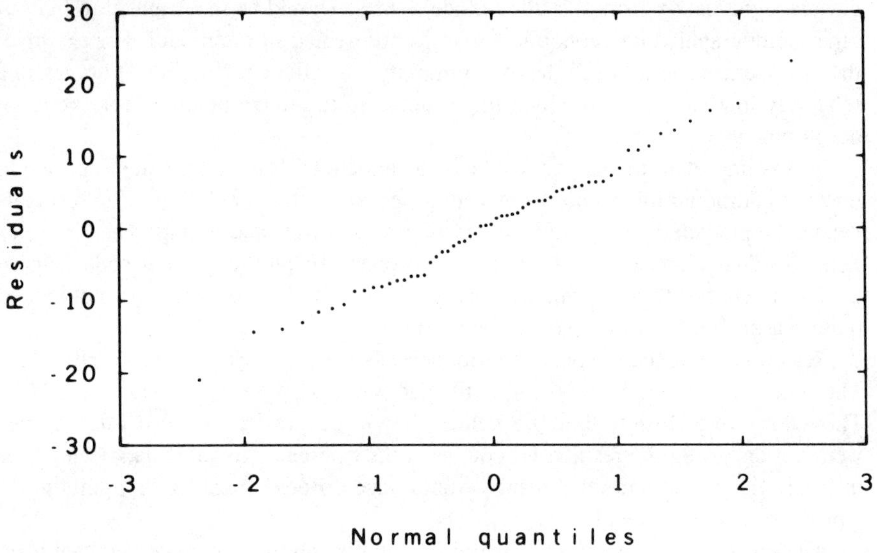


**Figure 20.10** Normal probability plot of the residuals.

of course, other issues to be considered for an effective promotion program, but the "forecasts" from a regression served as a valuable preliminary input.

## SUMMARY

The case studies in this chapter demonstrated that

- Regression models are useful for forecasting both time series and cross-sectional data.
- A significant portion of the variation for the dependent variable can be explained with only a single, well-chosen explanatory variable.
- Robust/resistant techniques are valuable tools for validating the strength of a regression relationship by providing some protection against outliers and unusual values.
- Diagnostic tools, such as residual plots, are helpful in identifying unusual values, suggesting transformations, and providing some direction for additional modeling.
- Confidence limits are necessary to put limits on the value being forecast with a reasonably high degree of confidence of being correct.

## USEFUL READING

BUTLER, W. F., R. A. KAVESH, and R. B. PLATT, eds. (1974). *Methods and Techniques of Business Forecasting*. Englewood Cliffs, NJ: Prentice-Hall.

CHAMBERS, J. C., S. K. MULLICK, and D. D. SMITH (1974). *An Executive's Guide to Forecasting*. New York, NY: John Wiley and Sons.

MAKRIDAKIS, S., and S. C. WHEELWRIGHT (1978). *Forecasting Methods and Applications*. New York, NY: John Wiley and Sons.

# Part 3

## Managing the Forecasting Function

CHAPTER **21**

# Selling the Forecast

As a consequence of their large investment of time and effort, it is not unusual for forecasters to believe that the constructed models and generated forecasts are end products in themselves. Of course, this is rarely true. Many forecasters tend to concentrate their efforts on the production of forecasts and not the marketing of them. The work shouldn't stop there: forecasts must be acceptable to management executives.

- This chapter is concerned with "selling" the forecast to your managers.
- It also stresses the principles underlying effective forecast presentations.
- An example of a nontechnical presentation is provided as well.

## PRINCIPLES UNDERLYING PRESENTATIONS TO MANAGEMENT

Your objectives in presenting a forecast should be:

- To gain the confidence of management executives.
- To gain acceptance of your forecasts.
- To gain acceptance of the methods you have used.

### What the Presentation Should Contain

A good presentation should have three basic parts—an introduction, the body of the presentation, and a conclusion. A typical plan for a presentation is shown in Table 21.1.

The introduction provides an overview of the entire presentation. We recommend that the introduction also include the proposed forecast for each key item and the

**Table 21.1** Organizing the presentation of a forecast.

A. Introduction
   1. Give an overview of the presentation.
   2. Indicate how the proposed view for each key series is related to previous views.

B. Body of presentation
   1. Provide specific economic rationale and assumptions, including sources of information.
   2. Link the proposed views to specific assumptions (about prices, competition, or sales plans, for example).
   3. Review each series, to provide
      a. An overview of methods used to set the final forecast.
      b. A highlight of each method with appropriate plots and tables.
      c. An assurance that checks and balances are operative.

C. Conclusion
   1. Integrate the proposed view with the long-range view.
   2. Summarize; and request approval of proposed view.

changes from the last forecast. The reasons for significant changes from the last forecast should also be reviewed. It is usually best to present a new forecast in the introductory stage of the presentation because this information is what an executive is awaiting, and to withhold it merely creates unwelcome suspense. An example of an overview is illustrated in Table 21.2.

The body of the presentation follows the introduction and is the most detailed part of the presentation. This part includes information about specific assumptions and their rationale. Sources of information should be clearly identified.

The final part of the presentation is the conclusion: at this place, the short-term

**Table 21.2** Forecast proposal for the year 19—.

| Forecast item | Current view | Proposed view | Difference: amount (percent) |
|---|---|---|---|
| Major products and services | | | |
| Product A | | | |
| Product B | | | |
| Product C | | | |
| Total revenues | | | |
| Total expenses | | | |
| Total capital expenditures | | | |

Reasons for changes

forecast is integrated with the long-term forecast. The consistency of these forecasts should be demonstrated. The key assumptions and forecasts are then briefly reviewed, and management approval of the forecast is sought through a formal sign-off.

### Gaining Acceptance by Management

Forecasters serve as *advisors* to managers. Typically, forecasters advise management about the future state of the economy with particular emphasis on the impact economic changes will have no demand for the products and services a firm sells. To be effective in this role, forecasters must gain the confidence of management personnel. The forecast presentation offers an opportunity to build confidence as a result of a thorough analysis of all relevant variables and a careful and clear persentation of data, assumptions, rationale, and forecasts. The result should be to impress decision makers with these qualities of the presentation rather than its length.

Presentations to executives generally should be *nontechnical* in nature and, since executives have a broad range of responsibilities and can devote only a limited time to a single area, it is essential to keep the length of the presentation to a minimum.

A forecaster's contacts with top management personnel are usually infrequent; it is important to present a well-documented and convincing presentation whenever the opportunity exists. A good track record of forecast accuracy goes a long way toward gaining acceptance by management. However good that record, ineffective presentations can seriously undermine managerial confidence in the professionalism of the forecaster. As W. E. Hoadley (1974) commented: "The primary skill of the business economist [forecaster] is selling useful forecasts to management. A fundamental premise on which this skill is based is that good ideas don't sell themselves; they are sold by competent people."

The presentation should be reinforced with easily understood graphic displays in the form of handouts, flip-charts, or slides. This material can be reproduced and placed in a binder which can be left with an executive for review at a later time. The assumptions upon which the forecasts are based and any additional backup graphs and tables that are pertinent should also be included in this package; any key ratios or reasonableness checks that the forecaster knows the executives consider important should be shown and explained.

The economic and corporate assumptions in the body of the presentation should include national and regional economic forecasts, employment and labor developments, building construction activity and interest rates, inflation rates, and agricultural or special industry conditions.

The economic assumptions are then followed by specific corporate assumptions related to price or rate changes, deposit and collection policies, advertising and special sales promotions, new or modified product or service offerings, competition and regulatory considerations, and so on.

## Preparing Assumption Statements

Assumption statements are critical to the forecasts and are essential in analyzing forecasting performance at a later date. Too often, assumptions are stated in such broad terms that they are not meaningful. To correct this problem, assumptions should be tested against the following standards:

- Assumptions should relate only to the future time periods.
- Assumptions should be stated as positive assertions of facts, in that they are assumed facts for the future.
- Assumptions should indicate whether their realizations will have a positive or negative impact on demand. Presumably, there should be some of each.
- Assumptions should indicate the amount or rate of impact, the timing of the impact, and the duration of the impact.

For example, here is a good statement of assumptions: "The new South Towers apartment complex will have a positive impact on demand. The complex will contain 1000 units with initial occupancy in July of 1980 and complete occupancy by December 1980, resulting in 950 main telephones." The example is specific enough to be evaluated and later verified. The objective of an assumption statement is to be as specific as possible. However, it is recognized that certain assumptions, such as the national economic outlook, are general assumptions which must exist for some specific detailed assumption to come true.

The assumption statements should be followed by a review of each of the key series for which a forecast has been made. The review includes an overview of the methods used to generate the forecasts, appropriate plots or tables, and reasonableness checks. A sample presentation format is shown in Table 21.3. This format avoids technical jargon but demonstrates the depth of analysis performed.

**Table 21.3** A worksheet to compare various forecasting techniques.

| | Forecast test | | Forecast bias (percent) | | Forecasts (thousands) | |
|---|---|---|---|---|---|---|
| Technique | 1 Year (percent) | 2 Years (percent) | Peak period | Trough period | 1980 | 1981 |
| Exponential smoothing | 1.09 | 4.41 | 1.35 | 0.70 | 795.5 | 871.7 |
| Regression: log revenues against time | 3.81 | 5.33 | 4.31 | −5.69 | 743.8 | 802.5 |
| Regression: log revenues as a function of employment | 1.11 | 1.63 | 1.82 | −0.75 | 778.8 | 840.2 |
| Turning point analysis—most likely scenario | — | — | — | — | 780.1 | 843.3 |

For each method employed, the intermediate forecast test results are presented, as well as the final forecasts for the end of the period. The forecast test is one of the most relevant measures of model performance and one of the easiest to understand. Evidence of over- or underforecasting at peaks and troughs provides a means for adjusting model forecasts to agree with the pending economic outlook. Graphical plots of actuals and forecasts provide a convenient way of demonstrating the reasonableness of the new forecast. Suitable graphical techniques might include the use of centered twelve-month moving total plots, unweighted moving averages (twelve-month or MCD), weighted moving averages, "robust smoothers," seasonally adjusted data, bar charts, month-by-year charts, and year-by-month charts.

### Providing Alternative Scenarios

In most cases, a single numerical forecast implies greater precision than can realistically be achieved. It is useful to provide executives with alternative scenarios for different sets of assumptions. An approach that has proved successful is to provide three scenarios (optimistic, most likely, and pessimistic), together with their associated forecasts. This provides management with a better understanding of the uncertainty in the forecast and helps *prevent surprise* should certain assumptions turn out inappropriate.

Additionally, alternative scenarios are valuable if there is unusual uncertainty in a business environment. This could be economic, competitive, or regulatory uncertainty, for example. Different scenarios are also of value when making policy decisions, when the sensitivity with which a model predicts the impact of exogenous factors is questioned, and when very different forecasts are obtained with different models for the same time series. Alternative scenarios, answering "what if" questions, are becoming common in most forecasting organizations. It is in answering these kinds of questions that the forecaster serves as an advisor to management.

## A PRESENTATION FORMAT

In this section, we shall apply the principles underlying effective forecast presentations to a practical forecasting problem. In the process, the following points will be illustrated:

- How multi-method forecasts are brought together in the forecast presentation package.
- How "turning point" forecasts can be subjectively developed, based on alternative economic outlooks.
- How reasonableness checks play an important role in supporting the proposed forecast.

- How sensitivity analyses using optimistic, most likely, and pessimistic scenarios can inform management about the uncertainty in the forecast.

The following forecast presentation is intended to illustrate the key points made so far. For purposes of illustration, we have used a simplified forecast of telecommunications toll revenues for one year into the future.

### Overview

The purpose of this presentation will be to gain management approval for a forecast of toll revenue for 1980. The overview is the place for a succinct summary of the entire forecast; therefore a plot of the revenue history (solid) and revenue forecast (dashed), as shown in Figure 21.1, or of the historical and forecasted percent changes (over the same period one year prior) in Figure 21.2, demonstrates a reduction in the growth of revenues is expected in 1980.

### The New Forecast

As briefly as possible, the forecaster next sketches details of the new forecast. These might be of the sort that follows: "The new forecast amounts to a 8.3 percent increase in revenue over 1979. The forecast growth rate is 1.5 percent higher than the previous forecast as a result of a change in the economic outlook. The timing of the expected recession can be deferred until late in 1980. As a result, the 1980 employment growth will exceed the previous expectations. This will impact revenue growth positively."

### Assumptions

What are the forecaster's reasons for the foregoing conclusions? They might be as follows:

"The U.S. Gross National Product is expected to decline by 1.1 percent in 1980. This translates to a 0.1 percent increase in U.S. employment nationwide. The company economists have provided forecasts of total nonfarm employment and nonfarm-less-manufacturing employment. In the analysis that follows, emphasis will be placed on the latter series. The economists have forecast a 0.2 percent growth in average regional nonfarm-less-manufacturing employment in 1980 compared to a 2.0 percent growth in 1979. The reduction in employment growth in 1980 will cause a corresponding reduction in revenue growth from 12.4 percent in 1979 to 8.3 percent in 1980.

"No changes in toll rates are expected in the forecast period. Competitors are expected to maintain their share of the total business toll calling market in 1980. The historical relationship between employment growth and revenue growth is expected to hold."

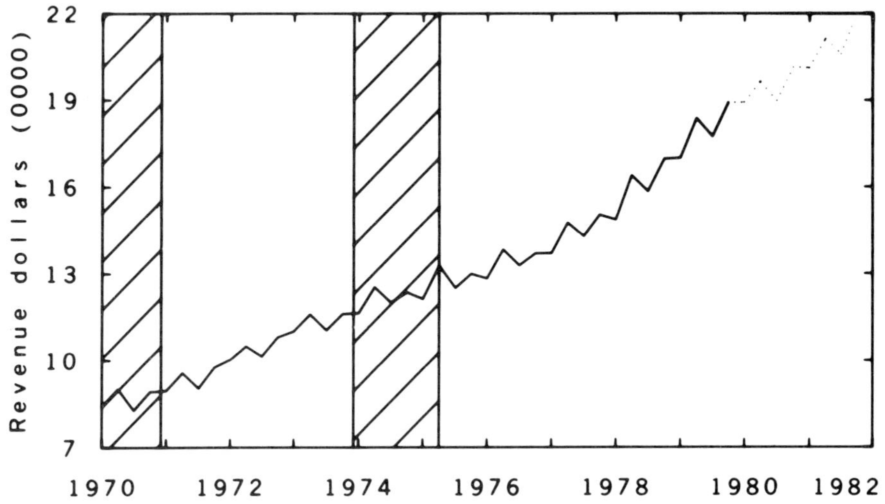


**Figure 21.1** A time series plot of the historical and forecasted toll revenue series.

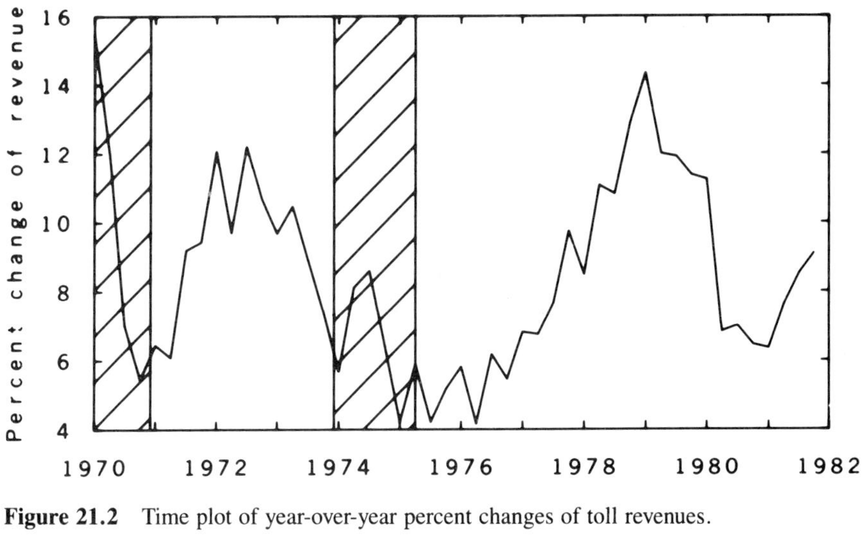


**Figure 21.2** Time plot of year-over-year percent changes of toll revenues.

## Forecasting Methods

Table 21.4 is an example of the kind of format that can be used to summarize the forecasts from the various methods used to arrive at the final forecast. The forecasts range from \$743,800 to \$795,500.

The exponential smoothing forecast did not capture the expected downturn in 1980 and its validity was discounted somewhat. The projection from the trend model

**Table 21.4** A summary of forecasts from various forecasting techniques.

| Technique | 1980 Revenue (thousands) |
|---|---|
| Exponential smoothing | 795.5 |
| Exponential trend line | 743.8 |
| Regression — revenue as a function of employment | 778.8 |
| Turning point analysis | |
| Control | 780.1 |
| Optimistic | 785.1 |
| Pessimistic | 774.1 |
| Selected forecast | 780.0 |

was also discounted; the level of the series in 1979 was considerably above trend and the series was not expected to return to trend in 1980. The projection from this exponential smoothing model had a very slight chance of being exceeded. The confidence limits from the trend model indicated there was only about a 2.5-percent chance that the actual results would exceed $795 thousand (see Table 21.5). The turning point and revenue–employment regression model forecasts took the economic conditions into account, however, and provided forecasts closer to the middle of the range.

Figure 21.3 shows additional information useful at this stage in the presentation—namely, the deviations-from-trend of revenues after seasonal adjustment of the series with the SABL procedure (Chapter 19). The dashed lines represent three alternative forecast scenarios subjectively determined.

The most likely turning-point forecast was one in which a peak would occur in the fourth quarter of 1979, with a peak-to-trough duration of six quarters. This is in agreement with the employment forecast, which is shown in Figure 21.4. The optimistic turning-point forecast was based on the possibility of a milder and shorter recession. The pessimistic forecast was based on a more severe, longer-lasting reces-

**Table 21.5** Confidence limits of the most likely forecasts.

| Technique | Lower limit | Forecast | Upper limit |
|---|---|---|---|
| Regression—revenue as a function of employment* | 776.4 | 778.8 | 780.0 |
| Exponential trend line† | 696.0 | 743.8 | 795.0 |

*Upper and lower limits based on optimistic and pessimistic employment scenarios rather than statistical confidence limits.
†Upper and lower limits are 95 percent confidence limits.

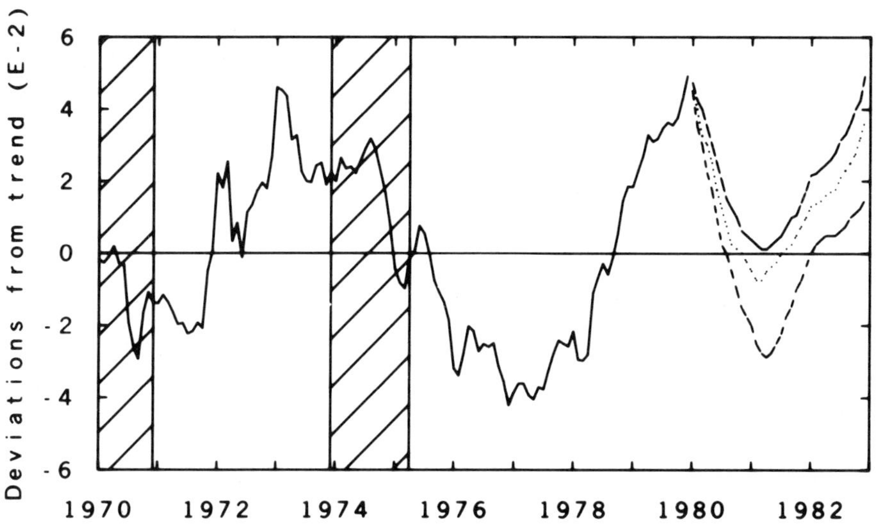


**Figure 21.3** The deviations from trend after seasonally adjusting the revenue series. The hatched areas correspond to recession dates determined by NBER.

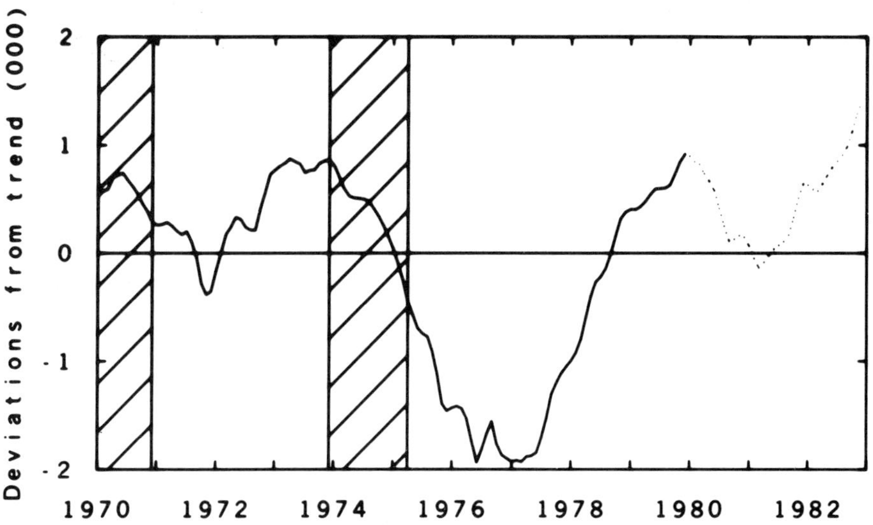


**Figure 21.4** The employment forecasts corresponding to the most likely scenario. The hatched areas correspond to recession dates determined by NBER.

sion. Given the economic conditions of high inflation, high interest rates, depressed building starts, and poor automobile sales prevailing at the time the forecast was made, the pessimistic forecast was a more likely alternative than the optimistic forecast.

The regression model forecast was based on the employment forecast. As such, it would be subject to the validity of that forecast and any intervening data revisions. While revisions in such forecasts have often been significant, still the forecaster felt that this model had the highest probability of precision given the expected turning point in 1980. However, the forecast was rounded upwards in the direction of the exponential smoothing projection to $780 thousand.

## Confidence Limits about the Forecast

Considering the range of forecasts from the various techniques, it would be helpful to provide management with alternative forecasts and confidence limits on the most likely forecasts; the format a forecaster might use for this is shown in Table 21.5. The trend model provides statistical confidence limits; the employment model confidence limits are based on alternative employment scenarios.

Forecast test results (Table 21.6) from the exponential smoothing, trend, and regression models are also helpful in estimating approximate confidence limits. Based on the uncertain yet deteriorating economic climate, the direction of the alternative forecast would be downward to $774 thousand. As mentioned earlier, the series was expected to turn downward but had not yet begun to (see Figure 21.3), and the exponential smoothing projection did not take the expected downturn into account. For this reason, the forecast was discounted to a greater extent than past history would suggest.

## Conclusion

Table 21.7 shows how a short-term forecast is related to a long-term forecast: it shows the historical annual growth in revenue and revenue per nonfarm employee. The 8.3-percent growth in revenue in 1980 is in reasonable agreement with historical performance and the existing long-term forecast. Because revenues were unusually

**Table 21.6** Forecast test results.

| Technique | Average absolute one-year-ahead percent error |
|---|---|
| Exponential smoothing | 1.09 |
| Exponential trend line | 3.81 |
| Regression—revenue as a function of employment | 1.11 |

**Table 21.7** Historical annual growth in toll revenues and revenues per nonfarm employee.

| | Percent change over prior year | |
|---|---|---|
| Year | Revenue | Revenue per employee |
| 1974 | 7.2 | 8.0 |
| 1975 | 4.9 | 8.6 |
| 1976 | 5.4 | 6.0 |
| 1977 | 7.8 | 6.7 |
| 1978 | 10.9 | 7.8 |
| 1979 | 12.4 | 10.3 |
| 1980 | 8.3 | 8.7 |
| 1981 | 8.7 | 9.2 |
| 1982 | 7.7 | 8.3 |

great in 1979, the projected year-over-year percent growth for 1980 may appear somewhat conservative.

At this point, management approval is requested through a formal sign-off. This presentation has followed the recommended format. The introduction has consisted of the new forecast, the change from the last forecast, and the reasons for changes. The body of the presentation has consisted of specific assumptions, an overview of the methods used, highlights of each method, and the presentation of alternative scenarios. The conclusion related the short-term forecast with the long-range forecast, and then management approval was sought.

## FORECAST PRESENTATION CHECKLIST

A. Pre-Presentation

____ Who is the presentation being made to?
____ What, specifically, is wanted of the audience?
____ When will the presentation be given?
____ Where will it be given?
____ Why is it important or necessary to make this presentation?
____ How will it be delivered?

B. Attention Stage of Presentation

____ Is the main purpose of presentation stated?
____ Is the content appropriate for the audience?

____ Does the content appeal to their interest or use?
____ Are audio-visual aids appropriate?

C. Overview Stage of Presentation

____ Are the key points outlined?
____ Is the schedule or process stated to the audience?
____ Is the outline of the approach to the subject clear from the point of view of the audience?
____ Are visual aids clear and readable?

D. Information Stage, or Body of Presentation

____ Does the forecaster have the attention of the audience?
____ Is information presented in an appropriate order (consecutive, topical, logical, or chronological)?
____ Are new words, phrases, or technical terms introduced and defined for the audience?
____ Can the audience be involved in the presentation (i.e., is there interaction)?
____ Is the supporting information understandable in terms of the knowledge or experience of the audience?
____ Is the information related to their needs and purposes?
____ Are specific examples and illustrations used?
____ Are visual aids clear, readable, and usable?

E. Review Stage of Presentation

____ Are the key points enumerated?
____ Was the audience reminded of the purpose of the presentation?
____ Were the overview visual aids used to reinforce the message?

F. Conclusion Stage of Presentation

____ Was the key purpose of the presentation reviewed?
____ Did the review relate back to the "attention" stage of the presentation?
____ Are the conclusions related to the audience's use, purpose, or interest?
____ Are the media used for the attention stage relevant also for the conclusion?

G. Post-Presentation

____ Was the makeup of the audience what it was expected to be?
____ Did the audience do what was desired of them?
____ Were there any environmental or logistical difficulties?
____ Were there any particular points or techniques that were particularly successful or unsuccessful?

## SUMMARY

Forecast presentations are valuablc opportunities to gain the confidence of management executives and to provide advice about the environment in which a firm operates.

- Presentations should usually be kept nontechnical and brief.
- They should consist of an introduction, a body of presentation, and a conclusion.
- Graphical methods for displaying and summarizing data, forecasts, and supporting detail should be an integral part of the presentation.
- Forecasts need to be documented with supporting detail about assumptions and uncertainties inherent in the forecasts.

## USEFUL READING

HOADLEY, W. E. (1974). Reporting Forecasts to Management and the Use of Forecasts as a Management Tool, in *Methods and Techniques of Business Forecasting*, Butler et al., eds. Englewood Cliffs, NJ: Prentice-Hall.

CHAPTER 22

# Tracking Results

The forecaster's responsibility to management does not end when the forecast is approved; an important part of it is just beginning. One of the forecaster's prime responsibilities is to *track actual data* as they become available, defend the forecast or alter it as need be, and update and validate any quantitative models which are used in the forecasting process. This chapter provides guidance in the following areas:

- The kinds of information that should be tracked on an ongoing basis.
- Specific graphical techniques that can be used to identify the need to revise forecasts.
- Tracking signals that can be used to generate reports of exceptions automatically when patterns of overforecasting or underforecasting are encountered.
- A method to determine whether inadequacies in the forecasting model or inaccurate forecasts of the independent variables are the primary causes of forecast errors.

## ROLE OF TRACKING

Forecasters track results not only to know where they are today relative to where they predicted they would be, but also to help make better forecasts. *Forecast tracking* consists of comparing recently published actuals against current forecasts and communicating the comparisons to higher management as appropriate. Clearly, it is necessary to monitor the assumptions on which the forecasts are based as well.

### Ongoing Communication with Management

In the previous chapter, emphasis was placed on the formal presentations that are periodically made to management. A forecaster should maintain ongoing communications with management on a less formal basis as well. These communications consist of written reports, memos, and personal conversations.

The purpose of ongoing communications is to keep management informed about current levels of results and forecasting performance as well as to recommend changes in forecasts when appropriate. Normally, forecasters should prepare a set of standard reports and analyses of current results and forecast performances. They should also strive to limit such reports to the minimum number necessary, since managers can easily become buried in reports from subordinates. If there are too many reports, an important change may be missed among the routine reports.

Rather, management should have confidence that the forecaster will issue timely reports of exceptions when unusual or unforecasted events occur. The forecaster should take the initiative at such times and not wait for a request from management. When managerial confidence is lacking, forecasters may find themselves being asked to issue daily and weekly reports full of data signifying nothing. This can be a tremendous drain on the productivity of both a forecasting organization and management.

The forecaster and manager should establish a minimal number of report dates, probably one a month, as actuals are received, and the forecaster should have the responsibility for issuing exception reports whenever necessary. The reports must provide accurate, concise, and timely analyses of results together with probable forecast revisions, if appropriate. By identifying changing forecast conditions and immediately advising management to adjust policies to cope with changed conditions, a forecaster will go a long way toward preventing management from being surprised by changes about which nothing can be done.

There will be times when the forecaster does not yet wish to change a forecast, yet it is probable that a change will be required if a short-term trend continues. The existing forecast, when issued, probably had a 50 percent probability of overrun or underrun. Several months later, it may be apparent that the forecast is frequently underestimating results and that actual results may well exceed the forecast. If the overrun is not large, the forecaster and manager may decide only to change the probability of overrun from 50 percent to—say—70 percent. However, managers usually want to know and use the new "most likely" forecast. The management decision about whether or not to change the forecast will be based on the information supplied by the forecaster and the impact the change would have on company operations.

## Monitoring Key Assumptions

It is usually worthwhile to look first outside the firm for changing conditions. Are the values for the independent variable(s) used in the forecasting models coming in as expected? Are the deviations from predicted values significant enough to cause concern? Why are the independent variables behaving as they are? The forecasts for the independent variables are key assumptions upon which the forecast of demand for the firm's goods or services are based. If these assumptions are not valid, a new forecast is required.

The larger a firm, the more likely it is that a communications breakdown will occur and that the forecaster will not be aware of marketing decisions or other internal policy decisions by various field and staff groups. Subsequent to the issuance of the latest forecast, the sales department may decide to stage a promotion for a given product; the accountant may become concerned about an increase in uncollectibles and recommend new deposit, credit, or collection practices; the research department may produce a new product that is competitive with an existing product; competitors may announce new offerings which appear superior to the firm's existing product line. Any or all of these kinds of changes can take place after the forecast has received management approval. If the impact of these changes is significant, the forecaster has the responsibility to advise management that exceptional events require a change in the forecast. By developing "pipelines" to key decision makers, the forecaster can minimize the frequency of forecast changes.

## TOOLS FOR TRACKING FORECASTS

A number of methods for identifying and evaluating significant differences follow. They include the use of ladder charts, prediction-realization diagrams, monthly and cumulative confidence limit charts, and tracking signals.

### Ladder Charts

A ladder chart is a simple yet powerful tool for monitoring forecast results. The ladder chart illustrated in Figure 22.1 is somewhat more detailed than those normally used. There are six items of information shown for each month of the year: average of the past five years; the past year's performance; the five-year low; the five-year high; the current year-to-date; and the monthly forecasts for the remainder of the current year.

The five-year average line usually provides the best indication of the seasonal pattern, assuming this pattern is not changing over time. By plotting the current year's monthly forecasts on a ladder chart, the forecaster can determine if the seasonal pattern in the forecast looks reasonable. In fact, this is a good check for reasonableness that can be done before submitting the forecast for approval.

The level of the forecast can be checked for reasonableness relative to the prior year (dashed line in Figure 22.1). The forecaster can determine whether or not the actuals are consistently overrunning or underrunning the forecast. In this example, the residuals are positive for three months and negative for three months. The greatest difference between actual and forecast values appears only in March and April, but

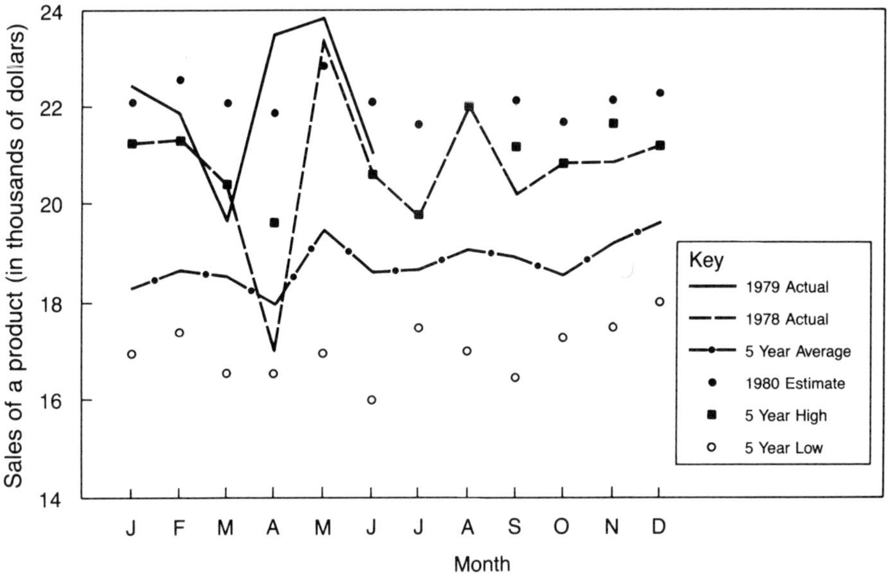


**Figure 22.1** Monitoring forecast performance with the use of a ladder chart.

here the deviations are of opposite signs: some additional research should be done to uncover the cause of the unusual March-April pattern. The forecasts for the remainder of the current year (1980) look reasonable, though some minor adjustments might be made. The ladder chart is one of the best tools for quickly identifying the need for major changes in forecasts.

## Prediction-Realization Diagrams

Another useful approach to monitoring forecast accuracy is the prediction-realization diagram due to Theil (1958). This diagram indicates how well a model or forecaster has predicted turning points and also how well the magnitude of change has been predicted given that the proper direction of change has been forecast.

If the predicted values are indicated on the vertical axis and the actual values on the horizontal axis, perfect forecasts would be represented by a straight line with a 45-degree slope. This is called the "line of perfect forecasts" (Figure 22.2). In practice, the prediction-realization diagram is sometimes rotated so that the line of perfect forecasts is horizontal.

The diagram has six sections. Points falling in Sections II and V are a result of turning point errors. In Section V a positive change was predicted while the actual change was negative. In Section II a negative change was predicted and a positive change occurred. The remaining sections involve predictions which were correct in sign but wrong in magnitude. Points above the line of perfect forecasts reflect actual

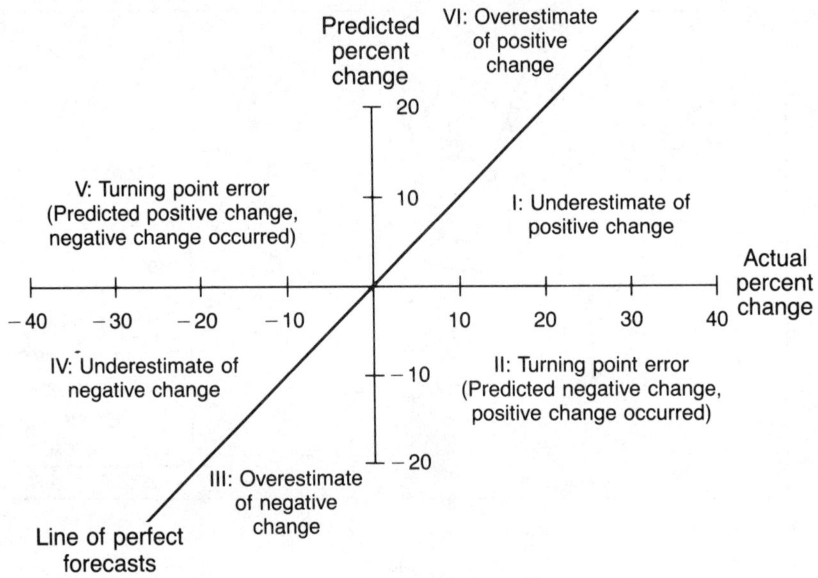


**Figure 22.2** A prediction-realization diagram.

changes that were less than predicted. Points below the line of perfect forecast represent actual changes that were greater than predicted.

The prediction-realization diagram can be used to record forecast results on an ongoing basis. Persistent overruns or underruns indicate the need to adjust the forecasts or to reestimate the model. In this case, a simple error pattern is evident and one can raise or lower the forecast based on the pattern and magnitude of the errors.

More importantly, the diagram will indicate turning point errors that may be due to misspecification or missing variables in the model. The forecaster may well be at a loss to decide how to modify the model forecasts. An analysis of other factors that occurred when the turning point error was realized may result in inclusion of a variable in the model that was missing from the initial specification.

Figure 22.3 illustrates a prediction-realization diagram for a model discussed in Chapter 20—main gain versus housing starts. The model is a regression of the annual change in main gain (over the same quarter the prior year) as a function of the annual changes in housing starts.

## Confidence Limits for Time Series Models

In Chapter 14, confidence limits were introduced as a way to express the uncertainty in the forecasts from simple linear regression models. Confidence limits and control charts play an important role in tracking forecasts for time series models (Platt, 1974).

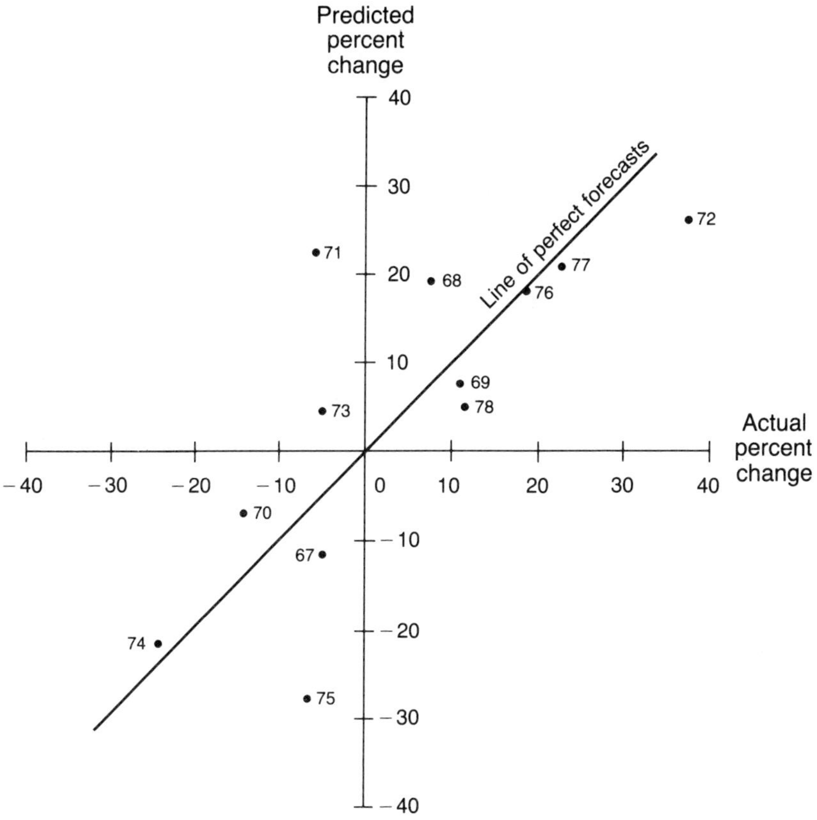


**Figure 22.3** A prediction-realization diagram for the main gain–housing starts model.

A simple method for the construction of *empirical confidence limits,* when no error distributions can be assumed, is described in Goodman and Williams (1971). The procedure is to go through the ordered data, making forecasts at each point in time. Then, the comparison of these forecasts with known actuals will yield an empirical distribution of forecasting errors. If the future errors are distributed like the most recent past forecast errors, then the empirical distribution of these errors can be used to set confidence intervals for subsequent forecasts. In practice, the theoretical size and the empirical size of the intervals have been found to agree closely.

In a regression model, it is generally assumed that errors are normally distributed with zero mean and constant variance. The variance of the errors is estimated from the sample data. The estimated standard deviation is calculated for the forecast period and is used to develop the desired confidence limits. While 95 percent confidence limits are frequently used, the range of forecast values for volatile series may be so great that it might also be helpful to show the limits for a lower level of confidence, say 75 percent. It is common to express confidence limits around the forecast; but, in the tracking process, it is more useful to deal with confidence limits around the forecast errors (Actual − Forecast) on a period-by-period or cumulative basis.

## Confidence Limits on Forecast Errors

An early warning signal is a succession of overruns or underruns. This is evident when the forecast errors are plotted over time together with their confidence limits and the forecast errors continually lie above or below the zero line. Even though the individual forecast errors may lie well within the monthly confidence band, a plot of the cumulative sum of the errors may indicate that their sum is outside their confidence band. This danger signal is evident in Figures 22.4 and 22.5. It can be seen that the monthly errors lie well within the 95 percent confidence limits for nine of the twelve months, with two of the three exceptions occurring in November and December. The forecast errors by themselves indicate that the monthly forecasts are reasonable. However, it is apparent that none of the errors are negative—certainly they do not form a random pattern.

The cumulative confidence limit plot confirms the problem with the forecast. The cumulative forecast errors are on or outside the confidence limits for all twelve months. This model is clearly underforecasting. Either the model has failed to

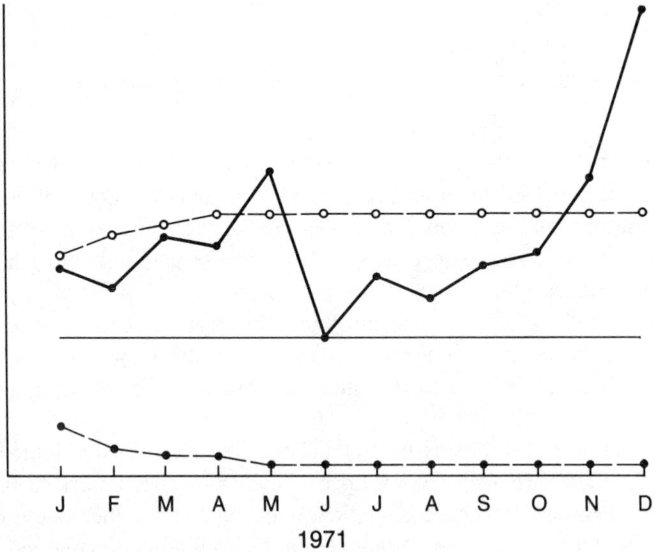


**Figure 22.4** Monthly forecast errors and associated 95 percent confidence limits for a time series model.

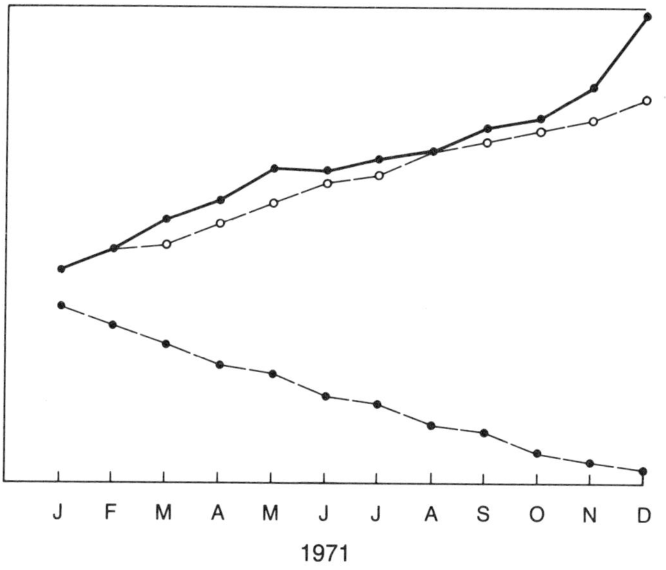


**Figure 22.5** Cumulative forecast errors and associated 95 percent confidence limits for a time series model.

capture a strong cyclical effect occurring in 1971 or the data are growing exponentially and the analyst has failed to make the proper transformation of the data in the modeling process. By using these two plots, the forecaster would probably recommend an upward revision in the forecast after several months. It certainly would not be necessary to wait until November to identify the problem.

A second monitoring danger signal is the appearance of an excessive number of forecast errors falling outside the confidence limits. For example, with 90 percent confidence limits, only 10 percent (approximately one month in a year) of the errors should be outside the confidence limits. Figure 22.6 shows a plot of the monthly forecast errors for a time series model. In this case, five of the twelve errors lie outside the 95 percent confidence limits. Clearly, this model is unacceptable as a predictor of monthly values. However, the error pattern is random and the annual forecasts from this model may be acceptable. Figure 22.7 shows the cumulative forecast errors and confidence limits. It is apparent that the annual forecast lies within the 95 percent confidence limits and is acceptable.

The conclusion that can be reached from monitoring the two sets of forecast errors is that neither model is wholly acceptable, nor can either be rejected. In one case, the monthly forecasts were good but the annual forecast was not. In the other case, the monthly forecasts were not good but the annual forecast was acceptable. Whether either model would be retained by the forecaster depends on the purpose for which the model was constructed. It is important to notice that by monitoring cumulative forecast errors, the forecaster was able to determine the need for forecast

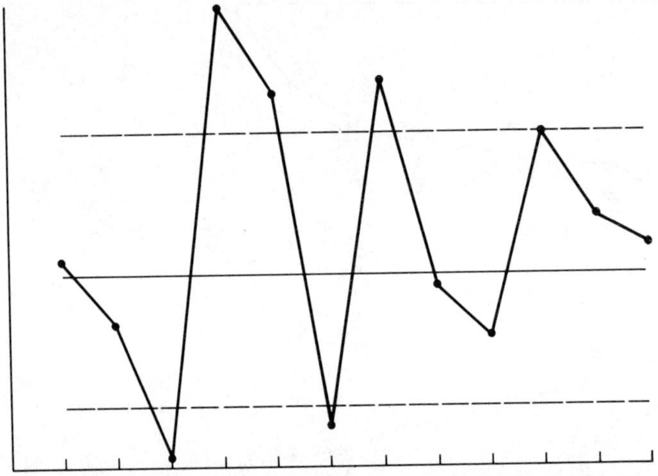


**Figure 22.6** Monthly forecast errors and confidence limits for a time series model.

revision much earlier than if he or she were only monitoring monthly forecast errors. This is the kind of early notification of forecast revision that management expects from the forecaster.

## Tracking Signals

The tracking signal, proposed by Trigg (1964), indicates the presence of nonrandom errors. The tracking signal is the ratio of two smoothed errors $E_t$ and $M_t$. The numerator $E_t$ is a simple exponential smooth of the errors $e_t$, and the denominator $M_t$ is a simple exponential smooth of the absolute value of the errors. Thus

$$T_t = E_t/M_t;$$
$$E_t = \alpha e_t + (1 - \alpha)E_{t-1};$$
$$M_t = \alpha|e_t| + (1 - \alpha)M_{t-1};$$

and

$$e_t = y_t - F_t,$$

where $e_t$ is the difference between the observed value $y_t$ and the forecast $F_t$ at period $t$. Trigg showed that when $T_t$ exceeds 0.51 for $\alpha = 0.1$ or 0.74 for $\alpha = 0.2$, the errors are nonrandom at the 95 percent confidence level.

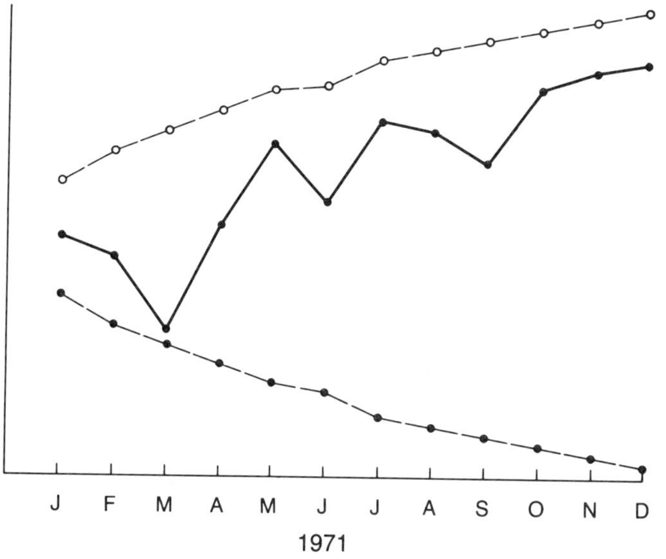


**Figure 22.7** Cumulative forecast errors and 95 percent confidence limits for a time series model.

Tracking signals are useful when large numbers of items need to be monitored. This is often the case in inventory management systems. When the tracking signal for an item exceeds the threshold level, the forecaster's attention is drawn to the problem.

Table 22.1 illustrates the use of tracking signals for an adaptive smoothing model of seasonally adjusted airline data. The tracking signal correctly provides a warning at time period 15 after five consecutive periods where the actual exceeded the forecast. Period 11 has the largest error, but no warning is provided because the sign of the error became reversed. It is apparent that the model errors can increase substantially above prior experience, without a warning being signaled, as long as the errors change sign. Once a pattern of over- or underforecasting is evident, a warning is issued.

## TRACKING THE MODEL

Tracking by confidence limits may work well for regression and time series models. This technique is generally not available for the more complicated multivariate time series and econometric models discussed in *The Professional Forecaster*. For single-equation models the calculation of confidence limits assumes perfect forecasts of the independent variable(s). Of course, this leads to a dilemma in the forecasting mode. Nevertheless, the confidence limits express the expected variation due to the

**Table 22.1** Trigg's tracking signal ($\alpha = 0.1$).

| Time period | Error | Smoothed error | Smoothed absolute error | Tracking signal ($T_t$) |
|---|---|---|---|---|
| 1 | −1.58 | | | |
| 2 | 2.54 | −1.17 | 1.68 | −0.70* |
| 3 | 5.24 | −0.53 | 2.04 | −0.26 |
| 4 | −0.51 | −0.53 | 1.89 | −0.28 |
| 5 | 0.59 | −0.42 | 1.76 | −0.24 |
| 6 | 2.26 | −0.15 | 1.81 | −0.08 |
| 7 | 1.49 | 0.01 | 1.78 | 0.01 |
| 8 | 1.31 | 0.14 | 1.73 | 0.08 |
| 9 | 0.43 | 0.17 | 1.60 | 0.11 |
| 10 | −7.73 | −0.62 | 2.21 | −0.28 |
| 11 | 11.57 | 0.60 | 3.15 | 0.19 |
| 12 | 8.98 | 1.44 | 3.73 | 0.39 |
| 13 | 3.82 | 1.68 | 3.74 | 0.45 |
| 14 | 4.17 | 1.93 | 3.78 | 0.51 |
| 15 | 1.06 | 1.84 | 3.51 | 0.53† |

*Note:* Example is taken from a seasonally adjusted simple adaptive smoothing model of airline data.
*Starting Value—Ignore.
†Exceeds 0.51—Warning.

model, but it must be realized that the actual uncertainty may be greater because of errors in the forecasts for the independent variable(s).

If the forecaster is interested in an "after-the-fact" evaluation of the forecasting performance, the model can be rerun with actual values for the independent variables in the forecast period (these are known as *ex post* forecasts). The realistic forecast is made by using predictions for the independent variables and is referred to as the *ex ante* forecast.

In Figure 22.8, the annual error is divided into its component parts, the part due to the model itself and the part due to the imperfect forecasts of the independent variable(s). If the major contribution to the error is the model, perhaps a better model can be built. If the major contribution to the error is the poor forecasts for the independent variables, the forecaster may want to seek better forecasts for these variables.

If good forecasts cannot be obtained, perhaps another variable can be substituted for which more accurate forecasts are obtainable. It is entirely possible that the original forecast is better than the *ex post* forecast because of compensating errors in the predictions of the independent variable(s). In this case, the forecaster has the right answer for the wrong reason. The forecaster should not place too much confidence in the model when this occurs.

The forecaster may also choose to compare residuals from the original model with those of the *ex post* model. If autocorrelated residuals, or some other residual

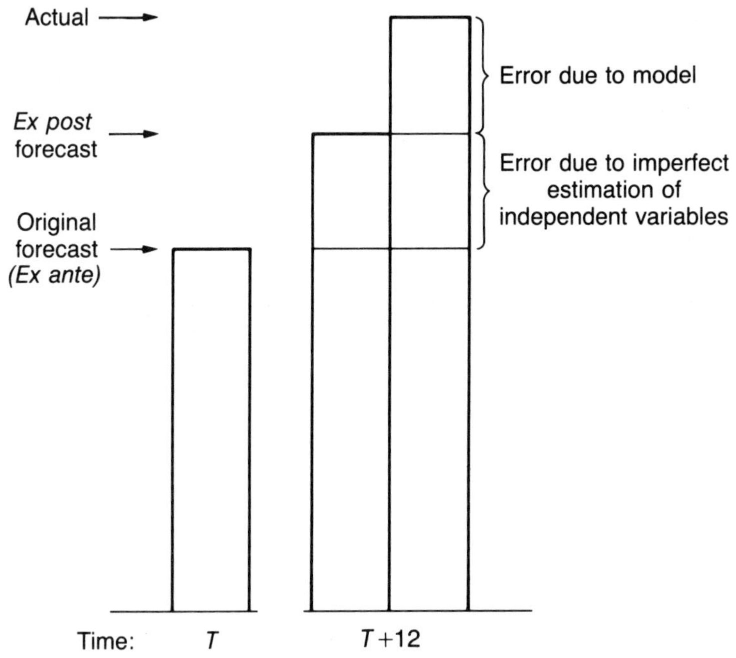


**Figure 22.8** Forecast performance analysis for demand models.

pattern, exist in the original model but not in the latter, the model itself may be a good one. Once again, improved forecasts for the independent variable(s) are needed.

## FORECAST TRACKING CHECKLIST

____ Are independent/exogenous and policy variables monitorable?
____ Are ladder charts used to highlight forecast deviations?
____ Are confidence limits developed about the forecast errors for time series models? Monthly or quarterly? Cumulative?
____ Is there a succession of overruns or underruns in the errors?
____ Are the monthly or quarterly forecast errors within the appropriate confidence limits?
____ Are the cumulative forecast errors within the confidence limits?
____ Has an *ex post* analysis been made on the accuracy of the model?
____ Was the major contribution to the forecast error due to forecasts of independent/exogenous variables? The model itself?

- ____ Can other independent/exogenous variables be used where better forecasts are obtainable?
- ____ Does the importance of the forecast warrant the expense of applying a Monte Carlo simulation for random sampling of errors?
- ____ Does the model "blow up" when extreme values are input for the independent/exogenous variables?
- ____ Was a sensitivity analysis performed under different scenarios?
- ____ Does the forecaster have a sound evaluation of the uncertainty that exists in the model's forecasts?
- ____ Is it helpful to talk to management in terms of percent errors rather than confidence limits?

## SUMMARY

- The tracking of results is essential to ensure the continuing relevance of the forecast. By properly tracking forecasts and assumptions, the forecaster can inform management when a forecast revision is required. It should not be necessary for management to inform the forecaster that something is wrong with the forecast.
- Tracking techniques include the use of ladder charts, prediction-realization diagrams, confidence limits about the forecasts and the residuals, and tracking signals that identify nonrandom error patterns.
- The tracking of results also helps the forecaster to better understand the models, their capabilities, and the uncertainty associated with the forecasts derived from them.

## USEFUL READING

GOODMAN, M. L., and W. H. WILLIAMS (1971). A Simple Method for the Construction of Empirical Confidence Limits for Economic Forecasts. *Journal of the American Statistical Association* 66, 752–54.

PLATT, R. B. (1974). Statistical Measures of Forecast Accuracy, in *Methods and Techniques of Business Forecasting*, Butler et al., eds. Englewood Cliffs, NJ: Prentice-Hall.

THEIL, H. (1958). *Economic Forecasts and Policy*. Amsterdam: North Holland Publishing Co.

TRIGG, D. W. (1964). Monitoring a Forecasting System. *Operational Research Quarterly* 15, 272–74.

CHAPTER 23

# Setting Goals for Forecasting Organizations

Successful forecasting organizations are those that have discovered how to apply traditional management philosophies and practices to what is essentially a nontraditional business discipline. The next three chapters develop specific managerial approaches to strengthening forecasting organizations. Emphasis will be placed on setting goals for forecasting organizations, establishing standards of performance, measuring performance, implementing new methods, and optimizing consultation with outsiders whose opinions can be helpful.

In this chapter, we shall offer suggestions to help managers:

- Improve their management of a forecasting organization.
- Evaluate forecasts presented for their approval.

## MANAGEMENT BY RESULTS

In planning this book, we realized that we believe a basic founding in management is necessary for anyone assuming control of a forecasting organization. A management framework that has been successfully applied in many forecasting organizations is *management by objectives* or *results:* a great deal of literature exists in this area and it is not our purpose in this chapter to describe management by results as an abstract skill. Instead, we shall endeavor to help you develop a management-by-results framework specifically for a forecasting organization. There are five key steps to consider in formulating management by results:

- Define the purpose of the job or organization.
- Define the major areas of responsibility.

- Describe a long-term objective for each area of responsibility.
- Establish indicators of performance.
- Establish short-term goals and measure performance relative to them.

You could spend many hours wrestling with the purpose of your job, no matter how simple that job. Developing meaningful indicators of performance can consume a great deal of time and result in much debate. Experience will cause you to reject some indicators and replace them with others more relevant. However, without these indicators you will find it difficult to manage effectively. Naturally, both the indicators and attendant levels of performance will change over time as the business evolves.

### Purpose and Role

What is the purpose of a forecasting organization? What is the role of the forecast manager? These are two questions that require considerable thought since it is difficult to build an organization unless you know what it is that needs to be accomplished. We have emphasized throughout this book that the responsibility of a forecasting organization is to *provide top-quality advice*—usually advice about future demand for a company's products and services. One role of a forecast manager is thus as an advisor to that company's managers. To fulfill the other part of the role, a forecast manager must manage colleagues and their work.

A primary managerial responsibility is to *establish goals* for the organization. In a *single* sentence, and to focus on the key reasons for the existence of the organization, the statement made in the preceding paragraph can serve as a start: "The responsibility of a forecasting organization is to provide top-quality advice to management about future demand for a company's products and services."

### Areas of Responsibility

Next, try to define the *major areas of* your *responsibility* in short, one- or two-word statements: these areas of responsibility might be "revenue," "capital expenditure forecasting," or other such areas. There are three areas that will be common for almost all managers—self-development, forecasting staff or personnel development, and resource management. For forecast managers, key areas of responsibility are likely to include forecast evaluation, measurement, monitoring, presentation, and forecaster appraisal and development. This chapter will emphasize *forecast evaluation*. Forecast measurement and monitoring are discussed in the next chapter. Forecast presentation and forecaster performance appraisal and development are equally important but the methods for achieving success in these areas are not restricted to forecast managers. Traditional management literature covers these subjects sufficiently. After struggling with the statement of purpose and areas of responsibility, it is worthwhile to review them with higher management to gain their concurrence.

## Objective Setting

Suppose you have determined the purpose and areas of responsibility of management; the next step is to develop a *long-range objective* for each area of responsibility. These objectives should be general enough to have long-range significance, and they should contain an indication of the goal that the actual work should accomplish. Some examples might be: "to improve the accuracy of . . . ," "to improve the productivity of . . . ," "to improve managerial and technical skills," "to improve the credibility of the forecasting organization," or "to ensure the continuing relevance of. . . ." What is implicit in all of these is a striving for improvement that can be translated into actual work.

These objectives are important because they provide the managerial direction and focus which subordinates can embrace and strive to achieve. Forecasters can see how their activities are related to the achievement of organizational objectives.

## Indicators of Performance

The next step is to define the *indicators of performance* for the organization. How will the organization know it is making progress toward the achievement of its objectives? What will be the yardsticks? For certain forecasts one indicator might be the percent deviation between estimate and actual. For personnel development, indicators might be the demonstrated ability of a forecaster to use a new technique or forecast a new product or service effectively.

The last step is the *quantification of a specific goal* for the next six to twelve months. If the goal is to improve the accuracy of a forecast series, a reasonable quantification may be to improve the accuracy to within 5 percent. For personnel development the goal may be to assume responsibility for forecasting revenues within the next six months.

The last two steps of the *five-step process* are usually the most difficult when meaningful indicators of performance and goals do not already exist. However, until the last two steps are achieved, it will not be possible to demonstrate explicitly that the organization is achieving its objectives. The key to success in the approach is to make the areas of responsibility, indicators, and goals *job-relevant*. They must truly measure the important requirements of the job. An emphasis on joint boss-subordinate goal setting and communications will increase the probability that the organizational goals will be internalized by the members of the organization. In this chapter, emphasis is placed on developing *meaningful indicators of performance* that can be directly applied to forecasting organizations in a business environment. Of course, the recommendations that follow can be modified to approximate the specific forecasting requirements of a firm or organization more closely.

## ESTABLISHING STANDARDS OF PERFORMANCE

How can a manager tell a good forecast from a bad forecast at the time it is presented for approval? This is a perplexing problem that many forecast managers have faced at one time or another. The extent to which this is a problem in an organization depends on the experience of the staff and the stability of factors in the economic environment. The manager's participation, because of its potential for "adding value," is particularly useful when dealing with new forecasters, new time series, and organizational or environmental situations causing uncertainty, discontinuity, or abrupt change.

After a forecast time period has elapsed, anyone can look back and determine how closely the forecast predicted actual results; it is always easy to do this after the fact. But how does a manager ensure that the superior forecasting performance will be achieved? What is needed is a process that, if followed, will increase the likelihood of good forecasting performance—standards of performance for forecasters that will increase the probability of improved forecast accuracy.

### Use of Checklists

The forecasting procedures presented in the first four chapters of this book can provide the framework for establishing these standards. We have also prepared a *manager's checklist* which can be used to measure a specific forecast relative to certain generic standards. This checklist is included at the end of this chapter, and its use by the beginning as well as the managing forecaster is recommended. Once the new forecaster becomes familiar with the process and performance standards, the manager will be encouraged to step back, lessen his or her forecast involvement, and jointly plan opportunities for the technical or managerial development of the beginning forecaster.

The checklist is general in nature and covers the essential elements that must be a part of an effective forecasting process. It is designed to assist the new forecaster in getting started and to remind the experienced forecaster to "cover all the bases." It begins with the *establishment of basic facts concerning past trends and forecasts*.

### Preliminary Data Analysis

To be satisfied that basic facts have been researched adequately, the forecaster should develop tables and plots of historical data (see the Flowchart). The data should be adjusted to account for changes in prices, administrative decisions, or other factors that would distort analyses and forecasts.

If appropriate, the data should be seasonally adjusted to give a better representation of trend-cycle. It is useful to maintain records about the National Bureau of Economic Research reference dates for peaks and troughs of business cycles. This provides the forecaster and the manager with an indication of the extent to which a company's time series are being impacted by the national business cycles. Knowing this relationship will be helpful when the forecaster reviews the assumptions about the future state of the economy and how these assumptions are reflected in the forecast numbers (Sobek, 1973). Outliers or other unusual data values should be explained and replaced, if this is warranted.

Tables and plots of percent changes provide an indication of the volatility of the series and are useful later in checking the reasonableness of the forecast compared to history. If possible, ratios should be developed between the forecast series and other stable time series—company or regional. These ratios should be shown in tables or plots. If some major change is expected in the forecast period, these ratios should help identify the change.

Whenever possible, there should be at least a decade of data available for review. It may not be necessary to show this much history when presenting the forecast to the forecast users, but it will be necessary to have this much data available to analyze the impact of business cycles. If possible, data back to the 1957–1958 recession is desirable since, with the exception of 1973–1975, and perhaps the 1980 recession, that was the last major recession. For relatively new products and services this is not possible.

There should also be available a record of forecasts and actuals for at least the past three years. This will allow the manager to know how well the organization has done in the past and suggest how the users may respond to the new forecast. It will also be possible to determine if any forecaster or all forecasters have a tendency to be too optimistic or too pessimistic over time.

## Causes of Changes

The next segment of the checklist deals with the *causes of changes in past demand trends or levels*. The first step is to identify the trend in the data. Regression analysis is an excellent tool to do this (see Parker and Segura, 1971; Wheelwright and Makridakis, 1980). A regression against time, as a starting point, will provide a visual indication as to whether the trend is linear or nonlinear.

There should be a plot of the series and fitted trend on a scale of sufficient breadth that deviations from trend can be identified clearly. The reasons for the deviations should be explained in writing. These explanations need to be specific. Was there unusual construction activity? Was there a change in corporate policy or prices? Did the deviations correspond to a regional or a national economic pattern? What was the source of the explanation? Did the forecaster develop the analysis or was it provided by someone else?

Finally, how certain is the forecaster that the reason or explanation stated is correct? Is the forecaster reasonably certain of the cause, or does it turn out that there is insufficient evidence to be confident that the true cause has been or can be identified? This documentation of history is an important step that can serve as reference material for all future forecasts and forecasters. It is particularly helpful to a new forecaster, and it improves productivity significantly. These steps are in essence part of the development of a demand theory for the series (see the flowchart).

## Reasons for Differences

The next segment of the checklist is concerned with the *reasons for the differences between previous forecasts and actual results*. This represents a slight difference from the normal forecast tracking or monitoring activities. At this stage, as a manager, you will be evaluating past forecasts instead of the current forecast.

What we shall call "results analysis" is useful to uncover problem areas, to identify the need for new or improved methods, and to determine the quality of the prior forecasts. This subject will be dealt with in the next chapter, on monitoring forecasting performance.

In "results analysis," a manager is looking for a pattern of overforecasting or underforecasting. The key to identifying the reasons for such deviations is the existence of written basic assumptions, which the forecaster has kept for review. These assumptions should be tested against the standards provided earlier in the book. Do the assumptions relate only to the future time periods? Has the forecaster used assumptions that state a positive assertion of facts that may hold true during the forecast period? Was the direction of expected impact stated? Presumably, there are both positive and negative assumptions in terms of their impact on the series being forecasted. Do the assumptions indicate the amount or rate of expected impact, the timing of the initial impact, and the duration of the expected impact?

Accompanying each assumption should be a *rationale* indicating why the assumption is necessary. The source of the assumption should be identified and the degree of confidence in the assumption should be stated. The forecaster may be absolutely certain that the assumption will prove correct. On the other hand, the forecaster may indicate that it was necessary to make the assumption, but that considerable doubt exists as to whether or not the future will be as assumed. Also included at the end of this chapter is a checklist that both forecaster and manager may find useful for documenting assumptions.

## Factors Affecting Demand

The next segment of the checklist is concerned with the *factors likely to affect future demand* and therefore the forecast. This is a refinement of the theory of demand.

Assumptions will have to be made about factors such as income, price, habit, price of competing goods, and market potential. In addition, the forecaster should demonstrate that there is a logical time integration between historical actuals and the short- and long-term forecasts. Time plots are very useful here. Also, there should be a logical time integration between related forecast items. The forecast should also be reasonably related to forecasts produced by other organizations in the company (if the forecasting function is not centralized in one organization), such as forecasts of economic conditions, revenues, and expenses.

### Making the Forecast

At this time, the forecaster should explain why the forecasting methodologies used represent the best methods available for the problem (see the flowchart). The use of *multiple methods* to arrive at the final forecast is highly recommended. The methods presented in this book and in *The Professional Forecaster* have been tested extensively in business applications and have proved to be practical.

Within limits, it is very difficult for a manager to "fine tune" the numbers presented with any degree of assurance that the changes are appropriate. However, the manager can carefully review the forecast assumptions for reasonableness. The assumptions are the heart of the forecast and considerable probing of these assumptions will satisfy the manager as to their appropriateness for the forecast period. The manager can also review the technical soundness of the analysis and be satisfied that no errors were made. Having performed these forecast evaluations, the manager can tell a good forecast from a bad one at the time the forecast needs to be approved, or subsequently.

This level of managerial involvement will generally only be required for extremely sensitive or important forecasts, for training new forecasters, for reviewing exceptional cases, or for spot-checking to ensure that the processes are being followed. The amount of analysis may seem overwhelming. However, most of the analyses are performed the first time for a given time series and are then updated as new results become available. Often, much of the data and graphic displays can be generated by computer with a small clerical support group.

## FORECAST STANDARDS CHECKLIST

STEP 1: Setting Down Basic Facts about Past Trends and Forecasts

____ Are historical tables and plots of data and percent changes available?
____ Has the forecaster base-adjusted data?
____ Have seasonal and calendar adjustments been made?

____ Have outliers been explained?
____ Have NBER cyclical reference dates been overlaid?
____ Are ratios to stable related series available in tables and plots?
____ Is there an adequate amount of historical data?
____ Have forecast-versus-actual comparisons been made for one or more forecast periods?

STEP 2: Determining Causes of Changes in Past Demand Trends

____ Are trend and cycles identified?
____ Is there a linear or nonlinear pattern?
____ Is there a plot of data and fitted trends?
____ Is the scale of sufficient breadth to see deviations?
____ Have deviations been explained in writing?
____ Are explanations about causes specific?
____ Has the source of explanations been identified?
____ Is the degree of certainty about explanations noted?

STEP 3: Determining Causes of Differences between Previous Forecasts and Actual Data

____ Are differences explained?
____ Are there any patterns to explanations?
____ Were there basic assumptions to review?

STEP 4: Determining Factors Likely to Affect Future Demand

____ Do the assumptions relate to the future?
____ Do the assumptions indicate direction of impact?
____ Do the assumptions indicate amount or rate of impact?
____ Do the assumptions indicate timing of impact?
____ Do the assumptions indicate duration of impact?
____ Are there rationale statements for each assumption?
____ Are the sources for a rationale statement identified?

STEP 5: Making Forecasts for Future Periods

____ Time integration: are long-term, short-term, and history all shown on one chart?
____ Item integration: are ratios of related items shown, as well as their history through the long-term forecast?
____ Functional integration: are related forecasts identified and relationships quantified?
____ Have multiple methods been used for key items and results compared?
____ Has the impact on the user of the forecast been considered?

## SUMMARY

- Managing an organization that utilizes quantitative methods requires above average technical competence: a background in management is recommended.
- Forecasters and managers alike may find that a jointly compiled checklist will help in the technical evaluation of forecasting models. (A sample checklist is included in this chapter.) The purpose of such checklists should be to establish standards for the forecasting organization. The forecaster should use the checklists in the preparation of the forecasts and have them available for subsequent review by the forecast manager if an exceptional circumstance makes this advisable.
- The philosophy of forecast evaluation is one in which primary emphasis is placed on the process rather than the numbers.
- If a proper forecasting process has been meticulously followed by the forecaster, the end result will be as good a forecast as can be developed. If not, a manager may need to find a better-trained forecaster.

## USEFUL READING

PARKER, G. G., and E. L. SEGURA (1971). How to Get a Better Forecast. *Harvard Business Review* 49, 6–16.

SOBEK, R. S. (1973). A Manager's Primer in Forecasting. *Harvard Business Review* 5, 1–9.

WHEELWRIGHT, S. C., and S. MAKRIDAKIS (1980). *Forecasting Methods for Management,* 3rd ed. New York, NY: John Wiley and Sons.

CHAPTER **24**

# Measuring Forecast Performance

There are two areas of forecast measurement that the manager should include in an organization plan.

- The first area is forecast monitoring, in which the manager hopes to identify and highlight, as soon as possible, the need for a forecast revision.
- The second area is results analysis, in which the goal is to quantify the accuracy of prior forecasts as part of an overall measurement of the effectiveness of the organization.

## FORECAST MONITORING: OBJECTIVES FOR THE MANAGER

A primary objective of forecast monitoring is to be able to *prevent surprising* a company with news about *unforeseen exceptions* to a forecast. The firm should have sufficient time to evaluate alternative courses of action and not be forced to react to unpredicted yet predictable events. A second objective of monitoring is to *predict* accurately a *change in the direction of growth*. This involves predicting the turning points in the economy and the demand for the firm's products. Quite often managers find it difficult to predict a downturn in demand and instead call for an upturn too soon.

### Responsibility for Preventing Unpleasant Surprises

Managerial control is a process that measures current performance, based on available information, and guides performance toward a predetermined goal. It is easy to see why few managers of a business find the exercise of managerial control as challenging as the forecast manager does. Forecast managers are in charge of a function whose primary output is wholly related to the future environment; being unable to change the environment, the manager must instead revise a forecast when it is evident that an original forecast or goal cannot be met. In effect, the forecast manager is changing some predetermined goal to approximate expected performance more closely.

The process of forecast monitoring provides the manager with an early indication that such changes in forecasts may be required. Through experience, a good manager will develop an improved ability to anticipate change and to advise management so that the firm will have time to adjust operations to changing conditions. This, of course, is a valuable attribute in a manager.

## Knowing When to Predict Changes

At a more demanding level, objectives of monitoring are to predict changes in the rate of growth, to predict the level of growth, and to minimize the impact of forecast changes. The ability to predict any speeding up or slowing down of growth with accuracy helps management to decide on proper timing of company plans and programs. An accurate prediction of the level of growth—the forecast numbers themselves—allows management to make sizing decisions about investment in facilities, numbers of employees, and appropriate financing arrangements. Last, it is necessary to minimize the internal disruption that results from changing forecasts too frequently. The forecaster could, after all, change a forecast every month so that the final forecast and the actual data would be almost identical. However, this does not serve the needs of forecast users. The forecast manager must endeavor to minimize the need to change forecasts. The more carefully thought out and thoroughly researched the initial forecast is, the less will be the need to revise it.

## Knowing What to Monitor

There should be a difference between what a forecaster monitors and what the manager monitors. Forecasters monitor a data base that consists of time series and assumptions for numerous geographic areas or products. They are primarily interested in the numerical accuracy of the forecasts and the reliability of the forecast assumptions.

The manager monitors a data base that is both more general and more selective. Included in this data base are the exceptional cases that forecasters uncover as a result of their detailed monitoring. The manager is primarily concerned with the implications the difference between the initial forecast and the evolving reality will have on the business for which the forecast is made. The manager should "know more" about that business and should generally be more aware of the significance of forecast changes on business performance than the forecaster.

The specific items that managers select to monitor will naturally depend upon their areas of responsibility. The items to be monitored should relate to the purposes and objectives of the organization. The indicators that are established in the organization plan are natural candidates for monitoring.

Once having selected the items to monitor, the manager may find the following principles helpful.

The manager should consider *monitoring composites* or groups of items. Composites often serve as indicators of overall forecast quality and are frequently used as a base for decision making. They are resistant to individual deviations which may be measurement aberrations and not managerially significant. For example, a forecast of total revenues might be on target, although forecasts of revenues accruing from sales of a product to residential or business users may need to be adjusted.

Another monitoring concept is to *compare the sum of the components to the whole*. This helps to ensure that there is a reasonable relationship between the more stable "top-down" forecast and the more volatile "bottom-up" forecast of many small components. For example, the sum of the individual product forecasts should be compared to a total product line forecast. In this way, the manager can be assured that both upward and downward revisions to the component parts are being made to keep them in reasonable agreement with the total forecast.

Another useful concept is to *monitor ratios* or relationships between different items. The ratio of a given geographic area's sales to total corporate sales is an example of this approach. Another example could be the ratio of sales to disposable personal income.

*Time relationships* are another thing to monitor. It may be appropriate to monitor changes or percent changes over time. The use of seasonally adjusted annual rates is an example, as is the ratio of first quarter to total annual sales.

In addition to monitoring on a monthly basis, consider *monitoring on a cumulative basis*. Compare the sum of the actuals since the beginning of the year with the sum of the forecasts. This has the advantage of smoothing out irregular, random, month-to-month variations.

In all cases it will be necessary to *monitor external factors*. These are the basis for key assumptions about business conditions or the economic outlook. Corporate policy assumptions also need to be monitored.

One critical area that the manager should monitor is *user needs*. It is possible that budgetary or organizational changes, new or discontinued products, or changes in management will cause changes in the forecast user's needs. Since forecasting is a service function, managers need to monitor user needs to be certain that the forecasting service being provided is consistent with evolving business needs. Questionnaires or periodic discussions with users will indicate if such changes have occurred.

A final concept worthy of consideration is the *monitoring of similar forecasts* in several geographic locations. This will help determine if a pattern is developing elsewhere which may impact your company or area in the near future. Are there areas of the country which generally lead or lag your area? The manager may discover that his or her area is not the only area with weak or strong demand. A national pattern may be emerging that needs to be tracked.

## RESULTS ANALYSIS

The second aspect of forecast measurement is *results analysis,* in which the goal is to develop meaningful ways of measuring the performance of the forecasting organization.

For any manager, improvement in organizational or staff effectiveness is dependent upon measurement. A forecast manager will find it useful to establish a forecast *measurement plan* to provide indications of overall performance that can be reviewed with upper management. A properly developed plan will show performance trends and highlight trouble areas.

### Developing a Measurement Plan

The measurement plan will provide managers with a tool to assist in evaluating both forecasts and forecasters. When a measurement plan exists, forecasters know that they have to explain forecasts that miss the mark. This will force forecasters to structure and quantify their assumptions so that there will be documented reasons to explain deviations from forecasts and actuals.

More importantly, adequate documentation enables the forecaster to learn from past mistakes. From reviews of these after-the-fact reports, it can be determined if the assumptions were reasonable at the time they were made. Which assumptions turned out to be incorrect? Why? Did the forecaster do everything possible to obtain all the facts at the time the forecast was made? Were all sources of information reviewed? Were there any obvious breakdowns in communications? Was the forecast methodology appropriate for the particular problem? The answers to these questions become the information needed to evaluate the forecast and the forecaster.

In reviewing forecasts that were particularly successful, it may be discovered that a forecaster has developed a new method or established new contacts which were responsible for the superior forecast performance. Perhaps the approach can be tried in areas where performance is not as good. The documentation of superior and substandard performance, which will result from the measurement plan, provides the needed inputs to determine areas where improvement in methods or data are required. This document can also be used to support requests for people, data, or other items needed to improve the performance of the organization.

The existence of a measurement plan will also be of value to the users of the forecasts. It will improve their understanding of the limitations that must be placed on the accuracy of the forecasts they receive. For example, suppose the forecaster considers a $\pm 2$ percent miss to be a good job for a given forecast and the measurement plan takes this into account. A user would then be foolish to plan on a 0.5 percent accuracy, which for other reasons is a desirable accuracy. By providing users with forecasting accuracy objectives, one is in effect providing a range forecast which can help users to scale their plans to differing degrees of forecast sensitivity. In addition, the credibility of the forecasting organization will be improved because it is capable of reporting on its own performance.

## Indicators of Forecast Accuracy

The development of a measurement plan begins with selection of the indicators that will be used to measure forecast accuracy. There are four generally used indicators: (1) absolute miss in forecasted change, (2) percent miss in forecasted change, (3) difference between total past sales and forecast, in percent, and (4) the difference in growth rates.

The most commonly used indicator is the percent deviation between estimate and actual. It is most useful when very large numbers are involved (for then, absolute differences between estimate and actual would not be as enlightening). However, when negative, zero, or relatively low levels of demand for a product are realized, the percent deviation can become very large and not very meaningful. In those cases the absolute difference is preferable.

The ratio of the deviation between estimate and actual to the "in-service" quantity of the series being forecast tends to put the forecast error in perspective. For example, a 100 percent deviation in forecasting the growth of sales may be only a 1 percent miss in the total sales. Or a 100 percent miss in forecasting the growth rate of Gross National Product (GNP) may be only a 4 percent miss in actual GNP. However, when dealing with very large numbers, such as GNP, a 4 percent miss can be very significant. In such cases, a useful indicator is the difference between the forecast and actual growth rates (Estimated percent growth rate − Actual percent growth rate). For example, the forecast could be for an 8 percent growth rate, while the actual growth rate is only 4 percent.

The forecast measurement periods are generally monthly, cumulatively, quarterly, annually, or long-term (5–6 years). To be useful to the manager, the measurement plan should cover all areas for which forecasters have responsibility.

## Developing Scores for Performance

It may be desirable to translate forecast errors into numerical scores. Then, the scores can be reviewed and trouble spots will become evident. To identify trouble spots, it will be necessary to have a uniform standard of performance. The score a forecast error receives must not take into account the difficulty of forecasting. If difficulty is taken into account, it will generally not be possible to identify trouble spots. They will be hidden as a result of the scoring system: of course, this will mean that the score is not a direct indication of the ability of the forecaster.

Some forecasters will be responsible for forecasting in series or geographic areas that are more difficult to forecast than others. Such forecasts may receive low scores. However, it is better to identify low scores in difficult areas and know the reasons for the low performance than to have uniformly good scores and not know where your performance problems lie. The manager can be sure that the forecast users will know from past experience where performance problems are and will not be quickly impressed if you dismiss possible problems simply because forecasts for them seem to score high.

The initial step in developing a scoring system is to establish an accuracy ratio. The *accuracy ratio* represents the ratio of the miss (Estimate − Actual) for a given forecast to the miss that will receive a satisfactory score. Suppose the manager has decided that a 10 percent annual forecast deviation for a series is satisfactory and should correspond to an (arbitrary) score of—say—96: for an actual miss of 10 percent, the accuracy ratio will equal one. If the miss is 20 percent, the accuracy ratio will equal two and the score would be significantly less, say 90. The manager decides on the allowable deviation and the scoring is taken into account by the *scoring curve,* which translates measurable results to a range of scores.

For internal use, a manager may also choose to develop a plan which measures the forecast accuracy of individual *forecasters* by attempting to incorporate a measure of difficulty into the scoring mechanism. One approach is to review historical records of forecasts and actuals, to determine the average miss and a measure of its variability (e.g., standard deviation) for each time series. It may be the case that the larger the variability the more volatile and difficult the series is to forecast. With a scoring curve, a one-standard-deviation miss could result in a score of 96 and a two-standard-deviation miss, a score of 90. The lower the miss relative to the measure of variability, the higher the score.

The advantage of this approach is that the current forecaster's accuracy can be compared with others who have predicted the same series. The difficulty is built into the index because difficult areas invariably have larger measures of variability of forecast misses. In practice, the measure of variability used in this process should be "resistant" to outliers (e.g., downweighting of extreme deviations), so the conventional standard deviation may not always be appropriate.

Since the current miss is divided by a historical variability measure, a large miss will not necessarily penalize a forecaster. This is illustrated in Table 24.1. The forecast miss in a given year in Region 1 was 300 and the forecast miss in Region 2 was 100. Region 1 had traditionally been more difficult to forecast than Region 2, and their variability measures of misses were 300 and 100, respectively. The accuracy ratio in both cases equals one and both forecasters receive the same score.

This approach measures only the relative forecast accuracy of forecasters. In assessing a forecaster's ability, several other responsibilities are also important. A

**Table 24.1** Using accuracy ratios to measure the forecaster.

| Measurement | Area 1 (a difficult area) | Area 2 (less difficult) |
|---|---|---|
| (Estimate – Actual) | 300 | 100 |
| Standard deviation of prior forecast misses | 300 | 100 |
| Accuracy ratio | $\frac{300}{300} = 1$ | $\frac{100}{100} = 1$ |

manager will want to judge a forecaster's ability to sell the forecast to users, documentation of forecast work, development or testing of new methods, and overall productivity.

## SUMMARY

Forecast monitoring consists of activities designed to prevent surprise for a company by highlighting the need for a change in the forecast.

- These activities include monitoring composites or group of items, the sum of the parts to the whole, ratios of related items, monthly and cumulative results, company and external factors, results in other locations, and user needs.

Forecast measurement is important for any forecasting organization for a number of reasons. Not the least of these reasons is the need to develop credibility in forecast users. There are two generic approaches that can be pursued.

- The first is to measure only the forecast, making no allowances for difficulty. This approach will identify trouble spots.
- The second approach is to measure the forecaster. In this case, it will be necessary to take relative forecasting difficulty into account to be fair to the forecasters.

CHAPTER **25**

# Implementing New Forecasting Methods

Managers in industry today expect quantitative analyses in support of forecast-dependent decisions. In view of this, and because a concern of every manager is to ensure that his or her organization does not become technically obsolete, a forecast manager must be responsible for ensuring that staff or organization members develop skills necessary to master any new technology.

- This chapter provides guidelines for the implementation of new forecasting methods.
- You will find it helpful to follow the implementation checklist provided at the end of the chapter.

## SELECTING OVERALL GOALS

The first step of the implementation checklist is concerned with selecting overall goals for quantitative modeling (Wheelwright and Makridakis, 1980, Chapter 15). Clearly, it is difficult to be successful in any area of the business without having decided what it is that needs to be done. Since quantitative models can be built for many uses and the specific requirements of a company will determine which methods are appropriate, it is important for a forecast manager to know the company's needs.

Elaborate quantitative models are often constructed with the goal of *improving forecast accuracy*. Since these models can give predictions that are more accurate than official company forecasts using less complex approaches, you should be prepared to work with new models.

Managers usually look for more than just a set of forecast numbers. They would like to *understand* the *relationships* that exist among the various series of interest and among corporate (internal) data and the external economic or market variables, what the relevant relationships are, and how they have been changing over time.

Models also provide management with the ability to *explore alternative scenarios*. Most likely, optimistic, and pessimistic scenarios for economic or market forecasts can be utilized to assess demand for a firm's products and services. This helps management generate necessary contingency plans before these are needed. The models can also provide estimates of advertising effectiveness and price elasticities that can be used to assess the impact advertising and pricing strategies may have on revenues.

Modeling may also be a way of *increasing* the *productivity* of a forecasting organization and reducing overall costs. There are numerous applications where extremely large numbers of forecasts have to be generated. For example, tens of thousands of forecasts are required to determine the cable-pairs requirements between the thousands of telephone switching offices throughout the nation. To attempt to provide all of these forecasts on a manual, one-at-a-time basis is not practical. Often, relatively simple "canned programs" incorporating time series models provide acceptable forecasts for the great majority of cases. The exceptions that warrant additional time and money can then be given the individual attention they deserve.

Forecasters may also want to *develop documentation of successful forecasting techniques* or models that work well in specific situations. When a request for a special forecast is received, the forecaster can review the documentation to determine the methods that will most likely provide the best results. Unsuccessful attempts should also be noted to avoid repetition of false starts.

A problem that most forecasters face is the need to *provide substantiation for the forecasts* presented to management or regulatory authorities. Good documentation is often required to satisfy reviewers who question the forecasting job that has been done. Forecast tests, stability tests, and simulations are a valuable part of the documentation package. In this regard, the forecaster can also use the forecast test as a criterion for model selection. If a given model's forecast test results in errors that are above the objective set by the forecaster, the model can be rejected.

Before starting the modeling effort, the key point is to determine carefully the specific goals that one hopes to achieve.

## OBTAINING ADEQUATE RESOURCES

Another prerequisite to successful implementation of quantitative forecasting methods is having adequate resources. First, the forecaster needs to be trained and experienced in the methods that are available for use. Clerical assistance may be required to gather, verify, input, and process the study data. Access to a time-shared, batch, or desk computer is required. Budgetary limitations for salary and equipment will also need to be determined. If you plan to build a forecasting system, you can expect expenses and costs for computer access to build slowly at first but to increase rapidly as the modeling effort intensifies. This aspect of modeling will be discussed again under computer processing considerations.

## Data Sources

The forecaster is often faced with a data collection problem when attempting to build forecasting models. Even when the appropriate independent variables can be identified, it is not always possible to obtain predictions for these variables. The acquisition of external data has significantly improved over the last several years as the number of computerized data sources has grown. Many consulting firms and university establishments are now forecasting many national economic series, and several also provide regional or state economic forecasts.

Many corporations and business firms have research group staffs that provide forecasts of economic/demographic variables for internal use. These departments provide services to the company's management that enhance and balance the often conflicting forecasts from the outside consultants. The advantage of using an internal organization is that company forecasts can be made consistent with the corporate economic outlook.

The government is also a data source. Census Bureau publications, the monthly *Business Conditions Digest,* publications of the Department of Commerce, vital statistics data from the Department of Health, and publications of the Federal Reserve Banks are all helpful. In addition, county and regional planning boards and associations are often interested in economic and demographic projections in connection with funding from the federal government based on population, employment, unemployment, income, and other statistics. These forecasts must be carefully reviewed to be certain that they provide a consistent viewpoint.

Finally, the National Bureau of Economic Research provides an analysis of the economic cycles and determines official dates for the beginning and ending of recessions.

## Data Files

It is not a purpose of this book to recommend ways to create a management information system involving system analysis, system design, and system implementation. However, certain data management considerations are worth mentioning. Very early in the forecasting project the need for *standardized naming and filing conventions* for data will become obvious. As more and more models are created and new time series added, lack of a standard naming convention and index can hamper progress significantly. As time goes on, the forecaster will not remember what the earliest shorthand computer names represent and undocumented printouts will become useless.

When models become part of the everyday forecasting process, it will be useful to establish a file containing the models and the commands necessary to execute them. In this way it will be relatively easy to update the models and generate new forecasts in a quick, efficient, and cost-effective manner.

Experience also suggests that *file updating and maintenance* should be the responsibility of a single group. Otherwise, there is no accountability for data integrity and this results in duplication, excess storage for items no longer necessary, and out-of-date data files.

When establishing a data management system, it is advisable to *establish password or security conventions* and access restrictions. This prevents unauthorized people from accidentally or intentionally using private information or erasing or destroying a data file. Most computer vendors can provide a capability for the protection of computer files.

## Computer Processing

If the forecasting organization does not have its own mini- or desktop computer, the forecaster may prefer to do all the work on an interactive time-shared mode on someone else's computer. This is the most expensive method of operation and should be discouraged as soon as the forecaster becomes familiar with the computer system. Some work can only be done effectively on-line, but there are many opportunities for savings by having the processing performed off-line or in a batch mode. Such processing can be done whenever computer time becomes available (during evening or night hours, for example) and the output is mailed back to the analyst. This can mean as much as a 75 percent reduction in computer charges. The cost-per-computation is much less with batch-work, and there are no charges for connection to the system. The batch mode of operation is not practical if decisions must be made before subsequent processing can take place or if it is of the essence to do the processing fast.

Of course, with the rapid introduction of on-site mini-computers with built-in statistical software packages, the above considerations may become a thing of the past.

## Statistical Software Packages

Statistical software packages are widely available for statistical design, modeling, analysis, and the interpretation of results. You should investigate the availability, quality, and performance of these, and their ability to satisfy your needs in your forecasting environment. No package will be everything to everybody. Some factors you should consider before selecting the appropriate software package have been discussed by Muller (1980):

- Packages provide economies of scale and considerable savings in time, effort, and cost.
- Acquisition cost may be nominal; however, investment in learning how to make effective use of it can often be substantial, as can the cost of keeping up with its modifications.

- Independent development is a major investment which may be beyond the means of most individual organizations.

There are numerous statistical packages in use by government, university, and industry forecasters. Some of the more widely advertised include:

BMDP (Biomedical Computer Programs). UCLA Health Sciences Computing Facility, University of California, Los Angeles, CA 90024.

CROSSTABS. Cambridge Computer Associates, Inc., 222 Alewife Brook Parkway, Cambridge, MA 02138.

IDA (Interactive Data Analysis). Graduate School of Business, University of Chicago, Chicago, IL 60637.

MINITAB. Pennsylvania State University, 215 Pond Lab, University Park, PA 16802.

OMNITAB. National Bureau of Standards, NBS Tech Note 552, U.S. Government Printing Office, Washington, DC 20402.

P-Stat. P.O. Box 285, Princeton, NJ 08540.

SAS (Statistical Analysis System). SAS Institute, Inc., P.O. Box 10066, Raleigh, NC 27605.

SIBYL/RUNNER (Interactive Forecasting). Applied Decision Systems, 15 Walnut Street, Wellesley Hills, MA 02181.

SPSS (Statistical Package for the Social Sciences). SPSS, Inc., 444 North Michigan Avenue, Suite 3300, Chicago, IL 60611.

## Terminals and Graphics Devices

There are numerous computer terminals on the market, ranging from wide-carriage (about 130 characters) terminals for plotting time series, residual plots, and scatter diagrams to highly portable, lightweight suitcase-sized terminals. In addition to the wide carriage, a usually desirable quality is to have a terminal capable of operating at higher speeds than the normal 100 baud rate. Terminals operating at 300 or 1200 baud increase the rate of computer output and lessen the time available for a forecaster to decide on the next step or the time spent in waiting for the on-line output. It is important that the host computer and the graphics terminal are compatible, unless the terminal carries its own intelligence and software. Graphics terminals are generally not standardized to be compatible with mainframe computers.

Another consideration is whether a maintenance or service contract is available in a lease. The nearest service center for the terminal may be many hours away, resulting in prolonged downtime whenever the terminal breaks down.

Modern terminals are reasonably quiet, but they can still disturb the normal office environment. Whenever possible, a soundproof computer terminal room should be provided. This prevents distraction and also serves as a strategy room where forecasters can discuss the model results and alternative approaches.

## ENLISTING CONSULTING SERVICES

In recent years there has been a considerable increase in the number of firms and organizations providing consulting services in statistical analysis, econometric model building, computer applications programs, and a variety of technical courses. These firms have attempted to fill a demand for new, improved, and more sophisticated services than were available "in-house" or at nearby universities. These services consist of economic forecasts, demographic projections, timely forecasts, data base management systems, computer applications programs, technical assistance in building models, and training or educational services. This section offers items for consideration to maximize the value of consulting assistance.

### Economic and Demographic Forecasts

Until recently, forecasters faced a great problem in obtaining forecasts for economic variables for their models. After spending effort in selecting the best variables to include in the model, the forecasters would lack the expertise needed to generate consistent and informed forecasts of the economic variables. This problem is no longer serious when dealing with national economic variables, since forecasts for most of these variables are available from a number of consulting firms.

At the local or regional level, however, there are few organizations regularly preparing economic forecasts. The manager should consider the desirability of obtaining consulting help to generate the necessary forecasts if national variables are inadequate. It is best to check within the firm for such advice before looking outside.

Demographic forecasts are also generally available at the national level but less so at the regional or local level. Since the funding for an increasing number of government programs is dependent upon the local makeup of the population, local and regional planning agencies are beginning to gain expertise in preparing forecasts of births, deaths, migrations, and racial composition. Unfortunately, the forecasts prepared by these agencies may not always be objective, since projections of increased population mean more federal funds.

In many models, the market potential will be a function of the size of the population, the number of households, or the age distribution of the population. Therefore, demographic forecasts are increasing in importance and outside consulting help may be required.

Even when economic and demographic forecasts are available, they may not be published when the forecasting organization needs them. Local or regional forecasts are seldom provided as frequently as national economic variables are. Therefore, timeliness and detail are things for which the assistance of a consultant may be needed.

## Data Base Management

Almost all quantitative forecasting methods rely on the availability of computer software. As the scope of the forecasting job expands, the number of data files grows and data management becomes a serious problem. Consultants can sometimes recommend improved systems for storage and access which can minimize costs.

Most large corporations have organizations that develop the necessary computer programs to utilize quantitative methods. However, obtaining the priority to get a program completed when required is not always possible. Fortunately, many time-shared computing firms offer a library of application programs to users. The majority of the programs are available without paying a surcharge for access. If the forecasting organization requires a specific kind of program that is not generally available, consulting assistance may be required.

## Modeling Assistance

In many cases, only a small number of forecasters in an organization in one location use quantitative methods regularly. When it is not possible to hold periodic conferences among forecasters, outside consulting opinion may occasionally be required to ensure that the analyses being performed are technically correct. This approach may be more desirable than "farming out" technical problems since the forecasters will be increasing their quantitative skills by regularly working with consultants.

## Training or Educational Services

The forecast manager should be concerned about preventing technological obsolescence in the organization. Therefore, some form of periodic training will be required to maintain and expand quantitative skills. For large organizations, this training can be developed internally. For smaller organizations, training is usually provided externally.

The company should be wary of one- or two-day general training sessions sponsored by a consultant. Quite often these sessions present only those applications which will generate additional revenue for the consultant's firm by stimulating time-shared computer usage. While new programs or methods may well be interesting, the consultant's motivation for teaching them may be to establish the consultant's preeminence as "leader in the field." The methods may not yet have been proved successful in business applications. The classes may provide little or no hands-on practice, and the backgrounds of the students may be so varied as to make effective training impossible. For these reasons, it is good practice to attend one or two sessions before committing the firm to a contract for such services.

The role of consultant in quantitative forecasting methods is to help a company implement methods or techniques that will improve the quality and accuracy of the forecast. However, the company must be wary in selecting a consultant and in evaluating the services it receives for the dollars spent. The consultant is in business to make money. Failure to specify exactly what services are required can be a costly mistake. Generally speaking, the consultant must first learn about the specific industry, the markets it serves, the company, and the series to be forecast. This is often learned at the expense of the company before any productive work is forthcoming. Be sure to evaluate the consultant's reputation and experience in solving your kind of problems.

Consultants often sell the use of data files, forecast files, and application programs. In addition to the *per diem* expenses for consulting, a firm may find that it has a large bill for computer use generated by the consultant while experimenting with the company's time series. The best way to avoid needless expense is to define the services required very carefully and to monitor progress with indicators of performance.

## COORDINATING MODELING EFFORTS WITHIN THE FIRM

Quantitative analysis is an endeavor where two minds are better than one. Members of the group should be encouraged to brainstorm alternative approaches to problem solving. They should also share the results of their work with others, since progress is synergistic.

Periodic conferences are ideal mechanisms to coordinate quantitative methods. Participants should be encouraged to make presentations of their latest work. In this way successes can be transmitted throughout the company, misconceptions can be corrected, and, equally valuable, methods that haven't worked can be discussed.

Designation of technical coordinators, whose responsibility it is to assist all model builders, has proved to be a successful way of keeping the implementation project on schedule.

## DOCUMENTING FOR FUTURE REFERENCE

Documentation of results is one of the key aspects of any project. It is also the area that is most disliked and easiest to postpone, since it is often done after a forecast has been made. A documentation system such as that covered in the checklist is an effective way of solving the documentation problem. Documentation that takes place while the project is progressing can be planned ahead of time and monitored throughout the project. The establishment of literature, model, data, forecasts, software, and billing files will go a long way toward organizing the project and demonstrating to management the necessary control mechanisms for cost effectiveness.

## PRESENTING MODELING WORK FOR MANAGEMENT EVALUATION

The presentation of model results for evaluation by a company's managers is an important part of the implementation of quantitative methods. Experience has shown that it is best to do this in two different presentations. The first presentation should explain the approach taken, the alternatives considered, and the results from the model when only actual data are used. The purpose of this meeting is to assure management that the methodology is reasonable. Higher management should be encouraged to ask questions so that they understand the strengths and weaknesses of the particular quantitative method or methods presented.

The first meeting should not be one in which higher management is asked to approve a forecast based on a methodology foreign to them. There may be a natural reluctance to accept the methodology because it is tied in with a presentation that is essentially the selling of a forecast. The primary concern of management will be the forecast numbers and their implications for the company's performance in the future. For these reasons, management's evaluation of the quantitative method needs to take place in a separate meeting. After gaining acceptance of methodology, the model results can be incorporated in the normal presentation of the forecast to management.

## IMPLEMENTATION CHECKLIST

A. Identify a Task or Product. (What are your needs?)

____ Are models to be used for short-term or long-term forecasts?
____ Are models to be used to solve "What if" questions?
____ Are models to be used to determine elasticities?
____ Are models needed at all?

B. Priorities. (Identify these on the basis of your needs.)

____ Which quantitative techniques are useful?
____ Should they be implemented?

____ In what order?
____ What is the implementation schedule?
____ How does quantitative analysis fit into total job responsibility?

C. Identification of Resources.

____ Is management interest and support available?
____ Is money available for computer time?
____ Do job responsibilities allow time to meet implementation schedule?
____ Is clerical assistance available to maintain files?
____ Is economic data available for modeling?
____ Is modeling expertise available for consultation?

D. Data Base Management.

____ Who will enter and update data files?
____ Who will identify and correct outliers in data?
____ Will an ongoing program of documentation of outliers be implemented?
____ Will appropriate time series be base-adjusted, if necessary, on an ongoing basis?
____ Will seasonally adjusted data be created and updated periodically?
____ Will files be maintained at the local, area, or company level?

E. Terminal and Processing Considerations.

____ Are high-speed terminals available?
____ What is the carriage width?
____ Is a graphics device available?
____ Will modeling be done on-line or by batch processing to save money?

F. Intracompany Coordination of Modeling Techniques.

____ How many individuals in the company will be using quantitative techniques?
____ Can intracompany communication through seminars (and so on) reduce the redundancy and increase the effectiveness of quantitative modeling?

G. Documentation of Modeling Work for Future Reference.

____ Will modeling work be documented for future reference by others engaged in quantitative analysis?
____ Will files be organized for different aspects of modeling work?

1. Literature File: for publications about work in the modeling field, including journals and textbooks on mathematics, statistics, and economics, literature from vendors, modeling studies done by others, and so on.
2. Model File: about types of models developed, any changes and reasons

for change, including information on statistical tests, estimation of parameters, forecast tests, and simulations.
3. Data File: about types and sources of data, as well as explanations of adjustments and transformations.
4. Forecasting File: containing records on forecasts, forecast errors and monitoring information, and any analyses of forecast errors.
5. Software File: about available computer programs.
6. Billing and Related Expense File: about costs related to modeling work.

H. Presentation of Modeling Work for Management Evaluation.

____ What kind of feedback on modeling results should be sent to higher levels of management?
____ How should this be done, and how often?

## SUMMARY

We recommend a management-by-results approach for implementing new forecasting methods.

- A specific methodology should be selected for on-the-job implementation; deadlines should be established and the resources that will be made available to complete the project should be specified.
- Training courses improve the likelihood that new techniques are implemented; however, the value of training is often dissipated because of lack of specific on-the-job reinforcement. Making the implementation of new methods as routine as you would any other job requirement is the surest way to achieve success.
- An implementation plan should indicate the methods to be implemented and indicators of progress to ensure that the plan does not die from lack of follow-up. Considerations that should be incorporated into the plan are highlighted in a sample manager's checklist included in this chapter.

## USEFUL READING

MULLER, M. E. (1980). Aspects of Statistical Computing: What Packages for the 1980's Ought to Do. *American Statistician* 34, 159–68.

WHEELWRIGHT, S. C., and S. MAKRIDAKIS (1980). *Forecasting Methods for Management,* 3rd ed. New York, NY: John Wiley and Sons.

# Appendixes
# Bibliography
# Index

# Appendix A

**Table 1** Standardized Normal Distribution

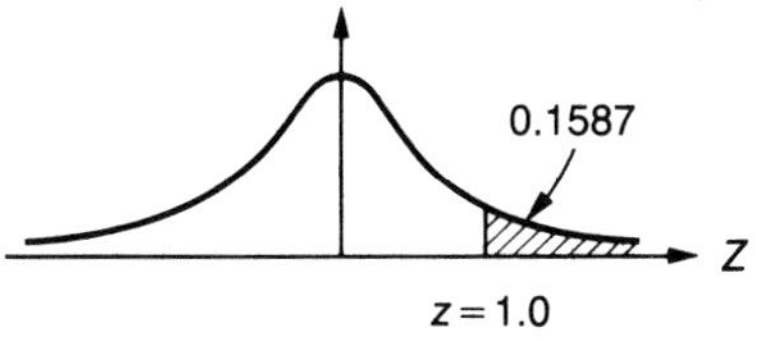


| z | .00 | .01 | .02 | .03 | .04 | .05 | .06 | .07 | .08 | .09 |
|---|---|---|---|---|---|---|---|---|---|---|
| 0.0 | .5000 | .4960 | .4920 | .4880 | .4840 | .4801 | .4761 | .4721 | .4681 | .4641 |
| 0.1 | .4602 | .4562 | .4522 | .4483 | .4443 | .4404 | .4364 | .4325 | .4286 | .4247 |
| 0.2 | .4207 | .4168 | .4129 | .4090 | .4052 | .4013 | .3974 | .3936 | .3897 | .3859 |
| 0.3 | .3821 | .3783 | .3745 | .3707 | .3669 | .3632 | .3594 | .3557 | .3520 | .3483 |
| 0.4 | .3446 | .3409 | .3372 | .3336 | .3300 | .3264 | .3228 | .3192 | .3156 | .3121 |
| 0.5 | .3085 | .3050 | .3015 | .2981 | .2946 | .2912 | .2877 | .2843 | .2810 | .2776 |
| 0.6 | .2743 | .2709 | .2676 | .2643 | .2611 | .2578 | .2546 | .2514 | .2483 | .2451 |
| 0.7 | .2420 | .2389 | .2358 | .2327 | .2296 | .2266 | .2236 | .2206 | .2177 | .2148 |
| 0.8 | .2119 | .2090 | .2061 | .2033 | .2005 | .1977 | .1949 | .1922 | .1894 | .1867 |
| 0.9 | .1841 | .1814 | .1788 | .1762 | .1736 | .1711 | .1685 | .1660 | .1635 | .1611 |
| 1.0 | .1587 | .1562 | .1539 | .1515 | .1492 | .1469 | .1446 | .1423 | .1401 | .1379 |
| 1.1 | .1357 | .1335 | .1314 | .1292 | .1271 | .1251 | .1230 | .1210 | .1190 | .1170 |
| 1.2 | .1151 | .1131 | .1112 | .1093 | .1075 | .1056 | .1038 | .1020 | .1003 | .0985 |
| 1.3 | .0968 | .0951 | .0934 | .0918 | .0901 | .0885 | .0869 | .0853 | .0838 | .0823 |
| 1.4 | .0808 | .0793 | .0778 | .0764 | .0749 | .0735 | .0721 | .0708 | .0694 | .0681 |
| 1.5 | .0668 | .0655 | .0643 | .0630 | .0618 | .0606 | .0594 | .0582 | .0571 | .0559 |
| 1.6 | .0548 | .0537 | .0526 | .0516 | .0505 | .0495 | .0485 | .0475 | .0465 | .0455 |
| 1.7 | .0446 | .0436 | .0427 | .0418 | .0409 | .0401 | .0392 | .0384 | .0375 | .0367 |
| 1.8 | .0359 | .0351 | .0344 | .0336 | .0329 | .0322 | .0314 | .0307 | .0301 | .0294 |
| 1.9 | .0287 | .0281 | .0274 | .0268 | .0262 | .0256 | .0250 | .0244 | .0239 | .0233 |
| 2.0 | .0228 | .0222 | .0217 | .0212 | .0207 | .0202 | .0197 | .0192 | .0188 | .0183 |
| 2.1 | .0179 | .0174 | .0170 | .0166 | .0162 | .0158 | .0154 | .0150 | .0146 | .0143 |
| 2.2 | .0139 | .0136 | .0132 | .0129 | .0125 | .0122 | .0119 | .0116 | .0113 | .0110 |
| 2.3 | .0107 | .0104 | .0102 | .0099 | .0096 | .0094 | .0091 | .0089 | .0087 | .0084 |
| 2.4 | .0082 | .0080 | .0078 | .0075 | .0073 | .0071 | .0069 | .0068 | .0066 | .0064 |
| 2.5 | .0062 | .0060 | .0059 | .0057 | .0055 | .0054 | .0052 | .0051 | .0049 | .0048 |
| 2.6 | .0047 | .0045 | .0044 | .0043 | .0041 | .0040 | .0039 | .0038 | .0037 | .0036 |
| 2.7 | .0035 | .0034 | .0033 | .0032 | .0031 | .0030 | .0029 | .0028 | .0027 | .0026 |
| 2.8 | .0026 | .0025 | .0024 | .0023 | .0023 | .0022 | .0021 | .0021 | .0020 | .0019 |
| 2.9 | .0019 | .0018 | .0018 | .0017 | .0016 | .0016 | .0015 | .0015 | .0014 | .0014 |
| 3.0 | .0013 | .0013 | .0013 | .0012 | .0012 | .0011 | .0011 | .0011 | .0010 | .0010 |

*Source:* Based on *Biometrika Tables for Statisticians*, Vol. 1, 3rd ed. (1966), with the permission of the *Biometrika* trustees.
*Note:* The table plots the cumulative probability $Z > z$.

**Table 2** Percentiles of the *t*-Distribution

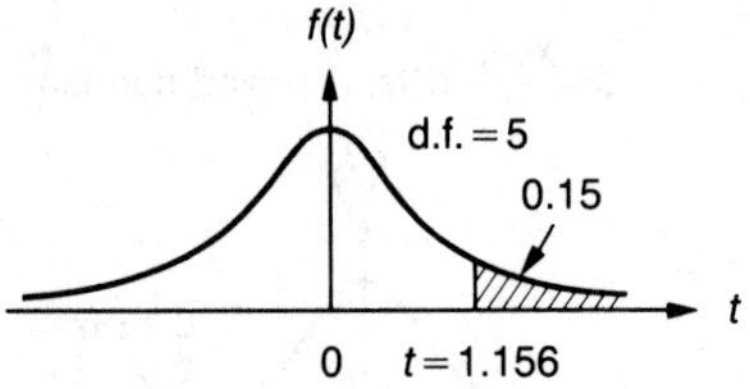


| Degrees of freedom | Probability of a value at least as large as the table entry | | | | | |
|---|---|---|---|---|---|---|
| | 0.15 | 0.1 | 0.05 | 0.025 | 0.01 | 0.005 |
| 1 | 1.963 | 3.078 | 6.314 | 12.706 | 31.821 | 63.657 |
| 2 | 1.386 | 1.886 | 2.920 | 4.303 | 6.965 | 9.925 |
| 3 | 1.250 | 1.638 | 2.353 | 3.182 | 4.541 | 5.841 |
| 4 | 1.190 | 1.533 | 2.132 | 2.776 | 3.747 | 4.604 |
| 5 | 1.156 | 1.476 | 2.015 | 2.571 | 3.365 | 4.032 |
| 6 | 1.134 | 1.440 | 1.943 | 2.447 | 3.143 | 3.707 |
| 7 | 1.119 | 1.415 | 1.895 | 2.365 | 2.998 | 3.499 |
| 8 | 1.108 | 1.397 | 1.860 | 2.306 | 2.896 | 3.355 |
| 9 | 1.100 | 1.383 | 1.833 | 2.262 | 2.821 | 3.250 |
| 10 | 1.093 | 1.372 | 1.812 | 2.228 | 2.764 | 3.169 |
| 11 | 1.088 | 1.363 | 1.796 | 2.201 | 2.718 | 3.106 |
| 12 | 1.083 | 1.356 | 1.782 | 2.179 | 2.681 | 3.055 |
| 13 | 1.079 | 1.350 | 1.771 | 2.160 | 2.650 | 3.012 |
| 14 | 1.076 | 1.345 | 1.761 | 2.145 | 2.624 | 2.977 |
| 15 | 1.074 | 1.341 | 1.753 | 2.131 | 2.602 | 2.947 |
| 16 | 1.071 | 1.337 | 1.746 | 2.120 | 2.583 | 2.921 |
| 17 | 1.069 | 1.333 | 1.740 | 2.110 | 2.567 | 2.898 |
| 18 | 1.067 | 1.330 | 1.734 | 2.101 | 2.552 | 2.878 |
| 19 | 1.066 | 1.328 | 1.729 | 2.093 | 2.539 | 2.861 |
| 20 | 1.064 | 1.325 | 1.725 | 2.086 | 2.528 | 2.845 |
| 21 | 1.063 | 1.323 | 1.721 | 2.080 | 2.518 | 2.831 |
| 22 | 1.061 | 1.321 | 1.717 | 2.074 | 2.508 | 2.819 |
| 23 | 1.060 | 1.319 | 1.714 | 2.069 | 2.500 | 2.807 |
| 24 | 1.059 | 1.318 | 1.711 | 2.064 | 2.492 | 2.797 |
| 25 | 1.058 | 1.316 | 1.708 | 2.060 | 2.485 | 2.787 |
| 26 | 1.058 | 1.315 | 1.706 | 2.056 | 2.479 | 2.779 |
| 27 | 1.057 | 1.314 | 1.703 | 2.052 | 2.473 | 2.771 |
| 28 | 1.056 | 1.313 | 1.701 | 2.048 | 2.467 | 2.763 |
| 29 | 1.055 | 1.311 | 1.699 | 2.045 | 2.462 | 2.756 |
| 30 | 1.055 | 1.310 | 1.697 | 2.042 | 2.457 | 2.750 |
| (Normal) ∞ | 1.036 | 1.282 | 1.645 | 1.960 | 2.326 | 2.576 |

*Source:* Abridged from Table IV in Sir Ronald A. Fisher, *Statistical Methods for Research Workers,* 14th ed. (copyright © 1970 by University of Adelaide, a Division of Macmillan Publishing Co., Inc.) with the permission of the publisher and the late Sir Ronald Fisher's Literary Executor.

**Table 3** Percentiles of the Chi-Squared Distribution

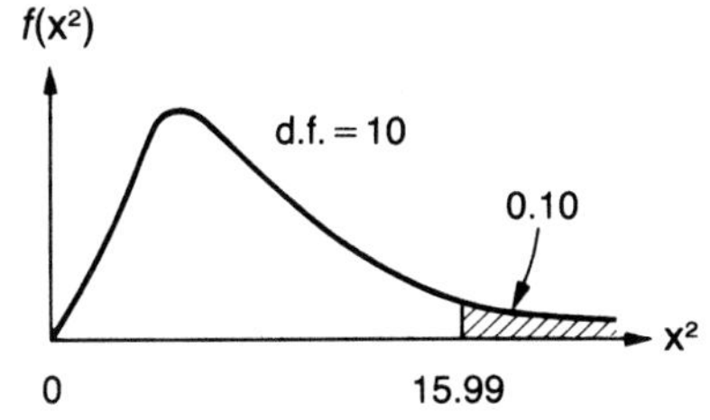


| Degrees of freedom | Probability of a value at least as large as the table entry | | | | | | | | |
|---|---|---|---|---|---|---|---|---|---|
| | 0.90 | 0.75 | 0.50 | 0.25 | 0.10 | 0.05 | 0.025 | 0.01 | 0.005 |
| 1 | 0.0158 | 0.102 | 0.455 | 1.323 | 2.71 | 3.84 | 5.02 | 6.63 | 7.88 |
| 2 | 0.211 | 0.575 | 1.386 | 2.77 | 4.61 | 5.99 | 7.38 | 9.21 | 10.60 |
| 3 | 0.584 | 1.213 | 2.37 | 4.11 | 6.25 | 7.81 | 9.35 | 11.34 | 12.84 |
| 4 | 1.064 | 1.923 | 3.36 | 5.39 | 7.78 | 9.49 | 11.14 | 13.28 | 14.86 |
| 5 | 1.610 | 2.67 | 4.35 | 6.63 | 9.24 | 11.07 | 12.83 | 15.09 | 16.75 |
| 6 | 2.20 | 3.45 | 5.35 | 7.84 | 10.64 | 12.59 | 14.45 | 16.81 | 18.55 |
| 7 | 2.83 | 4.25 | 6.35 | 9.04 | 12.02 | 14.07 | 16.01 | 18.48 | 20.3 |
| 8 | 3.49 | 5.07 | 7.34 | 10.22 | 13.36 | 15.51 | 17.53 | 20.1 | 22.0 |
| 9 | 4.17 | 5.90 | 8.34 | 11.39 | 14.68 | 16.92 | 19.02 | 21.7 | 23.6 |
| 10 | 4.87 | 6.74 | 9.34 | 12.55 | 15.99 | 18.31 | 20.5 | 23.2 | 25.2 |
| 11 | 5.58 | 7.58 | 10.34 | 13.70 | 17.28 | 19.68 | 21.9 | 24.7 | 26.8 |
| 12 | 6.30 | 8.44 | 11.34 | 14.85 | 18.55 | 21.0 | 23.3 | 26.2 | 28.3 |
| 13 | 7.04 | 9.30 | 12.34 | 15.98 | 19.81 | 22.4 | 24.7 | 27.7 | 29.8 |
| 14 | 7.79 | 10.17 | 13.34 | 17.12 | 12.1 | 23.7 | 26.1 | 29.1 | 31.3 |
| 15 | 8.55 | 11.04 | 14.34 | 18.25 | 22.3 | 25.0 | 27.5 | 30.6 | 32.8 |
| 16 | 9.31 | 11.91 | 15.34 | 19.37 | 23.5 | 26.3 | 28.8 | 32.0 | 34.3 |
| 17 | 10.09 | 12.79 | 16.34 | 20.5 | 24.8 | 27.6 | 30.2 | 33.4 | 35.7 |
| 18 | 10.86 | 13.68 | 17.34 | 21.6 | 26.0 | 28.9 | 31.5 | 34.8 | 37.2 |
| 19 | 11.65 | 14.56 | 18.34 | 22.7 | 27.2 | 30.1 | 32.9 | 36.2 | 38.6 |
| 20 | 12.44 | 15.45 | 19.34 | 23.8 | 28.4 | 31.4 | 34.2 | 37.6 | 40.0 |

*Source:* Based on *Biometrika Tables for Statisticians*, Vol. 1, 3rd ed. (1966), with the permission of the *Biometrika* trustees.

**Table 4** *F*-Distribution, 5 Percent Significance

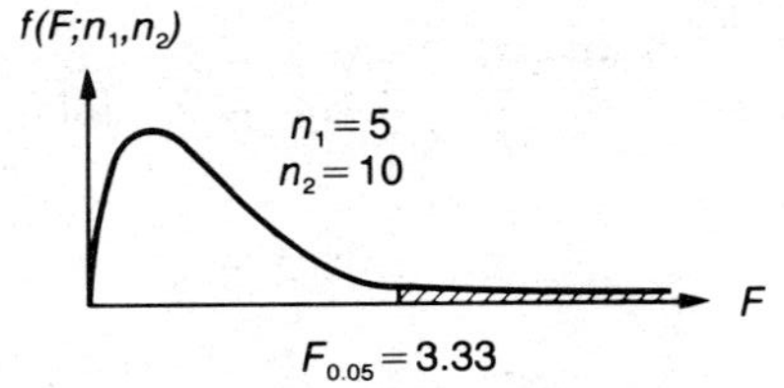


| | Degrees of freedom for numerator | | | | | | | | | | | | | | | | | | |
|---|---|---|---|---|---|---|---|---|---|---|---|---|---|---|---|---|---|---|---|
| | 1 | 2 | 3 | 4 | 5 | 6 | 7 | 8 | 9 | 10 | 12 | 15 | 20 | 24 | 30 | 40 | 60 | 120 | ∞ |
| 1 | 161 | 200 | 216 | 225 | 230 | 234 | 237 | 239 | 241 | 242 | 244 | 246 | 248 | 249 | 250 | 251 | 252 | 253 | 254 |
| 2 | 18.5 | 19.0 | 19.2 | 19.2 | 19.3 | 19.3 | 19.4 | 19.4 | 19.4 | 19.4 | 19.4 | 19.4 | 19.5 | 19.5 | 19.5 | 19.5 | 19.5 | 19.5 | 19.5 |
| 3 | 10.1 | 9.55 | 9.28 | 9.12 | 9.01 | 8.94 | 8.89 | 8.85 | 8.81 | 8.79 | 8.74 | 8.70 | 8.66 | 8.64 | 8.62 | 8.59 | 8.57 | 8.55 | 8.53 |
| 4 | 7.71 | 6.94 | 6.59 | 6.39 | 6.26 | 6.16 | 6.09 | 6.04 | 6.00 | 5.96 | 5.91 | 5.86 | 5.80 | 5.77 | 5.75 | 5.72 | 5.69 | 5.66 | 5.63 |
| 5 | 6.61 | 5.79 | 5.41 | 5.19 | 5.05 | 4.95 | 4.88 | 4.82 | 4.77 | 4.74 | 4.68 | 4.62 | 4.56 | 4.53 | 4.50 | 4.46 | 4.43 | 4.40 | 4.37 |
| 6 | 5.99 | 5.14 | 4.76 | 4.53 | 4.39 | 4.28 | 4.21 | 4.15 | 4.10 | 4.06 | 4.00 | 3.94 | 3.87 | 3.84 | 3.81 | 3.77 | 3.74 | 3.70 | 3.67 |
| 7 | 5.59 | 4.74 | 4.35 | 4.12 | 3.97 | 3.87 | 3.79 | 3.73 | 3.68 | 3.64 | 3.57 | 3.51 | 3.44 | 3.41 | 3.38 | 3.34 | 3.30 | 3.27 | 3.23 |
| 8 | 5.32 | 4.46 | 4.07 | 3.84 | 3.69 | 3.58 | 3.50 | 3.44 | 3.39 | 3.35 | 3.28 | 3.22 | 3.15 | 3.12 | 3.08 | 3.04 | 3.01 | 2.97 | 2.93 |
| 9 | 5.12 | 4.26 | 3.86 | 3.63 | 3.48 | 3.37 | 3.29 | 3.23 | 3.18 | 3.14 | 3.07 | 3.01 | 2.94 | 2.90 | 2.86 | 2.83 | 2.79 | 2.75 | 2.71 |
| 10 | 4.96 | 4.10 | 3.71 | 3.48 | 3.33 | 3.22 | 3.14 | 3.07 | 3.02 | 2.98 | 2.91 | 2.85 | 2.77 | 2.74 | 2.70 | 2.66 | 2.62 | 2.58 | 2.54 |
| 11 | 4.84 | 3.98 | 3.59 | 3.36 | 3.20 | 3.09 | 3.01 | 2.95 | 2.90 | 2.85 | 2.79 | 2.72 | 2.65 | 2.61 | 2.57 | 2.53 | 2.49 | 2.45 | 2.40 |
| 12 | 4.75 | 3.89 | 3.49 | 3.26 | 3.11 | 3.00 | 2.91 | 2.85 | 2.80 | 2.75 | 2.69 | 2.62 | 2.54 | 2.51 | 2.47 | 2.43 | 2.38 | 2.34 | 2.30 |
| 13 | 4.67 | 3.81 | 3.41 | 3.18 | 3.03 | 2.92 | 2.83 | 2.77 | 2.71 | 2.67 | 2.60 | 2.53 | 2.46 | 2.42 | 2.38 | 2.34 | 2.30 | 2.25 | 2.21 |
| 14 | 4.60 | 3.74 | 3.34 | 3.11 | 2.96 | 2.85 | 2.76 | 2.70 | 2.65 | 2.60 | 2.53 | 2.46 | 2.39 | 2.35 | 2.31 | 2.27 | 2.22 | 2.18 | 2.13 |
| 15 | 4.54 | 3.68 | 3.29 | 3.06 | 2.90 | 2.79 | 2.71 | 2.64 | 2.59 | 2.54 | 2.48 | 2.40 | 2.33 | 2.29 | 2.25 | 2.20 | 2.16 | 2.11 | 2.07 |

**Table 4** *(continued)*

| | Degrees of freedom for numerator | | | | | | | | | | | | | | | | | | |
|---|---|---|---|---|---|---|---|---|---|---|---|---|---|---|---|---|---|---|---|
| | 1 | 2 | 3 | 4 | 5 | 6 | 7 | 8 | 9 | 10 | 12 | 15 | 20 | 24 | 30 | 40 | 60 | 120 | ∞ |
| 16 | 4.49 | 3.63 | 3.24 | 3.01 | 2.85 | 2.74 | 2.66 | 2.59 | 2.54 | 2.49 | 2.42 | 2.35 | 2.28 | 2.24 | 2.19 | 2.15 | 2.11 | 2.06 | 2.01 |
| 17 | 4.45 | 3.59 | 3.20 | 2.96 | 2.81 | 2.70 | 2.61 | 2.55 | 2.48 | 2.45 | 2.38 | 2.31 | 2.23 | 2.19 | 2.15 | 2.10 | 2.06 | 2.01 | 1.96 |
| 18 | 4.41 | 3.55 | 3.16 | 2.93 | 2.77 | 2.66 | 2.58 | 2.51 | 2.46 | 2.41 | 2.34 | 2.27 | 2.19 | 2.15 | 2.11 | 2.06 | 2.02 | 1.97 | 1.92 |
| 19 | 4.38 | 3.52 | 3.13 | 2.90 | 2.74 | 2.63 | 2.54 | 2.48 | 2.42 | 2.39 | 2.31 | 2.23 | 2.16 | 2.11 | 2.07 | 2.03 | 1.98 | 1.93 | 1.88 |
| 20 | 4.35 | 3.49 | 3.10 | 2.87 | 2.71 | 2.60 | 2.51 | 2.45 | 2.39 | 2.35 | 2.28 | 2.20 | 2.12 | 2.08 | 2.04 | 1.99 | 1.95 | 1.90 | 1.84 |
| 21 | 4.32 | 3.47 | 3.07 | 2.84 | 2.68 | 2.57 | 2.49 | 2.42 | 2.37 | 2.32 | 2.25 | 2.18 | 2.10 | 2.05 | 2.01 | 1.96 | 1.92 | 1.87 | 1.81 |
| 22 | 4.30 | 3.44 | 3.05 | 2.82 | 2.66 | 2.55 | 2.46 | 2.40 | 2.34 | 2.30 | 2.23 | 2.15 | 2.07 | 2.03 | 1.98 | 1.94 | 1.89 | 1.84 | 1.78 |
| 23 | 4.28 | 3.42 | 3.03 | 2.80 | 2.64 | 2.53 | 2.44 | 2.37 | 2.32 | 2.27 | 2.20 | 2.13 | 2.05 | 2.01 | 1.96 | 1.91 | 1.86 | 1.81 | 1.76 |
| 24 | 4.26 | 3.40 | 3.01 | 2.78 | 2.62 | 2.51 | 2.42 | 2.36 | 2.30 | 2.25 | 2.18 | 2.11 | 2.03 | 1.98 | 1.94 | 1.89 | 1.84 | 1.79 | 1.73 |
| 25 | 4.24 | 3.39 | 2.99 | 2.76 | 2.60 | 2.49 | 2.40 | 2.34 | 2.28 | 2.24 | 2.16 | 2.09 | 2.01 | 1.96 | 1.92 | 1.87 | 1.82 | 1.77 | 1.71 |
| 30 | 4.17 | 3.32 | 2.92 | 2.69 | 2.53 | 2.42 | 2.33 | 2.27 | 2.21 | 2.16 | 2.09 | 2.01 | 1.93 | 1.89 | 1.84 | 1.79 | 1.74 | 1.68 | 1.62 |
| 40 | 4.08 | 3.23 | 2.84 | 2.61 | 2.45 | 2.34 | 2.25 | 2.18 | 2.12 | 2.08 | 2.00 | 1.92 | 1.84 | 1.79 | 1.74 | 1.69 | 1.64 | 1.58 | 1.51 |
| 60 | 4.00 | 3.15 | 2.76 | 2.53 | 2.37 | 2.25 | 2.17 | 2.10 | 2.04 | 1.99 | 1.92 | 1.84 | 1.75 | 1.70 | 1.65 | 1.59 | 1.53 | 1.47 | 1.39 |
| 120 | 3.92 | 3.07 | 2.68 | 2.45 | 2.29 | 2.18 | 2.09 | 2.02 | 1.96 | 1.91 | 1.83 | 1.75 | 1.66 | 1.61 | 1.55 | 1.50 | 1.43 | 1.35 | 1.25 |
| ∞ | 3.84 | 3.00 | 2.60 | 2.37 | 2.21 | 2.10 | 2.01 | 1.94 | 1.88 | 1.83 | 1.75 | 1.67 | 1.57 | 1.52 | 1.46 | 1.39 | 1.32 | 1.22 | 1.00 |

*Source:* Reproduced with the permission of the Biometrika Trustees from M. Merrington and C. M. Thompson, "Tables of percentage points of the inverted beta (F) distribution," *Biometrika* 33(1943), 73.

**Table 5** The Durbin-Watson Test Statistic $d$: 5 Percent Significance of $d_1$ and $d_\mu$

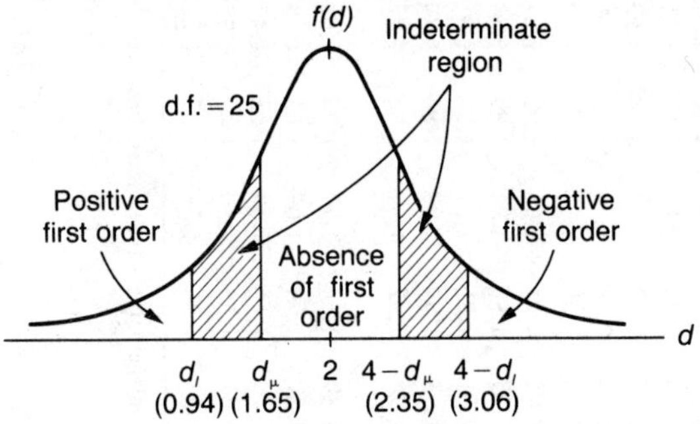


| Degree of freedom | $k = 1$ | | $k = 2$ | | $k = 3$ | | $k = 4$ | | $k = 5$ | |
|---|---|---|---|---|---|---|---|---|---|---|
| $n$ | $d_l$ | $d_\mu$ | $d_l$ | $d_\mu$ | $d_l$ | $d_\mu$ | $d_l$ | $d_\mu$ | $d_l$ | $d_\mu$ |
| 15 | 0.95 | 1.23 | 0.83 | 1.40 | 0.71 | 1.61 | 0.59 | 1.84 | 0.48 | 2.09 |
| 16 | 0.98 | 1.24 | 0.86 | 1.40 | 0.75 | 1.59 | 0.64 | 1.80 | 0.53 | 2.03 |
| 17 | 1.01 | 1.25 | 0.90 | 1.40 | 0.79 | 1.58 | 0.68 | 1.77 | 0.57 | 1.98 |
| 18 | 1.03 | 1.26 | 0.93 | 1.40 | 0.82 | 1.56 | 0.72 | 1.74 | 0.62 | 1.93 |
| 19 | 1.06 | 1.28 | 0.96 | 1.41 | 0.86 | 1.55 | 0.76 | 1.73 | 0.66 | 1.90 |
| 20 | 1.08 | 1.28 | 0.99 | 1.41 | 0.89 | 1.55 | 0.79 | 1.72 | 0.70 | 1.87 |
| 21 | 1.10 | 1.30 | 1.01 | 1.41 | 0.92 | 1.54 | 0.83 | 1.69 | 0.73 | 1.84 |
| 22 | 1.12 | 1.31 | 1.04 | 1.42 | 0.95 | 1.54 | 0.86 | 1.68 | 0.77 | 1.82 |
| 23 | 1.14 | 1.32 | 1.06 | 1.42 | 0.97 | 1.54 | 0.89 | 1.67 | 0.80 | 1.80 |
| 24 | 1.16 | 1.33 | 1.08 | 1.43 | 1.00 | 1.54 | 0.91 | 1.66 | 0.83 | 1.79 |
| 25 | 1.18 | 1.34 | 1.10 | 1.43 | 1.02 | 1.54 | 0.94 | 1.65 | 0.86 | 1.77 |
| 26 | 1.19 | 1.35 | 1.12 | 1.44 | 1.04 | 1.54 | 0.96 | 1.65 | 0.88 | 1.76 |
| 27 | 1.21 | 1.36 | 1.13 | 1.44 | 1.06 | 1.54 | 0.99 | 1.64 | 0.91 | 1.75 |
| 28 | 1.22 | 1.37 | 1.15 | 1.45 | 1.08 | 1.54 | 1.01 | 1.64 | 0.93 | 1.74 |
| 29 | 1.24 | 1.38 | 1.17 | 1.45 | 1.10 | 1.54 | 1.03 | 1.63 | 0.96 | 1.73 |
| 30 | 1.25 | 1.38 | 1.18 | 1.46 | 1.12 | 1.54 | 1.05 | 1.63 | 0.98 | 1.73 |
| 31 | 1.26 | 1.39 | 1.20 | 1.47 | 1.13 | 1.55 | 1.07 | 1.63 | 1.00 | 1.72 |
| 32 | 1.27 | 1.40 | 1.21 | 1.47 | 1.15 | 1.55 | 1.08 | 1.63 | 1.02 | 1.71 |
| 33 | 1.28 | 1.41 | 1.22 | 1.48 | 1.16 | 1.55 | 1.10 | 1.63 | 1.04 | 1.71 |
| 34 | 1.29 | 1.41 | 1.24 | 1.48 | 1.17 | 1.55 | 1.12 | 1.63 | 1.06 | 1.70 |
| 35 | 1.30 | 1.42 | 1.25 | 1.48 | 1.19 | 1.55 | 1.13 | 1.63 | 1.07 | 1.70 |
| 36 | 1.31 | 1.43 | 1.26 | 1.49 | 1.20 | 1.56 | 1.15 | 1.63 | 1.09 | 1.70 |
| 37 | 1.32 | 1.43 | 1.27 | 1.49 | 1.21 | 1.56 | 1.16 | 1.62 | 1.10 | 1.70 |
| 38 | 1.33 | 1.44 | 1.28 | 1.50 | 1.23 | 1.56 | 1.17 | 1.62 | 1.12 | 1.70 |
| 39 | 1.34 | 1.44 | 1.29 | 1.50 | 1.24 | 1.56 | 1.19 | 1.63 | 1.13 | 1.69 |
| 40 | 1.35 | 1.45 | 1.30 | 1.51 | 1.25 | 1.57 | 1.20 | 1.63 | 1.15 | 1.69 |
| 45 | 1.39 | 1.48 | 1.34 | 1.53 | 1.30 | 1.58 | 1.25 | 1.63 | 1.21 | 1.69 |
| 50 | 1.42 | 1.50 | 1.38 | 1.54 | 1.34 | 1.59 | 1.30 | 1.64 | 1.26 | 1.69 |

**Table 5** *(continued)*

| Degree of freedom, $n$ | $k = 1$ | | $k = 2$ | | $k = 3$ | | $k = 4$ | | $k = 5$ | |
|---|---|---|---|---|---|---|---|---|---|---|
| | $d_l$ | $d_\mu$ | $d_l$ | $d_\mu$ | $d_l$ | $d_\mu$ | $d_l$ | $d_\mu$ | $d_l$ | $d_\mu$ |
| 55 | 1.45 | 1.52 | 1.41 | 1.56 | 1.37 | 1.60 | 1.33 | 1.64 | 1.30 | 1.69 |
| 60 | 1.47 | 1.54 | 1.44 | 1.57 | 1.40 | 1.61 | 1.37 | 1.65 | 1.33 | 1.69 |
| 65 | 1.49 | 1.55 | 1.46 | 1.59 | 1.43 | 1.63 | 1.40 | 1.66 | 1.36 | 1.69 |
| 70 | 1.51 | 1.57 | 1.48 | 1.60 | 1.45 | 1.63 | 1.42 | 1.66 | 1.39 | 1.70 |
| 75 | 1.53 | 1.58 | 1.50 | 1.61 | 1.47 | 1.64 | 1.45 | 1.67 | 1.42 | 1.70 |
| 80 | 1.54 | 1.59 | 1.52 | 1.63 | 1.49 | 1.65 | 1.47 | 1.67 | 1.44 | 1.70 |
| 85 | 1.56 | 1.60 | 1.53 | 1.63 | 1.51 | 1.66 | 1.49 | 1.68 | 1.46 | 1.71 |
| 90 | 1.57 | 1.61 | 1.55 | 1.64 | 1.53 | 1.66 | 1.50 | 1.69 | 1.48 | 1.71 |
| 95 | 1.58 | 1.62 | 1.56 | 1.65 | 1.54 | 1.67 | 1.52 | 1.69 | 1.50 | 1.71 |
| 100 | 1.59 | 1.63 | 1.57 | 1.65 | 1.55 | 1.67 | 1.53 | 1.70 | 1.51 | 1.72 |

*Source:* Reprinted with permission from J. Durbin and G. S. Watson, "Testing for Serial Correlation in Least Squares Regression: II" *Biometrika* 38(1951), 159–77.

# Appendix B

Time series data used for examples in the text

Toll revenue volumes for the telecommunications example (REV) for a given region

| | 1969 | 1970 | 1971 | 1972 | 1973 | 1974 |
|---|---|---|---|---|---|---|
| 1 | 21821. | 25157. | 27163. | 30653. | 34306. | 35120. |
| 2 | 25490. | 29910. | 31927. | 35349. | 38617. | 41843. |
| 3 | 25565. | 29082. | 30484. | 34388. | 37187. | 39401. |
| 4 | 27819. | 31526. | 33327. | 35342. | 40623. | 43236. |
| 5 | 26427. | 29165. | 31325. | 35585. | 38490. | 41350. |
| 6 | 26259. | 29508. | 31036. | 34040. | 36847. | 40786. |
| 7 | 24614. | 25886. | 28622. | 32044. | 35398. | 38596. |
| 8 | 25792. | 27840. | 30660. | 35063. | 37774. | 40991. |
| 9 | 26970. | 29082. | 31147. | 34365. | 37335. | 40425. |
| 10 | 28605. | 29900. | 31572. | 35634. | 39074. | 41656. |
| 11 | 28987. | 30651. | 34576. | 37389. | 39642. | 42991. |
| 12 | 27023. | 28678. | 31502. | 35060. | 37362. | 38881. |
| SUM | 315372. | 346385. | 373341. | 414912. | 452655. | 485276. |

| | 1975 | 1976 | 1977 | 1978 | 1979 |
|---|---|---|---|---|---|
| 1 | 36133. | 37656. | 41423. | 45238. | 50687. |
| 2 | 44003. | 46263. | 49410. | 52583. | 61547. |
| 3 | 41120. | 44386. | 46222. | 50869. | 57783. |
| 4 | 45671. | 47650. | 50690. | 56078. | 63420. |
| 5 | 43914. | 45748. | 48829. | 54799. | 60589. |
| 6 | 43167. | 44886. | 48112. | 53109. | 59672. |
| 7 | 40303. | 42753. | 45271. | 50974. | 57707. |
| 8 | 42452. | 44843. | 48678. | 53265. | 59672. |
| 9 | 42320. | 45203. | 49029. | 54213. | 59973. |
| 10 | 43825. | 45995. | 50191. | 56892. | 63458. |
| 11 | 44955. | 47341. | 51961. | 58695. | 65100. |
| 12 | 41121. | 43658. | 48199. | 54142. | 60500. |
| SUM | 508984. | 536382. | 578015. | 640857. | 720108. |

Monthly message volumes for the telecommunications example (MSG) for a given region

| | 1969 | 1970 | 1971 | 1972 | 1973 | 1974 |
|---|---|---|---|---|---|---|
| 1 | 7600. | 8391. | 8775. | 9851. | 11003. | 11638. |
| 2 | 7630. | 8244. | 9079. | 10268. | 10988. | 11575. |
| 3 | 8131. | 9388. | 10017. | 10893. | 11874. | 12456. |
| 4 | 8104. | 8946. | 9719. | 10285. | 11609. | 12437. |
| 5 | 8207. | 9102. | 9638. | 10858. | 11986. | 12807. |
| 6 | 8577. | 9594. | 10343. | 11408. | 12067. | 12651. |
| 7 | 8150. | 8946. | 9404. | 10159. | 11242. | 12101. |
| 8 | 8583. | 9333. | 10175. | 11321. | 12393. | 12855. |
| 9 | 8662. | 9491. | 10205. | 10993. | 11845. | 12685. |
| 10 | 8862. | 9340. | 9916. | 11293. | 12311. | 12973. |
| 11 | 8175. | 8961. | 10003. | 10946. | 11885. | 11955. |
| 12 | 8444. | 9084. | 9583. | 10510. | 11307. | 11739. |
| SUM | 99125. | 108820. | 116857. | 128785. | 140510. | 147872. |

| | 1975 | 1976 | 1977 | 1978 | 1979 |
|---|---|---|---|---|---|
| 1 | 12330. | 12572. | 13621. | 15299. | 17092. |
| 2 | 12029. | 12857. | 13681. | 15195. | 16894. |
| 3 | 12972. | 13882. | 15172. | 16782. | 18210. |
| 4 | 12759. | 13531. | 14285. | 15552. | 17746. |
| 5 | 12810. | 13375. | 14561. | 16364. | 18176. |
| 6 | 13286. | 14110. | 15277. | 16939. | 18100. |
| 7 | 12488. | 12869. | 13828. | 15115. | 16853. |
| 8 | 13054. | 13897. | 15402. | 17052. | 18498. |
| 9 | 13162. | 13997. | 15257. | 16777. | |
| 10 | 13266. | 13690. | 15032. | 16928. | |
| 11 | 12044. | 13474. | 14700. | 16498. | |
| 12 | 12377. | 13171. | 14190. | 15539. | |
| SUM | 152577. | 161425. | 175006. | 194040. | 141569. |

Number of business telephones for the telecommunications example (BMT) for a given region

| | 1970 | 1971 | 1972 | 1973 | 1974 | 1975 |
|---|---|---|---|---|---|---|
| 1 | 491,195 | 502,336 | 504,071 | 511,665 | 518,522 | 517,100 |
| 2 | 493,068 | 503,013 | 503,785 | 512,555 | 518,797 | 516,520 |
| 3 | 495,482 | 504,042 | 505,736 | 513,653 | 519,290 | 516,136 |
| 4 | 498,042 | 505,292 | 507,537 | 514,959 | 520,869 | 515,213 |
| 5 | 499,660 | 504,720 | 507,267 | 514,576 | 519,606 | 513,040 |
| 6 | 499,004 | 504,378 | 506,704 | 515,345 | 520,006 | 512,909 |
| 7 | 499,602 | 503,571 | 507,436 | 515,712 | 519,274 | 512,306 |
| 8 | 500,065 | 503,158 | 508,378 | 517,240 | 520,072 | 512,918 |
| 9 | 502,858 | 505,757 | 510,861 | 519,132 | 521,234 | 514,679 |
| 10 | 502,468 | 504,828 | 511,251 | 519,159 | 520,631 | 514,246 |
| 11 | 502,589 | 503,905 | 510,768 | 518,610 | 519,474 | 513,864 |
| 12 | 502,504 | 503,434 | 510,505 | 518,296 | 517,935 | 512,591 |
| SUM | 5,986,540 | 6,048,433 | 6,094,300 | 6,190,904 | 6,235,709 | 6,171,521 |

| | 1976 | 1977 | 1978 | 1979 |
|---|---|---|---|---|
| 1 | 512,615 | 512,286 | 515,163 | 520,438 |
| 2 | 512,553 | 512,363 | 515,423 | 521,051 |
| 3 | 512,702 | 512,626 | 516,766 | 522,419 |
| 4 | 513,165 | 513,296 | 517,439 | 523,345 |
| 5 | 510,701 | 511,400 | 515,357 | 521,849 |
| 6 | 510,229 | 511,621 | 515,885 | 522,547 |
| 7 | 510,610 | 511,656 | 516,345 | 522,333 |
| 8 | 510,771 | 512,889 | 517,708 | 523,943 |
| 9 | 512,981 | 514,907 | 520,203 | 526,622 |
| 10 | 513,713 | 515,563 | 521,043 | 526,921 |
| 11 | 512,950 | 515,422 | 520,522 | 526,194 |
| 12 | 512,042 | 514,829 | 519,938 | 525,297 |
| SUM | 6,145,032 | 6,158,857 | 6,211,791 | 6,282,958 |

Nonfarm employment for the telecommunications example (NFRM) for a given region

| | 1970 | 1971 | 1972 | 1973 | 1974 | 1975 |
|---|---|---|---|---|---|---|
| 1 | 7063 | 6926 | 6866 | 6977 | 6985 | 6792 |
| 2 | 7092 | 6929 | 6871 | 6995 | 6974 | 6763 |
| 3 | 7157 | 6982 | 6960 | 7059 | 7024 | 6782 |
| 4 | 7202 | 7007 | 7000 | 7102 | 7064 | 6801 |
| 5 | 7221 | 7059 | 7062 | 7149 | 7130 | 6865 |
| 6 | 7282 | 7112 | 7122 | 7224 | 7196 | 6903 |
| 7 | 7191 | 7050 | 7020 | 7154 | 7135 | 6866 |
| 8 | 7189 | 7022 | 7083 | 7191 | 7149 | 6900 |
| 9 | 7140 | 6973 | 7045 | 7148 | 7080 | 6806 |
| 10 | 7106 | 6982 | 7120 | 7181 | 7087 | 6818 |
| 11 | 7102 | 7000 | 7149 | 7204 | 7080 | 6827 |
| 12 | 7116 | 7024 | 7164 | 7200 | 7022 | 6839 |
| SUM | 85861 | 84066 | 84462 | 85584 | 84926 | 81962 |

| | 1976 | 1977 | 1978 | 1979 |
|---|---|---|---|---|
| 1 | 6666 | 6645 | 6804 | 6993 |
| 2 | 6665 | 6662 | 6816 | 7011 |
| 3 | 6715 | 6718 | 6903 | 7065 |
| 4 | 6758 | 6781 | 6984 | 7122 |
| 5 | 6781 | 6847 | 7055 | 7196 |
| 6 | 6837 | 6920 | 7137 | 7269 |
| 7 | 6883 | 6916 | 7086 | 7220 |
| 8 | 6868 | 6948 | 7133 | 7235 |
| 9 | 6806 | 6920 | 7102 | 7202 |
| 10 | 6816 | 6957 | 7142 | 7243 |
| 11 | 6834 | 6980 | 7188 | 7267 |
| 12 | 6845 | 6998 | 7192 | 7272 |
| SUM | 81474 | 82292 | 84542 | 86095 |

Nonfarm less manufacturing employment for the telecommunications example
NFMA, for a given region

| | 1970 | 1971 | 1972 | 1973 | 1974 | 1975 |
|---|---|---|---|---|---|---|
| 1 | 5275 | 5282 | 5295 | 5393 | 5413 | 5365 |
| 2 | 5279 | 5279 | 5285 | 5391 | 5393 | 5344 |
| 3 | 5336 | 5326 | 5361 | 5443 | 5436 | 5365 |
| 4 | 5403 | 5365 | 5406 | 5495 | 5479 | 5393 |
| 5 | 5439 | 5418 | 5465 | 5534 | 5540 | 5457 |
| 6 | 5489 | 5465 | 5507 | 5589 | 5588 | 5483 |
| 7 | 5463 | 5457 | 5469 | 5558 | 5570 | 5474 |
| 8 | 5429 | 5397 | 5472 | 5560 | 5558 | 5478 |
| 9 | 5380 | 5335 | 5420 | 5506 | 5486 | 5362 |
| 10 | 5400 | 5350 | 5491 | 5541 | 5511 | 5374 |
| 11 | 5411 | 5368 | 5516 | 5562 | 5525 | 5387 |
| 12 | 5427 | 5421 | 5548 | 5586 | 5531 | 5417 |
| SUM | 64731 | 64463 | 65235 | 66157 | 66031 | 64897 |

| | 1976 | 1977 | 1978 | 1979 |
|---|---|---|---|---|
| 1 | 5267 | 5231 | 5365 | 5527 |
| 2 | 5252 | 5237 | 5370 | 5528 |
| 3 | 5286 | 5276 | 5437 | 5575 |
| 4 | 5325 | 5332 | 5514 | 5631 |
| 5 | 5340 | 5389 | 5578 | 5696 |
| 6 | 5382 | 5442 | 5636 | 5748 |
| 7 | 5458 | 5472 | 5624 | 5727 |
| 8 | 5418 | 5475 | 5636 | 5730 |
| 9 | 5342 | 5436 | 5603 | 5686 |
| 10 | 5358 | 5468 | 5641 | 5725 |
| 11 | 5375 | 5490 | 5673 | 5758 |
| 12 | 5406 | 5527 | 5693 | 5777 |
| SUM | 64207 | 64776 | 66768 | 68109 |

# Bibliography

[numbers in brackets refer to page numbers in this book]


AFIFI, A. A., and S. P. AZEN (1979). *Statistical Analysis—A Computer Oriented Approach,* 2nd ed. New York, NY: Academic Press. [**175, 220**]

ANDREWS, D. F., P. J. BICKEL, F. R. HAMPEL, P. J. HUBER, W. H. ROGERS, and J. W. TUKEY (1972). *Robust Estimates of Location: Survey and Advances*. Princeton, NJ: Princeton University Press. [**79, 158, 209**]

ARMSTRONG, J. S. (1978). *Long-Range Forecasting: From Crystal Ball to Computer*. New York, NY: John Wiley and Sons. [**15**]

Intended for the producers of long-range forecasts in the areas of social, behavioral, and management sciences.

ASCHER, W. (1978). *Forecasting—An Appraisal for Policy Makers and Planners*. Baltimore, MD: The Johns Hopkins University Press.

Intended for users of forecasting in both the public and private sectors. Examines long-range forecasting accuracy in the areas of population, economy, energy, transportation, and technology.

BARR, A. J., J. H. GOODNIGHT, J. P. SALL, and J. T. HELWIG (1976). *A User's Guide to SAS 76,* Raleigh, NC: SAS Institute, Inc. [**68, 84**]

BECKER, R. A., and J. M. CHAMBERS (1977). GR-Z: A System of Graphical Subroutines for Data Analysis. *Proceedings of Computer Science and Statistics, Tenth Annual Symposium on the Interface*. National Bureau of Standards Special Publication 503, 409–15. [**52**]

BELL, D. (1976). *The Coming of Post-Industrial Society—A Venture in Social Forecasting*. New York, NY: Basic Books.

For students and researchers interested in social forecasting.

BELSLEY, D. A., E. KUH, and R. E. WELSCH (1980). *Regression Diagnostics*. New York, NY: John Wiley and Sons.

BOWERMAN, B. L., and R. T. O'CONNELL (1979). *Time Series and Forecasting*. North Scituate, MA: Duxbury Press. [**94, 98**]

A textbook for applied courses in time series and forecasting. Part II discusses the forecasting of time series described by trend and irregular components. The exponential smoothing approach to forecasting such time series is discussed there.

BOX, G. E. P. (1953). Non-Normality and Tests on Variances. *Biometrika* 40, 318–35. [**207**]

BOX, G. E. P., and D. R. COX (1964). An Analysis of Transformations. *Journal of the Royal Statistical Society,* B 26, 211–43. [**121**]

BOX, G. E. P., and G. M. JENKINS (1976). *Time Series Analysis—Forecasting and Control,* rev. ed. San Francisco, CA: Holden-Day. [**97, 125, 215, 241, 249, 260, 266**]

BRELSFORD, W. M., and D. A. RELLES (1981). *STATLIB—A Statistical Computing Library*. Englewood Cliffs, NJ: Prentice-Hall. [**160**]

BROWN, R. G. (1959). *Statistical Forecasting for Inventory Control*. New York, NY: McGraw-Hill Book Co. [**95**]

BROWN, R. G. (1963). *Smoothing, Forecasting, and Prediction of Discrete Time Series*. Englewood Cliffs, NJ: Prentice-Hall. [**95, 97, 98**]

BUTLER, W. F., R. A. KAVESH, and R. B. PLATT, eds. (1974). *Methods and Techniques of Business Forecasting*. Englewood Cliffs, NJ: Prentice-Hall. [**37**]

Compilation of papers in business forecasting with emphasis on microeconomic forecasting in government, industry, and academia.

CENTER for the STUDY of SOCIAL POLICY (1975). *Handbook of Forecasting Techniques*. Menlo Park, CA: Stanford Research Institute; Reproduced by the National Technical Information Service, Springfield, VA, 1975; also a two-part supplement, 1977.

Report discusses twelve basic methods of forecasting suitable for long-range forecasting. A supplement (in 2 parts, 1977) contains brief evaluations of seventy-three forecasting techniques.

CHAMBERS, J. C., S. K. MULLICK, and D. D. SMITH (1971). How to Choose the Right Forecasting Technique. *Harvard Business Review* 49 (July–August), 45–74.

CHAMBERS, J. C., S. K. MULLICK, and D. D. SMITH (1974). *An Executive's Guide to Forecasting*. New York, NY: John Wiley and Sons. [**16, 26, 29**]

A nontechnical, nonmathematical treatment of forecasting aimed for decision makers. Concerned with how techniques can be used.

CHATTERJEE, S., and B. PRICE (1977). *Regression Analysis by Example*. New York, NY: John Wiley and Sons.

These authors view regression analysis as a set of data analytic techniques that are used to help understand the interrelationships among a given set of variables. Emphasis is not on statistical tests and probability computations, but rather on informational analysis techniques as a prelude to developing regression equations. Chapters 1 and 2 deal with simple linear regression.

CLEVELAND, W. S., D. M. DUNN, and I. J. TERPENNING (1978). *The SABL Seasonal Analysis Package—Statistical and Graphical Procedures*. Computing Information Service, Bell Laboratories, 600 Mountain Ave., Murray Hill, NJ 07974. [**248**]

CLEVELAND, W. S., D. M. DUNN, and I. J. TERPENNING (1979). SABL—A Resistant Seasonal Adjustment Procedure with Graphical Methods for Interpretation and Diagnosis, in *Seasonal Analysis of Economic Time Series,* A. Zellner, ed. Washington, DC: U.S. Government Printing Office. [**248**]

CLEVELAND, W. S., and S. J. DEVLIN (1980). Calendar Effects in Monthly Time Series; Detection by Spectrum. *Journal of the American Statistical Association* 75, 489–96. [**274**]

COHEN, M. (1976). Surveys and Forecasting, in *Methods and Techniques of Business Forecasting,* W. F. Butler, R. A. Kavesh, and R. B. Platt, eds. Englewood Cliffs, NJ: Prentice-Hall.

CONFERENCE BOARD (1978). *Sales Forecasting*. New York, NY: The Conference Board. [**22**]

DAGUM, E. B. (1976). Seasonal Factor Forecasts from ARIMA Models. *Proceedings of the International Statistical Institute, 40th Session, Warsaw, 1975*. Warsaw: International Statistical Institute, 206–19. [**244**]

DAGUM, E. B. (1978). Modeling, Forecasting, and Seasonally Adjusting Economic Time Series with the X-11 ARIMA Method. *The Statistician* 27, 203–16. [**244**]

DANIELLS, L. M. (1980). *Business Forecasting for the 1980s–and Beyond*. Boston, MA: Harvard Business School.

A selected, partially annotated bibliography.

DAUTEN, C. A. and L. M. VALENTINE (1978). *Business Cycles and Forecasting,* 5th ed., Cincinnati, OH: Southwestern.

A text dealing with business fluctuations, forecasting economic activity and sales, and proposals for achieving economic growth and stability.

DEVLIN, S. J., R. GNANADESIKAN, and J. R. KETTENRING (1975). Robust Estimation and Outlier Detection with Correlation Coefficients. *Biometrika* 62, 531–45. [**222, 223**]

DIXON, W. J., and M. B. BROWN (1979). *BMDP-79 Biomedical Computer Programs P-Series*. Los Angeles, CA: University of California Press. [**68, 84, 122, 220**]

DRAPER, N. R., and H. SMITH (1981). *Applied Regression Analysis,* 2nd ed. New York, NY: John Wiley and Sons. [**153, 158, 178**]

DURBIN, J., and G. S. WATSON (1950). Testing for Serial Correlation in Least Squares Regression: I. *Biometrika* 37, 409–28. [**165, 354–55**]

DURBIN, J., and G. S. WATSON (1951). Testing for Serial Correlation in Least Squares Regression: II. *Biometrika* 38, 159–78. [**165, 354–55**]

EBY, F. H., Jr. and W. J. O'NEILL (1977). *The Management of Sales Forecasting*. Lexington, MA: Lexington Books, D.C. Heath.

Provides the sales forecaster with an understanding of both the general management of the forecasting operation and of specific forecasting procedures.

ENRICK, N. L. (1979). *Market and Sales Forecasting-A Quantitative Approach*. Huntington, NY: Krieger Publishing Co.

ERICKSON, B. H., and T. A. NOSANCHUK (1977). *Understanding Data*. Toronto, Canada: McGraw-Hill-Ryerson Ltd. [**48, 78, 108, 119, 120**]

EZEKIEL, M., and K. A. FOX (1959). *Methods of Correlation and Regression Analysis*. New York, NY: John Wiley and Sons. [**199**]

FELS, R., and C. E. HINSHAW (1968). *Forecasting and Recognizing Business Cycle Turning Points*. National Bureau of Economic Research. New York, NY: Columbia University Press.

Two papers dealing with the problem of recognizing peaks and troughs in business cycles.

FILDES, R., and D. WOODS, eds. (1978). *Forecasting and Planning*. Farnborough, England: Saxon House.

Conference papers intended for business practitioners who deal with the application of advanced forecasting techniques in practice.

FIRTH, M. (1977). *Forecasting Methods in Business and Management*. London, England: Edward Arnold Ltd.

Describes the applicability, usefulness, and limitations of a range of formal forecasting techniques for general managers. Aimed at students heading for management careers in forecasting as well as practicing managers interested in recent developments in forecasting.

FISHER, R. A. (1960). *The Design of Experiments,* 7th ed. Edinburgh, Scotland: Oliver and Boyd. [**223**]

GEURTS, M. D., and I. B. IBRAHIM (1975). Comparing the Box-Jenkins Approach with the Exponentially Smoothed Forecasting Model Application to Hawaii Tourists, *Journal of Marketing Research* 12, 182–88. [**30**]

GILCHRIST, W. (1976). *Statistical Forecasting*. New York, NY: John Wiley and Sons.

The author describes a number of forecasting methods, including linear trend models, growth curves, adaptive methods, and other extensions.

GOODMAN, M. L., and W. H. WILLIAMS (1971). A Simple Method for the Construction of Empirical Confidence Limits for Economic Forecasts. *Journal of the American Statistical Association* 66, 752–54. [**311**]

GRANGER, C. W. J. (1980). *Forecasting in Business and Economics*. New York, NY: Academic Press.

GRANGER, C. W. J., and P. NEWBOLD (1977). *Forecasting Economic Time Series*. New York, NY: Academic Press. [**30, 274**]

GROFF, G. K. (1973). Empirical Comparison of Models for Short-Range Forecasting. *Management Science* 20, 22–31. [**30**]

GROSS, C. W., and R. T. PETERSON (1976). *Business Forecasting*. Boston, MA: Houghton-Mifflin.

Develops framework for forecasting process. Emphasizes business forecasting at the firm or industry level.

HARRISON, P. J. (1965). Short-Term Sales Forecasting. *Applied Statistics* 14, 102–39. [**95**]

HARTWIG, F., and B. E. DEARING (1979). *Exploratory Data Analysis*. Sage University Paper on Quantitative Applications in the Social Sciences, 07-016. Beverly Hills, CA: Sage Publications. [**48, 78**]

HOADLEY, W. E. (1974). Reporting Forecasts to Management and the Use of Forecasts as a Management Tool, in *Methods and Techniques of Business Forecasting,* Butler et al., eds. Englewood Cliffs, NJ: Prentice-Hall. [**295**]

HOGG, R. V. (1979). Statistical Robustness: One View of Its Use in Applications Today. *The American Statistician* 33, 108–15. [**220**]

HOLT, C. C. (1957). *Forecasting Seasonals and Trends by Exponentially Weighted Moving Averages*. Pittsburgh, PA: Carnegie Institute of Technology. [**95, 98**]

HUBER, P. J. (1964). Robust Estimation of a Location Parameter. *Annals of Mathematical Statistics* 35, 73–101. [**209**]

HUBER, P. J. (1973). Robust Regression: Asymptotics, Conjectures, and Monte Carlo. *Annals of Statistics* 1, 799–821. [**210**]

INTRILIGATOR, M. D. (1978). *Econometric Models, Techniques, and Applications*. Englewood Cliffs, NJ: Prentice-Hall. [**15**]

JENKINS, G. M. (1979). *Practical Experience with Modeling and Forecasting Time Series*. Jersey, Channel Islands: GJ&P (Overseas) Ltd. [**143**]

JONES, H. and B. C. TWISS (1978). *Forecasting Technology for Planning Decisions*. New York, NY: MacMillan.

A two-part book on the practice and methodology of forecasting for corporate planning.

KALLEK, S. (1978). An Overview of the Objectives and Framework of Seasonal Adjustment, in *Seasonal Analysis of Economic Time Series,* A Zellner, ed. Washington, DC: U.S. Government Printing Office. [**240**]

LEWIS, C. E. (1975). *Demand Analysis and Inventory Control*. Lexington, MA: Saxon House/Lexington Books.

Book contains a variety of short-term forecasting techniques, including adaptive filtering for use in production planning and control systems.

LING, R. F., and H. V. ROBERTS (1980). *User's Manual for IDA*. Palo Alto, CA: The Scientific Press. [**71**]

MACAULEY, F. R. (1930). *The Smoothing of Time Series*. Cambridge, MA: National Bureau of Economic Research. [**239**]

McGILL, R. J., J. W. TUKEY, and W. A. LARSEN (1978). Variations of Box Plots. *The American Statistician* 32, 12–16. [**81, 82**]

McLAUGHLIN, R. L. (1962). *Time Series Forecasting*. Marketing Research Techniques Series, No. 6, Chicago, IL: American Marketing Association.

McNEIL, D. R. (1977). *Interactive Data Analysis*. New York, NY: John Wiley and Sons [**48, 68, 78, 84, 108, 119, 220**]

MAKRIDAKIS, S., and M. HIBON (1979). Accuracy of Forecasting: An Empirical Investigation. *Journal of the Royal Statistical Society* A 142, 97–145. [**30**]

MAKRIDAKIS, S., and S. C. WHEELWRIGHT (1977). Forecasting: Issues and Challenges for Marketing Management. *Journal of Marketing,* 24–38.

MAKRIDAKIS, S., and S. C. WHEELWRIGHT (1978). *Interactive Forecasting—Univariate and Multivariate Methods*. San Francisco, CA: Holden-Day. [**71**]

Contains numerous examples and programs to illustrate a wide variety of forecasting methods, including all the smoothing methods. Chapter 3 treats the topic of autocorrelation analysis with many examples.

MAKRIDAKIS, S., and S. C. WHEELWRIGHT (1978). *Forecasting Methods and Applications*. New York, NY: John Wiley and Sons. [**15, 94, 98**]

Chapter 5 describes the techniques of simple linear regression. Chapter 8 includes a discussion of autocorrelation analysis. Chapter 12 examines problems associated with predicting business cycles and turning points, and describes the use of leading indicators.

MAKRIDAKIS, S. and S. C. WHEELWRIGHT, eds. (1979). *Forecasting,* New York, NY: North-Holland Publishing Company.

A collection of readings covering the most current concepts and knowledge about forecasting.

MALLOWS, C. L. (1979). Robust Methods—Some Examples of Their Use. *The American Statistician* 33, 179–84. [**208**]

MASS, N. J. (1975). *Economic Cycles: An Analysis of Underlying Causes*. New York, NY: John Wiley and Sons.

The book provides an overview of existing theories of economic cycles and develops a general framework for evaluating the impact of social and economic factors on economic cycles of various periodicities.

MICHAEL, G. C. (1979). *Sales Forecasting*. American Marketing Association Monograph Series No. 10. Chicago, IL: American Marketing Association.

Oriented to business decision-makers who have a need of forecasts, and would like to be more comfortable in choosing the most effective forecasting technique. A Forecasting Decision Matrix is provided as a useful tool in comparing major forecasting techniques.

MILNE, T. E. (1975). *Business Forecasting—A Managerial Approach*. London, England: Longman Group Ltd.

Aimed at the nontechnical or managerial reader interested in practical aspects of forecasting. Covers a wide range of approaches including subjective methods.

MONTGOMERY, D. C., and L. A. JOHNSON (1976). *Forecasting and Time Series Analysis*. New York, NY: McGraw-Hill Book Co. [**93, 94, 95, 98**]

MOORE, G. H. (1975). The Analysis of Economic Indicators. *Scientific American* 232 (January), 17–23.

A general account on the use of economic indicators.

MOORE, G. H., and J. SHISKIN (1972). Early Warning Signals for the Economy in Statistics, in *Statistics, a Guide to the Unknown,* J. M. Tanur et al., eds. San Francisco, CA: Holden-Day. [**128**]

MOORE, R. W. (1978). *Introduction to the Use of Computer Packages for Statistical Analyses*. Englewood Cliffs, NJ: Prentice-Hall. [**174**]

MOSTELLER, F., and J. W. TUKEY (1977). *Data Analysis and Regression*. Reading, MA: Addison-Wesley Publishing Co. [**91, 120, 148, 150, 229**]

MULLER, M. E. (1980). Aspects of Statistical Computing: What Packages for the 1980's Ought to Do. *American Statistician* 34, 159–68. [**338**]

NEWBOLD, P., and C. W. J. GRANGER (1974). Experience with Forecasting Univariate Time Series and the Combination of Forecasts. *Journal of the Royal Statistical Society* A 137, 131–65. [**30**]

NIE, N. H., C. H. HALL, J. G. JENKINS, K. STEINBRENNER, and D. H. BENT (1975). *SPSS: Statistical Package for the Social Sciences,* 2nd ed. New York, NY: McGraw-Hill Book Co. [**68, 84**]

NIE, N. H., C. H. HALL, M. N. FRANKLIN, J. G. JENKINS, K. J. SOURS, M. J. NORUSIS, and V. BEADLE (1980). *SCSS: A User's Guide to the SCSS Conversational System.* New York, NY: McGraw-Hill Book Co. [**71**]

PARKER, G. G. and E. L. SEGURA (1971). How to Get a Better Forecast. *Harvard Business Review* 49, 6–16. [**323**]

PLATT, R. B. (1974). Statistical Measures of Forecast Accuracy, in *Methods and Techniques of Business Forecasting,* Butler et al., eds. Englewood Cliffs, NJ: Prentice-Hall. [**310**]

PLOSSER, C. I. (1979). Short-Term Forecasting and Seasonal Adjustment. *Journal of the American Statistical Association* 74, 15–24. [**244**]

RAO, V. R. and J. E. COX, Jr. (1978). *Sales Forecasting Methods: A Survey of Recent Developments.* Cambridge, MA: Marketing Science Institute.

Review of sales forecasting literature, with particular focus on recent methodological developments. Also contains a semi-annotated bibliography of articles and books on sales forecasting.

REID, D. J. (1971). Forecasting in Action: A Comparison of Forecasting Techniques in Economic Time Series. *Proceedings, Joint Conference of the Operations Research Society,* Long-Range Planning and Forecasting. [**30**]

ROBERTS, H. V. (1974). *Conversational Statistics.* Hewlett-Packard University Business Series. Palo Alto, CA: The Scientific Press. [**191**]

RYAN, T. A., B. L. JOINER, and B. F. RYAN (1976). *Minitab Student Handbook.* North Scituate, MA: Duxbury Press. [**71**]

SAS (1980). *SAS/ETS User's Guide, Econometric and Time Series Library.* Cary, N.C.: SAS Institute, Inc. [**175**]

SHISKIN, J. (1957). *Electronic Computers and Business Indicators.* Cambridge, MA: National Bureau of Economic Research. Occasional Paper 57.

SHISKIN, J., and H. EISENPRESS (1957). Seasonal Adjustments by Electronic Computer Methods. *Journal of the American Statistical Association* 52, 415–49.

SHISKIN, J., and C. H. LAMPART (1976). Indicator Forecasting, in *Methods and Techniques of Business Forecasting,* W. F. Butler, R. A. Ravesh, and R. B. Platt, eds. Englewood Cliffs, NJ: Prentice-Hall.

A detailed account on the use of indicators in economic forecasting.

SHISKIN, J., and G. H. MOORE (1967). *Indicators of Business Expansions and Contractions.* Cambridge, MA: National Bureau of Economic Research. [**128, 137**]

SHISKIN, J., A. H. YOUNG, and J. C. MUSGRAVE (1967). *The X-11 Variant of Census Method II Seasonal Adjustment Program.* Technical Paper No. 15, U.S. Department of Commerce, Bureau of the Census. Washington, DC: U.S. Government Printing Office. [**239, 242**]

SILK, L. S., and M. L. CURLEY (1970). *Business Forecasting—With a Guide to Sources of Business Data*. New York, NY: Random House. [**135**]

SOBEK, R. S. (1973). A Manager's Primer in Forecasting. *Harvard Business Review* 51, 1–9. [**129, 323**]

SULLIVAN, W. G., and W. W. CLAYCOMBE (1977). *Fundamentals of Forecasting*. Reston, VA: Reston Publishing Co. [**15, 101**]

Intended for the nonstatistical reader interested in applying popular forecasting techniques, and their strengths and weaknesses. Includes computer listings.

THEIL, H. (1958). *Economic Forecasts and Policy*. Amsterdam: North Holland Publishing Co. [**309**]

TRIGG, D. W. (1964). Monitoring a Forecasting System. *Operational Research Quarterly* 15, 271–74. [**314**]

TRIGG, D. W., and A. G. LEACH (1967). Exponential Smoothing with Adaptive Response Rate. *Operational Research Quarterly* 18, 53–59. [**95**]

TUKEY, J. W. (1977). *Exploratory Data Analysis*. Reading, MA: Addison-Wesley Publishing Co. [**48, 78, 81, 83, 91, 108, 119**]

VELLEMAN, P. F., and D. C. HOAGLIN (1981). *Applications, Basics, and Computing for Exploratory Data Analysis*. North Scituate, MA: Duxbury Press. [**220**]

VELLEMAN, P. F., J. SEAMAN, and J. E. ALLEN (1977). *Evaluating Package Regression Routines*. Technical Reprint 877/008-010. Ithaca, NY: New York State School of Industrial and Labor Relations, Cornell University. [**175**]

WALLIS, W. A., and H. V. ROBERTS (1966). *Statistics, A New Approach*. New York, NY: The Free Press. [**178**]

WALSH, J. E. (1962). *Handbook of Nonparametric Statistics*. Princeton, NJ: Van Nostrand Co. [**192**]

WHEELWRIGHT, S. C., and D. G. CLARKE (1976). Corporate Forecasting: Promise and Reality. *Harvard Business Review* 54 (November-December), 40–64.

WHEELWRIGHT, S. C., and S. MAKRIDAKIS (1980). *Forecasting Methods for Management*, 3rd ed. New York, NY: John Wiley and Sons. [**15, 16, 18, 26, 30, 95, 188, 323**]

Aimed at the practitioner seeking to understand a wide range of forecasting methods along with major advantages and disadvantages. Addresses organizational, behavioral, and qualitative approaches as well.

WINTERS, P. R. (1960). Forecasting Sales by Exponentially Weighted Moving Averages. *Management Science* 6, 324–42. [**95, 101**]

WOODS, D., and R. FILDES (1976). *Forecasting for Business*. New York, NY: Longman.

Aimed for the practicing manager and student of forecasting interested in the tools and framework necessary to produce a good forecast without becoming a statistician/econometrician.

YOUNGER, M. S. (1979). *Handbook for Linear Regression*. North Scituate, MA: Duxbury Press. [**175**]

# Index